BECAUSE ALL IS
ONE

Three Rungs Yet One God, "Living God". D'kula Had — "all is one", attaining one name — one's rung, yet — "You" — end of heaven to end of heaven. God", Elohim, "God" – above, Elohim Hayim, "Living God". Eli, "my rung in the mystery of Elohim Hayim, "You". you are my God: I will search for you. although they are three, it is you", atah, "my God"; Eli, are here: Elohim, "God"; (Zohar 2.140a)

(Psalms 63.2)

BECAUSE ALL IS
ONE

Rabbi Ariel Stone

Copyright © 2019 by Rabbi Ariel Stone.

ISBN: Softcover   978-1-7960-5860-4
          eBook   978-1-7960-5859-8

All rights reserved. No part of this book may be reproduced or transmitted in any form or by any means, electronic or mechanical, including photocopying, recording, or by any information storage and retrieval system, without permission in writing from the copyright owner.

The views expressed in this work are solely those of the author and do not necessarily reflect the views of the publisher, and the publisher hereby disclaims any responsibility for them.

Scripture quotations marked KJV are from the Holy Bible, King James Version (Authorized Version). First published in 1611. Quoted from the KJV Classic Reference Bible, Copyright © 1983 by The Zondervan Corporation.

Any people depicted in stock imagery provided by Getty Images are models, and such images are being used for illustrative purposes only.
Certain stock imagery © Getty Images.

Print information available on the last page.

Rev. date: 10/16/2019

To order additional copies of this book, contact:
Xlibris
1-888-795-4274
www.Xlibris.com
Orders@Xlibris.com
802107

CONTENTS

FOREWORD..ix
INTRODUCTION..xv
Seeing the Meaning of a Life..xv
Spirit and Flesh...xvi
Dream and Compromise..xviii
Hope and Reality...xix
"Seeing Is Believing"..xxi
What Moses Saw..xxv
The Place Where One Begins to See..xxix
Turning to See: Exile and Return..xxxvi

PART I - ALEF–DALET–NUN-YUD: THINGS HIDDEN AND REVEALED
Chapter 1 Apples of Gold in Vessels of Silver..............................1
             Adonai: Surface and Depth..2
             The Sefirot: A Theology of Mutual Need....................6
             Becoming a Self, facing an Other.............................14
             Memory and Belonging..19
             Remembering the Way Home..................................22
Chapter 2 The Theology: Balancing Paradox............................26
             The Stakes...26
             Old-New Theological Questions...............................29
             The Balance..34
             The Blessing Is in the Struggle.................................38
Chapter 3 Medieval Mystical Insights to Inform a New
          American Jewish Theology...42
             Ancient Wisdom as a Path to Redemption...............43
             Is Kabbalah Jewish? – Specific, Individuated Community.45

Wholeness as Healing from Alienation 47
Seeing the Link Between Heaven and Earth 50

PART II - YUD-HEY-VAV-HEY: "GO TO YOURSELF"

Chapter 4 For the sake of unifying All 57
    Lekh L'kha: to oneself, to the world 57
    Unifying the Self Leads to Unifying the All 60
    Unifying the Self Through Learning 64
Chapter 5 Torah Study as Ascent 66
    YHVH: Meaning in the Middle Ground 66
    What Avram Saw 70
Chapter 6 Ascending the Sefirot Toward Meaning 76
    Vision and Limitations 81
    Grasping the Ladder 85

PART III - TEN LESSONS IN THE SEFIROT

Summary, Preparation, and a Warning............................... 89
Chapter 7 Three 90
Chapter 8 Three Worlds of Human Existence 93
Chapter 9 Ten.. 96
    Sefirot as Aspects of God 97
    Sefirot as Vessels 98
    Sefirot as Aspects of the Human 99
    The Human Being as Sefirah 101
Chapter 10 Do not Say, "Water, water!" 105
Chapter 11 The Ten Sefirot 107
    Malkhut – The Gate of Belonging 107
    Yesod – The Gate of Embodiment 130
    Hod – The Gate of Hoda'ot 148
    Netzakh – The Gate of Endurance 163
    Bridging: Reaching Beyond Hod and Netzakh
    Toward Tif'eret 182
    Tiferet – The Gate of Connecting Below with Above 185
    Din – The Gate of Judgment 200
    Hesed – The Gate of Mercy 233

*Bridging: Integrating All That Has Come Before,
Rising Toward the Heights..................................248
Binah – The Gate of Understanding............................251
Hokhmah – The Gate of Wisdom..................................277
Keter – The Gate of Transcendence............................299*

Part IV - Conclusion - Ehyeh: What Will Yet Be Seen
Chapter 12 Teshuvah: Beginning to See 321
Chapter 13 The River Kevar......................................326
Chapter 14 Get Going: The End of Exile 329
Chapter 15 Standing in the Light 334

Endnotes..337

FOREWORD

by Rabbi Dr Byron L. Sherwin

This work is highly informed by the academic study of Jewish mysticism. Some scholars date the inception of the academic study of Jewish mysticism in America to 1938, when the founder of the field, Gershom Scholem of The Hebrew University of Jerusalem delivered a series of lectures at The Jewish Institute of Religion (JIR) in New York City, which evolved into his now classic work, *Major Trends in Jewish Mysticism.* However, decades later, b the time Ariel Stone was a student at JIR, the study of Jewish mysticism was not taken seriously, neither academically nor theologically, at that institution. When Ariel began to think about composing this work, she did not take Jewish mysticism very seriously either. But, as this study attests, things changed. She changed. That change is an important feature of her spiritual autobiography that remains secreted between the lines of this book.

In Scholem's opening lecture, he delineated a number of characteristics of Jewish mysticism, some of which he found to be peculiar to Jewish mysticism. Two of these are relevant to the present discussion. According to Scholem, unlike other mystical traditions (such as Christian mysticism) Jewish mysticism always has been a monopoly of males, devoid of a feminine perspective. Another unusual characteristic of Jewish mysticism identified by Scholem is the severe reticence of Jewish mystics to reveal autobiographical data. This, according to Scholem, explains the severe paucity of mystical diaries in

Jewish literature, as contrasted with, for example, Christian mystical literature.

When Ariel Stone began to contemplate the nature of the academic project that would evolve into this book, I recommended that she include a distinctly autobiographical dimension. Precisely because of her sensitivity to female gender orientation, because of the absence of such an orientation in Jewish mysticism and theology, and because of her dissatisfaction with this longstanding state of affairs, I further recommended that she strive to break boundaries and to establish new precedents by becoming one of the first female Jewish mystical theologians. Rather than jump on the opportunity to be a pioneer of modern Jewish mystical theology and spirituality, and the author of an exceedingly rare Jewish mystical diary, her reaction to my proposal was to burst out laughing. Such a reaction was not unlike that of the first Jewish woman, Sarah, when told that she would become the first Jewish mother. After catching her breath, Ariel informed me of her then current conviction that Jewish theology and mysticism were barely worth serious study or reflection, that neither mysticism nor theology were poignant nor relevant to the burning issues of the day, that Judaism would never be liberated from its androcentricity, and that Jewish identity, and that the details of her personal "journey" were nobody's business but her own. However, this book demonstrates that her laugh was not her last word on the subject.

In this work, Ariel's indisputable scholarly depth and erudition, particularly in Jewish mystical theology, not only demonstrates her vast learning and analytic skills, but also the all-important ability to apply them to vital, visceral, perennial, and contemporary issues of Jewish meaning, identity, and community. What she once considered peripheral is now considered essential.

Like many of the authors of the Jewish mystical and other texts she studied in the process that led to the composition of this work, Ariel in effect has produced a mystical autobiography, a spiritual diary, without revealing the intimate features of her own personal quest and journey. Ariel gently but firmly employs the fruits of her own intellectual, spiritual, psychological and personal transmigrations to instruct her reader in ascending the ladder of spiritual ascent. Ariel leads her readers from where she has been to where she is now, and to where she hopes they will also arrive: from exile to wholeness, from fragmentation to oneness, from self-alienation to intimate relationship, from self-deception to revelatory clarity. Like its predecessors in Jewish mystical literature, this work conceals more than it reveals about its author's life and personality, but it reveals more than it conceals about its author's journey in grappling with the identical existential problems that may be besetting the reader. What the author offers is her roadmap, a travel-guide to confronting these issues for the reader/seeker who wants to have the luxury of reading a roadmap composed by someone who already has made the arduous and perilous journey up its rungs, and has surprised herself along the way.

In this erudite, insightful and forcefully written manifesto, Ariel Stone draws upon her years of diligent study, hard-won lessons of living, insights garnered from years of rabbinical listening and counseling, and years of intense personal introspection, to produce a guide-book for the contemporary Jewish (and perhaps also the non-Jewish) person who seeks an end to their spiritual homelessness and who wants to find a path to individual identity, Jewish meaning and caring community through an encounter with various forms of learning rooted in a Jewish framework, especially a Jewish mystical one. But this is not the Kabbalah of Hollywood dilettantes or faddists. This is the real stuff. This work shows how obscure ancient and medieval mystical texts and ideas can resonate with contemporary relevance as we face the existential challenges that confront us each day. It demonstrates how the wisdom of the past can forcefully address the perplexities of the present.

The questions that evoke the spiritual journey described in this volume are both personal and perennial: Where is meaning to be found? Who am I? Why am I here? Where am I going? To what can I aspire: How can I acquire "directional signals" for my quest from my religious tradition? How can I overcome the roadblocks deterring me from becoming who I can become …and more. Ariel Stone powerfully and vividly demonstrates both *that* and *how* the authentic teachings of the Jewish mystical tradition, coupled with insights from biblical, talmudic and other aspects of Jewish tradition and wisdom, and peppered with insights drawn from a wide variety of western cultural resources, can offer a roadmap to spiritual homecoming, wholeness, oneness, meaning, intimate relationships and community. Using the esoteric teachings of the medieval kabbalist Joseph Gikatilla on the *sefirot* (the divine emanations) as the foundation, framework and springboard for her exposition, Ariel deftly unpacks the esoteric ideas and places them in the service of the practical. She moves easily from penetrating the mysteries of the Godhead to portraying the often equally mysterious workings of the human psyche in daily relationships.

This book is an invitation for searching, studying exploring, learning, grasping, discovering, recovering, creating, climbing, engaging, relating, knowing, being, becoming, entering, encountering, unifying...and more. It is an invitation to which you should RSVP, for you have little to lose, but much to acquire. This work is a potent antidote to "spiritual homelessness." According to the Talmud,

if a person tells you "I have not searched, yet I have found," do not believe. If a person tells you "I have searched, yet I have not found," do not believe. But if a person tells you "I have searched and I have found," believe.

These pages are Rabbi Dr. Ariel Stone's heart and soul. Believe her, because she has searched and she has found. How she did so may elude you - but that she has, should not elude you.

Rabbi Dr Byron L Sherwin
Distinguished Service Professor
Vice President for Academic Affairs Emeritus
Spertus Institute of Jewish Studies
Chicago, Illinois

"Out of chaos He formed substance, making what is not into what is. He hewed enormous pillars out of ether that cannot be grasped." — Sefer Yetzirah 2.6

These eerie, dark pillar-like structures are actually columns of cool interstellar hydrogen gas and dust that are also incubators for new stars. The pillars protrude from the interior wall of a dark molecular cloud like stalagmites from the floor of a cavern. They are part of the "Eagle Nebula" (also called M16 -- the 16th object in Charles Messier's 18th century catalog of "fuzzy" objects that aren't comets), a nearby star forming region 7,000 light-years away in the constellation Serpens. (http://seds.org/hst/M16Full.html)

INTRODUCTION

What need is fulfilled with the creation of the human being, body and soul? Why were human beings given two different longings, one for good and one for evil? After they were implanted in the human, how can they be controlled by the human power of choice, and by what strength?[1]

Seeing the Meaning of a Life

How does one express the meaning of a life?

On even the simplest cemetery headstones, one finds etched the deceased's name and, below it, two dates, that of birth and that of death. Between them is usually a line. Life may be starkly summarized by the idea of what one does with one's line – that small, straight line, which sums up the distance between a birth and a death. What is symbolized by that simple short line connecting the two most important dates in a life?

Jewish spiritual inquiry leads directly to the question of the meaning of life. So much about our purpose is unclear; so little that we would rely on is truly certain. One of the more disturbing questions we come to ask about our existence is *Why? What am I here for?* The human being lives a curious existential quandary: "The substances composing man's body belong to two worlds, namely, the world below and the world above."[2] In the story of human creation we are described in a way that suspends humanity between the opposites of *afar min ha'adamah,* "dust of the earth," and *nishmat hayyim,* "the breath of life."[3] Created to reflect God's image, but made of corruptible flesh and will, we are physical beings with spiritual longings, suspended between worlds. The Talmud relates a story in which an Arab merchant takes Rabbi Bar bar Hana on a journey into the wilderness, to see "the place where heaven and earth kiss."[4] If we knew how to look, we would see that each human being is that place, and we would come to understand the meaning of our lives. Beholding that illuminating sight, however, is literally the journey of a lifetime.

That wilderness Rabbi Bar bar Hana had to enter in order to see the place where everything is one is a striking metaphor; life itself is a wandering, as each of us, caught between heaven and earth, traverses a wilderness of uncertainty. Jewish mysticism offers us the vision of human life as journey, in which each step challenges us to find our balance among the opposites of a human life: spirit and flesh, dream and compromise, hope and reality. One's very sense of self is itself essentially a balance, between that which one can know of one's own inner thoughts and the outside influences that profoundly shape us. We make our way through all that is part and parcel of human nature: between sadness and joy, between what we have and what we want, between what is and what may yet be.

This study explores the doctrine of a central mystical tradition, the Ten *Sefirot* of the Kabbalah, to reveal ancient teachings which offer new perspectives for the challenges of balancing the demands of our lives. Jewish tradition has a long acquaintance with questions that we might assume to be the unique burden of the modern individual; but we are still asking the spiritual questions and facing the existential dilemmas that once preoccupied the authors of ancient books of Jewish wisdom: the Torah, the Talmud, and the mystical *Zohar.*

Spirit and Flesh

The author of Ecclesiastes wrote that "the eye is not satisfied with seeing."[5] It is human nature to imagine that which does not yet exist in one's experience; such is a central talent of the artist. Judaism teaches that each human being is the artist creating his or her own human life.[6] We are capable of believing that there yet exists something so far not beheld, a faith that clouds will clear and clarity will extend beyond the eye to the heart. But it is also human nature to be distracted: on the eve of the day when the ancient Israelites had been promised a revelatory moment to sweep away confusion forever, according to ancient tradition, they fell asleep while waiting at the foot of Mt. Sinai.

The heart seeks to see, and the heart flees from seeing. Still, the Psalmist asserts that "God is near to all who ... [seek] with sincerity."[7] Jewish tradition urges us to act in ways that reflect God's image and, by so doing, to redeem the failings of the flesh. Passively experiencing life, carrying the divine image like a mask held before one's face, empties it of meaning; such is not an acceptable response to the gift of life. Actively using both one's body and one's will in the pursuit of meaning is the response which redeems human life out of the wilderness of uncertainty.

The Jewish question of what one is meant to do with one's life is both asked and answered within the behavioral system of *mitzvot*. With the *mitzvah* system as guide to using one's body and spirit meaningfully, one faces a world of suffering and uncertainty from a certain framework which orders one's being in the world. One encounters the suspicion, anger, and hatred which rule human relations on nearly every scale of existence with a steady awareness that trust, happiness and love is yet possible – and a way to act to strengthen that vision.

For any observant Jew, the *mitzvot* help to order chaos. For the mystic, there is yet a more profound potential: "the foundational meaning of doing the *mitzvot* is the healing of the world, and the drawing forth of desire and will from above to below."[8] An individual's acts, when they are part of a larger structure of meaning, translate the individual life into a living link between heaven and earth, between spirit and flesh – and, in the doing of the mitzvah, between the individual and the world beyond the self. In every *mitzvah* that heals some hurt in the world, we heal the brokenness of our lives, for we who are part of the world.

Dream and Compromise

One of the more frustrating aspects of human existence is the distance between *kavvanah* and *keva,* between "intention" and "fixed form". In an ideal world, one's heart would always be with the work of one's hands; in reality, we participate in social compromises that may feel hypocritical. In Jewish terms, a central example of the tension between one's mood and one's obligation is expressed during the fulfillment of the *mitzvah* of prayer. In the Talmud, it is written that one who makes prayer *keva,* or a "fixed task" – in other words, one who recites by rote but whose heart is not in it – is not genuinely praying. Some examples of unacceptable prayers follow:

> R. Jacob the son of Idi said in the name of R. Oshaiah: Anyone whose prayer is like a heavy burden on him. ... Rabbah and R. Joseph both say: Whoever is not able to insert something fresh in it. R. Zera said: I can insert something fresh, but I am afraid to do so for fear I should become confused.[9]

When one is unable to summon one's best intention, one's *kavvanah,* but is still engaged in fulfilling one's obligations according to the proper *keva,* or form, is this not sufficient? Are obligations soulless and hypocritical if unaccompanied by the proper feeling? Are feelings themselves enough, or must there be a proper form? The Talmudic sages leave the question open.

In the modern American Jewish community, this quandary may be expressed as the choice between remaining alone with one's own individual preferences, and joining a community even if one's heart is not always in it. This is a perennial Jewish conundrum; some rabbis preferred private prayer to that of the group, and some mystics taught that God was best sought in solitude. Yet the rabbis also recognized that holiness is evoked by the prayer of the community, and mystics discovered that companionship, and a good teacher, lead to the deepest of mystical insights. Is one's presence in community, even in an imperfect situation, more valuable than individual acts? What is the value of compromising one's own desires in order to take one's place in the human community? Jewish tradition does not give a single answer. Jewish mysticism recognizes both a desire for the perfect, uncompromised, personal experience and also that one does not achieve one's dreams alone. As the Hasidic saying goes, "A prayer which is not spoken in the name of all Israel is no prayer at all."[10]

Hope and Reality

> A central tenet of Jewish mysticism is that neither our personal state of being, nor that of the world of which we are a part, is whole: the world as we know it is broken, and suffering. The Jewish response to that brokenness is not despair, and certainly not cynicism, but, rather, a rededication to wholeness, and working toward the vision of the healing that brings wholeness, as the highest meaning of a life. The stubborn belief in the human capacity to heal the world is at the heart of Jewish mystical spirituality. "There is a task, a law, and a way: the task is redemption, the law, to do justice, to love mercy, and the way is the secret of being human and holy."[11]

The Talmudic Sage Akiba taught that hope is the quality that purifies human beings from the sin of despair. The Hebrew root letters *k.v.h.* can be built into two words: "hope" and "purifying ritual immersion":

> Rabbi Akiba said, "How fortunate are the people of Israel – before Whom are you ritually cleansed, who purifies you? Your father in heaven, as it is said, "I will sprinkle purifying water on you and make you pure" (Ezekiel 36.25), and it is said, *mikveh Yisrael,* "God is

the Hope of Israel" (Jeremiah 17.13): Just as a *mikveh* purifies from sin, so does God purify Israel.[12]

Reality may be overwhelming, and life a whirlwind of confusion and misery. The Jewish path toward healing is found in the work of hope: of nurturing in oneself the ability sincerely to envision, strive for, and believe in the better world yet to be. The human search for meaning may all too often seem to be best summarized as too much like "a blind man searching in a dark room for a black cat that isn't there."[13] But Jewish mystical teachings hold out the promise of a future day of illumination. The path to wholeness is found through working toward the unified world, in which the meaning and purpose of existence will be seen clearly, even as the ancients said, "through a looking glass that shines brilliantly."[14] For Judaism, the source of all meaning and purpose is God; for the mystics, the closer one draws to God, the Source of Unity, the closer one comes to one's own wholeness, as part of the All which is One.

The purpose of a life is to seek that closeness, and to become whole oneself, as one comes as close as possible to the Source of Wholeness, of the oneness of All. In so doing, as part of the world, one does one's small but necessary part to unify the world with God.

> "God is near to all who call him, to all who call him with sincerity." What does *be'emet*, "sincerity" mean (*emet*, in Hebrew, also means "truth")? As it is written, "Give truth [*emet*] to Jacob"[15] meaning one must know how to unify the Holy Name exactly as it should be, and know the service of the Holy Name. And what does it mean to know how to unify the Holy Name? It is to establish the world as one.[16]

As the prophet Zekharyah (whose name means "God remembers") declared, "On that day YHVH will be one and the Name will be One."[17]

The mystical teachings – that life has transcendent meaning, and that meaning can be found in the healing and unifying potential of each act – parallel the place of the *mitzvot* in the life of a mindful Jew, as mystical practices are predicated upon the *mitzvah* system. Even as the *mitzvot* guide human behavior, mysticism holds insights that guide one's inner intentions. Mysticism offers support to anyone who is willing to keep an eye on the hope and possibility of wholeness even as life, in all its fullness, remains fragmented and distracting in its daily challenges, because the mystical path offers a way toward unity. Mystical vision not only heals the fractured individual sense of self experienced by so many, but also rebuilds weakened communities and communal structures of meaning. Here, the mystics teach, is the secret, difficult to discern and also to learn, of knowing "how to unify the Holy Name." In that secret is the most awesome of insights: that human acts are needed not only by the world, but also by God. It is in this vision of human potential that we will seek in Jewish action, thought, and belief.

"Seeing Is Believing"

> Moses said, "They will not believe me, nor will they listen to me; they will say 'God did not appear to you.'"[18]

Near the beginning of the epic Biblical story of the Exodus, an Egyptian prince named Moses, who had discovered that he was really an Israelite, was hiding from Pharaoh in the Midianite wilderness. Imagine his situation: nothing was as he thought it to be. His former status as an adopted son of Pharaoh had been replaced with that of fugitive; one day privileged, the next he belonged to the enslaved people who labored outside his former palace. Literally overnight, everything that Moses knew to be true about his life had completely changed, and now all he knew was that he had no certainty about his life, or what was true.

Was it because his earlier, certain preconceptions about his life and the experiences he was likely to have had been so completely stripped away from him that one day, while herding his father-in-law's sheep, he was able to see something that no one had ever seen before?

> He looked, and here was a bush aflame in fire, and the bush was not consumed. Moses said, "I will turn aside and see this amazing sight – why is that bush not burning up?" YHVH saw that he had turned aside to look, and God called to him from the midst of the bush, saying "Moses, Moses", and Moses said "Here I am."[19]

No wonder he worried that no one would believe him. Most of us tend to disbelieve reports of other people's eye-witness experience if the story invites us to venture outside the world of our normal expectations. "Seeing is believing," as it is said. If ever there was a phrase in the English language that would deny validity to mystical speculation on the question of *what might be* rather than *what is,* here it is. Pragmatic, guarded, conservative, it is a hedge against going along with a witness' report: let me see for myself and then I'll believe. Such an attitude seems to limit severely one's tolerance for the "what if" of speculation, interpretation, exploration, and wondering. Yet in our own lives we know that seeing is not necessarily understanding: much that seems apparent at first glance is not. And what does it really mean to see?

Much scholarly inquiry into Jewish mysticism identifies hearing, not seeing, as the primary sensory perception of Jewish spirituality.[20] After all, *Shema Yisrael,* "Hear, Israel," is the primary Jewish declaration of faith. God spoke words that created the world, presuming a capacity to hear, not see; at Mt. Sinai the Israelites heard Ten Utterances that defined the covenant relationship into which they were entering.

Yet it is also said of that moment that, during the theophany at Sinai, the people "saw the thunder."[21] This was no ordinary experience of human senses: "They saw what is ordinarily heard, and heard what is ordinarily seen."[22] At the moment of the greatest impact upon the limited human ability to perceive God's presence – the revelatory moment of Sinai – sight and hearing were scrambled. The extreme spiritual experience caused the Israelites to experience a blending of normally separate sensory perceptions.

> All the people saw the thunder [literally, *kolot,* "voices"] and the lightning, and the voice of the shofar, and the mountain in flames, and the people saw and were shaken, and retreated.[23]

Scientists studying the human brain's sensory capacity describe a different use of the senses, called synesthesia, in which the normal barriers that exist in the brain between neural stimuli are somehow lowered. As a result, people report being able to see speech, or hear color. It is as if their minds literally become more open, less prone to categorize and more flexible in sensing, as if more than one brain center might process a sensory perception.

The revelation is experienced by the senses in a way unlike any other sensory use of the brain.

What would it mean, then, to see God, if such sight is unlike any other use of one's eyes? It is an intensely personal perception, limited by one's physical senses; and it is beyond what we typically mean by "seeing."

> The voice was in the singular, as it is written: "I am YHVH your [singular] God" [which is to say that] what each of the Israelites saw was the root of his or her own being. With their own eyes, each saw the spark of the divine Soul above which is within each one. And they did not need to "believe" the commandments, only to "see" the voices. That's how it is when God speaks.[24]

"You saw with your own eyes," Moses tells the people, reminding them of the miracles of their Egyptian rescue, yet unquestioned belief in the unseen God is obviously *sine qua non.* The issue of seeing and believing has been curiously contradictory in Jewish theology from the beginning. According to the canonized text of the Hebrew Bible, normative ancient Israelite belief is that God cannot be imaged,[25] yet the Bible itself clearly refers to God as having a corporeal presence. The divine body cannot be seen, for it would be overwhelming to human eyes, but that does not negate the fact that there was such a body.[26] God tells Moses, "You cannot see me and live,"[27] but a closer look at this and other ancient texts reveals a more complicated idea of what may and may not be seen.

> There is a perennial clash between the view that God is not susceptible to portrayal by images ... and the basic religious need to imagine the divine in figurative representation. ... The problem of the visionary experience of God represents one of the major axes about which the wheel of Jewish mystical speculation in its various permutations turns. Indeed, literary evidence attests that the religious experience described in the different currents of Jewish mysticism from Late Antiquity through the Middle Ages is overwhelmingly visual.[28]

What does it mean to "see" God? In the English language, the verb "to see" encompasses many meanings other than that which imprints the retina of the human eye: to understand, to become enlightened, to visualize mentally, to comprehend – all these are ways of "seeing." Talmudic rabbis taught that *giluy Shekhinah,* an immanent but not necessarily visual sense of God's presence, is achievable in "normal" life; one need not be a mystic, need not seek out the paranormal or the supernatural in order to "see" God's presence, that is, to feel a sense of connection to the Divine. Such a sense was assumed to be available to any Jew, through the simple technique of fulfilling daily *mitzvot* with an inner intention of experiencing God's presence: "it was expected that the people at large cultivate a sense of the immediate nearness of God."[29] Yet there is a tradition which asserts an actual sight of God: "a handmaid was able to see at the Sea that which Isaiah and Ezekiel and all the prophets never saw."[30]

For the Jewish mystics that sought to explore more deeply, the desire to behold what the handmaid saw is primarily expressed in visual terms. This is true both in narratives of antiquity such as those of the ancient mystics called the *yordei haMerkavah,* the "descenders to the Chariot" who sought to duplicate Ezekiel's vision of a divine chariot (described but never named in the first chapter of that prophetic book), and in the development of the medieval schema called the *Sefirot,* which occupies a central place in this study.

What Moses Saw

At the beginning of his spiritual journey toward God, the greatest and most successful Jewish spiritual seeker of all time, Moses, saw a revelatory sight that is famous in the Western religious tradition: the burning bush. The burning that did not destroy the bush is often interpreted as a miracle, that is, as a way for God to get Moses' attention. But an eye sharpened by the vision of a mystic might see something inexpressibly more:

> the fire which burned *in* the bush without burning the bush, is nothing other than a small-scale manifestation of God. This humble manifestation resembles the larger one that would take place at the same mountain not long thereafter, when the Israelites received law at Sinai.[31]

Moses has the vision of a mystic. His ability to see what is there – not his ability to imagine implications or possibilities, but merely to see what was before his eyes – enables him to experience a startling moment of contact with God and gives him the certainty of a future vision to follow, toward Sinai and for the rest of his life. How did Moses see, not the surface impression of a burning bush, but the deeper reality that the bush was not burning? How did he manage even to be willing to believe that he might see something so utterly unexpected, so outside his human experience? From what did he have to look *away* in order to look *at*?

Jewish tradition takes care to emphasize that Moses was a human being, not an angel or a demigod. What happened to him, then, could happen to anyone; on any day, anyone might begin to achieve the kind of vision that will offer a promising path toward a secure sense of life's meaning. It is said that the real miracle of the bush was that Moses stopped and was attentive to what he saw, long enough to realize that the bush was not burning. We modern human beings are surrounded and bombarded by visual stimuli. How can we be alert to echoes of that bush in our own lives? How shall we slow down our lives, and learn to pause long enough to really see what is before our eyes? How does one see what one does not expect to see?

In our seeing there is much that goes unseen: often when we are looking for something small and necessary we look right past what we seek. Scientific study of the nature of human sight indicates that we simply cannot see what is before us if we have no referent for it in our experience or, at least, in our imagination. Even when we do clearly see what is before us, we may yet miss it if our minds are busy categorizing what we are seeing. Clear seeing and efficient categorization are useful and necessary, but there is another kind of seeing, a kind that allows us to see what we cannot categorize, cannot expect.

From his visual perspective, Moses was able to see that "no place is devoid of God's presence, not even a thorn-bush."[32] This is the kind of seeing that allows one to see that which might be. Rather than being a seeing that defines, it is a seeing that "involves letting go."

> When I see this way I sway transfixed and emptied. The difference between the two ways of seeing is the difference between walking with and without a camera. When I walk with a camera I walk from shot to shot, reading the light on a calibrated meter. When I walk without a camera, my own shutter opens, and the moment's light prints on my own silver gut. ... The secret of seeing is, then, the pearl of great price. If I thought he could teach me to find it and keep it forever I would stagger barefoot across a hundred deserts after any lunatic at all. But although the pearl may be found, it may not be sought. ... Although it comes to those who

wait for it, it is always, even to the most practiced and adept, a gift and a total surprise.[33]

On one level, then, what one sees depends on one's ability, like Moses', to see that which is not already assumed, not yet categorized. It is easy to miss what one does not expect; it is more difficult to see what one has never seen before. This is literally true of the way the human brain works, and it is also emotionally true. It is extremely difficult to be able to see and recognize that which is outside one's experience. To accept that one will see something new in the world requires a sort of humility, a willingness to believe that one has not already "seen it all." For Jewish interpreters, Moses' ability to see was a sign of his moral virtue as well as of his sensitive intellect. Regarding the phrase, "I must turn aside to look,"

> R. Simeon b. Lakish said: He turned his face to see, as it is said: "And when YHVH saw that he turned aside to see." (Exodus 3.4) When God saw this, He said: This man is worthy to tend Israel.[34]

The "turning aside" enabled Moses to see. This movement of turning, associated in Jewish tradition with *teshuvah*, with "turning" back to the path toward God, implies a movement away from what is expected, from what is already known and seen and categorized. It is the prerequisite for God's calling out to Moses, and the beginning of the role that will define the meaning of Moses' life.

That kind of seeing requires a willingness to bend, to be ready for new directions, to newly be able to see that which has been there all along. Torah scholar Aviva Zornberg notes the profound symbolism inherent in the physical motion: "the neck in torsion – an image for desire, a counterimage to the stiff-necked intransigence of those who set themselves against the new."[35]

This mystical kind of seeing is not dead with Moses, not frozen in time with the canonization of the *Tanakh*. Mystics seek it every day, and those who are open to it find that mystical sight is available to anyone. Annie Dillard describes her experience of seeing in this way:

> Then one day I was walking along ... thinking of nothing at all and I saw the tree with the lights in it. I saw the backyard cedar where the mourning doves roost charged and transfigured, each cell buzzing with flame. I stood on the grass with the lights in it, grass that was wholly fire, utterly focused and utterly dreamed. It was less like seeing than being for the first time seen, knocked breathless by a powerful glance. ... Gradually the lights went out in the cedar, the colors died, the cells unflamed and disappeared. I was still ringing. I had been my whole life a bell, and I never knew it until at that moment I was lifted and struck. I have since only rarely seen the tree with the lights in it. The vision comes and goes, mostly goes, but I live for it, for the moment when the mountains open and a new light roars in spate through the crack, and the mountains slam.[36]

So was Moses "knocked breathless by a powerful glance" at meeting God in the vision of the bush all aflame. It is this tree, this light, this seeing, that Jewish spiritual seekers have sought ever since. This is the mystical yearning of all life: this vision of light, this chance to be "lifted and struck," to ring with the light of God's presence.

The image of a tree all alight is among the most ancient of Jewish images: the *menorah,* the seven-branched lampstand. In the Torah's description, the large gold menorah, which is crafted for the *Mishkan*,[37] is carefully modeled on the living almond tree:

> Six branches issued from its sides: three branches from one side of the lamp-stand, and three branches from the other side of the lamp-stand. There were three cups shaped like almond-blossoms, each with calyx and

> petals, on one branch ... and so for all six branches. ... on the lamp-stand itself there were four cups shaped like almond-blossoms, each with calyx and petals.[38]

Atop its seven "branches," seven lamps were to be lit regularly to illuminate the sacred space. The lamps themselves were vessels that held olive oil and a wick. Why were they attached to a *menorah*, a lamp-stand shaped like a large sculpted tree? Perhaps to evoke the memory of another tree on fire.[39]

The *menorah* not only sheds the light by which the priests do the work of Israelite ritual; its light, burning from within a tree that is not consumed, reminds us of the light that is "utterly focused and utterly dreamed ... less like seeing than like being seen for the first time." This is the light of God's presence. In Jewish tradition, it is the *or ganuz*, the "hidden light," which is the epitome of seeing and being seen.

The mystical search begins.

THE PLACE WHERE ONE BEGINS TO SEE

> We shall not cease from exploration
> And the end of all our exploring
> Will be to arrive where we started
> And know the place for the first time.[40]

To embark on a spiritual journey, to define the line between one's date of birth and date of death, one must start with oneself, and an assessment of the place where one finds oneself. One seems to stand alone, in an existence demarcated partly by one's physical body, and partly by one's spiritual vision. This conjuncture of heaven and earth constitutes the human sense of self.

But what is a self? Western philosophical thought posits two possibilities: one may see one's selfhood either as that of an independent individual, bearing the weight of one's world on one's own shoulders all alone; or one may see one's self as part of an interlinked social network of individual selves, all affecting each other. In the social discourse of our time it is easy to feel disconnected and disempowered as an individual, since it appears unlikely that one individual can make a real difference in the meaningful questions and problems of the day. Yet we know that we are interconnected, because the fate of one is the fate of all: climate change will affect us all, regardless of our social rank or economic power. A story is told of a man in a lifeboat who begins to drill a hole under his seat. His companions, outraged, stop him. He is similarly outraged. What business is it of theirs if he drills under his own seat?[41]

The Jewish sages envisioned the world as a massive earthen raft, floating on an endless sea, with another endless sea up above. This precarious situation was anchored, they taught, by three pillars holding the world steady. The three pillars are still the essential, three-cornered stability of Jewish life: *Torah,* study; *avodah,* prayer; and *gemilut hasadim,* acts of loving kindness.[42] All three required human beings then, as now, to work together. No one person can hold or steady one of those pillars alone, just as no one can steady his or her own life alone. Such a philosophy which assumes human interconnection challenges the modern cult of individualism that predominates in Western society. The more ancient concept, however, may be coming back into currency. The sociologist Kenneth Gergen suggests that individualism is, at best, a passé concept, and, at worst, it has actually become destructive to our own survival as individuals and as a species.

> Western culture has long placed a strong value on the individual's self-determination (usually limited to the male). It is the good person, it is said, who makes his own decisions, resists group pressure, and "does it his way." It is the spirit of individualism to which the culture pays tribute for economic prosperity, military victories, and a strong democracy. Yet, the critics point out, this same cultural value has many shortcomings. In particular, it invites people to think of themselves as fundamentally isolated, alone to ponder and create their own fate. Because cooperating with others means "sacrificing

one's own desire" to the will of others, individualism also discourages cooperation and the development of community. A me-first attitude is also invited, because if we are all isolated individuals then self-gain is to be preferred to the gain of others. Indeed, propose the critics, if individualism remains the dominant value, the future well-being of the planet is jeopardized. We now possess the means for annihilating all human life, and values that stress independence, self-determination, and self-gain militate against cooperation for the good of all. They foster a context for destructive conflict.[43]

Modern Western culture teaches the foundational idea that each of us must be an autonomous individual, and thus, that the final authority rests with each of us; our decisions, to be valid, must be made by ourselves. Of course, each person has her own voice, which deserves to be heard. But the concept can be exaggerated out of all proportion or sensibility. The human self cannot, and is not meant to, carry all the weight of defining one's own human existence. Becoming one's self is self-defeating if it cuts one's self off from the other selves with which one shares life and the world.

Jewish mysticism asserts that underneath all the apparent individuals there is a unity, a Oneness that connects us all. In the spiritual journey toward one's own wholeness, one slowly begins to perceive the underlying connectedness of one's own life to all other life. In the recognition that all is One, we see that distinctions, which must be respected on the basic communal level of life, can be seen through, and unmasked as mere surface impressions. We exist in a world in which there are two kinds of perception, and two kinds of lived meaning-making which are complementary, not conflicting: communal and personal. That which we dream on our own is a private fantasy, free of the compromise of communal agreement. But Judaism teaches that we come closest to holiness in the midst of the community, by way of our connection to others.

> "Speak to the entire community of Israel and say to them, You shall be holy". (Leviticus 19.2) It is taught that these words were spoken in the midst of the people. Here is a hint that one reaches holiness by means of unification with all Israel. This is what is meant by the verse "for YHVH your God goes in the midst of your camp," meaning, when that camp is unified in a complete oneness.[44]

Finding the unity one shares with one's community requires recognition of the limits of the self, and the concomitant awareness that an individual's strength is drawn from one's individual connection to others, to the world, to the All. This requires being able to see beyond individual trees to behold the Forest.

Judaism teaches that God is reflected in each individual, and among all peoples as an immanent presence accessible throughout the world. But how to see that? How to access that hidden light? First comes a necessary recognition of the limits of the self, and the concomitant awareness that an individual's strength is drawn from one's individual connection to others, to the world, to the All. Like a tree, each person stands alone; yet, also like a tree, each person depends upon the environment that nurtures all. In Jewish tradition, this is the reality of life: in prayer, for example, one stands alone within the community in which prayer is offered, yet without the community one cannot fully evoke the holiness sought in prayer. Similarly, Jewish mystical insights are an invitation to consider the world as a dense web of interconnectedness. Inevitably, each human being is alone and isolated inside a physical body, but the self grows from the touch of a thousand different points of contact.

Out of millennia of searching for the unity of connection emerges the unifying world-view of the *Sefirot*. The theological speculation of Jewish mysticism that creates the doctrine of the *Sefirot* is called in Hebrew *kabbalah*, "received tradition." The *Zohar*, a recording of mystical speculation on the *Sefirot*, searches through the received tradition, yearning on each page to catch a glimpse of God such as that which Moses had. This sacred book, nearly 1000 years old, conveys a mystical vision of the "deep structure"[45] of the universe. Through its vision of the *Sefirot* as that structure, the *Zohar* presents a clear path toward understanding the place of human beings in it, that is, in the world. To discern the underlying structure of the universe is the first step toward finding one's own place within it. Exploring the *Sefirot*, then, is learning to envision the mystical unity, the wholeness, of the world, and of one's self.

"Clear" does not mean easy, nor does it mean simple; but there is a clarity of meaning that can be gained from a willingness to see what is taught and, even more fascinating, implied by the doctrine of the *Sefirot* explored in the *Zohar* as well as other Jewish mystical treatises. What is required of one who would seek clarity from its depths is the willingness to see that which is beyond one's prior experience, that which is unexpected – that which is beyond the self, and beyond the ordinary ways of seeing. Jewish mysticism offers, through contemplation of the *Sefirot*, a chance to see what Moses saw: to see the world and all of us within it interconnected in every aspect and function, every thought and act.

The journey toward a sense of wholeness and meaning is lifelong. It requires of each person a willingness to confront the self honestly and to assess, in a way as clear eyed as possible, the state of one's life, without hedging or avoidance. To move toward one's highest human potential requires holding on to this attitude as a first step. One must come to terms with the place where one is, if one hopes to understand one's place – and perhaps, even, to move from it.

The graph of the mystical *Sefirot*, depicted as a ladder on which one might rise toward one's best self and toward God, offers the conceptual focus for this journey. The spiritual path, as expressed through the *Sefirot*, is a way of visualizing one's progress, step by step, from inquiry, to knowledge, to understanding, and, finally, toward meaning. It is a lifelong journey. A successful encounter with each of the *Sefirot* as they echo within one's self and one's world requires all the integrity one can muster. The *mitzvot* offer guidance and support. This path has structure, and others have attempted to ascend. Some have even managed to leave signs along the way.

To rise, one must be willing to rise above rationality. While useful, it is only a part of life. Only 200 years ago, during the profoundly creative period we know as the Enlightenment and Romantic eras of European civilization, imagination became a quality more highly admired than the basic ability to see and quantify the phenomena of life. Imagination is the ability to conceptualize what the phenomena of life might signify in the vast scheme of things. To bring all of one's God-given faculties effectively to bear, especially in a quest for wholeness, one must welcome and use all one's abilities: the rational, the imaginative, the artistic, the emotional, and the creative. The creative is especially significant since that is the aspect in which, according to Jewish tradition, human beings most resemble their Creator.[46] One must be willing, in the spirit of the *Nishmat kol Hai* prayer's assertion, "All my limbs will praise," to resist the modern tendency to value science over imagination, to rank fact above faith. All "limbs," of the body and of the spirit, must work as one. This is an essential teaching of the *Sefirot:* all aspects of the diverse whole must move in harmony together. The world depends upon it. To reach such a place, one must suspend disbelief, to live with contradictions and to tolerate uncertainty; only thus is one able to withstand the reality of change, of growth, and of ascent.

To begin, we conjure up a dream: Jacob's dream of a ladder that was firmly rooted in the ground and yet reached the heavens. The ladder evokes the *Sefirot* and serves, as well, as a symbol of the distance between who we are and who we might become and, also, of the connection between the two. As its lengths are connected by rungs at regular intervals, it symbolizes the connecting link between opposites; as a ladder cannot function if each part is not stable and supported by every other part, so also the *Sefirot* need each other to balance and steady their existence: heaven and earth, good and evil, dark and light, one and many, spontaneity and planning, love and hate. The ladder has ten rungs. It is a visual evocation of the ascent of the *Sefirot*. But, at the same time, the ladder of ascent, the *Sefirot,* is also part of each of us.

The *Sefirot* echo the world as it is, and, as well, the Place in which we find our place. We rise toward that which is already a part of us; that is why it feels like coming home. That is also why it is so difficult.

We spend our lives avoiding ourselves, avoiding certain aspects of ourselves, at least, that we find unacceptable. Accepting ourselves fully and completely will be the first terribly difficult challenge on our way toward wholeness.

"Place" is a mystical expression for God, and the *Sefirot* are, finally, God. Our ascent of the ladder brings us toward God, but the ladder itself, the *Sefirot* by which we ascend, are also God. As we consider how the *Sefirot* express God, let us also keep in mind that everything we say will, by definition, be incorrect, at the very least by virtue of being incomplete. In the graph of the *Sefirot*, the "bottom" is that which is closest to us, that in which we ourselves have a part by virtue of our existence. It is the immanence in which we feel our part with God, each other, and the world. The "top" of the graph, which connotes the sense of being far away from us, is the mystic way of expressing the transcendence of God, which is beyond us, beyond our human comprehension, and beyond words. The "top" of this graph indicates an openness; the graph is not itself complete. This incompleteness at the far end of reality indicates the mystical recognition that we cannot speak of God, not fully and not correctly, and that is why the Psalmist writes *l'kha dumiyah tehila,* "to You silence is praise."[47] There is a place where there are no words. When we try to think of the word we need to express ourselves, but cannot bring it to consciousness, we are reminded that much cannot be expressed at any given moment. Yet we know that many words are spoken about God; Torah presents to us a God who is loving, angry, creative, regretful, impatient, awesome, and, most of all, communicative. This immanent God, the God we sense in our lives, is the one to whom we turn for comfort or in pain when we need to ask *Why?* even knowing that there is no answer to that question anywhere in life. That God is also real, and sought, in mysticism: *Eli atah v'odekha, Elohai arom'meka,* "You are my God and I will praise You, You are my God, I will exalt You."[48] We cannot help but speak our need, even when words fail us. Everything asserted in this work - about God, the world, the self, and human nature – is necessarily incomplete. A mystery will remain, a silent presence at the heart of the discussion. Yet we will speak many words, sometimes repeat them and strive to make them as accurate as possible, because we are trying to understand the meaning at the heart of life. Everything we say about God is also applicable to God's world. Everything we consider about ourselves is also applicable to God.

Everything we articulate will be wrong, because we are groping in darkness toward a half-concealed light. But it is only out of darkness that we can see light; it is only out of confusion that we can sense clarity; it is only out of homeless wandering that we can begin to understand what it means to come home.

Turning to See: Exile and Return

> It's bad enough to be in *galut* – it's worse to be in *galut* and not even know it.
> - the Kotsker Rebbe

The ancestors of modern Jews lived in *galut* – in exile. For many generations, the Jewish people lived in geographical exile, forced out of their ancestral home to wander precariously throughout Europe as a small, sometimes barely tolerated minority within hostile populations of medieval Christians and Muslims. Despite their homelessness and the attendant lack of power, the Jews developed and maintained a strong spiritual home, a secure place in the midst of terrible insecurity. They knew who they were and they maintained a strong sense of Jewish identity during 2000 years of exile. Their success was such that a recent victim of exile, the Tibetan Dalai Lama, came to leaders of the Jews to ask for advice and guidance, so that his people might survive what he feared would be their own lengthy exile. The Jews knew how to create a sense of home in the midst of utter uncertainty and with no clear sense of the future.

On the eve of the establishment of the modern state of Israel and fulfillment of the promise of the End of Exile, Jewish historian Yitzhak F. Baur described the home created by the Jewish people in *galut*:

> The most exalted speculations, the soberest rationalism, the grayest tones of everyday life – all remained bound

to the first realities of people, land, and Torah, past and future greatness, and the inexplicable sufferings of the Galut. The people are kept together by a national consciousness unique in the world. The land is the *real* land of Palestine, however veiled by religious imagination and mystery, however bereft by political circumstances of its beauty and productivity. And the much criticized Talmudic dialectic still leads always back to the miracle of the Torah. The religion renews itself in every generation through a strength that comes from the people and is at the same time mythos and purest intellect....a system of religious concepts – complete in itself, if overloaded – of which every representative of the tradition can give a clear account.[49]

For two millennia, the Jewish people knew that they were in *galut*, in exile. Yet, because of their rootedness in Torah, which allowed them to see clearly how they were connected to their memory, their people, and their God, they were able to create a sense of home within it.

Jews today live in a different kind of exile, one that many do not recognize. The modern Jewish condition is perhaps most striking when considered geographically: miraculously, a Jewish State of Israel exists again. In a sad irony, though, many Jews do not see it as home. They who are comfortable in their homes and neighborhoods, who get along well with the majority non-Jewish population around them, who in many places no longer struggle with legislated discrimination – these Jews do not see themselves in exile, in *galut*. The scattered residences of the Jewish people outside of the State of Israel are, rather, referred to as the *Diaspora*, Greek for "dispersed". Diaspora Jews speak of their destiny, Biblically mandated, to live among other peoples, to be a "light unto the nations," to bear witness to Judaism's insights and values.

Yet Jews today are in exile, in a very different way from the *galut* their ancestors knew, and possibly more difficult to survive. For varied reasons, among them the secularization of Western culture and the rise of the individual as a superseding social value, modern Jews have entered a new kind of exile. They live exiled not from the land where they do not live, but from the land carried by the Jewish people in their hearts.

> If I forget you, O Jerusalem,
> let my right hand forget her cunning.
> Let my tongue cleave to the roof of my mouth,
> if I do not remember you;
> if I set not Jerusalem above my chiefest joy.[50]

The Jewish *siddur* incorporated longing of the Babylonian exiles for Jerusalem into its prayers: after the chanting of the *haftarah*, "Have compassion upon Zion, for she is the source of our life,"[51] in the liturgy for a wedding, "soon may there be heard in the cities of Israel and the streets of Jerusalem the sounds of joy and of happiness"[52]; and in every ritual when the Torah scroll is taken out and read, the words of hope are repeated, "May the walls of Jerusalem be rebuilt."[53] Jews pray standing, facing Jerusalem, wherever they may be in the world, when the central *Amidah* prayer is recited. At the end of every Pesakh Seder it is declared, "Next year in Jerusalem!" In the middle ages Kabbalists developed an elaborate mourning ritual for Jerusalem's destruction, a ritual that was to be practiced monthly.[54]

For many generations of geographical exile, Jews carried "home" with them. Through Torah and Talmud study, thanks to immersion in social and religious norms, they knew *who* they were even if they did not know *where* they were. Now the situation is different. Jews are in spiritual exile, alienated from a clear and certain sense of Jewish selfhood. And in Jews' alienation from each other, what will happen to the memories that inform Jewish identity? Will the stories continue to be told?

The Talmud, which reached its final form in the first generations of the Second Exile, recorded the mythology of rabbis who understood that the underlying cause of their exile and suffering was their own people's alienation from each other. It was a distancing that reached, in its lowest form, *sin'at hinam*, "baseless hatred" and a lack of compassion for others, friends and enemies alike. The exclusion of God's presence from among the people was inevitable:

> R. Judah b. Idi said in the name of R. Johanan: ... "The Divine Presence left Israel by ten stages ... it ascended and abode in its own place, as it says, I will go and return to my place."[55]

The theology is symmetrical and places the onus directly on the people's choices to act: to fulfill the *mitzvot* or not, to do justice in the world or not. Since God's presence is established by justice, the lack of justice among the people drives the Divine Presence from the people, into exile. As an inevitable consequence of their exile from each other and from God, the Jewish people found themselves in exile from their homes and their land.

Judaism teaches that the world is in human hands, to create or to destroy, to guard or to waste. Jewish mystics, seeing the condition of exile, experience it not only as a geographical hardship but also as a spiritual wandering in the wilderness. Through the *Sefirot,* a mystic can seek to redress the condition of exile, for herself, for her people, and for God. The number of stages by which Israel and the Divine are distanced are ten, precisely the same as the number of *Sefirot,* the levels on the ladder of Jacob's dream, by which the mystic seeks to overcome and repair that estrangement.

> The glory of the Eternal went up from the midst of the city and stood upon the mountain which is on the east side of the city. "And from the wilderness it went and abode in its own place," as it is written, "I shall go and return to my place until they make *teshuvah.*"[56]

God is distanced by our acts, and we wander in the wilderness of those transgressions. Both we and God suffer, for the world's Oneness is broken and the All is incomplete. The image of Moses turning to look, doing *teshuvah* in order to see, offers a perspective on the first step toward wholeness in the world, and in one's self: first, there must be a recognition of the need for *teshuvah,* for turning away from the vision before one's eyes so that one might see the redemptive potential in the world.

The recognition of exile must be a communal awareness. Until the Jewish people recognizes that the cause of exile is part of each individual as well as all, the wilderness wandering of each of us, and of our communities, far from God's presence, and far from wholeness, will not end.

> If a man could see his own faults, he would not look the same way at the faults of others. This is what is written: a man sees all faults except his own. ... the remembrance of one's own faults and sins is a sign of the redemption [*ge'ulah*] of the soul, even as it is written, *karvah el nafshi ge'alah,* "bringing redemption to my soul."[57]

The first step toward redemption is to look toward one's own perfection, rather than find faults in others; and this personal redemption will be the first step in the general end of exile. We have come full circle in the mystical balance of the individual and the community: to save oneself, one must start by seeking the communal good; to redeem the world, one must start with oneself.

"Everything a person does leaves its imprint on the world ..."

> Even a human word, yes, even the voice, is not void, but has its place and destination in the universe. Every action here below, if it is done with the intention of serving the Holy One, produces a "breath" in the world above, and there is no breath which has no voice; and this voice ascends and crowns itself in the supernal world.[58]

The first step on the path towards redemption is to look towards one's own perfection, rather than find. Our acts, and even the words we utter, have an impact; with the right intent, they ascend, like the angels going up and down the ladder in Jacob's dream. One should perhaps think of the self not as a self-contained work of art but, rather, as part of an artistic collective with a shared higher purpose: "The purpose of man's service is to 'give strength to God', not to attain one's own individual perfection."[59]

One begins by learning to look for the hidden light that will enable one to see what is, not only what appears to be. One begins by seeing that one is in darkness; only then can one begin to discern light. The first step toward personal redemption is seeing one's own ethical faults rather than those of others. Similarly, the first step toward coming home is to acknowledge that one is *not* at home – one is in exile. Exile separates the Presence of God from the people, who, according to the Torah, were used to perceiving that presence in their midst regularly.

Jewish tradition holds that one does not overcome loneliness alone; one does not escape exile individually. There is a famous Hasidic story, told by the Rebbe of Tzantz, about a man lost in a forest who wanders for days. He finally finds another man there and, relieved, asks him how to get out. "I too am lost," says the second man. "I can only tell you that the paths I have tried lead nowhere. Let us join forces and look for the way together." So it is with us, said the Tzantzer Rebbe. We, too, are lost. Let us hold hands, and look for the way together.

Upon Beginning, A Prayer

> *b'shem yikhudo shel Kud'sha Berikh hu v'Shekhintei* – "in the name of the unification of the Holy Blessed One and the Divine Presence."[60]

Before the ancient holy ones began to pray, it is said, they prayed for one whole hour "that they might pray properly." A mystical attitude toward one's prayer and acts, including the act of study offered in this work, is summoned by first reciting, "This I do for the sake of the unification of the Holy Blessed One and its Presence." This "prayer before praying" gives voice to a universal human longing for the linking of earth and heaven, of child and parent, of light and darkness. It is a prayer for the end of alienation, the end of homelessness. Jewish mysticism teaches that it is possible to act for the realization of this prayer; indeed, that such healing is the purpose of human acts. Through every act, compassionately undertaken, and through every mindful word and intention, one rises toward unification and thus toward healing, belonging, home.

May this study offer to readers a step toward that rising.

PART I

Alef–Dalet–Nun-Yud: Things Hidden and Revealed

CHAPTER 1

Apples of Gold in Vessels of Silver

The mystical journey begins with oneself, with a readiness to open one's eyes and one's heart. It begins "in trying to overcome hardness of heart, in cultivating a sense of wonder and mystery, in unlocking doors to holiness in time."[61] The doors to holiness are everywhere; to see them, one opens oneself to a seeking beneath surface appearances, and toward the mystery beyond. We begin to consider how to seek beneath the surface with a teaching on the nature of the divine name *Adonai* offered by the medieval mystic Rabbi Joseph Gikatilla:

> *Adonai* [*alef dalet nun yud*] is the ark for the Name YHVH. ... .the name *Adonai* does not contain everflow and blessing except from the blessed Name YHVH, and one cannot enter into the realm of YHVH without going through the Name *Adonai*.[62]

Consider the Ark built by the Israelites during their wilderness wanderings. Carefully and devotedly crafted, it was a vessel of wood overlaid all about with gold, which carried the stone tablets of the Israelites' covenant with God. Surface beauty notwithstanding, by itself the Ark was just a vessel. What gave the Ark meaning and made it holy was what the vessel contained. So it is, also, with us.

Adonai: Surface and Depth

In daily life, we are surrounded by vessels, outer shells that mask inner realities. Surface appearances can be, however, quite convincing: American popular culture emphasizes the value of artificially created appearances. The essence of marketing is to manipulate perception by creating attractive surface impressions. What appears to be reality may only be a façade; often we do not understand the meaning even of that which is seen.

This perceptual predicament is no less true with regard to religious teachings. The great mystic Moses Cordovero warned his readers not to judge the book of books, the Torah, by its "cover":

> Come and see: a garment is visible to all. Those fools, when they see a man in a garment that appears good to them, seek no farther. They think that the garment is the actual thing. [However], the essence of the body is the soul. Just so, the Torah has a body. The commandments of the Torah are called the "body" of the Torah. This body is clothed in a garment made up of the stories of the Torah. ... all the words and stories are garments.[63]

Surface appearance is only a garment. This is the essence of a mystical approach: one approaches what seems to be concrete reality knowing that the visible is a veil.

> The wise king said, "a word fitly spoken is like apples of gold in vessels of silver."[64] ... a golden apple overlaid with a network of silver, when seen at a distance, or looked at superficially, is mistaken for a silver apple, but when a keen-sighted person looks at the object well, he will find what is within, and see that the apple is gold.[65]

One must read beyond appearances to discern beyond the distracting surface to the reality within, to see, as it were, beyond *Adonai* to YHVH.

For generations, Kabbalists have transmitted the sober truth from teacher to student: one must prepare oneself if one would seek beyond the veil. For some, discovering the discrepancy that exists between the apparent and the real causes intolerable intellectual stress, and, in extreme cases, psychic trauma. Exploring the hidden without appropriate preparation may lead not to redemptive visions of possibility but disbelief, disillusionment, and disaffection. The mystic investigation of Torah always dispels long-held impressions, and challenges deeply seated, and needed, beliefs.[66]

Another danger of the investigation of the hidden is that one who seeks the deeper meaning at the heart of life may be tempted to dismiss the surface level of appearances as evil, or, at the very least, as meaningless. For Jewish mystical tradition, this is a clear sign of going dangerously astray. The "silver vessel" level of the world's apparent reality must be respected; it is the level on which we live, the level on which every life is guided and judged by ethics and defined by the morality of one's choices. One may not reject surfaces in the quest for depths; an individual is expected always to consider *ma'arat ayin*, "the impression of the eye", in considering the ethics of one's own behaviors. Judaism does not negate any aspect of God's creation; wholeness is not achieved by amputation.

How to see the wholeness, and not just the surface? How to respect the vessel and yet proceed beyond the doorway? One must first contemplate a closed gate if one would ascertain how to open it. For the mystics, one cannot approach the truth of YHVH, with all the hidden knowledge implied by that Name, without perceiving and coming to understand, and appreciate, the Ark of surface impressions symbolized by the Name *Adonai* spelled out the way it sounds, with four Hebrew letters: *alef-dalet-nun-yud*. This name opens the doorway to the mystical vision of the world which is expressed by the *Sefirot*.

This first name of God, the first gate approached by those who seek by way of the *Sefirot*, is the vessel that is the surface level of our lives. If we are to see the evidence of God's presence in the world at all, we must seek it in the surface level of life, in the world of everyday errands and shopping and business and friendly relationships and family interactions. This level of life, filled with veils and hidden levels, is vitally important: it is the place where we live out the choices of our lives. This is the level of life the mystics call *asiyah,* "doing" in the most prosaic sense of the word, and it is at this level that we learn to look for hints of the golden apple. The opportunity to connect with God comes about by recognizing God's presence in Creation, and acting upon that vision. At first, one sees a piece of garbage flung along one's path; but with mystical study and practice, one learns to see the presence of God, waiting to be realized, in the release of all its potential power. That power is realized in the simple, world-affirming act of recycling or properly disposing of that garbage, and thereby healing one small part of the world.

Adonai is a Name of God that is neither hinted at nor veiled; it is the actual spelling out, in Hebrew letters, of the Hebrew word that means "our Master." It is an aural "veil" for the unsayable, for it is the Name of God used in prayer and ritual, by religious convention, whenever Jews vocally refer to the unpronounceable, ultimate Name YHVH. The collection of letters *alef dalet nun yud,* which can mean either God or a much lesser master, is the beautiful silver vessel of ordinary reality which holds the golden apple of deeper meaning within it. It anchors al that is to come, the way a tent peg socket is the foundation of the entire structure of a tent.

> The first of the gates and the keys by which one enters into the Name, may it be blessed, is the name called *Adonai.* It is the last of all the levels of God, from above to below. It is the true unifying foundation of wholeness. ... *Adonai* contains the same root as *adney hehatzer* (the foundations for the pillars in the courtyard).[67]

This spelled-out Name *Adonai* symbolizes everything significant about this initial level of our investigation of the *Sefirot.* The letters indicate a Name of God, which would seem to offer a welcome clarity and concreteness, except that this name is used primarily to vocalize another name of God that is spelled not at all in that way. Naming is an inexact exercise at best – to name a person may seem to evoke her essence, but a name can be changed, and no name belongs uniquely to one person. The God of the Jews is called by many names and, of course, can be called on without a name's being used at all.

When we imagine our own created self as a reflection of the attribute of *Adonai,* we see that a human being, too, is made up a surface appearances and deeper levels of meaning. A human being is also only partly named, and only sometimes nameable. And, the mystics, assert, human beings, too, are vessels which are meant to carry, and transmit, a sacred essence. The Torah declares that we are created in God's image, and one of the mystics' most provocative inferences from this statement is that, since each human beings reflects God, God can be understood, in a way, as a reflection of us. The similarity is no more certain, or perceptible, than that between a flower and its rippled, vague image in a moving stream, but it is there, and for Jewish tradition it has compelling force.

Rabbi Abraham Joshua Heschel has written that a human life's value is that we are messengers of that which we reflect; but alas, he writes, we have forgotten the message.[68] The impact of our lives on the world is the delivery of a message of which we are unaware, in all its confusing ambiguity. We do not know the effect of our actions across space and time, but, as physicists have discovered and ethicists have long taught, no energy, and no act, is wasted. Human deeds have an effect throughout the systems of which we are a part: of the world, of the self, which is of the world, and of God.

Mystical Jewish teaching claims a part for the self not only in the world, but also in the Place from which the message of our lives comes forth. One's goal is to experience the deeper meaning of human life, beyond the veil, knowing oneself to be part of an embracing and empowering human community, grounded in the ultimate foundational stability which is God. one must be willing to learn to see what a theology of the *Sefirot* teaches: that each human being is surrounded by the invisible links that connect each of us to all other human beings, and each one, in turn, to the world. Each of us affects all of the world through our own natural condition of interconnectedness in the way that a stone thrown into a pond creates ripples that affect the leaf floating halfway across, and disturb the snail on the other side; that the quality of one's interconnectedness, and the ethics of one's choices, touches and influences everything else in ways that the individual will never know. And that all of this is part and parcel of a Oneness that we call by many names.

The Sefirot: A Theology of Mutual Need

Once one is ready to consider existence not as whether, but how, one is connected to all life, one can begin to explore the *Sefirot* for insights into the self and its place in the world. Connections are part of every aspect of our lives: on a baseball field, outfielders choose their position vis-à-vis everyone else on their team; when a Jew walks into a sanctuary to participate in communal prayer, she looks for the right empty seat. As one finds one's place in any community, one is dancing one's part in a giant and complex waltz, in which each person's position and behavior affects everyone else's.

The *Sefirot* offer a visual example of this.[69] The mystics vary in their precise teachings regarding the nature of the *Sefirot*, but within the variations a well-known graph of ten attributes, emanations, or characteristics are depicted. They are variously defined as aspects of reality which all reflect each other, and all depend upon each other. The *Sefirot* are the world, the human community within it, and as well, a "map" of the characteristics of God, according to human perception, as deduced from the Torah. Each *sefirah*, each level, depends upon the others.

The reflections continue endlessly, in endless variations; one sees echoes of the *Sefirot* in patterns everywhere. The inner essence of the human being created in God's image is depicted in the many sefirotic aspects. An individual's place within the *Sefirot* may also be seen as occupying any one *sefirah* at the moment: in this way, the sefirotic system itself represents all of the individuals in any given group situation in which one finds oneself. Systems theory, especially as developed into theories of family dynamics, show clearly that the role each part plays in any group is influenced by the other parts being played in that group. The whole system is an interactive organism. Each individual, each aspect, each group, encounters life as a part of many systems, many groups, and within a larger whole in which all human beings find themselves.

This system is interactive: each person in any group, each aspect of any system, exists in a constant state of giving and receiving. The *Sefirot* are depicted as both receiving the *shefa'*, the Divine Flow, from God, and also transmitting it onward. The health and effectiveness of the entire system depends on each part fulfilling both of these functions: taking in, and giving forth. This encompassing All is that which the human being dimly senses and longs for; one attaches actively and mindfully to the All of the *Sefirot* (to which one is already attached, but passively), according to the mystics, by *devekut,* the act of cleaving as closely as possible to God. And there is that above which longs for the attaching as well.

The medieval mystic Ibn Gabbai relates the teaching of Rabbi Isaac the Blind, who identified the essence of "the religious life of the enlightened ones and those who contemplate [God's] name" as *uvo tidbakun,* "and to Him you shall cleave."[70] In so cleaving, one opens and strengthens the channels of the flow that one seeks to take into oneself: a *shefa',* an abundance, an "everflow" of harmony within oneself, and unity with others.

> The worshiper ought to contemplate and intend during his worship to unify the great name and join it by its letters and include in it all the [supernal] degrees and to unify them in his thought, ... And the reason that it is said: "and to him you shall cleave" is to hint at thought, which must be free and pure of everything and subdued, cleaving above in an everlasting and forceful cleaving, in order to unify the branches to [their] root without any separation. And thereby will the person who unifies cleave to the great name.[71]

The one who, in prayer and in the acts that follow it, seek to unify the great name is undertaking the mystic's most important task: the respond to the *tzorekh gavoha,* the "need above".[72]

This theurgic approach to Jewish mysticism asserts that, since human beings are part of the *Sefirot* which are part and parcel of God, God is, therefore, influenced by human actions. There is a need "on high", a need of God, that can only be answered by humanity. "More than the calf wants to suck, the cow wants to give suckle,"[73] offered one mystic, employing a Talmudic saying to explain God's need for the human beings God created.[74] This is an ancient theme, detectable in Biblical passages that express in the words of one scholar "the desire of the transcendent God to become immanent on the earth this God had created".[75] The mystical expression of that longing is embodied in human beings. Here is where physical ideas of imaging must be left behind: human beings are not a static image of God, not simply patterned upon Biblical accounts of divine emotional or physical manifestation. A human being achieving *devekut* is, rather, a link between heaven and earth, that is, an interruption of dimensions, through which God literally comes into existence in the world.

Three variations on the mystical goal of *devekut* are developed in Jewish thought. The first envisions *devekut* to be, in the Talmudic image, like the sticky cleaving of two dates.[76] Maimonides describes the human intellect at its highest realized potential coming as close to the Divine intellect as possible – yet each intellect, the human's and God's, retains its separate character. Or, as other mystics assert, *devekut* is actual union between the human and God: the human spark swallowed up in the Divine bonfire, the single drop of water within the sea. Turning the idea over again for a third time, other mystics define *devekut* is a reunion between the human soul and its source, to which it longs to return; this reconnection of the part to the whole follows upon the belief that a human is, literally, *helek eloha mima'al,* "part of God above".[77]

Devekut as an indirect connection was anciently defined by some Talmudic authorities, such as the school of Rabbi Ishmael, to be *imitatio dei:* thus, they taught, one could achieve *devekut* by choosing "to walk after [i.e. to emulate] the attributes of the Holy One, blessed be He. As He clothes the naked ... as He visits the sick ... as He comforts mourners ... [so ought you to do likewise]."[78] In contrast, the school represented by Rabbi Akiba's teachings maintains that an actual attachment to God is possible:

> In this world Israel cleaves to the Holy One, Blessed be He, as it is said: "You that cleave unto God" [Deuteronomy 4:4]. However, in the time-to-come they will become like [God]. For as the Holy One, blessed be He, is a consuming fire, as it is written – "The Lord your God is a consuming fire" [Deuteronomy 4:24], so shall they be a consuming fire as it is written: The light of Israel shall be for a fire, and his Holy One for a flame" [Isaiah 10:17].[79]

Techniques for achieving *devekut* are not clearly defined in Talmudic literature, but the implication from the Rabbinic teachings regarding *imitatio dei* is that one comes close to God through fulfilling the *mitzvot*. The Torah names those who keep the *mitzvot* as *d'vekim b'Adonai*, "you who cleave to God."[80] First among those *mitzvot* for many scholars is study of Torah, "which is equal to them all"[81] for Torah study undergirds and supports the fulfillment of the entire *mitzvah* system.

The *mitzvah* of prayer is the second central activity in *devekut*. During prayer, one attempts in thought, speech and act to cleave to the *Sefirot*:

> This is how a person merges himself with these qualities in thought, speech and action. For thought is the meditation we mentioned, speech is reciting the verse, and action is coming to the *beit Knesset* and bowing towards the sanctuary. Before the *Amidah*, he stands in the *beit Knesset*, his mouth a wellspring flowing with prayer, unifying *yesod*, the source of the wellspring, and

the well into which is opens, which is the *beit Knesset*. And he rectifies the *Shekhinah* with all the power of his concentration during prayer.[82]

To pray with the appropriate *kavvanah* is to connect oneself directly to the flow of *shefa'*: "*Barukh* is comprised of every power, from the source of life, from life, and from the light of life. It is blessing; it blesses; and is blessed, like the source of a stream (*berekhah*) that is blessed."[83] This drawing forth of the *shefa'*

> is the most important activity that man can engender within the Godhead. When thought ascends or when the two wills are joined, the gulf between man and God is abolished. ... The *Sefirot* become inextricably linked to one another; they are all comprised together, and they ascend in this unified state to *En-Sof*. ... This event, which represents the peak of mystical activism in Kabbalah, is portrayed as the underlying purpose of reciting prayers and blessings.[84]

These efforts at unification respond to the disarray in the *Sefirot*, which is seen as the deeper significance of the disorganization of the world; the *Sefirot*, like us, are alienated from each other, and aspects of life are out of balance above as below.

"The deeds below awaken the deeds above, the awakening below brings about the awakening above."[85] The mystic's task, and the goal of the mystical experience, is to realign the *Sefirot* through the fulfillment of *mitzvot* with the appropriate *kavvanah*. By way of the *mitzvot*, the mystic is able to nurture the *tzorekh gavoha*: the doing of the *mitzvot* creates energy in the *sefirotic* system, added by the human being doing the *mitzvah*. The energy activates the *sefirah* closest to the meaning of that *mitzvah*, which responds with its own burst of energy. As the exponential energy of the interlinked *Sefirot* are activated, the *shefa'*,0 or divine abundance of emanation that empowers and nurtures all creation, flows with renewed power throughout all the *Sefirot* and the world. God achieves immanence in the world.

This idea of theurgic mysticism is this: God needs human acts, human doing, in order to be fully manifest in the world. In the kabbalistic system, the human impulse which stimulates action comes from below, in the lowest, nearest regions, which are identified with the *sefirah Malkhut,* associated with the Community of Israel. Bringing the presence of God into the world from on high begins from the lower level. This power of the lower to act upon the higher is expressed in the mystic interpretation of the nourishment of the Garden of Eden:

> [N]o shrub of the field was yet on earth and no grasses
> of the field had yet sprouted, because God had not sent
> rain upon the earth ... but a flow would well up from
> the ground and water the whole surface of the earth.[86]

The lower flow that wells up from below is the "feminine waters" according to the mystics; it precedes the upper flow identified with the rain, the "male waters". The more powerful partner in this linkage, the "upper" God on high, is dependent upon the weaker partner, the "lower," mere human, mystic.

This drawing of God into the world clearly is for the sake of the world, which depends upon the constant flow of *shefa'* for life; and to the mystics, it was also clear that it was also for the sake of God. God's presence in the world is like the embers of a once blazing tree: sparks hidden in fragments, trapped in husks of smoldering materiality. The human task is contemplative, which is to say that every physical act, every ritual act, every moment of human existence should be lived with *kavvanah:* an abiding awareness of the ongoing task of looking for sparks of holiness everywhere, and that God is depending upon human help to emerge fully into the world. In so many words, the God of the mystics needs human beings to bring God fully into Wholeness.

This is the essence of the Jewish mystic's relationship with God: we need each other. The human being who sets out on the path to Wholeness through her life's acts achieves her own wholeness on the way.

God and humanity share in the same Oneness, and so as a human being focuses upon the ethics of living a unified life with her community, she is, through the sparks released in her acts, regularly kindling the fire on the altar of her own heart, as well as that of the primordial burning bush – a fire that, someday, will warm the entire world.

For the mystics, a human being can affect God – for good or for ill – because humans partake of the same *sefirotic* selfhood. The teaching that human beings are created in God's image develops new and fascinating depths. God is the *Yotzer,* the Artist who fashions, and the human is the *yetzirah,* the artwork.

> *vayivra' Elohim et ha-adam b'tzalmo,*
> "God created the human in God's own image,"
> *b'tzelem Elohim bara' oto,*
> "in the image of God they were created"
> *zakhar unekevah bara' otam*
> "male and female God created them."[87]

We are created in the *tzelem,* in the Image, of the unseen God. In cognate languages to ancient Hebrew such as Aramaic and Akkadian, *tzelem* indicates a statue, physically shaped to resemble the god whose presence it harbored in Canaanite and Sumerian religious traditions. Israelite religion rejected physical statues of God made of wood or stone, and replaced them with something more profound: "human beings are a sort of statue of God....in [this] theology human beings are what Israelite religion has in place of divine statues."[88] The ethical regard for the *tzelem* which is Judaism is the human being follows, then, from the fact that it is only through the human that God is properly revered.

For the mystics it is perfectly clear that by studying the artwork one gains insight into the Artist.

> Job said "out of my flesh I see God" (Job 10.9), for when a person considers his appearance and body, he can begin to learn something about God. We find in the Gemara (*Yevamot* 49b) that Menashe confronted

Isaiah, "your teacher Moses said that *man may not see Me and live,* and you have said *I beheld God on a great and mighty throne*"...it is impossible to see God because God is different from everything else....Isaiah saw God in the way that we see the physical; we see the outer layer, the clothing, as it were.[89]

"In the way that we see the physical," that is, through the level of the physical, we see echoes of deeper levels, deeper layers of reality. The physical body is only the beginning of our explorations into understanding the reality of our lives and the Life of the World. But although it is "only" the surface layer, it is to be respected; it is God's creation, and "in the way of the physical" it bears God's image. We must take great care of the physical vessel, nurture it and sustain it, if we would seek out its teachings, and if we expect it to help us go beyond it.

God does not actually have hands, or eyes, or feet, rather "there is a [part of the] world which is called Hand of God, Eyes of God, Feet of God, and all the rest of the body parts. There is no actual form of shape or appearance like this in the Upper Realms, nor can such even be imagined, God forbid; *v'ayn lo guf v'lo d'mut,* "has no body nor likeness," etc.[90] Rather, in the lower world there is likeness, which connects to its root in the upper world. Our eyes, for example, are sustained from that part of reality which we associate with God's Eyes; they are called eyes not because of a physical likeness but in a likeness of function.[91]

We resemble God not in actual physical terms, but in our understanding of how our physicality interacts with the world. When a human being acts out of her "image-ness" to heal, or repair, the lower manifestation of the upper reality, in so doing, she is healing the *Shiur Komah* – the "measure of God"[92] in the world – as it is expressed in the anthropomorphism of the Torah, and its anthropopathism as well.

Just as in the upper world there is a compassion which is called *Ayna Pekikha* ["open eye"] which forever watches over the compassion of the world and its needs, and this is called Eyes [of God], just so referring to the rest of the body parts, which are named by their functions, not their likenesses. The point of the human's creation is to repair the *Shiur Komah*. When a person does a *mitzvah* with his own hand, the part of the world which is called "Hand of God" is repaired.[93]

It is our ability to do, to create, and to act upon the world in *imitatio Dei*, as God does, which creates the grounds for our potential perfection as human beings.

The attainment of *imitatio Dei* is not merely a pious desideratum. It is an imperative of the Halachah, and as such is embodied in Jewish Law. Thus, in enumerating the positive commandments of the Torah, Maimonides places the commandment to emulate the Almighty to the best of our ability as eighth in the list.[94]

Mysticism seeks the deeper awareness of *imitatio Dei* in the act of fulfilling the *mitzvot*, for it is not only "the means whereby we can attain true perfection" but to go beyond the desire to perfect the human, toward the perfection of God.

What does it mean to be *helek Eloha mima'al*, a part of God in the world? First we must ask what it means, in Jewish mystical terms, to be a self. Here is the first step of the mystical journey. In order embark on the mystical path of the *Sefirot* toward wholeness, one must start where one finds oneself, with oneself. One must start on the ground where one stands and realize that wherever one is standing, one is a messenger of God.

Becoming a Self, facing an Other

"If I am not for myself, who will be for me? If I am only for myself, what am I? and if not now, when?"[95]

What is the human self? A moral quandary, an existential puzzle, a psychological problem which resists resolution. Something of the self remains forever hidden: "the roots of existence are never plain, never flat: existence is anchored in *depth*."[96] One's personal meaning is inextricable from the group meaning of which one is a part: one self-defines as an American, a Jew, a mother, a member of a book group, a sister, a registered Democrat, a vegetarian – and the meaning of one's life is a mixture of all these characteristics of self, and of the self which is so much more than their sum. And, as systems theory teaches, we can only grasp the true nature of a human being, or of a tree, in its living context: "one cannot study the life of a tree by *excavating its roots*."[97]

> This is what is the matter with us: we are bleeding at the roots because we are cut off from the earth and sun and stars. Love has become a grinning mockery because, poor blossom, we plucked it from its stem on the Tree of Life and expected it to keep on blooming in our civilized vase on the table.[98]

There is an inescapable paradox inherent in human life. In the search for a stable sense of self in the world, although we are surrounded by people, we may be bleeding at the roots, wandering from loneliness to uncertainty, and back again. We make bad choices out of the longing for certainty: "the devil you know," it is said, "is better than the devil you don't know." We may choose to stay with an unhappy relationship rather than risk the unhappiness of being lonely. We may fight change rather than chance a new horizon's promise. We may wonder at what may be beyond a gate, yet never muster ourselves to step through, and to see.

The self itself is a paradox. Not even the idea of a self can exist by itself. On the most basic level, one can only communicate one's individual sense of being by using communally-agreed upon sounds called language. I cannot say "I" unless you understand what I mean by that word. Ironically, the idea of what an individual is comes, as do all commonly-held ideas conveyed by a common language, from the culture which defines it. The very idea that we think about the individual self in socially conditioned, that is, communally-defined ways, is sobering. "What exactly is this 'inner self' we are supposed to be true to?

> What does it include and what does it exclude? What if it turns out that this true self includes some fairly nasty – or, even worse, banal – characteristics, traits

we would prefer not to think of as really *us*? What if many of our deepest and most personal thoughts and desires are actually products of the latest fads and fancies purveyed by the media? .... What if the whole notion of the innermost self is suspect? What if it turns out that the conception of inwardness presupposed by the authenticity culture, far from being some elemental feature of the human condition, is in face a product of social and historical conditions that need to be called into question?[99]

Selfhood has its limits, and maintaining oneself by oneself is a burden that the self was never meant to carry alone. One longs for something outside the self to trust. Sociologist Robert Bellah and his colleagues, studying American individualism and community, note that when one's ability to connect to others in significant ways weakens, one does not necessarily develop greater freedom to be oneself. The more one considers oneself an individual, independent of norms set by the community, the more one seeks validation: "when one can no longer rely on tradition or authority, one inevitably looks to others for confirmation of one's judgments. Refusal to accept established opinion and anxious conformity to the opinions of one's peers turn out to be two sides of the same coin."[100]

The medieval ethicist Eleazar Azikri saw the individual's place by the light of the menorah in the *Mishkan*. He compared the seven branches of the menorah to the seven branches of the primary ancestors: four Matriarchs and three Patriarchs: the Jewish version of a family tree. The light that their spiritual descendants are to regularly kindle in that menorah is called the *ner tamid*.

> We are commanded to bring pure olive oil to light the *ner tamid*, this means good olive oil, with a good smell, and it makes a good light. Similarly we bring ourselves, and if we are not good, i.e. if we are full of sin, then the light we create is smelly and nasty and no good for the

ner tamid ... one who is constant in service to God will be constantly refreshed, and will not dry out in the days of the sun, nor in those of the rains – then "God will be my salvation, and I will trust in his mercy forever," but if he will be inconstant in service, then God will be inconstantly present.[101]

The *ner tamid*, the "regularly kindled light," symbolizes a dependable, regular giving of the self to the other as the essence of community; an individual's choice to give only partially, in less than full participation, will cause the *ner tamid* to be improperly illuminated, and the entire community will suffer from loss of light. Only in the willingness to give oneself to caring for another, responding to and nurturing another's hunger for integration and meaning, can one achieve one's own sense of meaning, through the sharing of the struggle for wholeness that is also one's own.

Here is support for the self which must bear its own meaning. Each person builds a sense of self in community, learning to balance the conflict of internal desire and communal compromise by learning: in texts, in watching the role modeling of others, and by trial and error. If one is fortunate, one participates in building a community that supports the quest for balance and wholeness for each individual within it, and yet functions as a community.

The balance between the tendency to focus primarily upon one's own individual fulfillment, and that of securing the well-being of the community at the cost of one's own integrity, is difficult to find, and no easier to maintain. No martyrs need apply: the one caring must, as a prerequisite, care for herself.[102] Or, as expressed in a statement attributed to the Talmudic sage Hillel two thousand years ago: "They said about Hillel the Elder [that] when he would rejoice at the Joy of the Water Drawing Place he said: If I am here, everything is here, but if I am not here, who is here?"[103]

There is some indication that at the dawn of the twenty-first century we are emerging from the age of the glorification of the individual. For specific reasons, people do choose to come together to work for a common purpose.[104] Neighborhood associations form to share the security concerns of those who live on the same block; parents whose children attend the same public school band together to support its educational resources; people who share a love of the outdoors may become friends after meeting on an organized group hike. There are goals which are reached more easily as part of a group.

Modern individualist Americans are perhaps rediscovering an old truth: that if we focus only on ourselves, we will quite possibly begin to feel a sense of increasing distance from others. This insight, that something is wrong with the loneliness that comes with our sense of independence, is the first step toward overcoming our alienation from each other. If it is true that an authentic sense of self, and thus the capacity to truly appreciate and explore the meaning of our lives, is dependent upon the quality of our community, then much depends upon finding a way for the individual to find belonging in the group, and thus to rediscover one's meaning as a tent socket holding up the *Mishkan*: one among many, and all necessary.

In order to achieve a real integration of the self, one must find a way to accept one's past reality, one's past decisions and acts, at the very least as the necessary learning one did in order to arrive at the present point in time. We are made up of all that we have been, and all who are linked with our lives. Our efforts to build something of worth in this world require that we summon all that is within us. Jewish tradition records that the building of the *Mishkan* in the wilderness required a long list of different materials, and that each of the Israelites was needed to bring something in order for the *Mishkan* to be completed. The Izbitzer Rebbe taught:

> [I]t says in the holy *Zohar* (Shemot 148a) that these elements [the different elements of the *Mishkan*] correspond to the foundational elements found in the human being, meaning that one should deliver all one's elements and abilities to God, that God may rule over them according to the blessed divine will.[105]

In our essential structure, physically, emotionally and intellectually, and most of all, spiritually, we are each, and all together, a *Mishkan*, waiting to be constructed. Our task is to bring all the disparate parts together, into a structure raised to praise God, illuminated with the steady light of the communal *ner tamid*.

Memory and Belonging

For one who would explore a mystic's path to meaning, organized religious communities provide a meaningful framework for connecting to others not only in one's shared space, but also through time. The organized religious community is a communal expression of the preciousness of time; religious rituals reinforce the idea that life is to be lived mindfully. Each precious moment carries within it the potential for redemption.

> The communities of memory of which we have spoken are concerned in a variety of ways to give a qualitative meaning to the living of life, to time and space, to persons and groups. Religious communities, for example, do not experience time in the way the mass media present it – as a continuous flow of qualitatively meaningless sensations. The day, the week, the season, the year are punctuated by an alternation of the sacred and the profane. Prayer breaks into our daily life at the beginning of a meal, at the end of the day, at common worship, reminding us that our utilitarian pursuits are not the whole of life, that a fulfilled life is one in which God and neighbor are remembered first. Many of our religious traditions recognize the significance of silence as a way of breaking the incessant flow of sensations and opening our hearts to the wholeness of being.[106]

A community of memory is a community of the shared meaning conveyed by memory over time; Jewish meaning is transmitted with the memories that Jews retell over and over to each other, paradigmatically at the Pesakh Seder. How do Jews know what it means to be Jewish? Literally, by taking time to tell the stories which inform that meaning.

When God appears to Moses in their first encounter, speaking out of a burning bush that Moses turns to see, God shares the most intimate, and certainly least comprehensible, version of the Divine Name: *Ehyeh Asher Ehyeh,* "I will be (or "was", or "am") what I will be (or "was," or "am"). God goes on to say to Moses, *Zeh zikhri l'dor dor,* "My Name is my memory in (or "for," or "to") each generation." Theologian Rachel Adler describes the task of theology as focusing upon the *zikaron,* memory, in the stories we share with each other, and the archetypal myths that inform our sense of what it means to be Jewish. Each generation struggles with them until their meaning for that time is revealed.

This is the classic act of Torah study. It began with the work of the ancient scribe, who not only recorded the stories that became the Tanakh, but interpreted, as in Deuteronomy or Chronicles, and added, as in the early Aramaic translation of the Tanakh known as *Targum Yonatan.*[107] In this way, disparate stories became a corpus that transmitted meaningful guidance for Jewish life and belief; in each generation they are again considered, again interpreted, again mined for meaning.

The narratives that convey the Jews' sense of Jewish self-awareness, of collective *zikaron,* "memory," require not only a story teller but also a responsive audience. A story is related differently to different audiences. The story teller is conscious of the listeners' ability to hear and, thus, participate in, the story. Only in the dialogue between the two sides of teller and listener does the story reach its resolution and achieve its purpose. Recent scholarly inquiry into the development of printed Scriptural texts shows that for a long time, Jews transmitted and interpreted the Torah orally – as a story meant to be heard. The Hebrew verb for the reading of Torah itself, *k.r.',* preserves the sense of reading aloud.[108] To this day, the Torah is ritually read aloud as the high point of the Shabbat liturgy. The same verb is used to indicate the act of naming.

Memory is a vitally significant part of the foundation of the identity of an individual no less than a religious culture. The quality of Jewish time, and thus, lived Jewish reality, is grounded upon Jewish communal memory; what is not remembered is lost to the community, at least on the conscious level of self-understanding, as if it had never been. In the same way, as memories of what has been are shared with those who need to learn and own them, the common ground of meaningful belonging is prepared: theologian Rachel Adler points out that remembering is "re/membering", and re/membering "is the restoration of wholeness."[109] We cannot name the Jewish God if we do not remember the story of the covenant relationship; we cannot name ourselves within the Jewish community if we do not share those memories. "In every generation each Jew must see himself as if he himself went forth free from Egypt".[110] The mystical significance of memory will recur in our consideration of the Ten *Sefirot*.

A community of shared memory is a community with a clear framework upon which one can rely; those who find their place within it are those who find secure grounding in the sense of meaning it offers. This need not be the meaning of greatest popularity: fulfilled Jewish communities which constitute very small minorities in their societies can and do exist. The degree of their success depends upon the depth of the commitment of each individual to the community; this is Azikri's olive oil for the *ner tamid*. The Jew who is going to erev Shabbat services on Friday evening can't help but be aware of the fact that her journey toward the synagogue intersects with the worst rush hour of the American week. Even stranger is the trip to join with one's religious community for Yom Kippur, that sacred day when Jews fast and pray all day long. All around, the restaurants are open and businesses ply their regular trade. To attempt to balance both worlds equally will be a rather unsatisfying path. Only the one who is grounded securely in the sincerity of an inner integrity which is complete and whole will negotiate the alienation of American society successfully. And only she will know opportunities for deep, meaningful, and supportive belonging with a community that will give her a place to face, and learn, the lessons of her life. Such a person walks through the door of the synagogue and feels that it is home.

Remembering the Way Home

The paradox of the self is not, however, resolved. The ongoing challenge of each self, finding oneself within one's various communities, is, by way of living mindfully within those communities, to develop a wholeness, a sense of identity strong enough and deep enough to weather all the questions and storms of an individual life. This integration is not merely important for the individual and her inner sense of wholeness; as the mystics show us, it bears upon the well-being of the world.

To learn how to become oneself, among all the other selves of the world, is the everyday, mundane and deeply holy path which leads one toward a spiritual sense of oneness with the world, and with God. How to neither overestimate nor underestimate one's place in the world is not easy; to come to understand how one's needs and talents best fit against those of one's companions cannot be accomplished alone. One must keep before one's mind's eye both the image of the tent peg, and that of *Adonai,* in whose image one is created and before whom one stands. One must regain ancient memories to which one belongs, even if one has never heard them before, and so find the path that leads homeward.

Judaism teaches that the ideal of wholeness must apply to oneself precisely as it applies to one's surroundings. This idea is often expressed in Jewish spiritual terms. Even the Hebrew word for "peace," *shalom,* derives from the same root as the word "wholeness." This ultimate integration is an expression of wholeness on human and cosmic levels, which Jewish mystical tradition knows as Paradise. The paradox is that in order to be a whole self, we must reject the question for our own small individual sense of oneness, and become fully part of the all, and know it to be the Oneness to which we belong. To give up one's individual sense of oneness is to know the great oneness one becomes when one is part of the All.

There is a Hasidic saying: *Mi she ayn lo makom b'shum makom, yesh lo makom b'kol makom* – "If you don't have a place in any place, you have a place in any place."[111] The word *Makom*, "Place," is an ancient name for God. While a person may feel a lack of certainty of temporal place, the teachings of Jewish mysticism reassure that one's very being is intrinsically linked with God.

One must find one's place within the wandering itself. One who does not know is one who is ready to seek. To one who can admit uncertainty regarding the meaning of self and of life, the path toward meaning will open – and only to that one. Once again it is a paradox that most clearly reflects the human place: the certainty of an individual life is found outside of the individual. As Abraham Joshua Heschel put it,

> the meaning of our existence hangs on whether we can learn not to measure meaning in terms of our own mind, but to sense a meaning infinitely greater than ourselves. On the certainty of ultimate meaning we stake our very lives. In every judgment we make, in every act we perform, we assume that the world is meaningful.[112]

No one place on earth is The Place where one will finally find the meaning that will infuse one's life with purpose, unless all places are potentially The Place. "Earth's crammed with heaven, and every common bush afire with God!" wrote the poet, "but only he who sees takes off his shoes."[113] The poet reminds us that what Moses saw depended on his ability to turn to look, and suggests that every moment may be revelatory.

An ancient question posed to Rabbi Joshua ben Korkhah suggests hints that one must not only be ready to see, but to be seen:

> What did God see, that He chose to speak to Moses from within a thornbush? ... Why from within a thornbush? To teach you that no place is devoid of God's presence, not even a thorn-bush.[114]

Rabbi Joshua does not answer the more intriguing question: *what did God see?* But his colleague Rabbi Jose offers what is perhaps an answer later in the same text:

> R. Jose said: Just as the thorn-bush is the most difficult of all plants, and no bird that goes into it comes out in peace [or, "whole'], so was slavery in Egypt more difficult in God's sight than any other slavery in the world; as it is said: "YHVH said: I have seen, surely seen [*ra'oh ra'iti*] the affliction of My people." What is meant by the repetition of the word 'seen'? ... It is as if one took a stick and hit two people with it, and both felt the lash, and both knew the pain. Thus was the pain and slavery of Israel revealed and known before "the one who spoke and the world came to be". As it is said: "For I know their pains."[115]

God and the people of God's creation are linked, such that when one is hurt, the other feels the lash as well. What God sees is just what Moses and Abram both saw: the lack which is uncertainty, the readiness to see what has not already been seen and known, and the response to that seeing which comes out of compassion. For God, such a readiness to see what is not already seen and known is what the mystics call *tzimtzum,* the act of recognizing that a void is necessary if there is to be Creation to fill it.[116] For human beings, the same vision compels our willingness to make room, in order to let another person share one's space. A parent steps back and let a child make mistakes; a leader retires to let a new leader emerge; a person contains her personality's impact in a community, to allow others their own opportunity to act. One learns to see and feel the lash that falls upon another, not only upon one's own self.

Such a stance demands a willingness to live with an abiding sense of mindfulness, of the willingness to look at others, and to see oneself. "See, I offer you today a blessing and a curse"[117] declares the Torah, and the Kotzker Rebbe comments that the verse begins with "see" in the singular conjugation, but continues with "you" in the plural. Each one of us, he said, sees differently, and in our own way, the blessing and the curse that are presented before us all.[118]

CHAPTER 2

The Theology: Balancing Paradox

The Stakes

The grounding of our lives cannot be a foundation which we ourselves create; no individual self can create its own world without the danger of meeting a day on which one experiences a crisis of faith in oneself, and in one's self-sufficiency.

> The ideals we strive after, the values we try to fulfill, have they any significance in the realm of natural processes? The sun spends its ray upon the just and the wicked, upon flowers and snakes alike. The heart beats normally within those who torture and kill. Is all goodness and striving for veracity but a fiction of the mind to which nothing corresponds in reality? Where are the spirit's values valid?... It is such a situation that makes us ready to search for a voice of God in the world of man: the taste of utter loneliness; the discovery that unless God has a voice, the life of the spirit is a freak; that the world without God is a torso; that a soul without faith is a stump.[119]

In Torah study texts, lessons, and gatherings, Jewish teachers and students explore vital questions arising out of the modern American Jewish community's struggle to define meaningful Jewish existence. This study is based on the premise that while the questions may be drawn from political, sociological, and cultural categories of human awareness, the best answer is theological. If, as I have posited, the challenge is to balance self and other, individual and world, American and Jewish, and all the other complementary opposites between which we live, a mystical theology of connectedness, of a mutually-committed covenant, offers a promising path.

Theology is an articulation of the meaning of life from a religious perspective. Implicit in that statement is a method of constructing that articulation, which begins with God and the relationship between God and the world, and, more specifically, God and the Jewish people. Jewish theology proceeds from the core concept that we are not autonomous, independent, self-sufficient creatures, but that we live in interlinked, dependent, dense and all-surrounding webs of connectedness. In Jewish theology, we begin with the awareness that there is an Other in the world, and that our lives are defined in terms of self and other. Jewish experience is not autonomous but heteronomous: the source of authority for a Jew's existence reaches beyond the self to the self-defining realization that there is an other – and an Other.

This is not an abstract concept; it is interaction with the specific other who faces me that defines my moral existence, and teaches me of a commanding Other, called God. In a philosophy built upon such familiar Jewish ethical concepts, Emmanuel Levinas taught that "justice well ordered begins with the other"; justice cannot first be built abstractly as an idea, but must be birthed in the reality of human relationship.

Only by transcending individuality can a person touch God's presence. We are dependent for our moral existence upon the other who brings us out of ourselves, for only thus are we enabled to develop our own personal relationship with God. It is through recognizing another human being in all her need and beauty, face to face, that I become fully myself. The "face" of another human being whose need

I feel must not be a construct of my assumptions, created to conform to my comfort level. There is nothing more difficult than witnessing someone else's need, if it triggers our own sense of lack as well. But only on the day when I can truly see the Other as she truly is, can I begin to see myself clearly as well.

> To hear his destitution which cries out for justice is not to represent an image to oneself ... the face summons me to my obligations and judges me ... my position as *I* consists in being able to respond to this essential destitution of the Other, finding resources for myself. The Other who dominates me in his transcendence is thus the stranger, the widow, and the orphan, to whom I am obligated.[120]

The way we respond to our connectedness, not only that which we choose, but that which is beyond choice, such as family relationships or certain unavoidable existential realities, "has in many ways more in common with the older religion-linked versions of morality and a good society than with the modern Western liberal ideal."[121] To justify morality on a philosophical basis, rather than as a religious commandment, is a project of the modern era; philosophy can be intellectual and dry, though, while religion insists on personal connections, emotional loyalties, and the complete psychological commitment of faithful belief. While this can lead us toward a dangerous intolerance, it need not; we might discover, rather, that there is some profound and enduring human truth upon which the idea of connectedness touches. This "less individualist version of individuality" is defined not by an individual's assessment of some private sphere, but "becomes defined by responses to dependency and to patterns of interconnection, both chosen and unchosen."[122]

Old-New Theological Questions

Some question whether both the word and the concept of theology are foreign to Judaism. But Jews think about their religion, and detect a sense of internal meaning and coherence from its teachings; and when the answer makes a difference to the questioner's life, that is theology. Granted that thinking theologically is a Western concept, and other religions do it too, and the better question emerges: how the modern theologian will articulate what is distinctly Jewish in thought as well as in practice.

> Judaism is a way of thinking, as well as a way of living. The task of Jewish theology is to establish the nature and the parameters of Jewish religious thought, to articulate coherently the authentic views of Judaism, and to demonstrate how the wisdom of the Jewish religious teachings of the past can address the perplexities of contemporary Jewish existence in a manner that is compatible with the thought and life of the Jewish faith-community at a given juncture in time and space. The four criteria that characterize a valid Jewish theology are identical to those of any valid theology. These are: authenticity, coherence, contemporaneity, and communal acceptance.[123]

Ancient Israelites and modern Jews may not be very different from one another, as human beings live and die and wonder about their lives; but the presuppositions and categories of their religious thought are very different. As we consider the question of methodology, we come to the fork in the road which separates between Greek logic and the radically different Biblical mindset. The theologian deals with the problem of authenticity which is also common to every translator: how not to betray the meaning of the original insight or teaching, when it must be transmitted in a language or in categories of thought never dreamed of in the original utterance, or its context.

> The materials for the construction [of a Jewish theology] are the teachings about God and His relationship to man contained in the Bible and extended, elaborated on, and interpreted in the Rabbinic literature, in post-Talmudic thought down to the present day, and in the living experience of the Jewish people throughout the ages. The central methodological problem is that of discrimination. Not everything that has come down to us from the past is durable.[124]

The problem is one of a plethora of content; a tremendous amount of material exists in the Jewish family attic. How can we know what of the past is essential and what is merely definitive of a certain time or place? The situation of the modern Jew facing the traditional *siddur* is a good example: it has repetitions, garbled phrases caused by generations of Gentile typesetters' mistakes, and additions brought by the significant events that occurred during each generation of Jewish communities. The *siddur* has been described as the scrapbook of the life of the Jewish people: not everything in that *siddur* is timeless, but all of it together describes the history and formative experience of the Jewish people. How discern the most important refrains in all that varied song and story, that which is strong enough to continue to support the present, and welcome future additions?

And Jews are surrounded by much more than their own religious content. In an open society like America's, the contextual challenge for the modern Jewish theologian begins with the social pressure many Jews feel to avoid feeling fundamentally different. The story is related by a congregational rabbi of leading a discussion on Jewish questions of life and thought with a group of parents. After a discussion of Zionism occasioned by the approach of Israel's Independence Day, one mother was moved to ask, "Do all peoples have a homeland?" "That's the idea," was the response. "What about Christians?" she continued. "What's their homeland?" This fundamental difference between Judaism, a religious expression of essentially one extended tribal family, and Christianity, an evangelical religion, had become clear to her as never before. She had been taught only of the similarities the two monotheistic religions shared, and the so-called Judeo-Christian ethic. She had no sense of a way of thinking that was specifically Jewish, and that would require her to see herself as essentially different from her Christian neighbors.

The American liberal Jew's mindset tends to be shaped more by the founding documents of American society – the Puritan Mayflower Compact, the Deistic Declaration of Independence – than Jewish foundational texts. Often, the first condition of liberal Torah study must be reiterated: the perspective of the ancient Hebrews who are a modern Jew's spiritual ancestors is radically different. Many liberal American Jews are circling warily around the idea that Judaism's earliest antecedent beliefs are quite different from their Protestant-dominated American assumption about religion. The God of the Torah is not perfect, and not omniscient. The doctrine of monotheism, fully understood, challenges Jews to grapple with surprisingly sophisticated ancient teachings, such as Isaiah's insight that God creates light *and* darkness, good *and* evil.

Such Jews have assimilated far more of their religious thinking from the latent Christianity in American society than they have – or have had the opportunity to learn – from Jewish theological teachings. But it leaves them disturbed. They wonder how to defend or even explain the "vengeful Old Testament God" of Judaism, who "visits the iniquity of the fathers upon the children, even unto the third and fourth generations" in the book of Exodus[125] to their liberal, sophisticated post-Christian, atheist, or "spiritual, not religious" friends. They never think to question the mindset behind the question. The nearly universal assumption depicts the Jewish God as a highly anthropomorphized, personally involved deity who holds the Jewish people to unrealistic and arrogant standards, as with "the Chosen People" doctrine, and then regularly, if arbitrarily, blames and punishes the inevitable failures.

A rather different read of the text hardly ever occurs to American liberal Jews. Although it is there to be interpreted, it requires a radical openness, a willingness to see something other than what one expects, in order to comprehend what the ancient Hebrews understood about God in the Torah. One must turn the verse under consideration a different way, as the rabbis taught: *hafokh bah v'hafokh bah d'kula bah,* "turn it over and over again, for everything is in it."[126] For example, consider the verse in Exodus cited above another way: in situations like alcoholism, the sin of the alcoholic person who does not become healthy will affect the life and health of that person's children. A curse that falls on three and four generations is reasonable in the context of the ancient Israelites, who lived in tribally-organized human communities, very often with three and four generations of family living in the same tent, or in close proximity. Of course, then, three and even four generations would be hurt by the sins of the elders who ruled over their lives.

All depends on the effort it takes to make sense to modern American liberal Jews that one might consider the nature of God in a way that is very different from the way they have been conditioned to think about God in a society largely religiously shaped by Protestant values. Only then does one have the chance to consider that another way to learn about God is to discern God's presence, and will, in the way the world works. The statement "God willed it that way" is still applicable, but the thinking behind it is quite different. Rather than seeing the world set up as a board game and a deity arbitrarily moving pieces around, this construction sees everything that happens, even that which seems arbitrary, as inevitable occurrences to be accepted as the natural course of life and, therefore, as empirical evidence of God's presence in their lives. The typical modern liberal American is far more influenced by a species of Calvinist determinism, and a rather awful ideal of an arbitrarily caring, or not, God. One prays and hopes for a limited amount of divine compassion in the same way one hopes for lucky weather for the weekend, with about as much faith that one's prayers make a difference in the cosmos.

The ancient Hebrew understanding of God is radically different, and unfortunately most *siddur* translations into English do not illuminate this difference. American liberal Jews, usually without any Hebrew literacy in their intellectual arsenal, have no way to distinguish between the miserly Calvinist's view, and the Jewish mystical vision of the compassion flowing forth boundlessly from the Source of Creation, evoked as easily as in the recitation of a simple, heartfelt blessing.

There is an interesting insight available into the ancient Hebrew mind in considering the Hebrew word *olam*, which communicates both the concepts of the physical "world", and the temporal quality of "forever." God is referred to in the Hebrew of the Torah with similarly unbounded terminology. For the Torah, the world is not "that way" because God arbitrarily willed it to be that way, like an interior designer choosing between wood and stone for a floor. The world and the way it works are, rather, an ongoing opportunity to learn about the endlessly deep and profound way in which one small human intersects with, and participates in, Eternity.

We live in a modernity that is so different from past experience that at least one major Jewish thinker, Rabbi Yitz Greenberg, has suggested that we are living at the cusp of a "Third Era," which is as unlike the previous Rabbinic period as that period was unlike Biblical Jewish civilization. A major task, then, of a modern Jewish theology is to once again find the order that may be derived from apparent chaos. Judaism harbors within it the potential to address that which was not dreamed of by earlier generations and is outside the boundaries of Jewish experience; but which traditional truths must a Jewish theology uphold, and which can be challenged? Can a Jewish theology be authentic if it supports some traditional assumptions, such as the secondary status of women; can it be contemporary if it does not favor egalitarianism? How much communal acceptance is enough to stave off chaos? The way forward is not clear because it has never been orthodox, despite the insistence of conservative elements.[127]

> The nature and methodology of theology are more open questions in Judaism. Biblical and Rabbinic Judaisms embody a variety of theologies in forms that do not call themselves theology: narrative, prayer, law, and textual exegesis. Although in every period of post-biblical Judaism there have been influential theologies utilizing philosophical forms and categories ... there is no standard way of systematizing their Jewish content.[128]

The problem may not be with what is possible in Jewish thought, as much as with the structure of the methodology created to make it coherent. Adler warns of the burden an inadequate methodology places upon us as we think our way toward an authentic sense of Jewish meaning. *Halakhah,* for example, is created by "members of a Jewish male elite" who constructed the categories and method of classical *halakhah* to reflect their own perspectives and social goals and have held a monopoly on their application...classical *halakhah* [is] a methodolatrous system. The method becomes a kind of false god. It determines the choice of questions, rather than the questions determining the choice of method.

How does one succeed in the effort to see in a new way, when the permitted views are already legally defined? When one would seek a new way to understand the value of women's involvement in what were traditionally considered exclusively male areas of religious activity, Adler points out that "the Talmud's characteristic question" is "'how do we know that they are excluded?' The presumptions select the questions. The categories shape them."[129]

If the theologian must accord to tradition the respect of an equal partner in dialogue, as Martin Buber suggests, it is difficult to envision a discussion if one's interlocutor does not countenance it at all.[130] Here the theologian is rather like the first human, given the task of naming the animals and thus bringing them completely into being. If we cannot name a thing, it is not fully extant. The form of thinking adequate to the theological task is not detached conceptual thinking, then, but situational, sensitive to what is not yet spoken: "The beginning of situational thinking is not doubt, detachment, but amazement, awe, involvement."[131]

The Balance

A tangible symbol of the Jewish idea of justice is the *mishkal,* the scale; that simple device in which a central shaft balances two pans which hang from either end. The image of a scale in the hands of the goddess of justice is Roman. An older source which may well influence the ancient Jewish concept is that of the Egyptian goddess *Ma'at*, whose name connoted truth, order, and balance. She weighs the worth of a human life by placing the heart on her scales, and truth comes out in the balance.

In ancient Israelite practice, the *mishkal* was the basic tool of commerce. In one pan was placed a weight which reflected an agreed-upon value: a *shekel*'s worth of silver. In the other pan, a *shekel*'s worth of barley would be weighed out.

> Just scales, just weights and just measures you shall have; I am YHVH your God who brought you out of Egypt.[132]

In an agrarian society with an economy based on trade of unlike objects, the first step was an agreed-upon measure of value, the *shekel*'s worth of weight. The most basic expression of justice in this system is keeping one's thumb off the pan in which the weight is placed when the value of a sale is measured. The balance must be true, and just.

The Jewish communal experience is deeply rooted in both universal and specific justice; in the ideal, and in the application. The Biblical verse *tzedek, tzedek tirdof,* "justice, justice shall you pursue"[133] requires us to run after opportunities to establish justice among members of our community, and Rabbinic commentary asserted that the repetition of the phrase meant to ensure that both the ends which were desired, and the means by which they were reached, were just. The prophets declared that the value of our lives was based upon our treatment of the vulnerable members of our community. Attention to the specific needs of the individual for whose sake we exert ourselves in the cause of justice is part and parcel of the aspiration. Judaism values *tzedakah* more highly when it is carried out with *gemilut hasadim*, the kindness which seeks to avoid humiliation of the human being in need.

> Rabbi Yonah said: "happy is the one who gives to the poor" is not written here, but rather, "happy is the one who uses insight when giving to the poor" (Psalm 41.2),

meaning: consider this person carefully to understand how best to do the *mitzvah* with this particular person.[134]

It is the recognition of the fundamental human reality of interrelationship that shaped the writings of the Tanakh: "the ancient Hebrew writers developed a narrative art because only through narrative could they convey a view of human life as lived reflectively, 'in the transforming medium of time, incessantly and perplexingly in relation with others'."[135] The story of the Jewish search for meaning is told in stories of interaction – human with human and human with God. These are stories of acting in ways that are, or are not, rooted in justice, and the quality of justice expressed between human beings directly reflects upon the integrity of each actor's relationship with God, as well as with each other.

How are we to see clearly the relationships in which we are enmeshed? How to see the common humanity we share with neighbors? One passes homeless men and women on the street trying not to see them. One chooses and drops friends, and even membership in a community, for there is no vision of mutual responsibility. For Jews who contemplate their own place in the chosen, self-conscious Jewish community, the challenge of seeing what the American Jew has in common with those to her right or left on the religious spectrum is difficult enough to meet; how much more so is the effort to sense elemental links of connectedness between American and Israeli Jews.

A Jewish theology of balance and the principles that derive from it, proceeding from a Jewish conceptualization of God, embraces all of life and its meaning. Its truths and applicability must withstand the honest and thoughtfully considered existential challenges that emerge from every aspect of a Jew's life. The word "truth" in Hebrew is *emet*, a word spelled with the first, middle, and last letters of the Hebrew alphabet; truth in Judaism circumnavigates the world, open to all. A true theology of Judaism is constructed of a methodology enabling the learning from, and incorporation of, new truths that have yet to be discovered; a theology of balance recognizes that there are extreme imbalances in religious life at present, and new emphasis must be placed on the neglected side of the scale.

God is an eternal truth, but our understanding of that truth changes and grows. Thus the theologian faces new questions in the interface between the two, and one of her challenges is to articulate the sense of the dialogue between them and the new synthesis emerging from the dialectic. A theology growing from the *Sefirot,* a theology of wholeness, declares that all of life's religious attitudes, from belief to criticism to cynicism to doubt, are vital to the complete inclusiveness of the approach. Everything is as it has to be in the world that God created; whether or not the order of Creation makes sense to human beings may be intellectually stressful, but is not significant to Creation's legitimacy. For the mystics, since God created all that exists, everything is necessary: both the cherished teachings of Jewish tradition, and that which defies both the tradition and its teachings, have a place in the understanding of the world's structure, as the system of the *Sefirot* expresses that structure.

To put it in terms of mystical theology, some strong and necessary sparks of God are to be found within the criticism and the bigotry – one must dig deeply to see them, but they are there, because that is how this world is created to be. The good and the bad are confused, mixed up together in impenetrable thickets of history. Yet even in darkest, deepest exile, one may at any moment, in any situation, turn and see God's presence, even in a thicket, even in the midst of struggle.

A theology of balance, using the structure of meaning offered by the *Sefirot,* embraces all the imbalances; they are natural, and inevitable. The path toward rebalance and wholeness accepts opposites as part of a natural whole, and does not shy away from paradox and conflict, but sees the only meaningful path as leading right through the thicket of such difficulties.

Yet a theology of the *Sefirot* does not envision a neutral balance: at its foundation is *tzedek,* "justice", and, above justice, at the place of most perfect center balance, is located not neutrality but *Tiferet,* the *sefirah* of compassion. There is no neutrality at the heart of life, the mystics reveal: all revolves around compassion.

> What is our hope with our callousness standing like a wall between our conscience and God? Dark is the world to me, for all of its cities and stars, if not for the breath of compassion that God blew in me when he formed me of dust and clay, more compassion than my nerves can bear.[136]

One must remember to look, despite disappointment and sadness, in order to see. And one must be prepared to see what has never yet been seen, even at the moment of greatest blindness and most acute difficulty, even in the face of what one already knows with certainty.

> Abraham lifted up his eyes and looked, and he saw a ram caught in the thicket by its horns; Abraham went and took the ram and offered it up as a sacrifice in the place of his son. Abraham named the place *Adonai Yireh,* and it is called by that name to this day: in this place God was seen.[137]

At the last possible minute, Abraham lifted up his eyes and looked, and saw; Moses turned aside and looked, and saw. Somewhere in that thicket is the redemptive discovery, the path forward, which we will otherwise overlook.

The Blessing Is in the Struggle

One of the earliest insights of Jewish belief, conveyed in the story of Jacob's night encounter with the messenger of God by the river, is that the people of Israel finds meaning and purpose – blessing – not by avoiding the struggle but by plunging into it.

> Jacob was left alone; and there wrestled a man with him until the breaking of the day. ... Jacob called the name of the place *Peniel*: for I have seen God face to face, and

my life is preserved. The sun rose upon him as he passed over *Peniel*, and he limped upon his thigh.[138]

What did Jacob see that caused him to realize that he had been face to face with God? He struggled for his life by a river named Yavok, whose name derives from the Hebrew "wrestle". In order to find a way to cross over, he first had to commit to the struggle; only then did he find the blessing in it. The way to bridge that turbulent river was not easy, and it marked him for life; but in it he found an experience of the real presence of God.

The theologian has no recourse but to struggle with the outside sources which influence the Jewish seeker of the time. He or she must discover the place in which the seeker stands: to speak the language that the Jew understands[139] and respond to the situational need of the Jewish community of that time. Modern Jewish theology must help the radically self-conscious and self-centered Jew rediscover the communal truths that premodern Jews were born into and took for granted; it must show us a way to re-integrate the shattered vessel which was premodern Jewish community. While we should in no way idealize the shtetl, which in reality was often a destitute, desperate, and disease-ridden place, the nostalgia for that vanished way of life should not be dismissed, for it is really a longing for a secure sense of Jewish identity. At the beginning of the modern period, in the 17th century, the Eastern European shtetl's mostly Jewish population allowed its inhabitants to maintain a cultural insulation from non-Jewish influences that is no longer possible in the modern world. The world of predestined, certain Jewish identity and culture has been replaced by a world in which Jewish life cannot be based on any kind of cultural isolation.

In two thousand years of Rabbinically guided Jewish communities, theology, as a way of thinking about God and the meaning of life, was ideally more or less aligned with Jewish praxis, which is to say that what one did was more or less a direct reflection of one's beliefs. This is not true of the modern Western Jewish experience. In a world which has encouraged Jewish identity to fragment into a partial definition of self for many Jews, coherence and integrity become primary pathways toward meaning.

In 21st-century America, religious life is unrecognizable to traditionalists of even one or two generations ago. Where Jewish communities once cared for each other's physical as well as religious well-being, now "some communal practices were taken over by the secular state."

> Other practices were jettisoned by congregations because they appeared foreign and "Oriental." Still others were abandoned by individuals because they had come to see themselves as "private citizens" with minimal obligations to other private citizens. It became impossible to imagine a unified way to live as a human being, a citizen, and a Jew.
> We cannot simply resurrect the old premodern praxis, because it no longer fits us in the world we now inhabit. ... To be faithful to the covenant requires that we infuse the whole of our existence with our religious commitments. How is that to be done in our specific situation?[140]

Part of the answer is, in good traditional Jewish fashion, to look for familiar organizing principles that are part of the dominant culture, but in their own non-Jewish way echo Jewish principles and values. In a modern American Jewish congregation, there is a highly developed sense of personal responsibility regarding environmentalism: recycling, vegetarianism, and other practices which respect and conserve natural resources. Within the "green" philosophy are principles that are easily restated in Jewish terms. Beyond that, the fundamental stance of the Jewish individual who is committed to "recycling, reducing, and re-using" is far less self-absorbed and far more communally-conscious than the average American. Such a person is already living in a way that parallels Jewish communal norms. This person might be receptive to the idea that Judaism offers a praxis similar to that which already informs their lives, and that what Judaism can offer them is not so different – only that it is deeper, broader, and more enduring.

Jewish theology and praxis must be grounded in the soil in which Jews have always been rooted: Torah. It is in the act of study that the mystics find the possibility of revelation at all moments, that is, all moments when the student is prepared to look for what is not so easily seen – a bush that burns and is not consumed, a memory that demands the gift of the heart and yet does not diminish the giver. For the mystics, immersion in Torah study opens the door to that "convergence of interpretation and revelation," in the words of mysticism scholar Elliot Wolfson, which is Torah study at the level of its highest potential. Not from new inventions, but out of the plunging deeply into the communal memory conveyed by study, new Jewish visions of theology and of praxis will emerge.

And because study is an experience not of the individual but of the community, the individual immersing in study finds that the true spirituality of the Torah study experience requires the community. Rabbinic teaching holds that "when two study Torah together, the Divine Presence is with them."[141] The meaning of the modern Jewish community will not be found in building a physical *Mishkan,* but in creating the potential for revelatory contact with God – for seeing God, in the way that the Torah relates that Moses and Jacob did – in any space occupied by that Jewish community. This is not a new idea; it is received wisdom, in which we must find new depths and new teachings. In Part II Torah study is explored as means of ascent: grounding, guide, and path toward Jewish wholeness.

CHAPTER 3

Medieval Mystical Insights to Inform a New American Jewish Theology

Repairing the breaches, and healing the torn links that are meant to connect all human beings, is the goal of all acts of reaching beyond the self and into the world. In Judaism it is a given that "we all stood together at Sinai." In Kabbalah the longing to know before whom we stand compels us beyond the self toward others, and beyond the surface toward the depths. The medieval mystic ibn Gabbai relates the teaching of Rabbi Isaac the Blind, who identified the essence of "the religious life of the enlightened ones and those who contemplate [God's] name" as *uvo tidbakun,* "and to Him you shall cleave."[142] The one who cleaves becomes the link between upper and lower, between one and many, between all that is and all that might yet be seen.

One seeks as an individual, yet within a community's structure of meaning; the personal is inextricable from the communal. The term *kabbalah* itself means "that which is received" from others – those who came before, and from those who learn alongside one. One does not fruitfully study, mysticism or anything else, alone. Mystical insights which will inform a new theology for American Judaism include all these aspects: specific, differentiated community as an expression of individual wholeness, wholeness as a healing from alienation, and transmitted ancient wisdom showing the way to future communal redemption. And those insights will illuminate a way through our longing, toward home.

Ancient Wisdom as a Path to Redemption

The mystics teach this central, unifying truth in terms of exile and redemption: alienation from each other is a significant aspect of the human experience of exile. Exile in the geographical sense, which recalls traumatic destruction and dislocation, is intimately linked to exile in the spiritual sense. Home is destroyed and the Jews are sent away from the sacred place they built as a community, and through which they knew God's presence. In classical Jewish terms, Jews are in exile from God's presence because the sacred space was destroyed, and redemption is symbolized as the rebuilding of that sacred space in Jerusalem, and the restoration of God's presence there. Redemption, in Jewish tradition, is about rebuilding, restoring, and coming home – all acts that require interaction and communal connection. Jews cannot achieve redemption as individuals, but only as a meaningful community. Mysticism offers the individual a path to explore and heal the connections of one's own life and the life of the world, to set oneself on a path of practice which will restore them, and thus to find a way to connect to sacred community.

The book at the center of this mysticism, the *Zohar*, is itself a commentary on the Torah, interspersed with stories about a group of companions who delve into the holy mysteries of Torah study together. The *Zohar* – the Hebrew means "brilliance" or "splendor" – records mystical speculation about the nature of God, and the meaning of human life, which had been transmitted through generations only among small circles of initiates. Written in a mystifying form of the ancient language Aramaic, hinting at even more mystifying theological ideas, it cannot be studied without a guide. Despite its opacity, the *Zohar* is nevertheless an absolutely typical Jewish work. It epitomizes Jewish learning in every generation and in every field of study, because it both draws upon earlier wisdom, celebrates the synergy of shared learning, and encourages fascinating new insights.

Kabbalah is an attempt to read the Torah as God's biography. The early Hasidic masters, mystics that they were, saw a corollary: to study Torah was to consider the teaching of every verse for one's own self, created in the image of God. To inquire into one's own life is inevitably to consider one's impact in the world, one's reflection in the cosmos.

In Jewish terms, one lives one's essential connectedness through the three pillars of the world's existence and stability: *Torah, avodah,* and *gemilut hasadim* – study, prayer, and acts that fulfill relational responsibility.[143] Each of the aspects of this three-fold path to personal meaning leads one to others. Study – *Torah* in the widest sense – is traditionally done in *hevruta*, which provides the benefit of the synergy of shared learning. *Avodah,* prayer, including meditation, self-assessment, and other modes, traditionally requires a *minyan*, a group, to invoke holiness. Finally, acts of *hesed* (the core of the phrase *gemilut hasadim*) that fulfill relational responsibility demand that we first engage the other, especially if we are in a superior position to that other in power or position, to carefully ascertain what is required in each situation.

The Jewish framework of both concepts and acts which guide us along this path is the *mitzvah* system. A *mitzvah* is not, as popularly defined, a "good deed", nor is it merely a rigid list of imposed "commandments," which in 613 laws define the entirety of Jewish life. The *mitzvot* are the ever-evolving expression of the central Jewish idea of obligation. Life is a gift: what is one's responsibility in response? All *mitzvot* can be divided into two categories: *beyn adam l'adam,* "between human and human," those which pertain to one's relationship to others, that is, the world, and *beyn adam l'Makom,* "between human and God," those which have to do with one's link to God. The fundamental understanding that the *mitzvot* are equally an expression of individuality and community opens many mystical doors. For Kabbalists, the way is already prepared, and the wisdom already exists: our redemption is waiting to be discovered, by our own acts.

Is Kabbalah Jewish? – Specific, Individuated Community

The Hebrew word for tradition, far from being static and set, is *masoret*, "transmission." The word "Kabbalah" denotes "receiving." The term *m'kubal*, "kabbalist," was first applied to mystics of medieval Europe. The early Kabbalists portrayed themselves not as innovators but as faithful transmitters of that which had come before them.

The Kabbalists were, and their descendants are, profoundly conservative in their stance toward Jewish tradition. They seek to conserve the value of that which they study, to guard its meaning, and to protect it. The medieval creators of the mystical texts studied today were probably observant, and certainly knowledgeable, Jews who seem to have explored the mystical texts of earlier generations in small groups, just as the *Zohar* depicts Rabbi Shimon bar Yokhai doing with his students and learning companions. Scholars assume that it is quite possible that the *Zohar* itself was created as a result of such small group study, and that it is a product of more than one author.[144] Although they themselves were creating it, they saw it as the wisdom of the Talmudic rabbi who lived a millennium earlier, rediscovered in new expressions but drawn from ancient wells. This was the "old-new" essence of what they understood themselves to be transmitting.[145]

These students of mysticism considered the subject of their study to be sufficiently esoteric as to be kept secret from most of the Jews of their community. An old doctrine articulated in the Talmud forbids exploring mystical matters in groups – a ruling of which their small, devoted group of *havraya*, "companions," was aware, and sometimes suffered the consequences. Jewish tradition further forbids Kabbalah study until one is forty years old, is married, and has a beard.[146]

Through the prism of the Jewish traditional culture of sacred learning, one extrapolates several requirements for Kabbalah study: first, a mature Jewish adult is well-versed in basic Jewish knowledge. Second, one must be well-along in one's emotional and social development, be married, most likely have several children, and have a dependable way to support them. One's social connections, through friends and work, are well-developed by the age of forty. Third, one must be male – and that beard also connotes a certain maturity and level of Jewish observance. Kabbalah is not for just anyone; rather, in Jewish mystical tradition, such study is ideally reserved for the psychologically well-adjusted, communally responsible, learned, male, adult Jew.

A modern, egalitarian perspective questions the limits placed around the study of Jewish mysticism, once having recognized the justice of opening other doors to Jewish knowledge beyond their traditional bounds – to women, for example. Yet a progressive approach does not consist of wholesale condemnation of all distinctions, and effective judgment considers each aspect of the requirements for Kabbalah study on its own merits.

Since Jewish mystical writings are largely based on a deep grounding in Jewish sacred literature – Tanakh, Talmud, Midrash – it is unlikely that one will be able to appreciate mystical study in any depth without familiarity with those sources. Thus we reinterpret the bar to women's involvement with mysticism not as gender restriction but as an educational caution; in our own day, when education is egalitarian, so too should access be, finally, to the mystical texts.

Must the student of Kabbalah be a Jew? It is true that all religious cultures express a mystical element and that scholars find some interesting similarities between them.[147] Yet significant differences exist between mystical teachings, and certainly in behavioral expression. Jews and Christians encounter the same Torah with very different culturally-based assumptions. A two-thousand year old interpretative tradition has built upon itself, layer after layer, in both religions, in the choice of words in translations, in the direction of interpretative commentaries which betray their inevitable preexisting bias in the inner meanings they discover within the texts, and even in reactions to certain terminology. Christians call the Jewish holy texts an "old" testament, superseded by their own sacred texts. American culture, with its basically Christian religious sensibility, inherits many unarticulated assumptions about Jewish texts. An interpretative culture is a vast and complex sea of latent and patent assumptions, of which a student cannot be fully aware.

Jewish law commands one not to set a stumbling block before the blind; yet that is what one does if one ignores the assumptions, the expectations, the interpretative culture, and the intellectual and religious grounding of Kabbalah study. It is to invite the unprepared to encounter the incomprehensible. Worse, it is to empty the term of its meaning, for unless it is a transmission of received wisdom, it is not Kabbalah. The early sources warn of the dangers inherent in sharing mystical knowledge with the unprepared. Mis-study of the texts may or may not prove dangerous to those incapable of truly understanding them, but it certainly will be so to the texts themselves. The wisdom is both old and new. Unless it is old, there is nothing new in it.

Jewish tradition, nurtured by received wisdom, is grounded upon the assumption that what is received will be carefully, faithfully transmitted. When it is made accessible to all, it is cut off from the roots of the life it can no longer offer, and it is demeaned into superstition. Authentic study in Jewish tradition is inextricably linked to practice. To share in the received wisdom – that is, to become wise – is to become sensitive not only to one's own need to learn and discover, but also to one's attendant responsibility to the interlinkages of community that makes the study possible. The community is ideally founded and maintained according to the wisdom in which the individual seeks immersion.

The *mitzvah* of learning Torah as a Jew is to learn with one's whole self, to recognize that this is the ultimate goal of becoming a differentiated individual. One must leave behind the fear of being different in order to truly mature, and individuate – that is, to develop a specific identity. The sacred learning of Torah study is not academic; what one learns is embodied by the individual whose practice is informed by it, and by the community which is formed through it. One finds one's unique identity naturally in the unique and differentiated, or individuated, community which is, in its practice and its public face, different. Jewish learning leads to specifically Jewish growth.

Wholeness as Healing from Alienation

Recall our image of the ancient Israelite measure of value, the scale. Even as a scale will not function without both opposing pans suspended in a balance, Jewish ethics, or *musar,* does not function without a constant act of thoughtful balancing. *Musar* is part and parcel of Jewish daily life and law, and it is also a meta-ethic that informs and overarches it. It is an expression of a general sense of Jewish morality and also the attitude that focuses on the ethic of every behavioral gesture. *Musar* is the ultimate practice of balance in all dimensions. It is the source of the Jewish caricature: on the one hand ... yet, on the other hand ...

Jewish ethics recognizes and addresses "the tensions which exist between the ideal and reality"; it balances between the demands of a *mitzvah* and of its context.[148] This tension is regularly demonstrable in Jewish tradition in the meeting of form and content, of *keva* and *kavvanah* – and, for mystics, between the transcendent and the immanent, between the longed-for and the lived. Life, in all its constant uncertainty, is most vibrant in its creative potential in the space between a continuum's two poles – and in the discomfort of conflicting opposites when they meet. Each time, an ethical decision must be made not only on the basis of precedent but also on a close consideration of the matter at hand and its unique circumstances. "A living morality is not assessed as a system of values but, as Martin Buber has observed, in the way it determines an ought, and an ought not only in the here and now."[149]

These are the creative parameters of ethical Jewish choice. In the classic statement, "I set before you this day life and blessing, death and evil,"[150] the Torah is content to command in vague and general terms to choose life and leaves the details to be determined in the given situation. The struggle to live according to an ethical ideal is a daily reality. The *yetzer hara'*, the "evil impulse," is hard to control. Every day, every moment, we learn, we judge, we choose:

> Free will is given into the hand of each human being to improve his ways, to correct his behaviors, to straighten his paths, and to choose the path of life and good, as it is said, "See, I set before you this day life and good, death and evil" (Dev. 30.14), "choose life" (Dev. 30.19).[151]

For a mystical theology, being an ethical person is of ultimate importance, because of the power of human actions to bring God's presence more fully into the community. It is the ultimate act of personal responsibility, since no one, not even God, can do it for one. It is the ultimate act of prayer: to *be* the change we pray to see in the world. As Abraham Joshua Heschel is reported to have said after joining Martin Luther King's Selma march, if it was time to pray for equal rights, in this case it was his legs that were doing the praying.

> It is written (Ex. 23), *va'avadtem et Adonai Eloheykhem uvarekh et lakhmo,* "And you shall serve Adonai your God and each shall bless his bread." The beginning of the verse is in the plural and afterward it continues in the singular. This is because that which is related to matters of holiness must be done in the community of Israel and in the name of all Israel, and therefore it is written *and you (plural) shall serve.* But in matters of physicality, even when the community eats together, each one's eating is for his own body, and is not for the need of his companion. So we find that matters of Torah and prayer, even if one engages in them alone, they are in the name of (*l'shem* also means "for the sake of") all Israel, but matters of physicality, even if they are undertaken in a community, each one is an individual in this.[152]

This recalls the Talmudic teaching[153] that one who seeks to be judged on his own merit will find that his merit depends on others, and one who seeks to be judged on the merit of others will find his destiny dependent on his own acts. The acts, and the destiny, of the individual and the community are inextricably intertwined, since we are all interconnected within God.

According to mystical theology, any *mitzvah* that any individual does may tip the ethical balance of the entire world, and its fate, toward redemption. The opposite act, an *averah,* "transgression", may tip the balance of the world toward destruction; the Hebrew is related to the verb "to cross over", as in to overshoot one's boundaries, or to tip a scale out of balance by going too far. We may seem weak to ourselves, but even as the butterfly's wing reverberates across vast distances, we too are capable of tipping the world's balance toward redemption or destruction. We too echo throughout the world.

Seeing the Link Between Heaven and Earth

Having been created and put into this worldly place, the Jewish mystics understood God's command to the first humans "to till and to tend" the Garden to be an ongoing human task: to tend the place, and in so doing, tend the Place.

> [S]ince God is not just static being but also dynamic becoming, God needs us as we need God. ... we are here to be transparent vessels of [God's] power and creativity, the healthy and supple limbs, if you like, through which It enacts Its dance in the real. Without our conscious, willed, inspired participation, God is incomplete; God needs us to realize God's design in and for the world.[154]

As we are the limbs of a will of which God is the essence, we are all part of the same reality.

> *Lo yihiyeh b'kha el zar, el lo yihiyeh b'kha zar.* "There shall be no foreign [or strange] God among you," that is to say, God will not be foreign [or strange] within you.[155]

Once we arrive at the realization that to reflect God's image means to echo God's essence, then it follows that our inner sense of being, our soul, is an extension of God. Though we often consider the idea of God to be "foreign" to our own being, somehow different from us in essence and thus something to be discovered and figured out, in truth God is not strange or foreign to us – rather, God is of us. As the Kotsker Rebbe put it one night while considering the sleeping faces of his students, "How frail a dwelling for so great a God."

> Whatever is lacking in you, the same lack is in the *Shekhinah*, for the human being is a piece of God above (*helek Elohi mima'al*). Any lack in a part is a lack in the all, and the all feels the lack of the part.[156]

If each of us is a reflection of God individually, then it follows that all of us – the world itself, as the aggregate of all human actions and interactions – is also a reflection of God. Each of us generates either a positive or a negative ethical energy, and everything that happens does too – and all that reflects back at God. This is the meaning of studying Torah as God's biography: Torah seems to be a narrative of events or a collection of commandments, but is actually a window into the nature of God. Which is, also, of course, a view of our own nature – and a way to draw forth a sense of the meaning of our nature and our lives.

The realization that we are active conduits of energy from God and back to God gives each of us a vitally significant role in the life of the world. Our choices strengthen either the potential good of the world or the potential evil that is also inherent within it. Within us. Within God. The recognition that we play an active part in the life of the universe of which we are a part leads to a breathtaking definition of the purpose of the *mitzvot*.

> It is written, "and keep my commandments, and do (*asa'*) them" (Lev. 26.3). R. Hama son of R. Hanina expounded: 'If you keep the Torah,' [says God], 'I shall consider it as though you had made (*asa'*) the commandments,' [the text may also be translated]: "and make them." R. Hanina b. Pappi expounded: He told them: If you keep the Torah I shall consider it as if you had made yourselves.[157]

The mystical book *Sefer haYikhud* goes even further to assert:

> Whoever keeps my commandments, I regard as if he has made Me...literally, [since] whoever blemishes below, blemishes above, and whoever purifies himself below, adds strength ... above.[158]

The purpose of a human being is to imitate God and in so doing, quite literally and vitally to create God's presence in the world. We do so, however, as human beings, stumbling along, faced with the daily effort to balance that which is within ourselves. As heaven balances earth and day balances night, there are a good inclination and an evil inclination in the world – and, therefore, in human nature, which itself is a microcosm of the cosmos. The world is made up on every level of complementary balances between opposites that require each other for their own existence: male and female, light and dark; even a magnet has a positive and a negative polarity. It is a paradoxical predicament, the human situation.

We are inescapably both rational and spiritual, and we must balance these conflicting opposites in order to fully embrace our humanity. Not only are we ourselves like Jacob's ladder, linking heaven to earth in the ultimate dream of connectedness and certainty; in spiritual terms we often find ourselves standing upon a sort of ladder of purpose, and of exaltation, up which we are drawn, on some days, by a vision of the Eternal, toward the heights – only, on other days, to fall back. We are people who, in an age that has seen the collapse of confidence in science, seek certainty and a sense of meaning elsewhere – but where? We are rising and falling on that ladder which links heaven to earth, mostly falling. Some come to religion; others are attracted to the gods of patriotism, money, power, celebrity, acquisition, fads, cults, and other kinds of shallow belonging. Still others drown their sense of desperation in addictive behavior.

There are those who have the courage to live in this situation and find it in themselves to face uncertainty without resorting to hypocrisy or giving in to fear; who prefer difficult questions to the panacea of easy misfit answers. Some, for the sake of their children, if not for that of the child within themselves, want to engage in the search for real meaning, and come to understand by experience the truth that one can only follow that path by "doing justice, loving goodness, and walking modestly with your God."[159] They are the messengers of God whom we can see rising and falling, trying and failing, making the very journey of their lives a sacred pilgrimage. They are the legendary Thirty-Six of Jewish lore, the righteous for who sake the entire human world – miserable and corrupt as it is – continues to exist. Each one of us can aspire to become one of these messengers of God, these ordinary human beings who keep one eye on the ladder always. It is those Thirty-Six for whom the *or ganuz,* the Light at the End of the World, is waiting.

The saying that "it is always darkest before the dawn" is usually construed to mean that one's situation can seem desperately doomed before the light of relief appears. Darkness is often a metaphor for evil, for negative feelings of apprehension and even terror. But mysticism sees a more complex reality in darkness. The *Zohar* begins its interpretation of the Torah's account of creation:

> A spark of impenetrable darkness flashed within the concealed of the concealed, from the head of Infinity – a cluster of vapor forming in formlessness, thrust in a ring, not white, not black, not red, not green, no color at all ... it yielded radiant colors.[160]

It is darkness out of which light appears; darkness is the first condition. It is a necessary condition for light. Ancient Rabbinic commentary observes:

> The eye is composed of a white part and a dark part. One sees only through – only out of – the dark part."[161]

Anyone who has been on a stage under bright spotlights knows this experience. One who is in the light cannot see the audience; all is dark. Yet when one stands in darkness and looks into an area of light, everything is illuminated.

The Aramaic term for blindness is *sagei nahor,* "filled with light." This paradox of light, and of sight, is a powerful metaphor for much more. Creation itself is an act that comes out of darkness. The light that comes forth from the darkness is the original light of creation, appearing when, according to the Torah's account, God uttered the words *yehi or,* "let there be light."[162] This light appeared days before the sun and moon were created; it was a different kind of illumination. "The light created by the Blessed Holy One in the act of Creation flared from one end of the universe to the other."[163] With it one could see all of Creation; we might say, with it one could see creatively. "It is the light of the eye."[164] It is the artist's illumination, the intimation of a greater seeing, the hint of enlightenment.

> In you is the Source of Life;
> in Your light we see light.[165]

This is the light echoed in Moses' burning bush and memorialized in every *menorah*. It is this light we seek in our exploration of the *Sefirot*.

PART II

Yud-Hey-Vav-Hey: "Go To Yourself"

CHAPTER 4

For the sake of unifying All

l'shem yikhud Kudsha Berikh Hu v'Shekhintei, "for the sake of unifying the Holy Blessed One and the Shekhinah".

Lekh L'kha: to oneself, to the world

> The Eternal said to Avram, "Go forth [*lekh l'kha*] from your land, your birthplace, and your father's house, to the land that I will show you."[166]

One of the most famous commands in the Torah is that by which God spoke to a personbeing whom we know first as Abram and, later, as Abraham: *lekh l'kha*. This two-word Hebrew phrase is actually rather difficult to translate. It is possible that the first word is a verb, "go," and the second word is a verb intensifier, which is to say, the same verb, repeated for emphasis. In that case, *lekh l'kha* would convey the urgent meaning "Get going, go!" However, it is also possible that the second word is not a verb at all, but the word meaning "for yourself" or "to yourself"; in Hebrew, the letter *lamed* can be understood as a prefix meaning "for" or "to." Thus, the medieval Bible commentator Rashi[167] pointed out that the phrase can be understood not only as "Go forth" or "Get yourself going," meaning not to delay; the command can also be interpreted as "Go for yourself," or "for your own benefit, and your own pleasure."[168] The Torah, after all, does record a divine promise that Abram was to be blessed with wealth, a good name, and many offspring.

For a mystic, the passage reads differently, requiring a deeper plunge into the text, below the *peshat,* the surface level of apparent meaning. Consider that to speak of the Eternal One can be an evocation not of an ancient, unique personality, but a hint of a non-anthropomorphic, all-encompassing and unifying Oneness of life, which is always, Eternally, potentially present: an Eternity of, in, Oneness; a Oneness that contains and unifies Eternity in both time and space – and beyond, to all other imaginable dimensions. All is One. Avram, from this point of view, was suddenly touched by an intimation of a oneness, a wholeness that was so longed-for and welcome to him that he responded to it with a willingness to put everything else behind him. The alacrity of his response hints to the reader that he saw something so moving that he was focused only on the chance that he would be able to keep it. There is a sense of a moment when something opened his eyes, and he saw what he had never seen before.

Rashi suggests that it was for Abraham's own personal, material good that he was commanded to leave home. But the phrase *lekh l'kha* yields an even finer point of focus within this perspective, a point open to mystical interpretation, that is, to seeking even deeper levels of meaning to explore. Thus Hasidic thought reached for a deeper, hinted-at meaning of the command *lekh l'kha:* not Rashi's Go *for* yourself, but, employing the other possible translation of that letter *lamed,* "Go *to* yourself": "Every place that a person goes, he is going to his own self."[169] In other words, as you go about your own business, you are, in truth, encountering in the world around yourself a reflection of the world inside yourself. Or, put another way, if you would find the world, seek yourself. And if you would seek yourself, leave home: leave what you already know. Uncertainty is the required first step toward discovery.

To follow in Abraham's steps, one goes forth into the world for one's own benefit, to discover reflections of oneself in all that one sees and experiences. This accords with Jewish social justice rhetoric, in which one is a participant in either perpetuating or healing the brokenness of the society in which one lives. A mystical perspective puts it differently: one does not participate in the brokenness of the world, one comes to see that one is part of it. One seeks healing for the world because in so doing one finds healing for oneself. To learn to love someone else despite the flaws that annoy one is to learn to love oneself, despite those same flaws; to make room for another in the world is to keep a place open for oneself. One goes forth to find oneself in the world around oneself:

> Who is a true *hasid*, [one who does *hesed*, kindness]? one who is kind to his Creator." When a person does an act of loving kindness in this world below, he must intend it effect toward its parallel quality above. This is what it means to "show *hesed* to the Creator."[170]

By showing kindness to another human being, we add kindness to the entire world's store of it and thus increase the power of that attribute of kindness in God as well. Finding the ability to be kind to another opens us to the kindness in the world also there for us; to accept another flawed human being is, on some level, to come closer to accepting one's own flawed self. Thus we unify broken fragments in the world, and in ourselves.

When one finds evidence of brokenness – destructive behavior with no regard for consequences, an absence of human connection, the emotional pain and hopelessness of alienation – whether inside oneself or reflected in the world, "one must lift up the sparks" that one finds – sparks of God's presence, fragmented and out of balance and order, but there for the finding and the repairing. To find oneself in the world is to see that the world's brokenness is also one's own and that one's acts to make the self whole are also a gift of healing from one's self to the world. This mystical teaching echoes throughout the Kabbalistic exploration and development of the idea of the *Sefirot*.

Unifying the Self Leads to Unifying the All

What I have been describing as walking in Abraham's footsteps with mystical awareness accords with the basic teachings of Lurianic Kabbalah, which sees all of human experience reflected through *tzimtzum,* "withdrawal", *shevirat hakelim,* "the breaking of the vessels", and *tikkun,* "repair". *Tzimtzum* defines the initial act of God's creation of the world as a withdrawal of the Divine Self which fills the universe, so as to make room for Creation. In this small space, all of existence unfolds and finds its meaning. In human terms, as we imitate God, we learn that to enter the world creatively, we also must first withdraw, to make space for that which has yet to be. We step back from our own certainty that we already know, and allow a silence to occur, and wait and watch to see what is needed.

The doctrine of the presence of hidden sparks of the Divine in the world interprets Luria's second concept, *shevirat hakelim.* When the act of creation began, the divine flow came forth, meant to fill vessels made of its essence. But the flow of the divine essence was too powerful for the vessels:

> It [i.e., the vessel containing the lights within *Tiferet*] did not possess the capacity to bear the light, and [thus] these [vessels] shattered and "died," ... The light within them, that is, the [divine] vitality, departed [reascending] above to the womb of *Binah,* while the vessels [themselves] shattered and descended to the level of "Creation" [*Beri'ah*].[171]

The framework meant to convey God's abundance throughout the creation that would be nourished by it was not strong enough to bear the contact, and, when the vessels shattered, some of the divine light was trapped within them when they "fell to earth," as it were. The broken shards of the divine vessels are the material world as we know it, full of brokenness, unfulfilled potential, and tragedy; but within each shard of existence there is a potential discovery. A spark of divine light may be hidden within the experience of brokenness, despite the terrible suffering caused by the lack of fulfillment of meaning or potential; the spark that heals and redeems the world is found through a courageous engagement with the tragedy that all human beings come to know, not through the attempt to avoid it. To find a hidden spark of light and free it from the darkness is the mystic's understanding of the purpose of human life: in so doing, we repair the world, by restoring the fullness of God's presence in it.

The significance of Luria's doctrine not only helps us to look for a "silver lining" to ameliorate bad news; the human ability – and responsibility – to find and lift up the sparks that testify to the presence of God in the world, called *tikkun,* "repair." This powerful concept, applied far beyond its original meaning, energized the social justice movement of liberal Judaism in the 20th century.[172] And the lesson comes even closer to the core of the self and its purpose when one looks deeper into this mystic teaching: the sparks of possibility may be found everywhere, in any act, as long as it is undertaken with the appropriate intention. Luria and his followers taught that

> the project of human life is to separate the holy from the material world, and thus divest that world of all existence. *All existence will return to its original spiritual condition,* a state synonymous with the messianic age. ... The vision of redemption is a fundamentally spiritual one in which all things return to *olam hatikkun.* ... The responsibility for bringing all this about is a human one, not a divine one.[173]

To "lift up" the potential sparks that may be hidden, to allow them to add their brightness to the enlightenment of the world, is to add to the wholeness of the world through even the smallest, as well as more significant, carefully mindful acts.

Although Luria's definition focused upon spiritual *tikkun* in a way that rejected the physical world, interpreters of his doctrine found in it a compelling ethical teaching. The Talmud asserts that one who saves a life saves an entire implicit world[174]; for the mystics, every small act effects a small but profound step toward *tikkun*. If any act is pregnant with unknowable possibility, every act is potentially redemptive.

The more one's acts are in accord with this awareness, the more one acts with the power of one's undistracted *kavvanah*, and all one's interior "selves" are unified in that act. A Jew who is a soccer mom, social justice activist, loving daughter, Torah student, and small business owner – all aspects of the same busy woman – can by her awareness of this mystical teaching, of the importance of every small act, bring a quiet awareness to all that she does, in every aspect of her fragmented being. The more she knows herself to be a whole person, unified in her ability to focus her impact on the world, the more unified becomes her sense of self. By staying focused on the sense that she is able to heal the world, she is also able to heal herself if, whatever challenges comes to her, she is a Jew and she responds out of her sense of the Jewish mystical ethic that seeks healing and wholeness in the world and knows her power to help bring it about. The mystic seeks always to respond to life out of the awareness of the hidden sparks that may be redeemed when a person remains grounded and balanced in her own sense of self and purpose.

This concept is traceable in much of Jewish ritual. One example comes from the spring ritual of *sefirat ha'omer*. "Counting the *'omer*" is a traditional daily practice marking each day of the 49-day period between Pesakh and Shavuot. Originally an agricultural ritual, later overlaid with historical and religious layers of meaning, the *'omer* counting period is a time of anticipation, reflection, and, for historical reasons, even mourning.[175] Mystical practice developed out of a play on words – *sefirah* not only means "attribute [of God]", as the mystics use it, but also "counting" – offered a unique perspective on the traditional ritual of a short daily prayer in which one recites the count of the days that have passed since the first Seder evening. The mystics turned each day of *sefirah*, "counting", into an opportunity to reflect on the interaction and balance between each *Sefirah*, "attribute", and all others of the lower seven, which represent the created world. At the end of seven times seven, or forty-nine, days, each of the seven lower *Sefirot* has been contemplated in relationship to each of the other six and as a *Sefirah* existing in and of itself as well.

This ritual of meditation on an act of counting has ancient antecedents. Like naming, counting individuals is considered to have a real effect on them. Counting people is recognized as dangerous in the Tanakh; in several instances, in stories ranging from Moses to King David, taking a census of the Israelites is an act that must be atoned for. This awareness of the power of counting souls is reflected in the liturgy of the Days of Awe, which offers a famous image from the *Unetaneh Tokef* prayer: like sheep passing before their shepherd, "on Rosh HaShanah all the inhabitants of the world pass before [God]"[176] to be counted and judged.

A mystical awareness immediately creates the sense that such a potential for power must be seized on and correctly channeled if one is to increase the good in the world. And so, before the prayer that counts the days of the *'omer* and gives the mystic the opportunity to meditate on the relationship between the *Sefirot* in each day's prayer, one finds the opening *kavvanah*, an "intention" for the prayer's impact stated in so many direct words: *l'shem yikhud Kudsha Berikh Hu u'Shekhintei*, "for the sake of unifying the Holy Blessed One and the *Shekhinah*." This mystical formula, recited just before the fulfillment of the *mitzvah* of counting the *'omer*, harnesses the power of the counting in the actual unifying and balancing of the characteristics represented by the two *Sefirot* on which the mystic will meditate on that day, aspects both of the Holy One of Blessing beyond us and of the immanent presence of God among us. In our meditation, we envision a unity between the transcendent and the immanent, the unknown and the everyday; this is true whether we are speaking of aspects of God or of ourselves. It is true in applying the mystical mindset to connecting our own sense of judgment and kindness and also to understanding larger connections, and the consequences of disconnection, in the world: justice and the legal system, food banks and bureaucracy, safety and armies. Does a sense of connection exist between each ideal and the framework meant to contain and realize it?

As we will see in our exploration of the individual *Sefirot,* the practice of meditating upon attributes like *gevurah* and *hesed* is meant not only to better appreciate the aspects of God in the world and their unification. Such meditation also focuses on each individual's own sense of how these aspects of reality are reflected in his or her own being. How does my sense of self reflect, for example, my compassionate side and my judgmental side, and how might they be reconciled, balanced, and thus unified into the whole person I am meant to be?

Unifying the Self Through Learning

Jewish mysticism emphasizes the ancient teaching that the purpose of a human being is to imitate God. This is true both in one's acts in the world and in one's own inner sense of selfhood. The created human seeks to understand the Creator through the record of human awareness of being created: the Torah. To immerse oneself in Torah is to connect oneself to the source of life: *etz hayim hi lamakhazikim bah,* "She is a Tree of Life to those who hold on to her".[177] To devote oneself to Torah study is to fulfill one of the foundational *mitzvot* on which all else depends: *Torah, avodah,* and *gemilut hasadim,* "Torah, service, and acts of loving kindness."[178] Torah, for the mystics, is the center, informing and deepening the meaning of both *avodah* and *gemilut hasadim.*

The significance of learning is profound. To seek to unify the self through any *mitzvah* is, according to the mystics, to add to the strength of divine unity. Because we are inseparably part of the *Sefirot* system, whatever we do affects the entire system, for good or ill. For mystic doctrine, that which we experience as evil is a result of an imbalance in the *Sefirot.* That which energizes the *Sefirot* in a way that encourages the good encourages a balance for unity. Evil acts are not only those caused by imbalance, but also those which cause that imbalance.

Mystics see individual human beings as acting in the world not as selves standing alone, but as part of the whole that is the All of existence. For a human being to do evil is damaging not only to the victims, but also, ultimately, to the perpetrator, since the entire world suffers. Evil causes an imbalance in the *Sefirot* and impedes the flow of *shefa',* which should be transmitted through them when they are moving in the harmony of balance. We may visualize this concept as paralleling the physical construction of the human body: when veins, arteries, or neural pathways are blocked, organs, and limbs suffer an imbalance of that which should be flowing to them to keep them healthy. *Shefa'* nourishes and sustains the world; when its flow is impeded, even "the Holy One suffers."[179]

Through the *mitzvah* of learning, we can begin first to understand, and then see how to undo the damage we do. Through learning, we heal ourselves and our world, and we can even contribute to the healing of the Holy One, by learning acts that lead to wholeness. Torah study, prayer, and acts of loving kindness, with the appropriate *kavanah*, can unify the shattered and broken aspects of God in the world.

> Come and see: everyone who immerses ['*osek*] in the Torah establishes the world and maintains each and every thing in its proper form. ... In the Torah are all the things of the upper world and the lower world; all the things of this world and all the things of the world to come are in the Torah.[180]

Jewish mystical speculation is grounded in Torah and all that proceeds from the four-fold interpretation of that sacred text – *peshat*, the "simple" or surface level; *derash*, the "seeking" or investigating level; *remez*, the level of the half-hidden "hint" one can sometimes surmise; and *sod*, the hidden "secret" level of the text that might be glimpsed, but only in the sense that there is something that is yet beyond understanding.

CHAPTER 5

Torah Study as Ascent

YHVH: *Meaning in the Middle Ground*

> Meaning is not something you stumble across, like the answer to a riddle or the prize in a treasure hunt. Meaning is something you build into your life. You build it out of your own past, out of your affections and loyalties, out of the experience of humankind as it is passed on to you, out of your own talent and understanding, out of the things you believe in, out of the things and people you love, out of the values for which you are willing to sacrifice something. The ingredients are there. You are the only one who can put them together into that unique pattern that will be your life. Let it be a life that has dignity and meaning for you. If it does, then the particular balance of success or failure is of less account.[181]

Discovering the meaning of one's life is a lifelong process. It is not clear why we exist, or why we exist in a certain way: female or male, rich or poor, fearful or eager: how all the accidents of our personal and social experience of self are to be summed up into a synergy that might bring one to clarity of purpose, and meaning. For the Jewish mystics, to seek one's purpose is to seek one's place in the world, that is, in the All. What is clear in Jewish mystical teaching is that one will not "stumble across" the meaning of one's life: one searches actively, through learning, through relationships, and through the deeds one chooses to undertake in the world.

The sacred learning of Torah study opens the door for the mystics into a way of rising toward a clearer vision of possible meanings for one's life, and, in the process, a closer awareness of God. It is said that "all beginnings are difficult". That may well be true, but in this case it is the journey's continuation that brings us to a formidable challenge. In the middle of the journey we often have neither the clarity of hope nor the ability to see. Before we begin a journey up a mountain on a beautiful day, we can clearly see it in the distance, possibly even with a snowy top reflecting shining sunlight. When one reaches it, one will also surely see it clearly enough from up close. It is a curious thing that, while one is on the journey toward that towering peak, it is often not visible. It is hidden from view by the more modest rise and fall of the land over which one must travel and by the forests that vivify its flanks. Similarly in a spiritual journey, both the "rise" of a good day and the "fall" of discouragement can make it difficult to see our overarching goal, and "forests" of distractions may appear around every bend. The middle is an uncertain place, and we continue on faith that the journey will lead to the desired end – and that the journey, itself, is valuable.

The Name of God associated with the middle level of the *Sefirot* speaks of the uncertain view in the middle of the mystical exploration of a meaningful life; one sees "by way of a reflecting mirror that does not shine."[182] For those who are not standing at the revelatory beginning or anywhere near the final view a dedicated traveler might someday behold, the view is uncertain. If we consider birth the start of our journey, and death its destination, the size of this middle place is disproportionate: it is the vast majority of the path. Most of human life is spent in this unclear, uncertain middle ground.

Human life is lived with unanswerable questions. This place of uncertainty holds much existential anxiety for some, but artists and mystics seek it out because they see what Avram saw: that uncertainty is the first step toward discovery. The Name of God associated with this part of the path appropriately offers familiarity and uncertainty: it is the best-known Name and the least understood. It is the Name that brings together all the other Names, and yet it is unpronounceable. It has four letters and no vowels: *Yud Hey Vav Hey.* We cannot articulate this Name of God, any more than we can articulate those truths, longings, and moments of seeing that move us most deeply.

We once again confront the inescapable sense of paradox that is at the heart of our attempt to achieve awareness of God and of our own true self. For no obvious reason, some days seem bright and clear, other days are dark. Even on a clear day, witnesses to an event will recount it differently, from differing perspectives. How much more uncertain will we be about the most important things we think we know? Jewish tradition preserves a variety of conflicting teachings about the Sinai theophany that express the uncertainty of the human experience of this foundational moment of Jewish identity and belief. One of the most compelling is found in the commentary *Mekhilta deRav Ishmael*:

> "All": in one single utterance (*dibbur*), as no human being can speak; for it says: "And God spoke *all* these Words to say. ..." If so, why does Scripture go on to say, "I am the Lord your God. ... (Exod 20.2) You shall not have [other gods before me ...] (Exod 20.3)"? This teaches [us] that the Holy One, blessed be He, after having spoken the Ten Words in one single utterance, pronounced each Word by itself. I might have thought that all the other Words in the Torah were likewise spoken in one single utterance; hence Scripture says: "*These* Words". These Words were spoken in one single utterance, but all the rest of the Words in the Torah [were spoken] each one by itself.[183]

If God were to speak to us, after all, it would be "as no human being can speak." Some commentaries held that it was also as no human being could bear! A Talmudic tradition holds that God's first word caused the

Israelites' souls to leave their bodies, and they had to be resuscitated.[184] According to the Torah's text, the Israelites "fell back and stood at a distance. 'You speak to us,' they said to Moses, 'and we will obey; but let not God speak to us, lest we die'."[185]

What would one need to hear in order to know that one was in the presence of God? The Hasidic master Rabbi Mendel of Rymanov offered a piercing insight: all that Israel heard at Sinai was the first letter of the first word of the first Commandment, that is, nothing more than the silent aleph of *anokhi*, "I am."[186] One need not hear even the first word, the "I," spoken by God. One need hear only the intake of breath, perhaps; the opening of a mouth, as it were; one need sense only that nothing is about to become a spoken word.

> "To hear the *aleph* is to hear next to nothing; it is the preparation for all audible language, but in itself conveys no determinate, specific meaning. Thus, with his daring statement that the actual revelation to Israel consisted only of the *aleph*, Rabbi Mendel transformed the revelation on Mount Sinai into a mystical revelation, pregnant with infinite meaning, but without specific meaning."[187]

To be "pregnant with infinite meaning, but without specific meaning": this is not only a description of the meeting place between God and humanity. It is also a description of any of us if we were to be taken out of the continuum of our days, our journey toward becoming, in a sort of spiritual snapshot. Here is the middle of the journey, the inevitable grey area that will always exist at the border between black and white, neither here nor there, which is part of every moment of our lives.

This is also a wonderful and evocative description of the *Sefirot*, that is to say, of God. Recall that the deepest level of spiritual exploration is called *sod*, "secret": there is so much mystery in the human awareness of God, including the level at which the human mind is ignorant of its own perceptual limits. So much is possible in the meeting of the creative, alert, and questing human mind with the mystery that is beyond it, but it is impossible to predict until that meeting what meaning, what insight, what learning, will be brought into existence.

> Transcendent meaning is a meaning that surpasses our comprehension. A finite meaning that would fit perfectly our categories would not be an ultimate explanation, since it would still call for further explanation and would be an answer unrelated to our ultimate question. A finite meaning that claims to be an ultimate answer is specious. The assumption, for example, that the pursuit of knowledge, the enjoyment of beauty, or sheer being is an end in itself, is a principle we may utter, not a truth man can live by. Tell man that he is an end in himself, and his answer will be despair. The finite has beauty but no grandeur; it may be pleasing but not redeeming. Finite meaning is a thought we comprehend; infinite meaning is a thought that comprehends us; finite meaning we absorb; infinite meaning we encounter. Finite meaning has clarity; infinite meaning has depth. Finite meaning we comprehend with analytical reason; to infinite meaning we respond in awe. Infinite meaning is uncomfortable, not compatible with our categories. It is not to be grasped as though it were something in the world which appeared before us. Rather it is that in which the world appears to us.[188]

To be full of potential meaning, yet without specific meaning, is exactly how we meet the world, as well. To live in time is to know that tomorrow some potential will be realized that does not yet exist today.

What Avram Saw

> Rabbi Yitzhak said: There is a parable of one who wandered from place to place and saw a sparkling

> palace. He said: shall it be said that this house is without a director? The owner of the palace appeared to him and said, I am in charge of this palace. Similarly, because our father Abraham asked: shall it be said that this world has no director? the Holy Blessed One appeared to him and said, I am in charge of this world.[189]

Ancient midrash already credits Avram, who becomes Abraham, with the ability to reason out the questions that need to be asked in a meaningful life. Yet for the mystics reason is not the essential quality associated with Abraham; in the *Sefirot* system, the lesson of Abraham's life is linked to the *sefirah* of *Hesed*, a Hebrew word variously translated by the mystics as "grace," "free-flowing love," and "generosity."[190] This "right" side of the *Sefirot* is associated with the Name YHVH, the Name of God, which cannot be pronounced. The right side of the *Sefirot* is characterized by deep wells of wisdom, overflowing, loving generosity, and confident dreams of perfection. The Abraham of mystic vision watches the wilderness horizon so as not to miss seeing a stranger who might need his hospitality, and also the seeker whose personality compels others to change their lives and join him.

What did Avram see? The *Zohar* teaches that "gates began to open," which is to say that the created world began to be fruitful and fulfill its potential, when Abraham appeared, and the that the world reached its complete creation "through Abraham."

> The holy name was completed, becoming *Elohim,* and the name *Abraham* as well. As one was completed, so was the other. Then life was generated and the complete Name emerged. ... All remained suspended until the name of Abraham was created. Once that name was completed, the holy name was completed, as the verse concludes: *on the day that YHVH Elohim made heaven and earth.*[191]

Perhaps what Avram saw was, as the *Zohar* puts it, his capacity to make God's Name, *YHVH*, complete, through recognizing his own capacity to become Abraham. In the addition of the letter *hey* to his name, Avram announces in the most essential way his belonging to the path he has chosen to follow. His name proclaims his connection to the God *YHVH*, the God of what is articulated only through human participation. This name of God is far more than an utterance naming a particular personality; it is an invitation to consider what may yet be created in the light of what has been, and how the creative potential of a moment may be seen.

If we contemplate the three levels of the *Sefirot* not as ascent, but as yesterday, today, and tomorrow, this middle level is Here and Now. It invokes both memory and hope; it gathers up both past and future. The Name we find here is made up of what is better understood as a pictogram than as a set of letters that spell a word. The letters of this Name, *yud-hey-vav-hey*, can be seen as a list of the letters that are needed to spell out all forms of the Hebrew verb Be. *Hayah,* the past tense, requires a *hey* and a *yud. Hoveh,* the rarely used present tense, adds the *vav* to our list, and the future tense, *yihiyeh,* contains letters we already have, put together in a different way. Even as the Name draws together all Being in time, in the structure of the Ten *Sefirot* this Name draws together all the *Sefirot:* the yud is in *hokhmah,* the first hey in *binah;* the *vav,* with a numerical value of six, brings together the six *Sefirot* below *binah,* and *malkhut,* or *shekhinah,* is the place of the final *hey.*

This Name is sometimes referred to as the *shem Havayah,* "the name of Being," rather than pronounced with the substitute names such as *Adonai* ("our Lord") or *HaShem* ("the Name"). None of these articulations is actually an attempt to speak the letters as they are found.[192] This is an essential insight into the Jewish sense of God. This Name of God is not a name to be pronounced so much as it is a Name to behold; that it cannot be said is essentially because it is not an articulation but an awareness – of all that was, is, and will be, together in the same moment of thought.

This Name is a presentation, in a nutshell, of the problem of contemplating God without descending into the idolatry of defining

God. Any image of God is a diminishment of the All: for example, to use the male pronoun in reference to God is already idolatry, if idolatry defines God in any way that makes God less than All – if God is exclusively male, then God is not All.[193] For those who are uncomfortable with an exclusive vision of God as a male, or as a human figure, the *Sefirot* bring a very different and welcome perspective. Here the Name is unpronounceable, the vision is untranslatable; and, although Jewish mysticism does not deny the anthropomorphism and anthropopathism of the Tanakh, the Sefirotic vision of God is not precisely a vision of, or only of, Michelangelo's oversized old Caucasian guy with a long beard. The Name does indeed invoke *Avinu Malkeynu*, "our Father, our King", yet it does not let us rest there. It invites us to consider many conflicting ideas and visions of God, and thus it opens a gate toward a much different understanding of the Universe, which is, of course, nothing more or less than God – unknowable in its completeness and, at the same time, the Essence.

Certainly, one can know pieces of it; one can have moments of insight that are true, to us, on a profound and life-altering, life-completing level. But we will never be sure of the real truth of our insights, since we can contemplate the universe only out of our own limited perspective. To be human is to be limited – by our available energy, by our capacity for knowledge, by the built-in imperfections in the way we see, feel, think, and perceive. Much of what we think we might know about God, the mystics teach, we learn from careful reading of the Tanakh, our oldest and best source of information. The more closely we read, the more carefully we bring different insights together, the better the chance that we might come across a new spark to illuminate our lives.

Such insights are derived even from the smallest physical aspects of our being:

> When you count the small bones in your fingers [phalanges] you find that there are fourteen of them in each hand, and twenty-eight in the two hands taken together. The number twenty-eight in Hebrew is *khaf*

het, which spells *ko'akh*, "strength". Indeed, the hands are the instruments of man's strength, the tools with which he performs all his tasks.[194]

This teaching comes from the practice of *gematria,* in which words are calculated by their numerical values (each letter in Hebrew is also a number. *Alef* is one, *bet* is two, and so forth.) Certainly, this is a clever and interesting way of understanding the potential strength of the human hand – but there is more. We are created in God's image; God is also described as having "hands," and, paradoxically, it is these metaphorical "hands" which make manifest the inexpressible Name.

"[F]or I will see your Name in the work of your fingers" (Ps. 8.4), and this is proof that the work of the Heavens and all their hosts are by means of fingers, which is a way of referring to the *Sefirot,* through which the world was created, and they are ten. Five over against five, as proved in the text "my hand established the Earth, my right hand spans the Heavens" (Isaiah 48.13).[195]

In a religious tradition in which creation was initiated through a word, a religious awareness of a meaning may not be uttered, yet may be evoked in action. This is an insight into the peculiar semantic range of the word "word" in Hebrew. *Davar* can mean "word" or it can mean a tangible "thing." We cannot articulate the Name in a word, but we can, as it were, articulate it in acts. This is the mystical definition of Jewish ethics; although we cannot be sure of the effect of our acts, we must do what we can to act for the good – and every act may bring "the work of Your fingers" more fully into the world.

The ambiguity that manifests itself precisely where we most need certainty offers a teaching into the essential nature of life. The teaching offered by an unspeakable Name is this: there exists an unknowable level to God, as well as to the question of what our lives are about, and to the nature of the essential connectedness of all. There are several lessons here, the first of which is humility. Human vision is limited, understanding more so: there is much that is beyond knowing. There is a level of mystery that will never be unraveled. Wonderfully, it is mystery which, paradoxically, opens up room for hope. The fact that human endeavor cannot, with certainty, unravel the meaning of life and of the universe, by means of either science or religion, does not mean that there is no meaning.

The meaning is in the response to the gift of life: living a life of gratitude for the gift of the short time we each have in life. The heart of the Jewish response to life is to inquire not after one's rights, but after one's obligations. *Halakha,* the "path" or "law" of Jewish life, is founded on this axiom.

> [T]he law addresses each community member directly and specifies the obligations of one to one another and to God in detail ... failure to perform the law is the equivalent of abandoning the community.[196]

What Avram saw was not only the director of the world, and not only his own inner need to leave home to find himself; he also was able to confront uncertainty and respond with generosity, with compassion, and with love. If the first requirement of discovering oneself is to be willing to step into uncertainty, the second requirement is to see the world, and one's community, as full of the potential for love, and to respond to it.

CHAPTER 6

Ascending the Sefirot Toward Meaning

Ascending the *Sefirot* offers a path for discerning the meaning of one's life. As we have considered, the *Sefirotic* system can be seen as a way of understanding the world, our place in it, and our purpose, all at the same time. It is a way of comprehending the world that places a supreme value not on a single correct, lifelong answer for us to cling to, but on a way of seeing the world that allows us to bend, grow and change, all the while with a sense of unwavering security. Each *sefirah* is different and unique, but altogether they express one indivisible wholeness. As we contemplate each one and explore its reflection in our own sense of being, a clearer sense of self, with all its disparate parts, emerges. Sometimes we will muse upon questions: how do I express *netzakh* in my choices? Other times a shock of recognition will stop us: I had not realized the extent to which my desire for order, the *gevurah* tendency, was choking my desire to show love, *hesed,* to those I love. Exploring and learning the *Sefirot* and their interconnectedness shows us our own capacity for wholeness, within the healthy expression of all our conflicting, interconnecting selves.

That is the practice of *kavvanah,* of "directing oneself." Because each of us is a reflection of God, to direct our self toward wholeness is to assemble the image of God that we reflect. It is as if a choppy sea, full of chaotic waves, came to rest, the sky suddenly visible in the calm expanse of water where before there were only shards of partial reflection. As the lowest *sefirah, Malkhut,* reflects the highest *sefirah, Ayn Sof,* so does the Assembly of Israel associated with *Malkhut* reflect *Ayn Sof,* the transcendent, hidden God. But until a person is spiritually centered, with all her aspects drawn together into a serene wholeness, that reflection is garbled and broken up by the interference of physical, emotional, and intellectual distractions.

> The presence of God demands more than the presence of mind. *Kavanah* is direction to God and requires the redirection of the whole person. It is the act of bringing together the scattered forces of the self; the participation of heart and soul, not only of will and mind; the integration of the soul with the theme of the mitzvah.

It is one thing to be *for* a cause and another thing to be *in* a cause. It is not enough to help thy neighbor; "Thou shalt love they neighbor." It is not enough to serve thy God; you are asked "to serve Him with all your heart and with all your soul" (Deuteronomy 11.13). It is not enough to love Him: "thou shalt love ... with all thy heart, and with all thy soul, and with all thy might" (Deuteronomy 6.5-6).[197]

The mystic Isaac of Radvil wrote in the 19th century that the real meaning of the words *ra'u banekha,* "your children saw," at the Sea was not that the Israelites escaping from Egypt recognized their true God, but that they suddenly understood that they were one with the essence of the God that was saving them from Egyptian slavery.[198] They were not "for" their God but "in" their God and the acts through which that God was manifested. They "saw" that they were "your children," literally sharing the same divine essence. Jewish mystics seek that vision in every aspect of the *Sefirot.*

How can the *Sefirot,* understood as an imagined structure of the self, provide a discernible path for one who seeks to ascend? The *Zohar* gives us a clue by using the word *dargah,* "level" or "step," for *sefirah.* The *Sefirot* can be imagined as a succession of interconnected steps. Just as the rungs of a ladder are integral to it, and each riser and tread is an essential part of a staircase, so each *sefirah* is equally necessary to the wholeness and stability of the overall frame.

How can the *Sefirot*, understood as an imagined structure of the self, provide a discernible path for the one who seeks to ascend? The *Zohar* gives us a clue by using the word *dargah*, "level" or "step" for *sefirah*. The *Sefirot* can be imagined as a succession of interconnected steps. Just as the rungs of a ladder are integral to it, and each rise and tread is an essential part of a staircase, so each *sefirah* is equally necessary to the wholeness and stability of the overall frame.

The *Sefirot*, however, do not constitute an inanimate, unresponsive structure. They are the different parts of one's real, lived self, and they are in constant flux as they interact with each other – the choppy waves of the sea which is the lived sense of self. Consider how different we can be in varying situations that call forth different aspects of our personalities: with some people, one is a teacher, with others, a student; in some situations, one acts as a public person, whereas one might behave quite differently in private. When called on to respond to the acts of others, sometimes compassion is aroused, yet at other times, it is one's capacity for judgment (justified or not) that is most apparent. And all this time one is that same, single person, displaying all these characteristics and answerable for them.

The *Sefirot* are also the different parts of our human community. Obviously, as individuals we are shaped and molded by the people who are most influential to us: our parents, family members, close friends, teachers, and others. But such influence and our interconnectedness go much further. It is useful to consider the Observer Effect which we have learned from quantum physics: tells us, the act of looking at something already has an effect on that which is observed, and upon the observer as well. It happens to you and me all the time: when I know that you are staring at me, I begin to act accordingly, perhaps becoming self-conscious or awkward. Yet it would be worse to feel as if I were invisible. Just like birds that perch on a limb in relationship to the others of their flock,[199] we are positioned vis-à-vis the others in our life. We influence each other in uncountable ways in innumerable encounters, and none of us is unaffected.

The concept of the *Sefirot* is rather like a complex map of all of the interactions and influences which are the result of the layers of connectedness among us, and among the different parts of each of us. But learning the patterns of these links is only the beginning. Considering the *Sefirot* without also keeping in mind the idea of *shefa'*, the ever- flowing abundance that streams through them, is akin to taking a creature from the forest and pinning it to a wall in order to study it. The *Sefirot* are a mystical example of systems theory; we cannot look at any single *sefirah* in isolation from its "system" (i.e. the universe) and truly see it. It is a vessel for the *shefa'* that flows through it and that, in turn, influences what will go forth from it. Each *sefirah* transmits what it has received. Compare this to the job of our internal organs: each part of our physical bodies receives and then transmits. If something gets clogged, the physical system breaks down. This is exactly the same reality as what happens in a human group. Think of committee meetings or gatherings, which largely depend on communication flowing freely, each member receiving and transmitting information. Group action is terribly hobbled by a group member who keeps secrets or passes on inaccurate information, or who does not show up and is thus cut off from the rest of the group.

The connections of the *Sefirot* may be understood as a way of linking our individual selves with each other, and, widening our vision a bit further, with the world in which we live. Ultimately, the connectedness of the *Sefirot* shows us our place in history, as well; "When we want to understand ourselves, to find out what is most precious in our lives, we search our memory. ...That only is valuable in our experience which is worth remembering."[200] To engage in the learning and transmission of that memory is to re-member, to animate the potential limbs of the body of Jewish tradition into the "mighty arm and outstretched hand" that saves us from meaninglessness and placelessness. This is what is shining like the sun, in the palace that Abraham saw or out of Moses' bush: *zeh zikhri l'dor dor,* "This is My remembrance for every generation."[201] It is the light that breaks over us when we encounter the divine presence through the vital traditional *minhag* of Torah study, and thus, through becoming part of our people's memory, we form our own sense of self and place:

> Study is an invitation to the past, an entrée to memory. Learning is a means of acquiring authenticity, self-enrichment and self-transformation. through study, a link between a past otherwise destined to fade and an otherwise impoverished future is forged. In Heschel's words, one's 'total existence is, in a sense, a summation of past generation, a distillation of experiences and thoughts of his ancestors. The authentic individual is neither an end nor a beginning but a link between ages, both memory and expectation.'[202]

The *Sefirot* are a way of expressing that which cannot be uttered, since human beings cannot help but talk about that which grounds history and existence: God, and the human sense of connectedness to God. Like the salmon that seeks to return to the river in which it emerged into life, human beings are compelled toward the All out of which we emerge, in which we have our place, through which we are all part of the same whole: "the divine abounds everywhere and dwells in everything: the many are One."[203] This is the message of the *Shema: Adonai Ekhad*, "God is One," meaning unifier of all, that One-ness which links the many. Small Jewish children in prayer services teach mystical truth in signing the *Shema*, holding up one finger to signify *Adonai*, and for the world *Ekhad*, "One," tracing a circle in the air as far as their outstretched arms will allow. All is One.

In the ancient Rabbinic work *Pirke Avot* we are admonished, "Know what is *mim'kha*, above you."[204] Focusing on the word *mim'kha*, which literally means "from you," the Baal Shem Tov taught the insight that what we seek outside of us is also to be found within us. "Which is to say, know that what is above you, all comes from you."[205] Each of us is what links heaven and earth.

The ladder in Jacob's dream is both one's self and one's path. The *Sefirot* system offers a way to center on the different parts of the self and how one might see one's different attributes as rungs of a ladder one seeks to ascend. The *Sefirot* may be understood in one way as constituting three levels of human nature. The first and most foundational is our physical nature; it is expressed in the lower *Sefirot* (*Malkhut, Yesod, Netzakh,* and *Hod*). The next level of our existence is the emotional, which is associated with the middle level of *Sefirot* (*Tiferet, Hesed,* and *Gevurah*). Finally, at the highest and most developed level, we find the upper *Sefirot* (*Binah, Hokhmah,* and *Ayn Sof*), those of the intellect – and also what is beyond the intellect.

The *Sefirot* as a picture of the integrated and perfected self is not only about our physical, psychological, and intellectual nature; the *Sefirot* are variously associated with our physical body and with ethical qualities. Seen from the perspective of our creation in the image of God, the *Sefirot* are also a challenge to live up to our spiritual potential. And, if we remember that the *Sefirot* are also a map of the world, we can gain insight into our place in it by considering which place on the map we find ourselves inhabiting, and what our communal and social influence really is when seen in that context.

Everything is connected; as the *Zohar* says over and over, *d'kula had,* "all is One." That which we sense in ourselves is echoed in the world around us: in those with whom we feel a kinship of perspective and in those with whom we share a sense of destiny. Paradoxically, there is also an echo of connectedness to that with which we feel no conscious link – and even to that we would deny. We are not, after all, necessarily aware of, or willing to consider, all the relationships that affect our lives, yet there is still an effect. No less is there a link between each individual and the larger natural world of which each shares a part: there is no part of an individual's being or lived life that does not somehow affect othersת and the environment around us, in ways of which we are only partly aware, if at all.

Vision and Limitations

There are days when we feel in touch with the world and powerful, and other days when nothing seems to work and we are bereft. Kabbalah recognizes that human experience is frustrating even when we set out with the best of intentions, and the greatest of energies, determined to do something good in the world and realize our own personal potential. The well-known phrase "one step forward, two steps back" is expressed in mystical terms, here by the Besht, the founder of Hasidism, through the two states of *mokhin d'gadlut* and *mokhin d'katnut:*

> What is *katnut* ["lesser spiritual capacity"] and what is *gadlut* ["greater spiritual capacity"]? The former refers to when a man sits to study Torah without preparing [himself]; he is in *katnut,* his mind is not whole. But when he learns with preparation and exhilaration, then he achieves the level of *gadlut,* which is linked to the upper *dargot* [steps]. It is just the same with prayer and with every mitzvah which a person does – one does everything in a state of *katnut* or *gadlut.*[206]

There are two states of consciousness possible in a human being: expanded or diminished. We hope for the former, and constantly fall from it into the latter. This is what Martin Buber[207] characterized as the difference between the I-Thou state of awareness, in which God is blazingly present in all and all is harmonious and whole and One, and the I-It state of being, in which we perceive "through a glass, darkly" and life is fractured and confusing and annoying.

> Nevertheless, [the people] Israel are holy, and they do not fall from their level without strengthening themselves, aggrieved to their very souls for their fall into the state of lessened spiritual capacity, and they repent, and they are strengthened and they progress even further, running to do the will of their Creator – even while in a state of lessened spirituality.[208]

Recall the mystic Isaac Luria's explanation of the sense of incompleteness in our lives and the reality that our vision of life is obstructed by all that happens to us by means of his metaphor of the shattered vessels and the interrupted channels that are meant to link them; they are the *Sefirot* and their only partly realized interconnectedness. The light pours forth into the vessels, but the channels which should carry the flow freely toward us are compromised, blocked, broken. A blocked channel is like an eye turned away: nothing can be seen. Who among us has not been distracted when a sight before our eyes needs seeing? An eye that looks but does not see, or that sees but does not accept what it sees, suffers the results of the broken connections of Luria's mystical vision. The broken conduit can neither carry nor transmit what it has seen. The whole still exists, but in far less than its ideal form.: the vessels pour forth, and the channels carry on, but much is lost, and much is limping along. The system is characterized by the loss of its potential fullness, not by the promise of fulfillment. God appears, but we cannot see; messages pour forth to us from the universe, but we do not notice them.

Our own physical and spiritual creation is a reflection of the cosmos, and so experiences a similar reality. Because of blocked channels of understanding between phenomenon and perception, we may feel physical pain but not be able to fathom its source; we may know emotional distress without clearly apprehending its cause. Like the created world, like God, we, too, suffer from the lack of a clear sense of connection among all our aspects and among all the different dimensions of our days. And so we must live lives that constantly seek the balance between conflicting desires, among conflicting demands, but without understanding why. How might one attempt to become a more integrated person and not feel pulled this way and that by the need to answer more requests than be met? What is the way out of overscheduled days and overcommitted hours? How might we begin to center ourselves without becoming alienated from others and from our own inner sense of self?

The mystical symbol of Jacob's ladder appears in the Torah in the context of a description of such fragmentation of the self. The Book of Genesis[209] relates the significant trauma that occurred within the family of Isaac and Rebekah and their twin sons, Esau and Jacob, when Isaac plans to give the all-important blessing of the first born to Esau, and Rebekah sets about to deceive her husband into blessing Jacob instead. Jacob is torn between loyalty to his father, obedience to his mother, his own desire for the blessing, and the complexity of his relationship to his brother. We see his state of self most clearly in the language of the Torah itself when we follow Jacob into exile. He managed to receive the blessing from Isaac by an act of family subterfuge and has been banished from the family, journeying toward he knows not what. When night fell, the text relates, he chose a place to rest, "took from the stones of the place," and *vayasem m'ra'ashotav*, "placed it under his heads." The use of the plural here is striking.[210] His head, in other words, is not "together"; his sense of self is fragmented. He is far from having a sense of wholeness, and as he himself declares the next morning, without a sense of where he was. This is not just a geographical statement.

And it is specifically just at that time, when he is most pulled apart from his sense of self and center, that he is able to see most clearly a sense of purpose. That night, as his fragmented and divided self seeks rest, Jacob dreams a vision of a ladder.

> Jacob dreamed, and saw a ladder fixed on the earth, and its head reached to heaven; he saw the angels of God ascending and descending on it. The Eternal was beside him, and said: "I am the Eternal, the God of Abraham your father and the God of Isaac. ... behold, I am with you, and will keep you wherever you go" ... Jacob awoke from his sleep, and he said: "Surely the Eternal is in this place; and I knew it not." He was afraid, and said: "How full of awe is this place! This is none other than the house of God, and this is the gate of heaven."[211]

Following the lead of the Hasidim, who taught the insight that all the descriptions of the Torah can be seen as (among other things) projections of the inner workings of the self, we can see that Jacob found his truest sense of meaning only when he had truly "hit bottom." He lost all support, all enabling, for the self he had been, and only now can he see his real connectedness to his past, his family, and his world (symbolized by the appearance of God, identified as the same God of his father and grandfather), and his real potential, in the form of the ladder. In his dream, the ladder is *mutzav artzah,* "fixed upon the earth" and, directly contrasting to the plural "heads" used to describe Jacob, the ladder was standing with *rosho magia' hashamaymah,* "its head reaching toward heaven." Jacob became aware of eternity: his perspective widened beyond his own current predicament, beyond the narrow confines of his selfhood, and he was able to see his place as a descendant of his ancestors and of their actions and culture. Even when he awakened, Jacob was still filled with the sense that the meaning he had gained through this new perspective would not leave him. His awareness of self shifted from a sense of isolation to a new vision of his being as part of the whole of creation.

Ironically, when he awakened Jacob did something very human, and yet, what he did is not the best expression of the meaning of his dream. He mistook the holiness of a moment for that of a place. "This must be the house of God, and the gate of heaven", he exclaimed and set up a pillar – not yet realizing that one cannot step in the same stream, or dream, twice. He did not yet realize that the ladder was not located at that place. What he did not yet see is that he himself is the ladder, and the place is The Place: God.

Grasping the Ladder

In Figure 1 we see a graph of the *Sefirot* in their classic form, as described by the *Zohar.* Gershom Scholem explained the uniqueness – and the boldness – of the *Zohar*'s approach: "Where previously the vision could go no farther than to the perception of the glory of [God's] appearance on the throne, it is now a question, if the expression be permitted, of the inside of this glory."[212] This collection of attributes is meant – poorly and inexactly – to express the mystic's immersion in the inside, the essence, of the Holy. Because each of us is, individually, a reflection of God's image, it is also a representation of the spiritual interior of each human being. And because individuals and the world collectively reflect God, this is also a depiction of the essential nature of the world.

This graph is not, however, *true* in a way that would limit other expressions of the ideas contained within Kabbalah; other arranging concepts include a tree, a human body, and the three pillars that uphold the world. The ten *Sefirot* are portrayed in a balanced arrangement which locates three on the left, three on the right, and four in a middle position. According to the Kabbalah, creation is an ongoing process of the flowing forth of *shefa,* the eternal, overflowing divine abundance from which the energy of creation endlessly gushes from *Ayin,* through the channels that link the *Sefirot.*

Associated with each *sefirah* are many characteristics and attributes that must first be learned, then discerned in oneself, in one's community, and in one's world. One who would move to the next level must come to understand and master the expression of these attributes in one's own life, and there are dangers, obstacles, and traps. This journey upward mirrors life: if and when one successfully meets the first challenge, the next will be even more difficult. Each step will require all the knowledge and experience one has gained from everything that one has learned in the process of coming this far.

It has been observed that walking is the act of a successful succession of steps. To take a step, we must move forward, and in so doing, we lean forward and give up the stability of the place where we were standing still. As we lift one foot and move it forward through the air in front of us, we are off-balance, and we must trust that when we lower that foot, we will find a new balance and a stability that we can achieve only by having been willing to give up the former security of standing still. To take a physical step forward is a leap of faith. To take this mystical step forward is no different, and no more difficult.

PART III

Ten Lessons in the Sefirot

Figure 1. **The Ten Sefirot**

כתר
Keter:
Gate of Transcendence
First Ripple in Stillness of *Ayn Sof*
Keter – *Alef* –
All

בינה
Binah: Gate of Understanding
Impenetrable Mystery –
Palace of Reflection – Womb of
Existence – *Teshuvah* – Return to the
Deepest Source – Leah – the Higher
Feminine

חכמה
Hokhmah: Gate of Wisdom
Primal point – Spark of Existence
Deep Well – God's water
Hidden Torah

דין
Din: Gate of Judgment
Judgment (*Din*) – Severity
Measuring of Divine Love – The
Restraining Hand – Sarah – Evil
Isaac – Power (*Gevurah*) – evil is
part of the All – the *yetzer hara'*
complexity

תפארת
Tiferet: Gate of Connecting
Below with Above
polarity – The Blessed Holy
One – connection of
Shekhinah and *Tiferet*
balance above and below
Harmony – Perfect Center
Rakhamim

חסד
Hesed: Gate of Mercy
Grace – free-flowing Love of God
Greatness (*Gedulah*) – Mercy
Abraham – Generosity
Openheartedness
Right Hand

יסוד
Yesod: Gate of Embodiment
the Sign of the Covenant
Phallus – Covenant
Rectifier – stable personality
Joseph – *Tzaddik*
Foundation of Memory

הוד
Hod: Gate of *Hoda'ot*
thanksgiving – beauty
place of wonders and miracles – place
of *hoda'ot* – light of creation
Elohim Tzva'ot – prophecy
Aaron – acceptance
uncertainty

נצח
Netzakh: Gate of Endurance
Endurance – Eternity
Victory – Prophecy – the
Temple pillars named *Yakhin*
and *Bo'az* – balance
unity

מלכות
Malkhut: Gate of Belonging
Community of Israel
Indwelling Presence – Level
of the Physical – Speech
Rivers that lead to the Sea
Ethics – David – Rachel
Bride of God – Mother of
Lower Worlds
God's kingdom

Summary, Preparation, and a Warning

A mystic seeks *devekut,* that union in which one loses one's sense of distance from God and all of life becomes one unified all within the awareness of God as the source of all that is. Apparent differences and difficulties drop away in the presence of that light, and one becomes able, finally, to see one's own natural place within the all. We all are looking for the same thing, in essence: we seek the safety of home, the certainty of self-knowledge, and the peace of harmony and love in all our relationships. We want to know what our lives mean, and that we belong.

But human lives are lived with the discomfort of the lack of these desires. For both the mystic and the rest of us, the way toward the fulfillment of our greatest desire is the path of personal integration. The more a person discovers, accepts, and integrates about herself, the more her power to move toward her desire is unleashed; the more a community does the same, the safer each of the individuals within it will be.

Following ancient Jewish tradition, every year on Yom Kippur Jews make a concerted attempt to bring their individual lives into harmony with God and with others who share life paths and community. There are two kinds of connections we make: those of the individual vis-à-vis God and those of the individual vis-à-vis another individual or group. Both relationships are real and require responsible attention; each touches on only half of one's existence. Life is lived as the constant balancing of a three-way connectedness that is usually interrupted in one or more of one's links to life: oneself and oneself, all one's conflicting impulses; oneself and one's companion; oneself and God.

CHAPTER 7

Three

Three is a central number in Judaism; "On three things the world depends," taught the Rabbis of antiquity.[213] The *birkat haCohanim*, probably the oldest blessing recorded in the Torah, is recited in three phrases.

> May YHVH bless and protect you;
> May YHVH's face illuminate you in grace;
> May YHVH lift his face upon you and give you peace.[214]

The repeated use of the anthropomorphic "face" recalls the promise that, as long as the people of Israel merit it through their caring for each other, the *kheruvim* will face each other on the Ark and God's presence will be manifest. Interestingly, although in human terms the "lifting up" of the eyes is followed by "seeing," this blessing does not quite ask that God direct the divine gaze upon the one blessed.

The traditional Jewish liturgy develops three major themes: of creation, revelation, and redemption. And the twentieth-century philosopher Franz Rosensweig presented Judaism as a triangle of three interlocking points: God, Torah, and Israel.

In his commentary on the Torah, Rashi explains that God counted the Jewish people on three separate occasions "because of His love for them"[215]: when they escaped Egypt after the sin of the Golden Calf and at the completion of the Mishkan. For a mystic, it is easy to see how these three countings can be traced as an individual's spiritual journey through the three levels of the *Sefirot*. The Lubavitcher Rebbe Menakhem Mendel Schneerson demonstrated this in an interpretation of Rashi's comment:

> These three countings were an evolutionary process. In the first, the Jewish souls was awakened by the love of HaShem, in that they followed His commands with complete self-sacrifice, but their emotions were untouched. In the second, the soul began to work its influence on their outward lives in preparation for the building of the Tabernacle for Hashem's presence. But the impetus still came from the outside rather than from an inner desire. However, by the third counting, because they were now involved with the actual service of the Tabernacle, through their own action they brought Hashem into their midst.[216]

The lowest and closest level of existence, the physical, is touched first. This is true in a child's development as well as in an adult's spiritual growth. The second level of existence, the emotional, is symbolized by the sin of the Golden Calf. Even as the Torah's creation story teaches that human existence inevitably includes the broken connection with God, which is expressed by sin, the mystics insist that a spiritual journey undertaken with integrity cannot avoid full engagement with the human condition, with sadness and pain as well as joy. The third and highest level of human existence, the level represented in the *Sefirot* system as that of the intellect, is the summit of a person's spiritual ascent. Here one achieves a sense of understanding, a clarity regarding life's meaning and the serenity born of the sense of wholeness, of completion, which comes with the soothing of doubt. One has a purpose that finally comes from within, an "inner desire" that replaces the outer guidance, just as children mature and come to know their own hearts as they grow away from a parent's guiding hand.

The *Sefirot* system is the kabbalists' way of envisioning our existence, and our sense of interconnectedness, in three dimensions: world, self, God. The three modes of being can be envisioned as interlocking, or as emanating waves, or in many other ways.

> The system of *Sefirot* can be visualized as a tree or a man or a circle, in three triads or in three columns. According to the last image the *Sefirot* are divided into a right column, signifying Mercy, or light, a left column, signifying Severity, the absence of light, and a central column, signifying the synthesis of the right and left. Each *Sefirah* is a world in itself, dynamic and full of complicated mutual relations with other *Sefirot*.[217]

The *Sefirot* are ten; but the individual's mystical journey upward, inward, and outward is expressed in three levels of these *Sefirot*, associated with Names of God. And even as the ten *Sefirot* are really three levels of existence, the three Names are really One. The letters of the central name of God, which are arranged in different Names for each of the three levels, can also be arranged to spell *hey vav yud hey,* or *havayah,* "existence."[218] Here are the three worlds of human existence: as individuals who know themselves through relationships, as individuals who have a separate sense of self, and as individuals who seek a place to belong, to find wholeness through attachment to a sense of self as part of All.

CHAPTER 8

Three Worlds of Human Existence

hu (= *nistar*, the level of God, 3rd person) where one loses one's **intellect** sense of self (*devekut*) from *atah* up toward	*Ehyeh*
atah (*nigleh*, the level of self, 2nd person, own consciousness apart God as other, with whom from influence of others the self dialogues) **emotion**	*Yud-Hey-Vav-Hey*
from *ani* up toward *ani* the level of com (first person, the world, nation, etc., always present with one) influences upon the self **physical**	*alef-dalet-nun-yud*

The "lowest" level of the *Sefirot* in the preceding diagram, the level that may be understood either as closest or as farthest away, depending on one's sense of self, is the level of the physical: outer influences, inner drives, one's education, and the impact of world events all belong here. This level is of the simple but profound word *ani*, Hebrew for "I," the word by which one refers to oneself. This is the level of that which is physically apparent, and the name of God associated with this level is both most concrete, because it spells out the name of God in so many letters, and is most distant from the truth of God's Name, since that which is spelled out is not the Name but a respectful reference to it. This is not to say that God is not present here; but the use of the term *Adonai,* which is not God's name but is once removed from that intimacy, indicates a certain level of awareness that is explored in depth in the discussion of the *sefirah* called *Malkhut.*

The middle level represents the second dimension of human perception – that which is beyond the physical self. Recognizing the existence of an other in the world, and plumbing the true depth of all the implications of the existence of an other for selfhood, are the essence of revelation. One knows one's own self in a different way when there are other selves, even as a child with a new baby brother experiences a different attention as she becomes one of many rather than one alone. One's selfhood is no longer absolute.

This level of being and exploration promises the potential for awareness of God in a different way and calls on aspects of one's self-awareness in dialogue with an other. Emotions, emotional experience, and the controlling of emotions as they affect others are central to this level, which is, as a result, liable both to stormy upheaval and wild exaltation. The Name of God associated with this middle level is the Name that cannot be spoken; the unpronounceable Name *YHVH* is as ungraspable as the reins of the heart.

The highest level of mystical contemplation of God is symbolized by the Name that cannot be defined. As familiar as the word *Adonai* is to the praying, learning Jew, *Ehyeh,* "I will be," is the ultimately unfamiliar Name. This is the level of the intellect, which is the highest and most refined level of human being. It is also the most distant from any selfish sense of self. Here, nearing the most intense, if least understood, level of God's presence, the mystic experiences a state in which the human being loses the sense of separate selfhood. The meaning of the Name as a static state of here and now is lost in the vision of the potential of what will be, and one's selfhood is no longer important at all. In this place of the "first ripple," the self ceases to be an obstacle or a conundrum, and becomes an instrument of God's will. This is the self whose every word and act makes the world whole, and in so doing, creates a state of wholeness for oneself.

CHAPTER 9

Ten

> The Ten Words [*Aseret haDibrot*] correspond to the Ten Utterances [*Asarah Ma'amarot*] by which the world was created; the holy *Zohar* teaches that the word *ma'amar*, "utterance" refers to that which is hinted and hidden, and *dibbur*, "word," means that which is known ... the glorious presence of the Blessed Holy One fills the entire world, but before this, it was hidden.[219]

The *Sefirot* are ten attributes, or ten characteristics, or ten vessels, that are aspects of God, emanations of God, or reflections of God within the human sense of self. Through the millennium during which the *Sefirot* have been taught and written about, no single primary description of the *Sefirotic* system has emerged as the "right" one. Each of the various conceptions is correct from its own perspective; by accepting all of them simultaneously as equally potentially authentic, one opens the heart to the ability to learn from all of them. Such is the Torah study perspective – "turn it over and over, for all is within it" – and it is a necessary aspect of self preparation.

Sefirot as Aspects of God

The term *sefirah* is related to the Hebrew verb "to count"; thus the *Sefirot* system may be said to count the qualities, or attributes, of God. These qualities are derived from the evidence of the Torah and the Tanakh (Hebrew Bible): an early explication of the *Sefirot*, the "Gates of Light" of Rabbi Joseph Gikatilla, names each *sefirah* according to Biblical verses. In his description of the fifth *sefirah, Tiferet*, "glory," we find "Israel, in whom I will be glorified" (Isaiah 49.3).[220] The idea that God has definable attributes is the sort of claim about which Talmudic rabbis were wont to say, "If it was not written in the Torah, one could never assert it." Yet it is, indeed, written:

> YHVH descended in a cloud and was present to him there, and declared the Name of YHVH. YHVH passed before his face and called out, YHVH, YHVH, a compassionate and gracious God, slow to anger, greatly merciful, and faithful.[221]

God proclaims God's own divine nature. From this short declaration we discern the qualities of compassion, grace, anger, mercy, and faithfulness. In the *Sefirot* schema, all have their place, and they are elaborated through endless refractions of Torah. The idea that God is manifest in ten exists in religious sources much older than the first appearance of the *Sefirot*. Such ancient ideas as the ten sayings with which God creates the world in the Genesis account, and the ten utterances of Mt. Sinai, demonstrate a religious appreciation for the number. Rabbi Isaac of Acre, the first Jewish mystical source to describe ten *Sefirot* as aspects of God, takes pains to assert that these are not separate divinities in any way; they are differing aspects of God, experienced differently in different contexts and situations, but always One.

> "Their end is found in their beginning": just as many threads come out of the burning coal, which is one,

since the flame cannot stand by itself but only by means of one thing; for all the things [that is, the Sefirot], and all the attributes, which seem as if they are separate, are not separated [at all] since all [of them] are one, as the[ir] beginning is, which unites everything "in one word".[222]

To speak of the *Sefirot* as if they were a listing of God's attributes is not to assert that we have, in so many words and with a graph like the one we have been using,[223] defined God. Yet, inasmuch as we know these qualities within our own nature, and since Torah describes God as both angry and merciful, loving and punishing, the message is clear: the teaching that we are created in God's image does not ignore the powerful emotions that are an essential part of our creation. Therefore, they must somehow also exist beyond us; these emotions somehow have expression in the world of which we are an integral part.

This does not mean that we have a simple definition for God's nature nor that we even understand what we are asserting by saying that we and God share these essential characteristics; our vision is too weak. We cannot even gaze at the sun, much less the sun's creator. The first and last question of this study will remain, what does it mean to "see" God: how can we know what we might see if we could truly see?

Sefirot as Vessels

A different interpretative tradition preserved in the ancient book *Sefer haBahir* describes the *Sefirot* as vessels through which, or by way of which, the world was created:

> As we have said, *b'reshit*, "with beginning," and beginning can only mean wisdom, as it is said, *reshit hokhmah yirat YHVH*, "The beginning of wisdom is reverence for God."[224]

This play on words is grammatically possible because the word *b'reshit* can mean either "in the beginning" or "with beginning," since it is possible to translate the letter *bet* as "in" or as "with." It is mystically possible because of the multiplicity of interpretative possibilities encouraged by the traditional approach to Torah study. The elasticity with which the Jewish scholarly mind approaches the possible meanings of any word of Torah allows the mystic to take a step further and envision the words themselves as elements with cosmic reality. The world is literally created through intermediary vehicles – in their terminology, vessels – by which God created the world and that continue to function as a link between God and the world.

An example of this enduring image of a vessel by which the world was created and that continues to link God and the world, is the Torah.

> "The Torah and its commandments are the intermediary which links the lower image with the supernal one, by the affinity they have with both." As a result of the Torah's double affinity – with its divine source and with the persons who perform the commandments – it is able to function as a bridge between the two realms.[225]

The *Sefirot* as vessels similarly act both as receptors of divine emanation and as transmitters, or instruments, of that influx, and thus bridge the material and spiritual words as well as the upper and lower levels of the spiritual world. The conduits between each vessel are envisioned by the Kabbalists to function as the arteries and veins of a human body do: both to receive and to transmit energy along certain defined pathways to nurture and maintain the entire *Sefirot* system. The system, it is worth remembering here, encompasses the entire world.

Sefirot as Aspects of the Human

This third way of understanding the *Sefirot* emerges naturally from the concept that we are created in God's image. As the medieval mystic and ethicist Moses Cordovero put it, "A human being should resemble his Creator, and the secret [meaning] of the Upper Image [is that]...if a human being should resemble [God] in image but not in act, this would be a betrayal of His Image."[226] The idea has Talmudic roots:

> R. Hama son of R. Hanina further said: What means the text: You shall walk after YHVH your God? Is it, then, possible for a human being to walk after the *Shekhinah*; for has it not been said: For YHVH your God is a devouring fire? But [the meaning is] to walk after the attributes of the Holy Blessed One. As God clothes the naked, for it is written: "YHVH God made for Adam and for his wife coats of skin, and clothed them," so shall you also clothe the naked. The Holy Blessed One visited the sick, for it is written: "YHVH appeared unto him by the oaks of Mamre," so shall you also visit the sick. The Holy Blessed One comforted mourners, for it is written: "And it came to pass after the death of Abraham, that God blessed Isaac his son," so shall you also comfort mourners. The Holy Blessed One buried the dead, for it is written: "God buried him in the valley," so shall you also bury the dead.[227]

The mystics take this idea of imitating God further. If we, who reflect God's image therefore are understood to comprise the same attributes, the same *Sefirot*, as God, then to activate a lower *sefirah* in ourselves is to experience, in some way, a sense of resonance, even unification, with the Upper *Sefirah*. To act to fulfill one of the *mitzvot* in the foregoing Talmudic passage with a conscious sense that in so doing we are imitating God is to experience, in a mystical way, the presence of that divine attribute. One becomes oneself, the vessel bringing that attribute into the world, in a way bringing God more fully into the world, by the performance of the *mitzvah*. Kabbalistic tradition transmits a mystical interpretation of an ancient midrash: "Whoever keeps My commandments is as if he made Me."[228]

When one is seen as both receiving vessel and also transmitting conduit, the performance of the *mitzvot* becomes that which "holds the sefirotic structure in its position, as it was intended to serve as a bridge between the *Ayn Sof* and the world. ... the performance of the commandments not only preserves the sefirotic pleroma in its balanced and perfect state; it even *makes* it."[229] This depiction of the true nature of human value is developed in the anonymous *Sefer haNe'elam*:

> "And one who kills a person, what is the loss he brings about? He sheds the blood of that [man] and diminishes the form, that is, diminishes the power of the Sefirot." Man is therefore an extension of the Divine on earth; his form and soul not only reflect the Divine but also actually are divine. Its real meaning is not the fact, emphasized in Rabbinic sources, that man is a whole world, a world in itself, but that this micro-cosmos is a divine monad. Destroying a person is tantamount to diminishing not only the divine form on earth but, as this text puts it, divine power itself.[230]

The human position in the mystical understanding of the *Sefirot* remains central in all these configurations: whether as a reflection of divine attributes or as a part of a cosmic system in which each human being has a place and an active role or as an expression of divinity in the world, all these variations of mystical speculation recognize the power of human potential in the system and the human moral and religious responsibility to participate in "tilling and tending the Garden."

The Human Being as Sefirah

Mystics do not create new sacred text; rather, they "push the envelope," testing the limits of pre-existing interpretation. They seek to go further and deeper into the Torah's insights. The story of creation is well known and exhaustively interpreted in Jewish tradition, yet the mystics find deeper and more provocative meaning in it. A foundational concept for Judaism is derived from the verse, "God created the human in God's image, male and female."[231] For the mystics, this is an invitation to consider the mean of the claim that human beings are a reflection of God's image. A mirror reflects, imperfectly, a human being. What, exactly, is the human being imperfectly reflecting?

The mystical gate that is opened by this question (this will be defined at length later in this study) is opened by the teaching that God may be intellectually and spiritually grasped by human beings in human terms because of the ancient Jewish teaching that human beings are created in God's image. God is described in the Torah variously as loving, angry, judgmental, forgiving, and compassionate – and so are human beings. For the mystics, all that can be known about God is already contained in the apparently simple but amazingly complex and multileveled sacred text called the Torah, which, in Jewish terms, is the definitive account of what is real. In traditional Jewish terms it is understood that the entire world is patterned on this same basic "blueprint" of life. Even as modern scientists detect basic patterns that repeat not only throughout all life forms but also from the universe's structure to that of the subatomic world of an atom,[232] Jewish mystical tradition holds that Torah is the pattern at the heart of it all: "God looked into the Torah and created the world."[233] This is a declaration not of physics, but of the deeper spiritual level of reality.

The *Sefirot* are a path leading upward, like a ladder; outward, from the innermost sense of self; and inward, from that which is apparent toward that which is real. This study makes its way upward from a starting point that seems most accessible to modern Western Jews attempting to find their individual and communal meaning. It begins with an exploration of *Malkhut* as the Community of Israel. In ways both physically and socially necessary, every person is inseparably and by definition part of a group.

The Jewish people entered history as a community. The Ten Words were offered to the Israelite people as they stood as a group at Mt. Sinai to enter into the Covenant with God. By Jewish historical, religious, and philosophical definition, no individual Jew has a covenant relationship with God except as part of that which is understood to exist within the larger communal Covenant. To embark on this personal journey of spiritual exploration and growth, the individual must first be willing to lose that status, so as to see himself as part of the People of Israel. Each individual Jew is but part of the whole, a part that is precious and irreplaceable; it takes ten individuals to make a minyan for Jewish prayer, and holiness can only be evoked from within that minyan.

The ten lessons that follow explore each *sefirah* in ascending order, with some of its attributes:[234]

1. *Malkhut* – The Gate of Belonging
Attributes: Community of Israel – Indwelling Presence – Level of the Physical – Level of Speech – the rivers that lead to the Sea – Ethics – David – Rachel – Bride of God – Mother of Lower Worlds – God's Kingdom

2. Yesod – The Gate of Embodiment
Attributes: Sexuality in the Tradition and in the Zohar – Sign of the Covenant – Phallus – Covenant – Rectifier – Stable Personality – Joseph – Tzaddik – Foundation of Memory

3. Hod – The Gate of *Hoda'ot*
Attributes: Thanksgiving – Beauty – The Place of Wonders and Miracles – The Place of Hoda'ot – The Light of Creation – Elohim Tzva'ot – Prophecy – Aaron – Acceptance - Uncertainty

4. Netzakh – The Gate of Balance
Attributes: Endurance – Eternity – Victory – Prophecy – the Temple Pillars Named Yakhin and Bo'az – The Balance Between the Pillars that Support All Being: Beauty and Eternity, Kavvanah and Keva, Hod and Netzakh - Unity

5. Tiferet – The Gate of Connecting Below with Above
Attributes: polarity – The Blessed Holy One – The connection of Shekhinah and Tiferet – seeking balance above and below – Harmony – Perfect Center – Rakhamim

6. Din – The Gate of Judgment
Attributes: Judgment [Din] – Severity – Measuring of Divine Love – The Restraining Hand – Sarah – Evil – Isaac – Power (Gevurah) – Evil Is Part of the All – The Yetzer Hara' – Complexity

7. Hesed – Tthe Gate of Mercy
Attributes: Grace – Free-Flowing Love of God – Greatness (Gedulah) – Mercy – Abraham – Generosity - Openheartedness – Right Hand

8. Binah – The Gate of Understanding
Attributes: Impenetrable Mystery – Palace of Reflection – Womb of Existence – Teshuvah – Return to the Deepest Source – Leah – the Higher Feminine – Tent

9. Hokhmah – The Gate of Wisdom
Attributes: Primal Point – Spark of Existence – Deep Well – God's Water – Hidden Torah

10. *Keter* – The Gate of Transcendence
Attributes: First Ripple in Stillness of Ayn Sof – Keter – Alef – All

CHAPTER 10

Do not Say, "Water, water!"

Rabbi Akiba, on the greatest of mystics, compared God to a *mikvah*, a pool of sanctified water in which a Jew immerses to become ritually pure.[235] We plunge into the sphere of each *sefirah* as if immersing in such a pool of water; we explore the attributes of each *sefirah*, following the order listed. The order is not important, however; it is no more correct to start at any one place along a circle that at any other. In this way, at least, the clumsy choice of a circular image of each *sefirah* on our graph is appropriate. The immersion into the *sefirah* offers the opportunity to confront the different qualities of that *sefirah*, and how one's own self reflects them. But there is no intrinsic order to our consideration of the attributes of each *sefirah;* they are each a wave on the surface of the body of water into which we have entered. In a circular way, each one of them leads to any other, and all of them make the whole of the *sefirah*, as the mystics have sensed and as far as they have been willing to share.

Some ideas will recur more than once; we will meet them in one *sefirah*, and they will reappear in another, shedding a different light on another aspect of reality. Thus are the *Sefirot* linked to one another through a myriad of connected lines of insight and imagination; there is no one straight line that can be drawn or imagined to lead one directly toward one's spiritual quest.

This study of the Sefirot calls on varied sources, not all of them part of Jewish tradition, not all of them expected, perhaps. But if mysticism teaches that sparks of God are everywhere in the world, waiting to be found and redeemed, then perhaps a great wisdom is waiting to be discovered in an unlikely place; perhaps insight will sometimes be triggered by a news analysis, a marketing pitch, or a small, obscure poem.

It may seem strange to consider that only now, in Part III of this work, we are at the beginning, but this is what mysticism teaches: every moment is a beginning, full of unexplored potential. Every moment is a doorway into understanding – and misunderstanding. At this point, we have considered much, and we have learned nothing. As we begin, we do well to hear the story of Rabbi Akiba's warning to his companions who sought their own mystical experience: when attempting to immerse oneself in the deepest mystery, "Do not say, 'Water, water,'"[236] where there is no water. A *sefirah* is not really a *sefirah;* it is only an image, a metaphor meant to evoke an abstract concept: an emanation from God, which the world is created to reflect, right down to the level of each human being. We are reflections of the Image of God as a pool of water reflects the sky. The mystical images created and described by the mystics of Jewish tradition are only pale reflections of what inspired them. None of the images used in the Ten Lessons are as literally true as the revelatory truth of the connectedness they will evoke in the life of one who learns how to understand them.

CHAPTER 11

The Ten Sefirot

Malkhut – The Gate of Belonging

ATTRIBUTES: COMMUNITY OF ISRAEL, INDWELLING PRESENCE, LEVEL OF THE PHYSICAL - LEVEL OF SPEECH - THE RIVERS THAT LEAD TO THE SEA, ETHICS, DAVID, RACHEL, BRIDE OF GOD, MOTHER OF LOWER WORLDS, GOD'S KINGDOM[237]

> *b'shem yikhudo shel Kudsha Berikh Hu v'Shekhintey* – for the sake of the unification of the personal and the communal, the individual and the community, the People of Israel and God.

Community of Israel

To begin with oneself, but not to end with oneself; to start from oneself, but not to aim at oneself; to comprehend oneself, but not to be preoccupied with oneself.[238] God said it first: "It is not good for the human to be alone" (Gen. 2.18).[239] The *sefirah* of *Malkhut* is called "Community of Israel." Note that this *sefirah* is not called "the *individual* stands before God." Rather, the expectation here is clearly that, to "play" this "game," in order to follow the mystical path toward discovering one's own personal life's meaning, one must recognize that, when one is a Jew, one is not *only* an individual. *Malkhut* is the gateway to the other *Sefirot:* to take this first step, one must thoughtfully explore the way its attributes resonate within the self.

What does it mean to be part of a community, especially when each human community has certain distinct and unique characteristics? Some propose that all people can universalize their sense of identity by reducing it to being a member of the human community and nothing more distinctive. They claim that trouble inevitably begins between human beings when we refine our sense of self with adjectives that then differentiate us from one another, and that seem inevitably to distance us from one another. But a strongly developed sense of an identity, of what one *is,* can come to one's rescue in uncertain circumstances.

No community has recently faced a more conscious choice of identity development than have the Jews of the former Soviet Union. The social system of the Soviet Union, which was meant to create a new *homo sovieticus,* was for true believers the essence of their personal meaning. When the Soviet Union collapsed, not only were those who believed in its message bereft of a social system, but also their sense of the justification for their own personal existence was also in danger of collapsing. Ironically, the hardship of being a Jew in the Soviet system was that one was always defined as a Jew, and this identity became a gift in the days of chaos and uncertainty that followed the collapse of the Soviet Union in August of 1991. For some post-Soviets, on whose identity papers was the word "Jew" on the fifth line,[240] there was a clearly defined, if unformed, identity to fall back on and a community rich with historical meaning to support it. To be a Jew had meant to be part of a despised minority; one could in the past never escape that "fifth point." Now suddenly that identification had become a source of hope and inspiration.[241] When one follows a Jewish path, one's personal work to create life's meaning is only part of one's responsibility. For the mystics, one cannot ascend toward Oneness if one is focused only on oneself. In other words, as one rabbi put it, if someone tells you that he loves God but treats his fellow human beings hatefully, you will know that he is lying. The very arrangement of the *Sefirot* show us this fundamental truth: we are all connected to one another, and our individual well-being depends on the well-being of all of us.

Indwelling Presence

According to Jewish tradition, the way we treat one another in the communities we build will either create a sense of the *Shekhinah* – the indwelling, immanent Presence of God among us – or banish it. This *sefirah,* when we act in ways that allow us to stay "in sync" with it, keeps us connected to both heaven and earth, keeps us aware that, as Isaiah heard the angels sing, "the whole earth is full of God's glory."[242] As the Torah describes, the people of Israel become a community in the process of a shared spiritual journey toward such a sense of God's immanent presence. As individuals, they are linked to one another in the experiences and destiny they share; but it is in the context of the community that they develop their working definition of the ultimate meaning of life, expressed as their sense of the presence of God among them. *V'asu li mikdash v'shakhanti b'tokham,* "Let them make me a sanctuary that I may dwell among them."[243] The sanctuary is the creation of the community, as many generations of Jewish fundraisers who have quoted this verse know well. But the Hebrew word translated as "sanctuary," *mikdash,* derives from the word *kadosh,* "set apart, "sanctified," or, most commonly, "holy. The deeper meaning of this verse is that God does not exist among the people without the communally created place of holiness. As the mystics teach, God is the *Makom,* the Place of the world; but the context of the Biblical verse makes clear that it is the behavior of the people that makes that Place manifest, in the quality of their community. What is evoked by this community-building is the *Shekhinah,* the Presence of God, which dwells among and within the people as long as they remain a community worthy of the name.

As in the Torah's description of the building of the *mishkan* in the wilderness, the community is as strong as the gift – in commitment and in participation – of each individual who belongs to it. Thus is the community meaningful, perhaps even in the Biblical sense of holiness expressed by the Torah's declaration: "You shall be to me a kingdom of priests and a holy people."[244] In an interpretation of this verse, *Midrash Tanhuma*[245] notes that the holiness of the people proceeds from its connection to God, "For I your God am holy,"[246] and compares this acquired holiness to the relationship between a king and the woman he marries, who becomes a queen because she now shares his status. The intimacy of the marriage relationship in this example indicates a certain quality of closeness expected in the relationship between God and Israel, a closeness to be echoed in the people of Israel's relationships with one another. A holy Jewish community is made up not simply of people who come to the same place to pray but of people who recognize that the reality of community evokes a certain intimacy, a certain interdependency, if they would live the meaning of that prayer. A holy, that is, an authentic Jewish community evokes a sense of God's presence through the quality of each member's caring for the welfare of the others who join with them in their spiritual journey: "God's holy presence is made real through *tzedakah,* justice."[247] Justice is a quality that can be expressed only in community.

No authentic Jewish search for self takes place in isolation, or in rejection of others, or outside of the community of meaning. Of the necessity of relationships in the search for one's own personal sense of meaning, Heschel noted,

> Reflection alone will not procure self-understanding. ...
> The human situation is disclosed in the thick of living. In
> living, man relates himself actively to the world. Deeds
> are the language of living, articulating the uniqueness of
> human being, the insights of being human. The decisive
> form of human being is *human living.*[248]

As has been said, living is with other people. There is a paradox here: to seek one's own sense of personal meaning, one must recognize that one is not an isolate, is but dependent on human relationships, and that out of these relationships is created the quality of the humanity of one's community. At every moment we are balancing our existence between the sense of ourselves as individuals, with our individual responsibilities and perspectives, which cannot be reduced to any generalization, and the real need we have for one another, physically, psychologically, and spiritually.

We see in the *Sefirot* and their symbolism that balancing between polarities is an essential posture – of the cosmos, of God, of individuals, of humanity. Not unlike our physical sense that we are standing still even though we ourselves and everything else oscillate all the way down to the cellular level, we may feel that we stand consistently in one spiritual place, but the reality is that we are constantly called on to recalibrate, to reconsider, to choose. Paradoxically, our spiritual stability depends on our ability to learn and to change and grow as a result of that learning – to be receptive constantly to the *shefa'* and to be able to respond.

The Level of the Physical – The Level of Speech – The Rivers That Lead to the Sea

In Jewish tradition, the body of a human being is holy because it is descended from a creation of God, as we read in the story of Genesis. Abraham Joshua Heschel explains:

> The Biblical word that man was created in the image of God means two things to the Kabbalist: first, that the power of the Sefiroth, the paradigm of divine life, exists and is active also in man. Secondly, that the world of the Sefiroth, that is to say the world of God the Creator, is capable of being visualized under the image of man the created.[249]

The *Sefirot* system can be understood as divided into three realms: from the nearest to us (the "lowest") as we look upward, they are the physical, the emotional, and the intellectual. The lowest level of the *Sefirotic* system – *Malkhut, yesod, hod,* and *netzakh* – express the most basic human level of existence: the physical.

The most fundamental level – the basic goal – of a human being is simply to secure one's physical existence. Obviously, one must have one's basic physical needs met before one can seek spiritual growth, as the tradition teaches: *ayn kemakh, ayn Torah,* "If there is no bread, there can be no learning."[250] Traditional Jewish educational theory has always held that to learn effectively, one must first care for one's physical needs. Only then can the higher aspects of being human manifest.

The reverse of that truth is also worth noting: we are not only spiritual, nor do we fulfill our spiritual potential by ignoring the physical aspect of our being. The ancient Israelites did not hesitate to see God in the corporeal; therefore the corporeal must be capable of holiness. Mainstream Jewish thought does not teach the denial of the body and its needs. The Torah expresses disapproval with asceticism; it requires the *nazir*[251] to bring a sin-offering; Rabbinic Judaism provides for the physical and sexual needs of a wife; medieval Jewish ethics saw each limb of the body as a special vehicle with which to fulfill *mitzvot* and do God's will. The idea that the body is valuable and good follows naturally from the teaching that we are created by a compassionate God. The *Sefirot,* arranged in levels of the physical, the emotional, and the intellectual, clearly express that, to achieve wholeness, one must integrate all three levels of self.

The physical world is not just the province of us humans; it is part of the manifestation of God. The lowest of the *Sefirot* express God's presence in the world.

> [This] triad is the source of the psychic and physical existences – *Netzakh* is the lasting endurance of God, *Hod* His majesty, and *Yesod* is the stability of the universe, the seat of life and vitality. *Malkhut* is the kingdom, the presence of the Divine in the World. It is not a source of its own but the outflow of the other *Sefirot;* "of itself lightless, it looks up to the others and reflects them as a lamp reflects the sun." It is the point at which the external world comes in contact with the

upper spheres, the final manifestations of the Divine, the *Shekhinah,* "the Mother of all Living."[252]

The qualities associated with the physical aspects of God proceed naturally from the Torah's descriptions. We recognize God physically in *Yesod,* the life of the world; in *Hod,* those moments of grandeur which transfix us in awe; and in *Netzakh,* dependability, or that which endures far beyond human ken. Yet we can also see ourselves reflected in these images: the life we participate in and reproduce, the awe we experience in small interpersonal moments, and in the ability to envision – and to long for – that which is eternal, and participate in that which is enduring. "Let the work of our hands be enduring!"[253] pleaded the psalmist.

The physical level of the *Sefirot* encompasses the most basic and fundamental aspects of life. If the graph of the *Sefirot* (see Figure 1) were a tree, this level would constitute its roots. Yet, if we seek to fulfill only these needs and desires of the physical, there will be very little that will differentiate our human existence from that of all other life forms. To continue the tree analogy, there may be physical groundedness and security, but there will be no fruit. For us to be human beings, as Heschel taught, we must do more than be. We must be human. As the mystics would put it in *Sefirot*ic language, the physical level of our existence, our intentions, our words and our acts, must be integrated with the higher spiritual realm of our existence.

We come now to one of the most difficult questions of human existence: what does it mean to act out a human life?

> Human living is being-challenged-in-the-world, not simply being-in-the-world. The world forces itself upon me, and there is no escape from it. Man is continuously exposed to it, challenged by it, to sense or to comprehend it. He cannot evade the world. It is as if the world were involved in man, had a stake in man. The first thought a child becomes aware of is his being called, his being asked to respond or to act in a certain way. It is in acts

> of responding to demands made upon him that the child begins to find himself as part of both society and nature. ... he self is inescapably beset by the questions: what shall I do with my existence, with my being here and now? what does it mean to be alive?[254]

What does it mean to be alive? To be a human being is not, according to Jewish teaching, to be merely a being. Heschel asserted that "the attribute 'human' in the term 'human being' is not an accidental quality, added to the essence of his being. It is the essence. Human being demands being human."[255] Working one's way up the *Sefirot* has to start with physical integrity. But this means more than being fit and well fed. The way we deal with our physicality concerns so much more than that which we share with all life – breath, blood, and sinew.

> Being means striving to go on, to go along, to extend, to continue. Yet being human means to go beyond sheer continuity. Being human occurs, comes about in moments ... the enigma of human being is not in what he is but in what he is able to be.[256]

Human continuity on the physical level might mean, simply, that an infant is fed regularly and kept warm and safe. But infants do not become human without human touch and interaction. And an adult who clings to, or is trapped by, a physical routine may be said to be living, but without moments when one's being is called to creative choice, such an person hardly has a chance to act, or be, human, whether through offering the kindness of support by bringing a meal to a bereaved friend, or sharing the shelter of solidarity through standing up for an accused co-worker.

To come to terms with our physicality, to embrace it as a part of ourselves without letting it so distract us that we forget it is only part of us, and that it is only the initial step into spirituality, may be the single most difficult aspect of the journey of life. But, despite the difficulties, there is that in the very nature of being human which urges us onward.

We are not content with the boundaries of our own physical being. We are made of both earth and heaven; our bodies are physical, yet our best use of them is in our striving to reach our dreams.

Look at the graph of the *Sefirot* again (Figure 1). Consider the placement of *Malkhut* at the edge between the *Sefirot* system and the world of Creation. One of the names of *Malkhut* is *bat sheva*, "daughter of seven," because it receives all the flow from the seven *Sefirot* above it. It is also called *Be'er* and *Yam*, a "well" or "sea" of water, and, when all goes well, seven rivers flow from it to sustain all life. Consider the place of each human being at the edge between all that flows into the self – memories and habits, influences and coercions, desires and hopes and needs – and see how all that flows forth from one is utterly dependent on what flows into one.

Malkhut receives the flow she needs only when all the upper channels are clear and flowing freely; only then can she give forth what is needed for the seven rivers to water the earth (to use the kabbalistic metaphor). The significant insight here is not only environmental, although the parallel to clogging rivers either with dams or with pollution is compelling enough; it is also personal. If one does not receive that which nurtures and helps one to grow, how can one gather the positive energy inside oneself to join in building a better world? It is also physical: if one's own arteries are clogged, one's system will not be able to allow one to be a vessel for the onflowing *shefa'* to flow through oneself, in one's participation in the acts that make a human being truly human, and that bless the world.

Ethics

The Jewish story of human origins is a poignant one. In it, the Garden of Eden (that idyllic, perfect home) is lost before we can come to know its value. Similarly, in our own lives there is a longing for some long-ago time of a pre-intellectual garden of peace and wholeness. The mystic version of the creation story relates that, originally, all the *Sefirot* were harmoniously connected, and God's *shefa'*, the power that sustains the world, pulsed throughout creation vibrantly and joyfully. Then, after the human transgression of the Garden's balance, "barriers evolved thwarting the emanation of [God's] power.

> The creature became detached from the Creator, the fruit from the tree, the tree of knowledge from the tree of life, the male from the female, our universe from the world of unity, even the *Shekhinah* or the tenth *Sefirah* from the upper *Sefirot*.[257]

In this world, in which we are separated from God almost completely, however, there is still the presence of the *Shekhinah*, which can be evoked by our willingness to make a place for Her, that is, to act in harmony with the upper worlds. We can achieve that harmony by following and fulfilling the *mitzvot*, which, in Jewish tradition, is to act as one created in the Image of God.

That is the heart of the Jewish concept of ethics. It is an ethics based not on the rights of the other whose life we affect by our actions and attitudes; rather, Jewish ethics is based on one's personal obligation to behave like a human being in the fullest sense of the word.

Imitate your Creator. Then you will enter the mystery of the exalted form, the divine image and likeness. If you resemble the divine in body but not in deed, this distorts the form, and people will say of it: "A lovely form but ugly deeds." For the essence of the divine image and the exalted form is action. What good is it if one corresponds to the exalted form, but the actions of that likeness are not like unto those of the Creator? ....all Israel are responsible for one another. Truly, in each one is a portion of one's fellow. One who sins hurts himself and also hurts the portion of his fellow that is within him. ... it is well for each one of us to seek the well-being of his fellow, and to case a benevolent eye upon his fellow's good fortune, and his honor should be as dear to him as his own, for it literally is. For this reason we are commanded: "Love your neighbor as yourself." The Talmud describes three spheres of Jewish ethical life: the personal, the religious, and the social.[258] A Jewish *ba'al middot*, literally a "master of ethics," is constantly mindful of the ethical effect of her every individual word and deed in all three directions: on God, on the self, and on others. She remembers that the ethical virtues "are all *yir'at shamayim* ("reverence") and *derekh eretz* ("decency")."[259] She not only does God's will by fulfilling the *halakhah*, but also strives to remain constantly mindful of its essence: every act has either a positive or a negative effect on the world of which she is a part.

The development of Jewish ethical literature and its study are means to the creation of a certain kind of person.[260] The Hasidic master Rabbi Nakhman of Bratslav taught that the struggle to become the kind of person who truly reflects the Image of God is a lifelong journey toward the final product, or image, that one will have become at the end[261] and that the crux of the matter lies in the ethical value of each step of the journey. Such a path demands patience, acceptance of one's perception of only a partial understanding and of a reality in flux, and an abiding awareness that God is in the details, in every little detail – present and reflected through every blade of grass and every human being. The end and the means must justify each other. If they do not, there is something wrong with the means or the end. One must be able to recognize God's presence, and the expression of ethics, in both.

For Judaism, ethics is a prerequisite for achieving wisdom. Yes, there is room for one who is not wise – owing not to lack of study but to lack of native ability – to practice *musar,* the Jewish system of ethics. But a religious system that exalts learning as bringing one into the presence of God will value ethical behavior with learning above simple ethical behavior. Thus we see it in the *Sefirot* system of the *Zohar*, which places wisdom above, and as the culmination of, the balancing of all the "lower" attributes of human nature – judgment and mercy, compassion and endurance and understanding, and ethical behavior: all come before it and all must be within it.

Much of the Jewish ethical focus is on *mitzvot beyn adam l'adam,* "*mitzvot* between people." For the Talmud, a *ba'al middot,* an ethical person, is one who refrains from the temptation of believing that what is right for oneself must necessarily be right for others. The anonymous medieval author of the ethical tractate *Orkhot Zaddikim* warns, in a similar vein, against arrogance: "The behavior of others is not dependent upon *your* thoughts."[262] An ethical person is one who does not presume to know what relationship another human being has with God or to judge its quality.

> A pious Jew does not worry about his fellow man's soul and his own stomach; a pious Jew worries about his own soul and his fellow man's stomach.[263]

Jewish ethics encourages the mystical perspective, which sees the enhancement of the interconnectedness of all life, in all its diversity, as a religious imperative. Despite the multiplicity of created things, God is One; thus, all that we are in our individual and general complexity is also, essentially, One. Behavior that proceeds from this realization would therefore be that which respects diversity as respecting equally the different aspects of God, that is, the *Sefirot*.[264]

Spiritual life is superior to physical life. But the physical life of another is an obligation of my spiritual life.[265] That statement of the creator of the modern *musar* movement, Rabbi Israel Salantar, is also at the heart of the philosophy of the modern Jewish thinker Emmanuel Levinas. Levinas describes God as appearing to human consciousness (and especially in Jewish experience) "clothed" in values; and ... whatever the ultimate experience of the Divine and its ultimate religious and philosophical meaning might be, these cannot be separated from penultimate experiences and meanings. They cannot but include the values through which the Divine shines forth. Jewish religious experience can only be primarily a moral experience.[266] For Levinas, recognizing that there is an other whom we perceive already poses a moral question. Our response to God, and any other, creates the dialogic Jewish religious path toward transcendence of the self. "To hear a voice speaking to you is *ipso facto* to accept obligation toward the one speaking. ... Consciousness is the urgency of a destination leading to the other person."[267]

Malkhut is also the place of *tzedek*, "justice." The Kabbalists realized that, although justice as an idea is lofty, rooted in heaven above, justice can exist only down here in *Malkhut,* the "clearing house" where all the upper intentions, pulling this way and that, are balanced. It is where all the lower realities of the "real world" come to bear. Justice in this world of *Malkhut* is not of one single, perfect *sefirah* above it; it is arrived at in the *sefirah*, which receives from them all and must make sense, justly, of it all. Justice, therefore, cannot exist if all the attributes above *Malkhut* are not flowing freely and strongly. Compare the *Sefirot* system to a human community – the community of the world. We cannot act justly, even if we wish to do so, if all the channels of politics and bureaucracy and social mores and physical ability are not all interconnected and strengthening one another. That is why food aid rots on docks. It is why *a mensch trakht und Gott lakht*, "man plans and God laughs," as the Yiddish proverb puts it. And it is one of the reasons why evil exists for the Kabbalists: we are cut off from one another. The *shefa'* of hope, of kindness, and of the ability to care, cannot flow through us. From an isolated place of distrust and cynicism, we cannot help one another and so evil flourishes among us because we do not see how much each of us needs all the others.

If we cannot see the power that connection to one another gives to each of us to find healing for ourselves f and the world, we cannot be inspired by it toward a deeper sense of meaning. We may even reach a sense of conviction that there is no meaning outside the self and its wants. Curiously, as complex and capable as each of us is, no one is self-sufficient either physically or ethically. Even the essence of what a person is, is not about the person.

> Man is not his own meaning, and if the essence of being human is concern for transcendent meaning, then man's secret lies in openness to transcendence. Such is the structure of our situation that human being without an intuition of meaning cannot long remain a fact; it soon stares us in the face as a nightmare.[268]

Writing in 1965, Heschel was perhaps remembering the evil of the Holocaust, or reacting to the brutality of opposition to the Civil Rights movement; at the beginning of the 21st century, one may call to mind too many mind-numbing tales of more recent terrible deeds. The lowest expression of human being has taken many forms throughout history, but the shocking inability of the cruel to access their own humanity, much less their victims,' remains constant. The worst excesses of evil may be held in check – except for the occasional horrific outbreak – by a more stable social order in the neighborhood in which we live, but the despair of meaninglessness that leads to inhumanity is present among us too.

The *Sefirot* show us that we are all connected to one another; evil expressed anywhere affects all of us. An example: the injustice of the social system of which I am a part causes some human beings to be less valued and to value themselves less; when they express their sense of alienation through violence in my neighborhood, my safety, and probably the value of my house are endangered. I have not done anything to cause this situation as an individual. I just live here. Yet I am inescapably part of the whole, and the whole is affected by the harm done to any part of it.

Heschel, inheritor of the mystical teachings of a prominent early modern European Hasidic Rabbinic dynasty, depicts the human condition in a way that is clearly informed by the mystical insight that a human being must balance the good and the bad in human physical nature:

> The human situation may be characterized as a polarity of human being and being human. Being human is an imposition on human nature. It requires resistance to temptation, refusal to submit to immediate satisfactions. ... Notwithstanding the inner tension between the claim to be human and the craving to be animal, the alternative is hardly realistic. ... The opposite of the human is not the animal but the demonic.[269]

The *Sefirot* system, which shows us our inevitable interconnectedness, not only offers us a way to understand what is wrong with our world; it also shows us a way forward from it. We both see into the abyss and glimpse heaven. To set one's steps on the path of the *Sefirot* is to move away from the evil that is potentially present in human-merely-being and toward "significant being." As inspiration to help us refuse to despair at the overwhelming size of the system and our own insignificance, we have this teaching: that each of us is an essential part of the system, and, although we cannot heal it all, we are certainly capable of working on the potential of our own being, our own gift to the All. We are "challenged not to surrender to mere being. Being is to be surpassed by living."[270]

David/Rachel – Bride of God

Malkhut (Kingdom) is also known as *Shekhinah* (Presence). In early Jewish literature, *Shekhinah* appears frequently as the immanence of God but is not overtly feminine. In Kabbalah, *Shekhinah* becomes a full-fledged She: daughter of *Binah*, bride of *Tif'eret*, the feminine half of God. *Shekhinah* is "the secret of the possible," receiving the emanation from above and engendering the varieties of life below.[271] *Malkhut* is the place where the Male and Female of the Cosmos are balanced; here we find both King David and Mother Rachel. When we look at the *Sefirot* as God, we see *Malkhut*, "kingdom," as God's commanding presence. In the Biblical idiom, we are aware of "God above." This is the male expression of kingship, of dominance before which we bow in submission during prayer. This is the expression of *Malkhut*, which, we noted, is also named *be'er*, the "well" that gives forth waters.

But *Malkhut* is also called *Shekhinah*, the "Presence" of God among us. This aspect of God is linked to humanity and in this "position" receives the flow from above. This receptivity is associated in Kabbalah with the Feminine. Here is the ability to receive into oneself, to be a vessel, to know when to listen and take in that which flows forth. *Malkhut*, in other words, faces both "down," toward us, and "up," with us toward God. It is the place where heaven and earth meet. The mystic Elimelekh of Lizhensk compared the *Shekhinah* with the date, a fruit that is both male and female. The *Shekhinah* receives and also emits *hashpa'ah* ("influence," from the same root as *shefa'*, that which is emanated), and therefore it is both female and male in function.

> "[A]nd it was told to Tamar, saying" (Gen 38.13). The *Shekhinah* is called Tamar [date] in the holy *Zohar*, for the *tamar* is male and female, and it can be said that this is because the *Shekhinah* influences the upper worlds through the good deeds of Israel, and afterward she receives influence from the upper worlds and transmits that influence to Israel, and so she is called *tamar* because of being both male and female, transmitting *shefa'* to the upper worlds and receiving *shefa'* for Israel.[272]

Depicted in this way, the *Shekhinah* demonstrates the masculine and feminine qualities in each of us, as well as in the world and in God. This *sefirah* teaches that it is possible both to receive (the word *Kabbalah* itself, after all, means "receiving") and to give, and that these two abilities must be balanced if the divine flow is to emanate successfully from *Malkhut*.

The *Sefirot* balance a male side and a female side. The balance is seen both as upper–lower (the *Shekhinah* being the lower, female side opposite the male side above her) and right–left (the left side of the *Sefirot* being the female side, with *Binah*, the womb of the world, at its height). In both cases, balance is key: disunity between male and female is a major cause of disruption in the *Sefirot* and their ability to connect and thus to channel God's *shefa'* toward the world. The causes of disunity between the male and female aspects of God are found in echoes not only of gender relations among human beings, but in all human relations; and their healing must be similarly broad based. For example, the exile of the upper, male aspect of God from the lower, female aspect of God is a situation that mystically expresses the state of exile of the Jewish people from their homeland. In the book of Jeremiah, we read that as the Israelites are led away from their destroyed city by the Babylonians,

> [t]hus says the Eternal: A voice is heard in Ramah, lamentation, and bitter weeping, Rachel weeping for her children; she refuses to be comforted for her children, because they are not.[273]

The rabbis taught that God goes into exile with us, in the form of Mother Rachel, who herself is a symbol of that presence of God, the *Shekhinah,* that stays with us, suffering with us, even in exile. And we heal that exile, at least for a time, through bringing the male and female aspects of God's creation – ourselves – together in the opposite of exile. When lovers integrate their own inner male and female and unite sexually, with sensitivity and respect and care, at the time of greatest favor, on Shabbat, then our world is more complete, and our human exile from one another is temporarily stayed. And, the mystics teach, the upper, male aspect of God and the lower, female aspect, *Malkhut,* are united above, even as we unite below.

In the 18th-century Jewish shtetls of Eastern Europe, Hasidism brought Kabbalistic teachings into the awareness of many observant and educated Jews. In sophisticated circles of Jewish learning, the human ability to trigger the mystical unification between male and female was not seen as strictly the province of the male. In the genre of religious writings for, and often by, women, the author of the *Tekhine Imre Shifre* described a profound link between that unification, of the above with the below, with that *mitzvah* which paradigmatically belongs to women: that of lighting the Shabbat candles. In this anonymous teaching, the weekly act of lighting the Shabbat candles is the direct descendant of the High Priest's lighting of the menorah that stood in the Holy of Holies, next to the Ark of the Pact.

> [B]ecause the two souls shine on the Shabbat, [women] must light two candles. As it is written in the verse, "When you raise [*beha'alotekha,* here usually understood to mean "when you kindle"] the lamps, let the seven lamps shine against the face of [*el mul penei*] the candelabrum". [It seems that the verse] should have used a term for kindling rather than one for raising up; but by his kindling below the verse *means* raising up. ... [The priest] raised the arousal to the Upper World. All this was set out below, corresponding to the Tabernacle above. ... When the priest below lit the seven lamps,

he therewith caused the seven lamps above to shine. Therefore, by kindling the lamps for the holy Shabbat, we awaken great arousal in the Upper World. And when the woman kindles the lights, it is fitting for her to kindle [them] with joy and with wholeheartedness.[274]

The *Zohar* itself, from which the teaching clearly is derived, states that "the woman must light the candles, for the Lady [the *Shekhinah*] adheres to her and acts through her."[275] The "Bride of God" name invites other, even more provocative images to challenge those religious assumptions built on conventional ideas of theology. Inasmuch as *Malkhut* represents us, the community of Israel, we are, it might be said, on "the receiving end" of God's grace, at the bottom of the *Sefirot*. God is in the dominant position, above us – which makes us, the community of Israel, the Bride of God. Given that the normative Israelite community that stands before God in intimate relationship is patriarchal, that is, male, there arises from the beginning of Israelite religion "a deep tension in defining masculinity."[276] Without delving deeply into the analysis here, we note that mysticism explores every aspect of human sexuality as yet another key to the mystery of our creation and the mystery of God's existence. And while it is the male-female dyad that is most often invoked as the two complementary halves of creation that make it whole, our vision is not necessarily that narrow. Again, we return to the key phrase by which we seek to understand our existence:

> God created *ha'adam* in God's own image, in the image of God they were created; male and female God created them.[277]

In the *Zohar*, Rabbi Shimon teaches that "the *adam* of emanation was both male and female, from the side of both Father and Mother"[278] and, further, that "the word *adam* implies male and female."[279] *Let us make a human being* – mystery of male and female, entirely in supernal, holy wisdom. *In our image, according to our likeness* – to be consummated by one another.[280]

Remembering that God is understood as incorporating both male and female sides, we may also learn that none of us is complete unless we have embraced both our male and female sides. Modern biology has discovered what mystics sensed long ago and taught as a holy truth: each of us has within ourselves both male and female, even as each of us has within us the capacity for softness and for strength.

> And then all that has divided us will merge,
> And then compassion will be wedded to power,
> And then softness will come to a world that is harsh and unkind,
> And then both men and women will be gentle,
> And then both women and men will be strong,
> And then no person will be subject to another's will,
> And then all will be rich and free and varied,
> And then the greed of some will give way to the needs of many,
> And then all will share equally in the Earth's abundance,
> And then all will care for the sick and the weak and the old,
> And then all will nourish the young,
> And then all will cherish life's creatures,
> And then all will live in harmony with one another and the Earth,
> And then everywhere will be called Eden once again.[281]

Mother of Lower Worlds

Malkhut, situated at the "bottom" of the *Sefirot*, is closest to the created world and to us. *Malkhut* therefore serves as that vessel which receives all the *shefa'* of the upper *Sefirot* and, taking it all into itself, unifies it into one Presence of God, which pours into our world, strengthening and sustaining it. In this, *Malkhut* is the world's mother, the source of its sustenance and support.

Malkhut is between the upper and lower worlds, balancing in itself the downward energy from above and the upward longing from below, *Malkhut* is the sapphire platform described in a Biblical vision: "They saw the God of Israel; under His feet there was a likeness of a pavement of sapphire, like the very sky for purity."[282] It is "the place where heaven and earth kiss,"[283] where we reach beyond the physical to the spiritual aspect of our existence. All that which is above is gathered into the single meeting point with that which is below; if a human life is to be seen as modeled on the *Sefirot,* then *Malkhut* is for us the place where it all comes together: physical desires, emotional needs, intellectual awareness, ethical conscience, and the spiritual capacity for exaltation. For the *Sefirot* themselves, *Malkhut* is the place where all the upper *shefa'* that flows through all the attributes is gathered and becomes a unified community of God, integrated and balanced. Like the moon, *Malkhut* is said to have no light of its own, yet it stands in the place where it reflects perfectly all the light of all the suns above it to illuminate that which is below.

Malkhut is a starting place worthy of the lifelong, world-embracing journey toward and beyond the self, for it shows us our potential nurturing capacity for others as well as ourselves. *Malkhut* mothers all the worlds; like quarreling children brought together and reassured that all is well, in *Malkhut* all the conflicting aspects of a self, or of a world, can come together as one. *Malkhut* is the location for the atonement and wholeness that we must find for the imperfections rooted in the physical. In *Malkhut* we learn to use the physical as a vehicle for the ethical, so that every act of our hands and ears and mouths becomes part of the person each of us wishes to be.

In *Malkhut,* "kingdom," we bow to the reality that we are not king, but servant. We come to terms with the reality of our gifts and shortcomings and do what we can to perfect our individual existences by learning to balance our sense of selfhood with our interdependence with others, our responsibility for our community's behavior and fate. For the mystics, to perfect one's human existence is to become the Image of God as completely as possible; to balance one's different attributes and characteristics, actions, and potential, and thus to achieve their integration within oneself, the better to reflect God's Image into the world. The goal of self-perfection is to become a worthy vessel and to channel all that might flow into and through each one of us. Thus we bring about a greater flow of *shefa'* into the world, and we bring the world one small step closer to healing, by restoring it to the original state that God intended.

Kingdom of God

According to the mystical understanding of Jewish liturgy, the work of the *Shema* is to bring the female lower *Sefirot* part of God together with the male upper *Sefirot* part of God. However, the *Shema* offers more than that to us in our *Malkhut* place. The acceptance of our communal obligation is repeated each time the *Shema* is recited; liturgically, this utterance is "the acceptance of the yoke of the kingdom of heaven." We are back where we began, standing before the covenanted community of *Malkhut,* the kingdom, and making the choice to enter, which is to be obligated: one must be committed to the community, a member of the covenant people, in order to enter into the first *sefirah*. One must recognize that one's personal journey has, at every turn, an effect on the world, on others, on the processes of life of which one is a part. To understand this is not necessarily to accept it; many Jews would rather escape their sense of belonging to a very large and diverse family, to some of whom one would rather not be related.

To accept that one's life is interdependent with others, that the responsibility one bears for one's acts is partly because of their inevitable effect on others, is to begin to grasp the potential power inherent in this position. In a famous Hasidic story, a bird alighted in the top branches of a tall tree, and the townspeople were captivated by its beauty. They resolved to catch it and bring it down where it could be properly seen. How to reach it? They resolved to form a human ladder; the strongest stood at the bottom, and others climbed onto their shoulders, and others then climbed on to theirs, and so on. They nearly reached the bird: only one more small child was needed, and he began his climb up the shoulders, knees, and elbows. Then someone who could not see the progress that was being made became impatient with the whole thing. She decided that her place in the tower would not be missed, and she walked away. At first, no effect was visible, but the weakness of the missing support took its toll before too long, and, just as the child's hand was reaching out to the bird, the entire human tower fell apart.

To accept the obligation to be a part of the covenant community is to step through a door toward possibilities that one cannot see from the bottom position in which one begins. Just like the woman at the base of the tower, we cannot see above us – and what we can see is veiled and misleading. We must accept the connection on faith, before seeing where it will lead and what it will demand, even as the Israelites at Mt. Sinai said *na'aseh v'nishmah,* first "We will do" and after that "and we will listen."[284]

Jewish tradition teaches that the *Shekhinah* accompanies the exiles. Exiled as modern Jews have become from one another, their search for her is their search for one another, for the community in which she – the Indwelling Presence of God – is made manifest. Judaism maintains that the effort to invoke God's presence, and to sense the connection that evokes meaning for our lives, is not a challenge that anyone can meet alone. God may be immanently present in one's inner sense of spiritual fulfillment or harmony with the universe, but also, transcendently, in the self-judgment and communal assessment that takes place opposite the face of the other. Thus the root of the Hebrew word for prayer, *hitpallel,* is also used Biblically to denote judgment; Hebrew prayer assumes a focus both inward, on the self, and outward, on the community's response to the self.

The Talmud relates a story[285] that takes place in the years after the Roman destruction of Jerusalem and exile of much of the population of what had been the Kingdom of Judah. Rabbi Yose enters one of the ruined buildings to pray; there he meets Elijah the Prophet, who asks him what he is seeking. We can imagine the feelings that overwhelm Yose as he walks alone through the ruins of the holy city, the city in which God's presence is always to be found. Other stories are told of rabbis bursting into tears when they beheld what had become of the once glorious Temple precincts. Yose answers Elijah that he had sought to pray there; perhaps he hoped to connect to the former glory and the lingering sense of God's presence that might still cling even to the broken rocks.

> Eliyahu asked me, "My son, what sound did you hear in this ruin?"
> "I heard a heavenly voice which sighed like a dove and said, *Woe to the children whose sins caused me to destroy my house and burn my palace and exile them among the nations.*"

Rabbi Yose hears the sound of the tragedy that has occurred; alone in the ruins; he accesses only his own and his people's sad memories. It seems that the Talmud wishes to tell us in this story that it is for the person who seeks God's presence; Yose has only his own memories, his own thoughts, to bring to the moment. Elijah then tells Yose that the place to hear the voice of hope, of the future, is

> at the hour when Israel enters the synagogues and the houses of study and answers *yehei shmei hagadol mevorakh*, the Holy One blessed be He nods his head and says, "*Happy is the King who is praised in his house in this way.*"

The "answer" mentioned in this source is the communal response that is part of the *Kaddish* prayer. Different versions of this prayer are recited in the study house and in the synagogue. What Elijah is telling Rabbi Yose is that it is "in this way" – within the Jewish community that gathers together in study or in prayer – that he will access that sense of God's presence which he had sought in his solitary search through the ruins of that which was. Not only in the solitary search, although it is important, does one find God. One's individual spiritual search for the meaning of one's life is balanced by that which takes place within, and is supported by, the strength of the assembled community of study and prayer.[286]

Yesod – The Gate of Embodiment

ATTRIBUTES: SEXUALITY IN THE TRADITION AND IN THE ZOHAR, THE SIGN OF THE COVENANT, PHALLUS, COVENANT, RECTIFIER, STABLE PERSONALITY, JOSEPH, TZADDIK, FOUNDATION OF MEMORY

The mystical gateway that offers entry into the world of the *sefirot* opens onto a passage of great and transformative power. It can be no less if this is a path to God. Putting one's first foot forward on this path cannot but be a life-altering experience. That the initial steps are expressed in the language of the unifying and transcendent power of the erotic offers us the opportunity to confront one of the biggest contemporary obstacles to physical integrity: the misuse, abuse, and estrangement of many of us from our own sexuality. We cannot go further unless we first open ourselves to this question and seek its resolution.

> *b'shem yikhudo shel Kudsha Berikh Hu v'Shekhintey* – for the sake of the unification of the upper and the lower, the inner and the outer, the potential of thought and its fruition in the fertility of the physical.

Sexuality in the Tradition and in the Zohar

> The Zanzer Rebbe taught that one should be extremely careful not to permit physical desires to master oneself. To permit this will not only lead to embarrassment but will degrade one's value as a human being.[287]

It should be no surprise that, whether one begins with the creation story or the idea of the reunification of the lowest *sefirah*, with its upper partners, the initial and foundational *sefirotic* activity is erotic. Creation as experienced by human beings is a sexual activity. We must come to terms with its intimidating power; and this is no small challenge for American Judaism, for our attitudes about sexuality are informed not only by our own Jewish traditions of sexual modesty, but also by Puritan and other Christian influences on American culture.

The novelist and poet Audre Lorde explored the centrality of the erotic, and its fundamental importance in our physical and emotional lives, in a way that opens us to a taste of what might be a mystical appreciation of this most basic aspect of our humanity, and our divinity:

> The erotic functions for me in several ways, and the first is in the power which comes from sharing deeply any pursuit with another person. The sharing of joy, whether physical, emotional, psychic or intellectual, forms a bridge between the sharers which can be the basis for understanding much of what is not shared between them, and lessens the threat of their difference. Another important way in which the erotic connection functions is the open and fearless underlining of my capacity for joy. In the way my body stretches to music and opens into response, hearkening to its deepest rhythms, so every level upon which I sense also opens to the erotically satisfying experience, whether it is dancing, building a bookcase, writing a poem, examining an idea. ...
> This is one reason why the erotic is so feared, and so often relegated to the bedroom alone, when it is recognized at all. For once we begin to feel deeply all the aspects of our lives, we begin to demand from ourselves and from our lives pursuits that they feel in accordance with that joy which we know ourselves to be capable of. Our erotic knowledge empowers us, becomes a lens through which we scrutinize all aspects of our existence, forcing ourselves to evaluate those aspects honestly in terms of their relative meaning within our lives. And this is a grave responsibility, projected from within each of us, not to settle for the convenient, the shoddy, the conventionally expected, nor the merely safe.[288]

> Our "deepest rhythms" are those of our physical being-ness: the regular beating rhythm of heart and lungs, the driving rhythm of lovemaking, the cyclical rhythm of our bodily needs. This deepest sense of the salty river of our blood / winding through us, to remember the sea and our kindred under the waves, the hot pulsing that knocks in our throats to consider our cousins in the grass and the trees, all the bright scattered rivulets of life[289] is what we touch when we are looking for the pulsating rhythm of the Eternal within us and others, as when we pray in the evening prayer called *Ma'ariv Aravim* ("that which causes evening"): *el khai v'kayam, aleynu yimlokh l'olam va'ed,* literally translated as may the living and existing God rule for all and for always! And, in the context of this prayer about the God-driven rhythms of sun and moon, day and night, might also be understood as, May we feel the rhythm of the Living and Eternal God within us always.[290]

From this perspective, perhaps it is not surprising that the great mystic Rabbi Akiva declared the erotic *Shir haShirim*, the Song of Songs, to be the Holy of Holies for the people of Israel. And we can also understand the conventional avoidance of the text, the conservative Jewish insistence that it refers only to a metaphorical expression of love between Israel and God. The mystic desire to take the text at its provocative word and to delve deeper requires us, as Audre Lorde noted, to be ready to step beyond "the conventionally expected" and "the merely safe."

For Judaism, the body created by God and given to each of us necessarily has great religious significance.[291] This is true not only in the sexual sense. The customary blessing to be recited after eliminating waste from the body recognizes that we are created "with holes and orifices" and gives thanks that they all function properly. Eating and drinking, and all other physical human activities, become opportunities for blessing, and the spiritual realization which emerges is that, in every moment, on the most mundane and prosaic of levels, the potential exists either to enhance creation or to destroy it. Everything that exists can be a vehicle toward holiness or an opening for negation of that potential.[292]

The body is the locus of great power, which can create, or destroy and which we can channel into the world for good or evil. Sexuality is an essential and central aspect of that power. Sexuality, or the erotic, is at the heart of the mysticism of the *Zohar*, which is a work dedicated to mystical attachment to God.

> "Attachment to God, for the *Zohar*, is erotic attachment, whether referring to the kabbalist's own attachment to God by means of Torah, to *Shekhinah's* link to the upper "male" *sefirot* as God's bride, or in the rare passages where Moses becomes the kabbalistic hero and himself weds *Shekhinah*, entering the Godhead in the male role. The contemplative and erotic aspects of attachment to God are just different ways of depicting the same reality, quite wholly inseparable from one another.[293]

The first words of the *Zohar*, in its introduction, are from the Song of Songs, that book of the Bible which is a love song of great beauty and eroticism. The companions of the *Zohar*, who learn excitedly and teach one another passionately and have mystifying and exalting experiences related to their learning, are embodied in every way. They weep with joy when one produces an innovative mystical exposition on Torah, and one kisses another in happy appreciation for a new insight. In its exploration of sexuality as a central metaphor for God's creative activity and the human connection to God, the *Zohar* develops the idea, latent in rabbinic Judaism, of the necessity for a female "side" to God, paralleling that of the male. Even in a male-centered culture, male sexuality alone cannot generate life. For that which pours forth to be generative, there must be something to receive: a strong vessel is filled with sustenance, a fertile field is sowed with grain, and a womb provides the sheltered growing place for the emanation of life.

The Kabbalists, like people of all ages, were filled with wonder at the human reproductive process. Their teachings are in part a reflection on the links between love, its passionate fulfillment, and the flow of creative energies throughout the universe. ... The forces within our human make-up that lead us to bring forth new generations lie in a continuum with the power that brought us here in the first place. Thus the human soul and even the existence of the lower "worlds" altogether are depicted by Kabbalah as resulting from an act of sexual union within God, of the flow together of divine "male" and "female" energies.[294]

Thus the *Shekhinah*, which means "indwelling presence of God" and happens to be female in its Hebrew declension, becomes the feminine aspect of God, that which receives the flow from the upper *sefirot* which is channeled through *Yesod* and into her.

In the ancient Near East, the marriage of divine and human was one of the most important religious rituals. The *hieros gamos*, "divine marriage," was a way to bring together a god and the human community that depended on that god for life and sustenance. In one famous example, the king, representing the people, united with a woman representing the god. The Kabbalistic version of the divine coupling is clearly related:

> The King [*Tiferet*] and the Matronit [*Shekhinah*] were not only brother and sister, but twins; in fact, Siamese twins, who emerged from the womb of the Supernal Mother in the androgynous shape of a male and female body attached to each other back to back. Soon, however, the King removed his sister from his back, and she, after a futile attempt to reunite with him

in the same position, resigned herself to the separation and to facing the King across a distance.

By human standards a marriage between brother and sister would have been incestuous; not so in the heavenly realm: there, a *Zohar*ic text informs us, no incest prohibitions cold exist, and thus it was completely proper and licit for the King and the Matronit to marry. The wedding, a veritable *hieros gamos,* was celebrated with due pomp and circumstance. The Matronit, surrounded by her maidens, repaired to her couch set up in the Temple, there to await the coming of the groom. At midnight, the tinkling of bells he wore around his ankles announced the coming of the King. As he approached, he was accompanied by a host of divine youths, and the maidens of the Matronit welcomed him and them by beating their wings with joy. After singing a song of praise to the King, the Matronit's maidens withdrew, and so did the youths who accompanied him. Alone, the King and the Matronit embraced and kissed, and then he led her to the couch. He placed his left arm under her head, his right arm embraced her, and he let her enjoy his strength. The pleasure of the King and the Matronit in each other was indescribable.

... Some say, that as long as the Temple stood the King would come down from his heavenly abode every midnight, seek out his wife, the Matronit, and enjoy her in their Temple bedchamber. ... Others say that the King and the Matronit coupled only once a week, on the night between Friday and Saturday.[295]

Within Jewish tradition, human sexuality evokes most powerfully the reflection of God's creative image. For the mystics, this expectation that we reflect the divine reality defies the patriarchal suppression of the feminine half of life and brings an ancient expression of sexual equality back into overt Jewish consciousness and practice.

> In the Kabbalistic view, when the learned men, familiar with the heavenly mysteries, couple with their wives on Friday nights, they do this in full cognizance of performing a most significant act in direct imitation of the union which takes place at that very time between the Supernal Couple.[296]

It is traditional for Jews to gather on the eve of Shavuot, the Festival of the Giving of the Torah, when Israel and God entered into a mutual covenant and became, as it were, married. Jews who do not consider themselves mystical at all nevertheless spend the entire night of erev Shavuot studying, in line with the practice of Rabbi Shimon as described by the *Zohar*:

> Rabbi Shimon would sit and study Torah all night when the bride was about to be united with her husband. And we have learned that the companions of the household [i.e. the mystics] in the bride's palace are needed on that night when the bride is prepared for her meeting on the morrow with her husband under the bridal canopy. They need to be with her all that night and rejoice with her in the preparations with which she is adorned, studying Torah, from the Pentateuch to the Prophets, and from the Prophets to the Writings, and then to the midrashic and mystical interpretations of the verses, for these are her adornments and her finery.[297]

In so doing, they ready themselves, the community that embodies *Malkhut*, to relive the covenant moment with God on the morrow, and perhaps even to experience a sense of the intimate moment of unification themselves.

The Sign of the Covenant, Phallus

This *sefirah* is the place of the foundational covenant between God and the People of Israel, the basic mutual promise from which the history of the Jewish people flows. When the imagined arrangement of the *sefirot* are compared to the human (male) body, this *sefirah* of *Yesod* parallels the phallus, in all its symbolic glory as the source of the generative power of nature, and, of course, the male's central status in the patriarchal culture of the ancient Israelites. From the male perspective, the phallus is, indeed, the foundation of human life and the family; one ancient metaphor for intercourse compares the man to the farmer sowing seed. The woman is the field, fertile and ready to be plowed. It is this organ of generativity, of life, that bears the sign of the covenant with God initiated with Abraham, the *brit milah,* the circumcision.

That physical sign of the covenant is an evocation of mutual responsibility and mutual commitment. In his *Shaarei Orah,* the mystic Joseph Gikatilla writes of three levels of *brit:* learning, flesh, and language.

Drawing a parallel between his interpretation of *brit milah* and the Three Worlds of Human Existence,[298] Gikatilla links the first level of the *brit* with the name *Adonai,* that name which signifies hidden meanings and truths concealed in contradictions. This is the world of the ongoing process of looking behind the veil to discover God's word, as expressed by the Talmud. This essential Jewish activity – learning – is recognized as the heart and guarantor of Jewish existence. To learn Talmud is not only to read and consider, explore and discover previous generations' insights and teachings; it is also to be a part of Jewish community, since Talmud is studied in *hevruta,* in a learning group of two or more. Here is the interconnectedness of the *Sefirot: Malkhut,* the community of Israel, is expressed through *hevruta,* a microcosm of that community.

The second level of meaning of the *brit milah* is of the sign of the covenant "sealed in our flesh," for which we give thanks in, among other places, the second blessing of the *birkat hamazon,* the Blessing After Meals.

> [F]or the gift of the beautiful and wide-open land, and for bringing us out of Egypt, for redeeming us from a life of slavery, for your covenant sealed on our flesh, for your Torah that you teach us, for your laws that you have allowed us to know, for the life of grace and mercy you gave us, and for the sustenance through which you support us, every day and every hour.[299]

The physical sign here is one more among several of God's actions within the covenant relationship. Gikatilla also connects it to Shabbat, which is clearly a specific idea related to the Jewish covenant with God and to the rainbow, which is not. "When the bow is in the clouds, I will see it and remember the everlasting covenant between God and all living creatures, all flesh that is on earth."[300] The name of God that Gikatilla connects to this level of the *brit* is *El Hai*, "the living God," the God we appeal to on *Yom HaZikaron*, the Day of Remembrance, to "remember us unto life".[301]

The third level of *brit milah*, language, relates to the mouth. The word *milah* can refer either to the act of "circumcision" or to the spoken "word"; at the moment that the Sinai pact is created, God says to the Israelites, "by the mouth of these words I have cut a covenant with you."[302] When Moshe protests his unworthiness as a "mouthpiece" for God, he uses this same imagery: "I have uncircumcised lips, why should Pharaoh listen to me?"[303] The quality of one's speech is of enough concern even to be included in the Ten Words, the foundational utterance of Sinai: taking a false oath in God's name, as well as witnessing falsely against one's neighbor, are both proscribed.[304] The written Torah is associated with this level of the *brit,* as is the upper *sefirah* of *Binah*, Understanding.

The Hebrew word *milah*, "word," reverberates here:[305] one's word has a sacred quality to it. In Jewish law and tradition, vowing is not taken lightly. This awareness underscores the action at the beginning of a familiar Genesis story in which trustworthy action is required, in which recognizing the power behind the covenant of the flesh sanctifies the covenantal power of the word of the mouth.

> Abraham was old and had lived long, and the Eternal had blessed him in all things. Abraham said unto his servant, the elder of his house, that ruled over all that he had: "I pray you, put your hand under my thigh and swear by the Eternal, the God of heaven and the God of the earth."[306]

The story from which that text is drawn is Genesis' account of Abraham's concern with finding his son a suitable wife. He is *zakeyn*, "old," and he turns to the head of his household, a trusted servant also described as *zakeyn*. The two old men must have been through much together, and now Abraham is going to ask his servant (unnamed in the text) to act *in loco parentis* in one of the most difficult and important tasks of all – that of finding the right partner for his son. More, Abraham is entrusting his servant with the future of his family and all he has sought to build. Perhaps because he is all too aware of the significance of this task, or perhaps to clearly indicate to his servant the seriousness he sees in it, Abraham asks the servant to swear a solemn oath.

The American tradition in our own time calls for the witness in a court case to place his hand on a Bible and swear that his testimony will be true. In Jewish history, placing one's hand on the Torah in the Ark was sometimes required for an oath to be binding. In both cases, there seems to be a recognition of a sense that the fear of God will be on the person swearing, which is to say that he will be soberly aware of the consequences of his words and he will not swear lightly. But on what did one swear before there was a holy book on which to place one's hands? After all, a book is just a book; the words within it point to something that it represents. In this case, the source of value is not represented in a book but exists unmediated. Abraham's servant swears on the place of most important human power: the genitalia ("thigh" is a euphemism).

That passage and others throughout the *Tanakh* reflect the ancient Hebrews' recognition of the centrality and sanctity of human sexuality. The way we most powerfully resemble God, after all, is in our sexuality, which is the human quality through which we express our power to create life. God is the Creator; we reproduce that act of creation through our own bodies. In the male-centered culture which is described by the Torah's stories of the earliest Hebrews, it follows that it is specifically the male genitalia that have special power. In this the Hebrews were not alone; pillars were erected as representations of the great and powerful male god Ba'al by the Hebrews' closest neighbor, the Canaanites. The word *ba'al* is found in Hebrew in several specifically sexual connotations, such as the verb that refers to the male (not the female) in the act of intercourse. Not by coincidence, it is also the Hebrew word for "husband."

Covenant

The grounding reality of the Jewish people's sense of communal being comes from the moment when we stood before God at Sinai and entered into the covenant relationship. That spiritual moment of shared historical memory is expressed in a physical mark of our group commitment to God which is, however, quite personal. The ceremony of *brit milah,* ritual circumcision, is an ancient and powerful demonstration of the *brit,* the covenant between God and the Jewish people. Observance of *brit milah,* the "covenant of circumcision", has a curious inverse relationship with the Jews' sense of difference. Modern American Jewish mothers sometimes question its meaning and appropriateness; in stark contrast, newly liberated Jewish men in post-Soviet Ukraine endured many hardships, among them lack of anesthetic, to be circumcised as soon as it was no longer illegal.

Those Jewish men in Ukraine, alienated from their Jewish heritage by Soviet law for generations, nevertheless seemed somehow to understand the truth of an ancient midrashic saying they had no doubt never heard. "You are my witnesses," says God, "and I am God". This is to say, if you are not my witnesses, then I am not [God forbid], God."[307] Without having been told of the significance that the free Jewish world placed on the physical sign of the covenant, without any education in the powerful symbolism of *brit milah,* with their bodies, and at some risk, these men expressed the mystical awareness that the covenant of the physical sign of *brit milah* is the foundation of the Jewish world. This act of covenant, initiated by Abraham's choice to respond to God's call as he heard it, opened up an entire new world of potential for the Creation.

> When did that key open gates? When was it fit to be fruitful, to generate offspring? When Abraham arrived, as it is written, "These are the generations of heavens and earth *behibar'am*, when they were created" (Gen. 2.4). And we have learned: *BeABeRaHaM*, through Abraham. Whereas everything was concealed in the word *bara* [created], now the letters were transposed and rendered fruitful. A pillar emerged, generating offspring: *eiver*,[308] organ - holy foundation on which the world stands.[309]

EiveAiberr is also the name of the descendant of Noah who is Abraham's direct forefather, according to the generational lists preserved in Genesis 11.10-26. From a mystical perspective, this is yet another hint at the significance of the connection of this word and all it symbolizes in the story of the founder of the Jewish people.

There is a mystical teaching based on an interpretation of God's command to Abraham, *lekh l'kha*, as meaning "Go to yourself." When one searches for God, one finds that one is looking at oneself. Similarly, one cannot care for others if one does not care for oneself. I recently participated in a game in which a group of people, hold aloft olds a circle of material,

Rectifier, Stable Personality, Joseph, Tzaddik

> We have learned: there is a single pillar extending from heaven to earth, and its name is *Tzaddik* (righteous). This pillar is named after the righteous. When there are righteous people in the world, then it becomes strong, and when there are not, it becomes weak. It supports

the entire world, as it is written, "and righteous is the foundation of the world." If it becomes weak, then the world cannot endure.[310]

Yesod is also called *tzaddik*, or the "rectifier,"[311] the one who sets things on their proper course. Jewish mystical thought takes literally the teaching that "the *tzaddik*, [righteous one], is *yesod olam*, [an everlasting foundation]"[312]; the righteous one is the foundation of the world. There is a well-known popular teaching that the world is maintained, sinful as it is, is for the sake of thirty-six righteous people, who are anonymous and who themselves do not even know that they are among that saving remnant.

On the graph of the *Sefirot* (see Figure 1), *Yesod* is at the bottom of the nine upper *sefirot;* below it is *Malkhut,* open and waiting to receive the flow from above. *Yesod* balances and focuses the energies flowing into it, which will then be channeled down into the waiting vessel of *Malkhut*. The successful passing on of the flow through *Yesod* depends on *Yesod's* filtering strength – hence the association with a stable personality. *Yesod* is like a person who maintains a sense of his or her own personal balance even when immersed in the influences of significant relationships, and the emotional upheaval they can evoke.

For the mystics, this ability to balance and faithfully transmit that which it receives from the *shefa'* above is foundational to the world's existence, and it is synonymous with the ethical quality of righteousness. Everything depends on this one *sefirah*, which connects all that is above to that which is below – the community of Israel, and the world itself. *Yesod's* power to regulate great energies and properly, thoughtfully balance them is a teaching about the difficulty and necessity of the art of balance in our own lives. For the mystics, this is what it means to "uphold the Covenant" with God. Everything depends on it, including the perfect world "that is coming," that we bring about through perfecting ourselves.

> Rabbi Hiyya opened, "Your people, all of them righteous, will inherit the land forever" (Isaiah 60.21).

> Happy are Israel who engage in Torah and know her ways, for on account of her they will attain the world that is coming! Come and see: All of Israel have a share in the world that is coming. Why? Because they uphold the covenant on which the world is erected, as is said: Were it not for my covenant day and night, I would not have established the laws of heaven and earth" (Jeremiah 33.25). So Israel, who embraced the covenant and uphold it, have a share in the world that is coming. Moreover, they are therefore called righteous. From here we learn that anyone upholding this covenant, upon which the world is erected, is called righteous. How do we know? From Joseph. Because he upheld the covenant of the world, he attained the title Righteous.[313]

The *Zohar's* commentary on *parashat Noakh* includes a comparison of Noah to Joseph:

> What is "my bow"? As is said of Joseph, "His bow remained firm" (Gen. 49.24), for Joseph is called Righteous, so "his bow" is the covenant of the bow, contained in the Righteous One, covenant linking one with the other.

"The phallus of *Yesod* is often symbolized by the bow and is also the site of the covenant (the sign of circumcision)."[314] Recall the connection that the mystic Gikatilla made between the bow in the clouds and the covenant of the flesh; here is another perspective on the connection between memory and covenant. God sees the bow in the clouds, which is a sign of the covenant, and remembers the covenant. We take up the theme of memory now, mentioned briefly already above, in more depth.

Foundation of Memory

Yesod, the "lowest" of the nine upper *sefirot*, is the stable grounding on which they are balanced when all is well and the energy flows freely through the channels that connect each *sefirah*. *Yesod*, "foundation," grounds the entire *Sefirot* structure above and connects the upper worlds to *Shekhinah* and the worlds below. "The ninth *sefirah* represents the joining together of all the cosmic forces, the flow of all the energies above now united again in a single place."

> When gathered in *Yesod*, it becomes clear that the life animating the *sefirot*, often described in metaphors of either light or water, is chiefly to be seen as male sexual energy, specifically as semen. Following the Greek physician Galen, medieval medicine saw semen as originating in the brain (*Hokhmah*), flowing down through the spinal column (the central column, *Tiferet*), into the testicles (*Netsakh* and *Hod*), and thence into the phallus (*Yesod*). The sefirotic process thus leads to the great union of the nine *sefirot* above, through *Yesod*, with the female *Shekhinah*. She becomes filled and impregnated with the fullness of divine energy and She in turn gives birth to the lower worlds, including both angelic beings and human souls.[315]

Yesod gathers all the energy that has emanated from *Hokhmah* and been diffused throughout the *sefirot*, and from *Yesod* comes forth a focused, aimed energy that is the sum total of the entire *Sefirot* structure.

Much that is associated with *Yesod* offers mind-opening insights into the nature of life and of one's own individual life. *Yesod* is also called *Zakhor*, "remember." Much of the meaning of a human life derives from what is remembered; parents and teachers teach, early formative experiences influence and shape. As we have seen, our sense of personal identity is relational. We become ourselves, paradoxically, as we participate in the communities of our lives.

What we remember shapes what we become. The act of remembering is a central religious obligation for Jews; it suffuses the Jewish sense of the identity and purpose of community. Jews are to remember Creation and the Exodus from Egypt with every *Kiddush*. They fulfill that obligation through prayers that recall ancestors and significant events; in Jewish study, through exploring the teaching of generations of rabbis past; and through rituals of storytelling, such as that provided by the *Haggadah* of *Pesakh*. The child's *Pesakh* question, which is basically one of identity, is to be answered with a recital of the memory of the Exodus.

The historian Yosef Hayim Yerushalmi has written that memory is fragile and often problematic. Yet the command *zakhor et yom haShabbat*, "remember the Shabbat day", is so important that it is one of the Ten Utterances heard at Sinai: "[T]he Hebrew Bible seems to have no hesitations in commanding memory.

> Its injunctions to remember are unconditional, and even when not commanded, remembrance is always pivotal. Altogether the verb *zakhar* appears in its various declensions in the Bible no less than one hundred and sixty-nine times, usually with either Israel or God as the subject, for memory is incumbent upon both.[316]

Memory is part of the reflection between Creator and Creation, a reverberating wave that pulsates just as sound waves do, carrying the story of Jewish history. Interestingly enough, in the Torah the commandment is sometimes to remember to forget, such as in the case of Amalek. Sometimes in the course of the ebb and flow of relationships, forgetting, letting something go, is the wisest and most compassionate act.

Jews are commanded to *zakhor et yom haShabbat l'kodsho*, "remember the Shabbat and set it apart [from other days]".[317] The word *zakhor*, "remember," shares its root letters with *zakhar*, "male." For this reason, the mystics link the commandment *zakhor*, "with the word *zakhar*, "male." The female aspect of God, the *Shekhinah*, is linked with the word *shamor*, meaning "observe" or "protect." The mystics applied this interpretation to explain why there are differences in the two versions of the *Aseret haDibrot,* the Ten Utterances, which appear in the Torah.[318] Both words, they asserted, were uttered by God, as the first verse of the mystic Shabbat hymn *Lekha Dodi* declares: *shamor v'zakhor b'dibbur ekhad hishmi'anu El hame'ukhad,* "'keep' and 'remember' in one utterance, the One God caused us to hear." Both acts are necessary for correct fulfillment of the *mitzvah* of observing Shabbat. More, the two aspects must be unified for Shabbat to be fully celebrated: "in one utterance."

In the Hebrew mindset of the Torah, when the narrative mentions a mental state such as remembering, there is an assumption that a physical act will follow; for example, God remembered the Israelites and then moved to free them from Egyptian bondage.

> It is written, "I will remember my Covenant" ... .first there is remembering, and then *pakod pakadti,* "I will intervene" ... the "intervening" completing the previous "remembering". Similarly with Sarah it says: "And the Lord *pakad,* intervened with, Sarah."[319]

The mental act of remembering is the cause, and the physical act is the effect. When God remembered Sarah and intervened in her barren state, she became pregnant. *Zakhor,* the Jewish act of remembering as a commandment, is fully observed only when it is "pregnant," that is, accompanied by *shamor,* the act that shapes reality in accordance with the memory. The concepts of remembering and acting share a mutual dependence in Jewish theology.

When Moses encounters God by way of the burning bush, God tells Moses that the Name of God revealed to him there is *zeh shemi l'olam, v'zeh zikhri l'dor dor,* "this is my Name forever, my Remembrance for all generations."[320] In this context, who is doing the remembering? What does it mean to have Name set opposite Remembrance, like the two *kheruvim* facing each other atop the Ark?

From a mystical perspective, to fulfill the *mitsvot* is not only to do God's will, but also to act out literally God's name. God's name, as we have noted, cannot be articulated in a spoken word, but the mystical perspective insists that it can be and is articulated in acts. Every *mitzvah* may not offer up a clear and immediate link to that insight, though, because the Name one evokes by one's acts is hidden from human understanding, as is the *sefirotic* level of the act itself.

> Kabbalah teaches that God's Name is the source of the 248 positive commandments and the 365 prohibitions. There is an allusion to this in the verse, "This is My name [*shemi*] forever, and this is My remembrance [*zikhri*] from generation to generation." [There are two parts to the divine Name *Yud-Hei-Vav-Hei,* namely *Yud-hei* (whose *gematria* is 15) and *Vav-hei* (whose *gematria* is 11). The numeric value of *shemi* is 350 ... and that of *zikhri* is 237]. ... Now if you combine the value of *shemi* (350) with the value of *Yud-hei* (15) you get 365, which is the number of prohibitions. If you add the numeric value of *zikhri* to the value of *Vav-hei* (11), you get 248, which is the number of positive commandments. So you see that in a metaphoric sense God's Name *Yud-Hei-Vav-Hei* includes all 613 *mitzvot* (365+248).
> [The verse begins, "This is My name forever" (*l'olam*).] Since the word *l'olam* in this passage is written without the usual *vav*, it can be read *l'alem*, "to be hidden". This tells us that the 613 mitzvot that are included in the divine Name are spiritual *mitzvot* whose essence is completely hidden and beyond human understanding.[321]

The attempt to discern an underlying rationale linking all *mitzvot* is a common Jewish scholarly theme; this mystical perspective suggests that what they all have in common is beyond the ken of human beings. That which is Eternal, *olam*, is also hidden, *alem*. Similarly, that which is All, unifying all the variation and contradiction of human experience, is hidden from human perception. The limited human eye sees the conflicts but cannot see what links them in a larger wholeness.

> [M]odern Jewish historiography cannot replace an eroded group memory.... The collective memories of the Jewish people were a function of the shared faith, cohesiveness, and will of the group itself, transmitting and recreating its past through an entire complex of interlocking social and religious institutions that functioned organically to achieve this. The decline of Jewish collective memory in modern times is only a symptom of the unraveling of that common network.[322]

God's name itself comprises the elements that come together to create that wholeness. If the word *zikhri* is understood as a mental state, "my remembrance," what does it mean to say that *shemi* is the corresponding act? Is it to see God's name as manifest in action? In memorial services the prayer called *yikzor*, "God will remember" is linked to those members of the community who are dead. What does it mean to assert that God remembers, and how is that remembrance reflected in us, reflections of God who remember, and forget? What is the Name-evoking act required of the community so that God's remembrance will be manifest in the world and so that the lives of the past, which prepared the ground for their inheritors today, will be accounted for in the story of the generations to come?

Hod – The Gate of Hoda'ot

ATTRIBUTES: THANKSGIVING – BEAUTY – THE PACE OF WONDERS AND MIRACLES – THE PLACE OF HOD A'OT – THE LIGHT OF CREATION – ELOHIM TZVA'OT – PROPHECY – AARON – ACCEPTANCE – UNCERTAINTY

> *b'shem yikhudo shel Kudsha Berikh Hu v'Shekhintey* – for the sake of the unification of power and submission, of the right and the left, of *kavvanah* and *keva*

Thanksgiving

> *L'kha Adonai,* Yours, Adonai, is *haGedulah,* the greatness, *v'haGevurah,* and the power, *v'haTiferet,* and the glory, *v'haNetzakh,* and the victory, *v'ha Hod,* and the majesty.
> – from the liturgy of the Torah ritual

It was taught in a Baraita in the name of R. Akiba: "Yours, O Adonai, is the greatness [*Gedulah*]": this refers to the cleaving of the Red Sea. "And the power [*Gevurah*]": this refers to the smiting of the first-born. "And the glory [*Tiferet*]": this refers to the giving of the Torah. "And the victory [*Netzakh*]": this refers to Jerusalem. "And the majesty [*Hod*]": this refers to the Temple.[323] In the encounter with the third *sefirah, Hod,* we begin to rise toward ever more complex, ethereal, and fascinating levels of God, of the world, and of the self. We are beyond the linkage between heaven and earth, between the Jewish community and God; we have passed through the gateway, as it were, of the covenantal commitment, symbolized by the *milah,* which is part of *Yesod.* Rising requires that we leave ambivalence behind; replacing freedom of choice with a willingness and a desire to be part of Israel's covenant. Without that personal commitment of the self on the part of each seeker, there is no further rising.

Later there may be a recognition that each of us is a vital part of the whole, that it cannot be otherwise. We may be able to leave the illusion of individuality as the highest good behind. For now, we must work on ourselves as a necessary part of the whole with which we are covenanted. For now, attention must be paid to the details. The *sefirah* of *Hod* is, among other things, the place of noticing details. *Hoda'ot,* expressions of gratitude, come from this *sefirah.* For Jews, to express appreciation is a basic condition for reciting a *berakhah,* a blessing.

> It was taught: R. Meir used to say, A man is bound to say one hundred blessings daily, as it is written, "And

now, Israel, what does YHVH your God require of you?" (Deut. 10.12)[324]

Who can say that he has ever even noticed one hundred details of a day, much less realized its blessings? The commentary on this Talmud teaching offers these aspects of close reading of the verse "What does YHVH your God require of you":

> "What" in Hebrew is *mah*. Do not read *mah*, "what," but *me'ah*, "one hundred." "Require" in this verse is *sho'el*, written *shin alef lamed*. This spelling, without the expected *vav*, is called *haser*, "defective." If one adds in the *vav* so as to spell more correctly the word *sho'el*, one finds that there are one hundred letters in the Torah verse Rabbi Meir cited.[325]

The *Zohar* offers a deeper significance to be found in the act of blessing, derived from the Torah verse[326] that becomes the rabbinic prooftext for the blessing after meals:

> "You shall eat and be satisfied and bless YHVH your God" ... it is a blessing for nourishment – demonstrating satisfaction before the rung of faith, as is fitting, and then blessing it fittingly, so that this rung of faith will be saturated, blessed, and filled with joy from supernal life, as is necessary, in order to provide us with sustenance.[327]

For the mystics, the intentional act of saying a blessing does more than help us focus our scattered human attention on the varied subtle realities of our lives. The Torah text literally states that we are to "bless God," and the power of that blessing sustains God (an aspect of God manifest in the "rung" or *sefirah*), even as the food we have eaten sustains us.

The Religious Imperative of Beauty – The Place of Hoda'ot – The Light of Creation

There is an ethical assertion about aesthetics in Jewish practice: if you are going to do something, try to do it as well and as beautifully as you can. Religious obligations must be fulfilled with joy. Nearing the harvest festival of Sukkot, one puts one's whole heart into the preparations, despite one's fatigue after completing the observance of the Ten Days of Awe between Rosh HaShanah and Yom Kippur, which ends only five days before. One's *lulav* and *etrog* should be carefully chosen: one seeks the most graceful palm frond, the most pleasingly shaped citron. Similarly, no matter the pressures of the week, preparing for Shabbat means gracing the table with carefully polished silver candlesticks, a white tablecloth, the best food one can afford, and, most importantly, welcome guests.

This attitude is called *hiddur mitzvah,* the "beautification of the *mitzvah*." The meaning of the word *hiddur* is closely linked to *hadar,* which, in its turn, is the second half of a word pair that appears throughout Jewish sacred literature in reference to our sense of God's awesome and beautiful presence in the world: *hod v'hadar,* "beauty and glory." *Hod,* translated as "beauty" (also, just as correctly, as "glory," "grandeur," or "majesty"), indicates an appreciation for the aesthetic quality of one's fulfillment of *mitzvot. Hod* refers to the beauty one strives to create through the religious act, the beauty experienced by the human senses. The rabbis of the Talmud explained the verse *hod v'hadar l'fanav,* "glory and majesty are before Him"[328] as referring to the outer, visible aspects of God's presence.

The word *hod* describes a surpassingly beautiful grandeur associated primarily with God. A discussion in the Babylonian Talmud tractate *Berakhot* associates this beauty with an interesting feminine nuance. Rabbi Yokhanan transmits an interpretation attributed to Rabbi Shimon bar Yokhai: a description of the five "worlds" of human existence that proceed from a meditation on a feminine reference in Proverbs, a book traditionally attributed to King Solomon. (For clarity, I have italicized the description of the nature of each "world".)

R. Yokhanan said in the name of R. Shimon bar Yokhai: What is the meaning of the verse, "She opens her mouth with wisdom, and the law of kindness is on her tongue"? (Proverbs 31.26) To whom was Solomon alluding in this verse? He was alluding only to his father David, who lived in five worlds and composed a psalm [for each of them].

He abode in *his mother's womb*, and broke into song, as it says, "Bless the Lord, O my soul, and all that is within me (i.e. womb) bless His holy name". (Psalms 103.1)

He came out into *open air and looked upon the stars and constellations and* broke into song, as it says, "Bless the Lord, you angels of His, you mighty in strength that fulfill His word, hearing the voice of His word. Bless the Lord, all you His hosts" (Psalms 103.20-21).

He *sucked from his mother's bosom and looked on her breasts* and broke into song, as it says, "Bless the Lord, O my soul, and do not forget all His benefits". (Psalms 103.2) What is 'all His benefits'? R. Abbahu said: He placed her breasts at the source of understanding [the Hebrew for *gemulav*, "benefits" is linked to *gamal*, "weaned"]..

He *saw the downfall of the wicked* and broke into song, as it says, "Let sinners cease from the earth, and let the wicked be no more. Bless the Lord, My soul, *halleluyah*" (Psalms 104.35).

He *looked upon the day of death* and broke into song, as it says, "Bless the Lord, O my soul. O Lord my God, You are very great, You are clothed with glory [*Hod*] and majesty" (Psalms 104.1).

How does this verse refer to the day of death? Rabbah, son of R. Shila said: We learn it from the end of the passage, where it is written: "You hide Your face, they vanish, You withdraw their breath, they perish" (Psalms 104.29).[329]

The first reference is to the 31st chapter of Proverbs. This text is well known as *Eshet Hayil,* "Woman of Valor" and is recited aloud each Shabbat eve by religiously observant Jewish husbands in honor of their wives. The feminine orientation of the cited verse hovers behind the five worlds described by Yokhanan in the name of Shimon bar Yokhai: worlds of (1) the safety of the womb, (2) the freedom and awe that exalts human life, (3) sustenance from the breast, (4) the triumph of good over evil, and (5) the realization of mortality. The reference to *Hod,* here translated as "glory," occurs in the context of this last world.

This image of God sustaining the living and setting the limits of their days, acting toward God's children - humanity - with the kindness and wisdom of Proverbs 31, is that which causes David to burst into songs of praise. This mothering presence of God, which David praises all his life, shelters and feeds him, supports his steps toward the fulfillment of his life's meaning, asserts justice on his behalf, and is clearly still in control as he approaches death. The last citation, in Psalm 104, is cited in reference to the "fifth world" in which we all live: the world in which death is met. The Psalm opens with:

> Bless, O my being, *Adonai*!
> *Adonai*, my God, you are very great.
> Grandeur and glory you don.
> Wrapped in light like a cloak, stretching
> out the heavens like a tent-cloth.[330]

In the first verse, "grandeur and glory" translate the Hebrew phrase *hod v'hadar.* These terms refer to the trappings of majesty, but it will immediately become clear in the next line that God's royal robes and chariot are not the stuff of earthly majesty but the elements of the natural world."[331] Indeed, the entire psalm is one image of divine power and glory after another, expressed as controlling the patterns that govern life on the earth and nurturing the life of all. At the psalm's end, the grateful poet desires only, "Let me sing to *Adonai* while I live / let me hymn to my God while I breathe."[332]

The place of *hoda'ot*, praises of thanksgiving, is inextricably linked with awareness of the natural world. For the mystic, the presence of God is clearly visible not only in mountaintop vistas and grand waterfalls, but also in the lovingly tended Japanese maple in the front yard and in the spontaneous beauty of the grasses and weeds that thrive in a vacant lot. Neglect of the environment does not only imperil the planet's life; it also, inevitably, diminishes the presence of God.

The Light of Creation

For the Psalmist, God's *Hod* is not made of fine velvet or silk, or even the deep blue-violet *tekhelet* of earthly royalty and of the *tzitzit;* as a Jew is wrapped in a *tallit,* God is wrapped in a *Hod* that is light itself. It is the splendor of the sun-lit heavens, the brightness of the primordial light that shone from end to end of the universe when the world was created, but then was withdrawn, and now is stored away as a future reward for the righteous.

> Inner light in Jewish tradition is said to reflect the earliest memory of the world as well as that of each person. It shows clearly that all is One. When God said, "let there be light!" on Creation's first day, the light that came forth was too bright for God's creatures to bear. With it, a person could see "from one end of the world to the other." Such great light, revealing all the secret places of existence, would not allow for life as we know it. We creatures need to hide in order to exist. The light was set aside ... only in the future will such hiding no longer be needed. The light of the first day will be brought forth for all to see. In walking toward that future, we reclaim our ancient light, and our memory, and we return to our truest self.[333]

The *Zohar* teaches that "the radiance that shone and was treasured away"; the primordial light, hidden in *Yesod*, is also called *tov* – "good".[334]

This ninth *sefirah* is the place of the sign of the covenant between God and the Jewish people; the light that illuminates each human life and the entire world is kindled by the mutual link and commitment between God and the Jews. This connection nourishes both; God and the Jewish people are both transmitters who offer *shefa'* and are the vessels that receive it. Just as the Israelites in the wilderness brought the gifts of their hearts as material with which to build the Tabernacle, God's dwelling place among us, so too are we the ones who offer up the material of our gratitude and love, the *hoda'ot* which wraps God in *Hod*. *Ner Adonai nishmat Adam,* "the human soul is God's light."[335]

We weave the light with daily prayers of praise and thanks for life, no less than with beach clean-up days and endangered-species legislation. Those who dwell in *Malkhut,* the kingdom below, provide God's garment of light and *Hod* by joining in traditional psalms of praise and *hoda'ot* that express their meaning in contemporary terms: efforts to ban pesticides, increase fuel efficiency, and other measures meant to respect and enhance the life of the environment. All so that God's *tallit* may be glorious, and the light of enlightenment will shine through.

Elohim Tzva'ot

God is not only sweetness and light, not only praise and manageable glory. This *sefirah* is associated with the divine name *Elohim Tzva'ot,* "God of the hosts" of heaven; it is

> the essence of the attribute that draws judgment and might from the left side. It draws from *Binah* and from fear, and it fights the wars of the Lord of Hosts both above and below. As it is written: "On that day *YHVH Tzva'ot* will visit the hosts of heaven in heaven and the kings of the earth on the earth" (Isa. 24.21).[336]

The sense of overwhelming awe and terror that is also part of one's sense of God's presence is described in Isaiah's famous vision of God, which Jews recall in every liturgical recitation of the *Kedushah* prayer:

> In the year that king Uzziah died I saw the Eternal sitting upon a throne high and lifted up, and His train filled the temple. Above Him stood the seraphim; each one had six wings: with two he covered his face and with two he covered his feet, and with two he did fly. And one called unto another, and said: "Holy, holy, holy, is the Lord of hosts [YHVH *Tzva'ot*]; the whole earth is full of His glory." The posts of the door were moved at the voice of them that called, and the house was filled with smoke. Then said I: Woe is me! for I am undone.[337]

The sense of being in the presence of something overwhelming is truly just that: our human categories of the difference between logic and fantasy, our hope that a query will lead to understanding, even our desire to believe that all things are either good or evil, fail in the face of it. This is what Rudolf Otto called "the numinous" in his classic study *The Idea of the Holy*. In his investigation of various religious experiences of God's presence, Otto described a sense of "the *uncanny* ... aspects of mystery, awefulness, majesty, augustness, and 'energy'; nay, even the aspect of fascinating is dimly felt in it."[338] What is not mentioned in Otto's description of the *mysterium tremendum,* of the human sense of that which strikes us silent, is the *moral*. A close awareness of God, as described in the various encounters of the Torah, does not fit our sense of morality. It is not that such an experience is *immoral;* after all, our sense of ethics is rooted in our sense of our existence vis-à-vis God. A close encounter with God's presence, Otto seems to suggest, is neither moral or immoral; it is simply beyond the human capacity to categorize. The *Akedah*[339] is a possible example; the experience of Nadav and Abihu, the sons of the first high priest, Aaron, may be another.[340]

Aaron – Acceptance – Prophecy

In the Book of Leviticus, the Torah narrates an impenetrable and difficult story in which two of Aaron's sons are killed on the first day of their service as consecrated priests. Aaron's reaction has long been understood by Jewish tradition as the appropriate response to tragedy that goes beyond one's ability to understand: he is silent. His silence is a kind of humble acceptance: not of the tragedy, but of his own inability to judge the reason, or purpose, or cause, of that which breaks the heart. [I]t is said, "and Aaron held his peace". ... And thus it was said by Solomon, "a time to keep silence, and a time to speak". Sometimes a man is silent and is rewarded for his silence, at others a man speaks and is rewarded for his speaking. This is what R. Hiya b. Abba said in R. Yokhanan's name: What is meant by the text, "awesome is God out of your holy places" [*mi-mikdashekha*]? Read not *mi-mikdasheka* but *mi-mekuddashekha* [through your holy ones]: when the Holy Blessed One executes judgment on His holy ones, He makes Himself feared, exalted, and praised.[341]

There are times when there are no words, and there are times when the words we struggle to offer in the face of grief may do more harm than good. And there are times when we do not speak because we *cannot*. As God pointed out to Job, our understanding is limited.

Our acceptance of the fact that our own vision is humanly limited opens us to the possibility of humility. Paradoxically, it is only from such a place that the seeking Jew can achieve a closer sense of her connection to God, that which may lead to prophecy. Such is the case of Moshe's servant Joshua, a young man who served him devotedly but of whom the Torah never records any interest in power for himself. The *Zohar* asserts that this humility was the key to his strength: "Joshua prophesied from the *Hod,* Splendor of Moses, as it is written, "confer of your splendor [*mi- Hodekha*] upon him."[342] The verse continues, "so that the entire community of Israel may listen."[343] The entire community is able to hear the word of God only when the speaker of that word makes himself a small, undistracting channel of that word.

> *Hod,* or Majesty, is a place where a man yearns, and then is wholly subdued before the object of his yearning, dwelling beneath it.[344]

It may seem counterintuitive that humility is the primary quality necessary for prophecy. But this is exactly what is true of whom Moses, called the most humble of men, and the greatest of all prophets. Mysticism teaches that one cannot connect to God as long as one's "I" is in the way. One cannot possibly reach the level of true prophecy, in which one's mouth speaks God's words, if one's sense of self intrudes. The "I" is the expression of human self-awareness and arrogance. A true prophet never has the thought, "I shouldn't say that," since there is no sense of "I" involved; one who speaks God's words can know no moment of hesitant consideration, no apprehension of how such words will be received.

> The humility of the *sefirah* of *Hod* leads to the understanding that we cannot do it all, [and to] the acknowledgment that we have to accept ourselves as we are and be grateful for life as it has been given to us. Beauty lies in that which is, if only we open our inner eye to behold it. ... *Hod* is the other side of wisdom, the self that bows before the mystery of what is *as* it is, the self who submits to reality and rejoices in doing so.[345]

Hod leads to humility because the left leg to which it refers has an ability to *bend*. Jewish tradition understood already two thousand years ago that part of what makes human beings great is that we have knees and can choose to use them. Indeed, at least one particular ancient Israelite vision of heaven preserved in Jewish tradition includes the strange detail that angels do not have knees.[346] What this means is that they have no power of independent thought, not even at the level of an angel individually expressing the preference of whether to stand or sit! Angels have no free will; human beings do. When one reaches the humble ability to bend the knee *lifney Melekh Malkhey haM'lakhim,* before the Holy One, the Holy of all Holies, one is, in that moment of willing submission, greater than the angels, who have no choice or thought about whether they will praise God.

Through humility we return to the awe and gratitude with which we began. Joseph Gikatilla explains the verse, "The dew of Mount Hermon falls on the hills of *Tziyon*" as referring to the *Sefirot* of *Netzakh* and *Hod*. Dew is a blessing in an arid land; the Jewish liturgy makes repeated grateful reference to the falling of rain and dew in season. It falls from the mighty northern mountain on the relatively small and humble mountain on which Jerusalem stands. "They, too, represent the place of *hoda'ot* ['thanksgiving'] and they are the essence of the verse, 'for each knee will bend before Me.' As the rabbis taught, "One is obliged to bend the knee during the prayer *Modim*." For any blessing that is brought to the world comes from them."[347]

> The essence of serving God and of all the *mitzvot* is to attain the state of humility, that is, to understand that all your physical and mental powers and your essential being depend on the divine elements within. You are simply a channel for the divine attributes. You attain this humility through the awe of God's vastness, through realizing that "there is no place empty of it." Then you come to the state of *Ayin*, the state of humility. You have no independent self and are contained in the Creator. This is the meaning of the verse: "Moses hid his face, for he was in awe." Through his experience of awe, Moses attained the hiding of his face, that is, he perceived no independent self. Everything was part of divinity.[348]

Uncertainty

Theology is "faith in search of understanding."[349]

Mystery is an enduring constant at the deepest levels of human life. Social scientists may consider mystery a challenge to be overcome, a riddle has always been is and will remain a mystery. Social scientists may find mystery a challenge to be overcome, a riddle to be solved and therefore annulled. Theology is a different kind of inquiry science: in the face of mystery, a theological inquiry seeks meaning, but this meaning does not necessarily banish the mystery.

Meaning is sought in terms of the human understanding of what it means to make sense of life in any given era. In the current era, marked deeply by scientific inquiry, one of the first stances a theologian – a believer – takes is whether or not a meaning must be provable, and how much room will be allowed for that which cannot be demonstrated to be true; in other words, how much tolerance are we are able to allow ourselves in the face of the mystery we can never fully understand? In considering the meaning of existence, one must be willing to co-exist, however uneasily at times, with the uncertainty of human vision and the poverty of human answers to the questions to which theology seeks to respond. "The Torah speaks in the language of human beings,"[350] the rabbis of the Talmud explained. We are limited in our perception and our ability to articulate that which we do perceive; our language cannot possibly convey God.

The sea of humanity parts before an issue such as this: when we face the mystery of existence, does one's need for the support offered by spiritual belief cause one to disregard science, or does one's need for the facts offered by scientific inquiry lead one to doubt that religion can offer any support at all? To forge a path between these two poles is an uncertain effort, a reminder of the humility we should bring to our attempts at certainty. Our lives are full of impressions, not certain seeing.

Mystery is a sort of darkness. The teachings of mystical ethics maintain that one should remain humble regarding what one thinks one sees. A passage in Leviticus focuses on a person who observes something on the walls of his house, He reports to the priest: *nir'ah li,* he says: "it appears to me as something like *tzara'at.*" In his commentary, Rashi explains that "even if he is wise and knows that it is, he should say, 't seems to me,' not "I know'." A mystical gloss points out that *nir'ah li* indicates that one has seen the *tzara'at* with one's own eyes and not, for example, with the aid of artificial light. If one is in darkness, one cannot see; similarly, if one is in darkness brought about by physical or psychological distress, one cannot expect to be able to assess accurately the extent of the flaws in one's own life and surroundings, nor in that of others.[351] This awareness of, and respect for, the irreducible reality of uncertainty in the face of the mystery of life is clear in the earliest evidence of Jewish thinking about mystery, and, for some scholars, it is evident in the very structure of the central holy texts of Judaism. In his description of the development of the Torah, Biblical scholar Israel Knohl explains:

> The editors recognized that God's word is not uniform, but that God speaks in many voices and people hear God in many ways. They did not want to mar the divine revelation nor detract from its fullness, so they created a pluralistic book...They understood that the Torah does not have only one entrance, but rather, has many. Their actions paved the way for the continuation of multivocality and variation in later generations. The multivocal editing of the Torah set the tone for Jewish literature. The Torah starts with a debate between two contradictory accounts of Creation: the Priestly tradition (Gen. 1-2.4a) and the J account (Gen. 2.4b-3.24). The editors put them side by side since in each of them there is a divine truth. The editors of the Mishnah followed suit. This most important legal collection of post-biblical Jewish law starts with a debate about the appropriate time for reciting the *Shema* in the evenings. And the controversies continue, for all rabbinical literature is based upon debate. The editors of the Mishnah, and then of the Talmud, followed the model of the Torah. They put, side by side, different and contradictory views. They felt that all of them were the words of the living God.[352]

The traditional Jewish approach to theology, as Rachel Adler describes it, demonstrates a variety of methodologies: "[T]he nature and methodology of theology are more open questions in Judaism. Biblical and rabbinic Judaisms embody a variety of theologies in forms that do not call themselves theology: narrative, prayer, law, and textual exegesis."[353] This multiplicity of voices does not easily lend itself to clarity and certainty.

Acceptance of uncertainty, as the Hasidic interpretation of the Leviticus text, already noted, is an important theological teaching. The Talmud declares "that which an astute student will innovate in the future is already contained in the revelation at Sinai"[354] and, in that assertion, expresses the virtue of humility on the part of the sage who uttered it, in his demonstration of the knowledge that neither he nor his generation was the last word on the subject. This stance regarding knowledge of truth – in traditional terms, knowledge of God's will – is maximalist. By maintaining humility about what we do know, we keep the gateway open to learning more deeply, less anxiously. Paradoxically, it is only in an uncertainty that banishes arrogance that we are able to seek God. We know this because we are warned not to confuse our own necessary ideas about God – our functional clarity, a manufactured working hypothesis standing between us and incoherence – with the ultimate mystery of God. Idolatry, Rachel Adler suggests, consists of mistaking our necessary ideas about God's nature for the unknowable truth of God's nature. We create our ideas – of wood and stone or of salvation – and we convince ourselves that we know what we are talking about. A false, manufactured certainty about God does not open a path toward *devekut*. Only a willingness to let emptiness and silence exist, in which one can listen, and watch, and learn, will allow that path to emerge. "The best we can do is designate a special space for Him to appear in, *a space that looks empty to the ordinary observer.*"[355] *Hit'halekh l'fanai v'heyeh tamim*, "Walk before Me and be whole," said God to Abraham.[356] As we grope in the darkness and uncertainty, we tend to overlook, or dismiss, our power to shed light and the need for us to do so. But the mystics remind us that in this also we are reflections of God and therefore must consider that there is uncertainty above as well as below. When we struggle to become more whole in the face of darkness and uncertainty, God is also more Whole.

The case of Abraham is comparable to one who is beloved of the King, who sees that the King is struggling in dark alleys; the beloved of the King looked out and began to light the way for him from the window. When the King saw him, He said, "Why should you light the way for me from the window? Come and light the way from before me. ... Thus the Blessed Holy One said to Abraham, "Come, and light the way for Me."[357]

Netzakh – The Gate of Endurance

ATTRIBUTES: ENDURANCE – ETERNITY – VICTORY – PROPHECY – THE TEMPLE PILLARS NAMED YAKHIN AND BO'AZ – THE BALANCE BETWEEN THE PILLARS THAT SUPPORT ALL BEING: BEAUTY AND ETERNITY, KAVVANAH AND KEVA, HOD AND NETZAKH – UNITY

> *b'shem yikhudo shel Kudsha Berikh Hu v'Shekhintey* – for the sake of the unification of the Eternal and the momentary, humility and self-confidence, *keva* and *kavanah*

Endurance – Eternity - Victory

The fourth *sefirah, Netzakh,* is the fourth level of of being, the fourth attribute of Being, and the fourth level of rising. Partnering with *Hod,* these two *Sefirot* are represented by the two legs that are the foundation of the physical body's stability; spiritually, they reflect the faith that is the fundamental support of Jewish identity. The two legs, or pillars, are complementary, not identical. Where the *sefirah Hod* stands for the grandeur of God and the humility of the human who stands before God, the word *netzakh* means both "eternity" and "victory." The interpretation of *Netzakh* as "eternity" is explained by "the [Talmudic] school of R. Eliezer ben Jacob:

> Wherever [in Scripture] the expression of *netzakh*, *selah* or *va'ed* occurs the process to which it refers never ceases — '*Netzakh*'? Since it is written "For I will not contend for ever, neither will I be always wroth." (Isaiah 57) '*Selah*'? Since it is written: As we have heard, so have we seen in the city of the Lord of hosts, in the city of our God — God establish it for ever. *Selah*. '*Va'ed*'? Since it is written: The Lord shall reign for ever and ever.[358] Eternity, which lasts forever, is the pure opposite of human life and experience. As *Kohelet* wrote at the opening of his book, *hevel havalim, hakol hevel*, "Everything is ephemeral."[359] Human existence is fleeting, and that which we most treasure about our life is constantly slipping between our fingers: loved ones die, friendships fade into the distance of time and place, even the very memories of all we have cherished are lost. Eternity is associated only with God; yet in the fifth *sefirah* of *Netzakh*, some small reflection of eternity is placed within the human being, and within the world. God gave 10 spiritual elements of himself: the soul, facial features, the sense of hearing, seeing, smell, the speech of the lips, the movement of the tongue, the use of hands and feet, wisdom, and understanding.[360]

It is particularly poignant that this *sefirah* is also associated with victory; for here we are acutely reminded that victory is transitory, and that the distance between a human self and the Self of the World can be a very long path.

God created the human soul in His image. Just as God is not restricted to a specific name or to a specific place (rather, His dominion extends throughout), so too, the soul cannot be defined by a specific name or place, for its dominion extends throughout the body; not one part of the body is devoid of the soul. This is not to say that the essence of the soul is comparable to God, for God created it. However, the soul is Godlike only in the sense that it prevails over the entire body, just as God rules over the entire universe.[361] In the paradoxical way often associated with mystical interpretation, the place of human victory is also considered to be the place of human vulnerability. *Netzakh*, associated with the right thigh, is the place, according to the mystics, where Jacob was injured by the one with whom he struggled in his night encounter by the river Yavok. (The word for "struggle" in Hebrew, *ne'evak*, has the same root.)

> *A man wrestled with him until the rising of dawn, and he saw that he could not prevail against him* (Gen. 32.25-26). ... that night was the night on which the moon was created, yet Jacob remained alone, unaccompanied by anyone. Now, we have learned, one should not venture out alone at night, especially on the night when the luminaries were created, since the moon is defective, as is written, *let there be lights* [*m'orot*, spelled deficiently]. Yet that night he remained alone! Now, when the moon is defective, the evil serpent is empowered to prevail.[362]

On this night, the fourth day of the week of creation, the moon and sun and all the lesser lights of the sky were created. The spelling of the word *m'orot*, "lights," is called "defective" because it is missing an expected letter *vav*. This is not an uncommon occurrence in the Hebrew of the Torah, and in each occurrence there is an interpreted meaning. The absence of the letter *vav* is especially significant, since this is one of the letters of God's Name of Being. The spelling irregularity suggests that something is not quite whole: a door is open, and evil can find its way in.

In the *Zohar*'s interpretation of the episode by the Yavok river we can follow various aspects of *Sefirotic* interpretation and how they interact. Like any human being, Jacob is both a human role model and also a physical representation of the cosmos. Thus the evil that makes its way into the world on this night attacks not only vulnerable human beings but also all of creation. Jacob, however, is also associated with *Tiferet*, the *sefirah* that connects and balances judgment and mercy. In short,

Jacob was all that he had inherited from his father, Isaac (associated with the *sefirah* called Judgment, or *Din*), and grandfather, Abraham (the expression of the *sefirah* of Mercy, or *Hesed*), and so the evil saw that

> Jacob was strong on all sides....*so when he saw that he could not prevail against him, he touched the socket of his thigh* (Gen. 32.26) – a site outside the torso, one pillar of the torso.[363]

The evil could not touch the upper *Sefirot,* so it attacked *Netzakh,* associated with the right thigh. And in the morning, Jacob limped forth from his night encounter. This is the nature of human victory: endurance, through the scarring of all human striving. One may be too strong to be overcome, yet human beings are imperfect, and any small place of vulnerability may be wounded. Jacob called the place of struggle *Peni'el,* Hebrew for "the face of God," "for I have seen God face to face."[364] One does not come close to God – close to ultimate understanding – and survive unscathed; nor can one protet that which makes one vulnerable.

This kind of endurance in one's attempt to rise toward God means continuing through tears, through pain, and through heartbreak. This is illuminated in a teaching handed down in the name of Rabbi Menakhem Mendel of Kotzk which interprets a phrase of the *Shema*. We are commanded to keep the words of God *al levav'kha,* "upon your heart." Why is it written *"upon* your heart" and not *"in* your heart"?

> Let the words be laid upon the heart like a stone, and when the heart is opened, at some special moment, these words will enter. His meaning is that for most of us, the heart is closed and no such words can enter. One must not recoil from serving God, though, and let these words lie upon the outside of the heart like a stone, and in one single moment of awakening, when the heart opens, the words will enter inside.[365]

Human beings endure life by holding to the assumption that we are self-sustaining, whole, and indestructible. Paradoxically, as long as our hearts are "like a stone," whole and strong, God's word cannot enter, yet we are commanded to keep the words *on* our hearts. Then, one day the heart breaks; we come to know that we are not whole, or self-sustaining, or indestructible. And then, says the Kotzker, the words will enter *into* our hearts. Then the gates of our hearts will open; and then, only then, we will finally know what it means to love.

The willingness to continue is the endurance, the longing for an eternal truth, which finds expression in the *sefirah* of *Netzakh*. This is the meaning of human victory: it is in the refusal to fear the intensity and the pain, even when one is limping away from the most meaningful encounters of one's life. It is in the refusal to turn away, to take refuge in cynicism. Victory, in human terms, is in the willingness to continue to long to draw near to that which we cannot maintain: *devekut*, "cleaving," seeking the closeness to God that feels as if we're coming home.

Prophecy

"Pour down, o skies, from above, let the heavens rain down justice, let the earth open, and triumph [*netzakh*] and justice will sprout together."[366] The mystic Gikatilla sees in this prophetic erse the upper spheres of *Hesed* and *Gevurah*, drawing from the *shefa'* above.

> Then they pour their favors on the three Spheres below them which are *Netzakh* and *Hod* and *Yesod*, and from there, the pool, which is called *Adonai*, and is also known as *Tzedek*, will be blessed.[367]

Tzedek below reflects *tzedek* above, as a pool reflects the sky. The pouring forth of blessing from above is clearly seen in the rain falling from above to nurture the world:

> [T]he force of growth is drawn for the plants, the trees and the fruit-bearing trees, for it is from there that the

power for regeneration comes for all the descendants of the world. ... from there too comes the force for all that grows in the world of all living creatures – and all this happens as a result of *Netzakh* and *Hod* connecting with *Yesod*.[368]

The nurturing of all humanity is not merely a matter of physical sustenance. Prophecy is also the result of that which rains down from above:

Know that the two Names *Netzakh* and *Hod* form the place of nurture for the Prophets and it is from there that the Prophets draw their prophecies, each Prophet according to his power and his grasp.[369]

The prophets drew their capacity for prophecy from their ability to "bond with the lower spheres ... *Malkhut, Yesod, Netzakh* and *Hod*. ... it is through the medium of the four lower spheres that are called *Adonai*, an unrefined reflection through which the Prophets saw conjured images."[370] Most prophecies are only a vague image, seen "through a glass darkly." God speaks in riddles and appears in dreams. The only prophet to rise above this level of uncertain vision was Moshe, who reached the higher level of *Tiferet*, from which he was able to commune with the higher spheres associated with YHVH.

Gikatilla depicts the lesser awareness of God, which is called *Adonai*, as a sort of outer layer; within it, one reaches a more inner essence, called YHVH. In Torah, this is the mystical significance of the *ohel mo'ed*, the simple tent set up on the edge of camp of the Israelite wanderers of the Torah: the awareness of *Adonai* is the first, outermost level of sensing God.

The *Ohel Mo'ed* is the essence of *Adonai*. Moses our teacher, peace be with him, entered the *Ohel Mo'ed* and spoke with YHVH, which is the polished reflection of seeing face to face.[371]

The idea of the *ohel mo'ed*, a simple tent outside the camp, as the ultimate place of coming face to face with God stands in stark contrast to the *mishkan*, an ornate creation situated in the middle of the Israelite camp and entered only by the priests. In the *mishkan*, sacrifices are offered, incense is burned, correct ritual is carefully observed. In the *ohel mo'ed*, on the other hand, there are no priests who act as intermediaries between the people and God's presence, there are no Levites dedicated to its maintenance, and the tent itself is *outside* the camp rather than at its center.

> Now Moses used to take the tent and to pitch it without the camp, afar off from the camp; and he called it The tent of meeting. And it came to pass, that every one that sought YHVH went out unto the tent of meeting, which was without the camp.[372]

What is most compelling here is that anyone can at any time inquire of God. All that is required is the ability to enter the *ohel mo'ed*, to rise to the level beyond complexity, and to arrive at simplicity, and clarity.

This is a vision of God in which things become clearer and simpler as one draws closer. Yet the mystics understood how human beings approaching a king are easily distracted by the outer trappings of majesty. The mystics told parables comparing one who seeks God to one who seeks the king on his throne in a large, opulent palace.

> A king is in his palace, and all his subjects are partly in the country, and partly abroad. Of the former, some have their backs turned towards the king's palace, and their faces in another direction; and some are desirous and zealous to go to the palace, seeking "to inquire in his Temple", and to minister before him, but have not yet seen even the face of the wall of the house. Of those that desire to go to the palace, some reach it, and go round about in search of the entrance gate; others have passed through the gate, and walk about in the

> ante-chamber; and others have succeeded in entering into the inner part of the palace, and being in the same room with the king in the royal palace. But even the latter do not immediately on entering the palace see the king, or speak to him for, after having entered the inner part of the palace, another effort is required before they can stand before the king, at a distance, or close by, hear his words, or speak to him.[373]

Only one who can see past the rich surroundings and find a path through outer gates, inner antechambers, and veils of assumption and expectation will reach the clarity of the king's presence. Most of us wander around the palace, dazzled by the outer signs of majesty and awe. Grand canyons and mountain ranges, technological wonders, and opulent creations – all the outer manifestations of a presence we call God are not, themselves, God. They must be transcended before we can attempt to enter the real Presence without distraction.

> You must forget yourself in prayer. Think of yourself as nothing and pray only for the sake of God. In such prayer you may transcend time and enter the highest realms of the world of thought. There all things are one: distinctions between "life" and "death," "land" and "sea" have lost their meaning. But none of this can happen so long as you remain attached to the reality of the material world. Here you are bound to the distinctions between good and evil that emerge only in the lower realms of God. How can one who remains attached to his own self go beyond time to the world where all is One?[374]

The Temple Pillar Named Bo'az – The Interplay of the Physical Pillars of Being: Beauty and Eternity Pillars of fire and smoke led the Israelites out of Egypt and toward their meeting with God. There are comparisons in the Talmud of the *tzaddik* to the pillar on which the world's stability depends, but there is another, different famous text asserting that "upon three things the world depends,"[375] and those three things are acts. Here, the good deeds of exceptional human beings sustain the world, which has been created for the sake of the righteous.

This ethical understanding differs from the temporal-Biblical and other rabbinic-architectural interpretations, as it allows a dynamic affinity between the righteous and the existence of the world. An interesting parallel to these stances is found in a late midrashic compilation, *Aggadat Bereshit,* in which the righteous are described as causing the world to stand on its foundation – *"ma'amid 'et ha'olam 'al yesodo* ... this formulation ascribes a more active role to the pillar: the world does not just rest, but rather, is sustained by it."[376] Thus, it is not a righteous person but the righteousness of acts that upholds the world, and sustains the *Sefirot.*

Referring to the graph of the *Sefirot* (Figure 1), we see that *Netzakh* is located on the right side of the *Sefirot.* Above it we find *Hesed,* "mercy" or "grace," and above that we rise toward *Hokhmah,* "wisdom," in a more or less straight line we can imagine as a pillar. These three *Sefirot* are identified with the masculine side of God. The three *Sefirot* that make up the central pillar include *Malkhut* at the bottom, and above her, *Yesod* and *Tiferet.* This central pillar balances the divine qualities of the pillars on the left and on the right. *Hod* is situated on the left side of the *Sefirotic* system, the first of three left-side *Sefirot,* which is described as the feminine side of God. Above *Hod,* "beauty," is *Gevurah,* "strength," and further above is *Binah,* "understanding." Imagined as pillars, the *Sefirot* are the three necessary supports of the universe: *al shlosha devarim ha'olam omeyd,* "on three things the world depends."[377]

Netzakh and *Hod* are also associated with the two pillars that were central supports in the First Temple. The book of I Kings relates that an artist named Hiram, who worked in bronze, was brought to Jerusalem by Solomon to direct the work of creating the Temple. (The parallel account in II Chronicles expands his resume to the point that he seems appropriately talented to succeed his predecessor, the director of the Tabernacle building project, Bezalel.) *Yakhin* is the name of the right pillar and is associated with *Netzakh; Hod* is, logically, linked with the pillar on the left side, *Bo'az*.

> He set up the columns at the portico of the Great Hall; he set up one column on the right and named it *Yakhin*, and he set up the other column on the left and named it *Boaz*.[378]

The *sefirah* of *Netzakh* on the body's right side corresponds to the right leg of the human body, even as *Hod*, on the left side, corresponds to the left leg. As we have seen, there are two ways to consider the physical teachings inherent in mysticism: the emotions as an expression of *devekut*, and the acts as an ethical imperative.

Corresponding to the two kinds of relationship a Jew experiences toward God – *yir'ah*, fear, and *ahavah*, love – the two dominant emotions a mystic experiences on ascent are also fear and love. *Yir'ah* is the fear, not of punishment, but rather that which is associated with the awe one experiences in the act of attempting to come closer to God, and to link one's soul to the Divine Presence. *Ahavah* is the love that flows from the exaltation of that connection, once made. This *yirat shamayim*, "fear of heaven," is "the essential attitude that characterizes the religious personality."[379] Fear, and the love that follows it, are intertwined: without fear, one cannot rise; without love, one would not try.

Inspired by a love described by mystics in highly erotic terms, the soul seeks out its source. The *Zohar* interprets the Sinai revelation as a moment of great spiritual and erotic ecstasy:

> "O that he would kiss me with the kisses of his mouth" (Song of Songs 1.2): all that Israel saw at the time they saw within one light absorbing all those other lights, and they yearned to gaze....there is no passionate cleaving of spirit to spirit except a kiss, and a kiss is by the mouth – spring of spirit and its outlet. When they kiss one another, these spirits cling to each other, becoming one: thus, one love....They ascend in four letters – letters

upon which the Holy Name depends, upon which those above and below depend, upon which the praise of Song of Songs depends. Who is that? *alef, hey, bet, hey*[380]. They are a supernal chariot; they are companionship, cleaving, consummation of all.[381]

The *Song of Songs* is a gold mine of verses interpreted to celebrate the mystical love of God. In one verse, a singer beholds a (feminine!) presence, *mi zot olah min hamidbar*, "who is this coming up from the wilderness" *k'timrot ashan*, "like pillars of smoke." Who is she that comes up out of the wilderness like pillars of smoke, perfumed with myrrh and frankincense, with all powders of the merchant?

> Behold, she is the litter of Solomon; threescore mighty men are about it, of the mighty men of Israel.
> They all handle the sword, and are expert in war; every man hath his sword upon his thigh, because of dread in the night.
> King Solomon made himself a palanquin of the wood of Lebanon.
> He made its pillars of silver, the top of gold, the seat of purple, the inside being inlaid with love, from the daughters of Jerusalem.[382]

As we look at our graph of the *Sefirot*, we see that the two *sefirot* of *Hod* and *Netzakh* protect the sign of the covenant; this arrangement parallels the physical structure of a male human being, whose thighs protect the phallus. In sefirotic terms, it is the balance of beauty and endurance that protects the mutual commitment of God and the Jewish people. These two pillars, on which so much depends, are both beautiful and strong. The mystics see an allusion to them in the "Song of Songs," in which one lover speaks of the charms of the other:

His legs are as pillars of marble, set upon sockets of fine gold; his aspect is like Lebanon, excellent as the cedars.[383]

Kavvanah and Keva, Hod and Netzakh, Thanksiving

Keva, the "fixed form" or habit of our acts, is the shape of our reliability; every day we rise and speak our gratitude for life to God. More elusive is the attribute of *kavvanah,* "intention," the inner purpose we try to awaken within the habitual acts we perform each day. *Kavvanah* is the effort to pay attention; it is the opposite of rote behavior. The conflict between fixed prayer and the need to feel the meaning of one's prayer is ancient; it dates back to the halakhic definition of prayer content and time which preoccupied the Sages two millennia ago. This balance of complementary opposites speaks of the human need for both dependable, fixed markers for one's life, and the desire for spontaneity and joy. It cannot be resolved; the need for both *keva* and *kavvanah* is one of the basic paradoxes of human life.

The tension between *Hod* and *Netzakh* also manifests the difficulty of balancing the demands of physicality with those of spirituality. One's physical needs are not to be devalued; there is a holy purpose to life and a reason why our sense of inner spirit is clothed in a physical body. We are created according to God's will, after all; that is a clear teaching of the creation story in the book of Genesis. We are here physically for a purpose.

> The purpose of the soul entering this body is to display her powers and actions in the world, for she needs an instrument. ... Before descending to this world, the soul is emanated from the mystery of the highest level. While in this world, she is completed and fulfilled by this lower world. Departing this world, she is filled with the fullness of all the worlds, the world above and the world below. At first, before descending to this world, the soul is imperfect; she is lacking something.

By descending to this world, she is perfected in every dimension.[384]

Physicality is not an obstacle to be overcome, but a tool to be used toward the ultimate goal of the integration of the individual with God. There is no physical state that is not potentially holy, and there is no act that is not a potential vessel for ethical behavior.

> You can mend the cosmos by anything you do – even eating. Do not imagine that God wants you to eat for mere pleasure or to fill your belly. No, the purpose is to mend. Sparks of holiness intermingle with everything in the world, even inanimate objects. By saying a blessing before you enjoy something, your soul partakes spiritually. This is food for the soul. As the Torah states, "One does not live on bread alone, but rather on all that issues from the mouth of God." Not just the physical, but the spiritual – the holy sparks, spring from the mouth of God. Like the soul herself, breathed into us by God. So when you are about to eat bread, say the *motzi*: "Blessed are you, YHVH our God, sovereign of the world, who brings forth bread from the earth." Then by eating, you bring forth sparks that cleave to your soul.[385]

In order to rise toward God, we must rise beyond the level of the physical with all its distractions. But we do not rise beyond it by ignoring or negating it; rather, we are victorious over the physical level of existence when our physicality serves our higher human purpose. When we practice ethics at every level of our physical being, enduring every physical challenge and rising beyond it, then we can use the pillars of *Hod* and *Netzakh* as the supports that they are meant to be. Literally, as our legs help us to stand upright, they can support us in the struggle to "know before Whom you stand."[386]

Unity

The apparently fragmentary nature of a world that, Jewish tradition insists, is unified and One, is one more example of the contradictory opposites that must be balanced in a human life, and in which one lives and perceives one's reality. Kabbalah teaches that understanding the ultimate unity of the nature of God – the transcendent and immanent, the awesome and innate, the beyond and the within, and, most of all, the God of the essential unity of *Ayn Sof,* on one hand, and, on the other, the God of as many different manifestations as there are human beings – is the ultimate "mystery of the Faith." *You yourself were shown to know* (Deuteronomy 4.35) ... what is to be known? *That YHVH is Elohim* (ibid). This is totality of the whole mystery of faith, totality of above and below, totality of the whole Torah. In this mystery lies totality of the whole mystery of faith, certainly so! Totality of the whole Torah – mystery of Written Torah and mystery of Oral Torah, and all is one. Totality of mystery of faith, for it is the complete Name; this is the mystery of faith. And who is it? *YHVH is one and His name one* (Zechariah 14.9). *Hear, O Israel! YHVH our God, YHVH is one* (Deuteronomy 6.4) – one unification. 'Blessed be the name of His glorious kingdom forever and ever!' – another unification, so that His name may be one. This is mystery of *YHVH is Elohim,* when they are in one unity ... [T]otality of Torah is totality of above and below, for this name is above and that name is below, one being mystery of the upper world, the other mystery of the lower world. Therefore it is written: *You yourself were shown to know that YHVH is Elohim* – this is totality of all, and this a person must know in this world.[387]

In other words, both impressions of God are true, although they are opposite: one name specific, one general; one name signifying unity, the other conveying plurality even in its grammatical form. The true nature of God is not either/or, but rather both/and.

That might be a difficult concept for a rationalist, but for the mystics, it is one of the axioms of theology that God is All and therefore is that which unifies all – even that which, to us, seems contradictory. When we recite the *Shema* and proclaim that God is *ekhad,* we are not only saying that God is one and not two; one of the meanings of the Hebrew word *ekhad* is to unify. We are all part of the all that is God, and, as part of the all, we are connected to each other and to everyone and everything, else. In her novel *The Color Purple,* Alice Walker's character Shug explains her own theological insight, which is very much in line with that of the Jewish mystics:

> One day when I was sitting quiet and feeling like a motherless child, which I was, it come to me: that feeling of being part of everything, not separate at all. I knew that if I cut a tree, my arm would bleed. And I laughed and I cried and I run all around the house. I knew just what it was. In fact, when it happens, you can't miss it. It sort of like you know what, she say, grinning and rubbing high up on my thigh....God love all them feelings. That's some of the best stuff God did. And when you know God loves 'em you enjoys 'em a lot more. You can just relax, go with everything that's going, and praise God by liking what you like.
> God don't think it dirty? I ast.
> Naw, she say. God made it. Listen, God love everything you love – and a mess of stuff you don't. ... I think it pisses God off if you walk by the color purple in a field somewhere and don't notice it.[388]

The characters in the novel struggle with a problem many of us share: moving one's religious vision past the Western, culturally ingrained vision of God as an old white man.

Through the ideal of the *Sefirot,* each independent but all interconnected, we see the mystical expression of the idea that God is not separate from us, not another human being like us, only bigger. For the mystics, God is not only a coherent personality expressed in the Torah and other Jewish literature, but at one and the same time God is the Place in which each of us exists. We sense God – rather like the invisible "dark matter" theorized about and chased by physicists – as the synergy that blossoms between us when we are meaningfully connected to one another and the world. And we bring ourselves most fully into our potential for meaningful existence when we recognize our connectedness to each other and to God, and strengthen it, and build it.

Rabbi Tarfon said, "Akiva, whoever separates himself from you – it is as though he disconnects himself from Life itself."[389] It is in sharing one another's lives that we are connected to Life itself. God's presence is among us and between us, if only we build a connection to one another. "Let them build me a sanctuary that I may dwell among them."[390] Modern Jewish theologians such as Heschel, Buber, and Levinas emphasize the Jewish teaching that God is manifest most clearly not in the human reflection of the Holy (which is, after all, an expression of potential that may go unrealized) but in the human relationship; God may be in you and in me, but it is the synergy of the God manifest between us and among us that makes for holiness. In *Who Is Man?* Abraham Joshua Heschel teaches that the need to be connected is a fundamental and necessary aspect of being human.

The authentic individual is neither an end nor a beginning but a link between ages, both memory and expectation. Every moment is a new beginning within a continuum of history. ... Only he who is an heir is qualified to be a pioneer.[391] In our own time, the continuum is interrupted. So many examples come easily to mind if we consider how people relate to each other – or fail to – in ways that show clearly the lack of connectedness we suffer, and its costs: the political "depersonalization" of an election opponent; the "impersonal" approach of large-scale businesses that try to create robots to convey a human touch; corporate leaders whose allegiance to the bottom line or stock prices discourages empathy among staff. We know how much we have lost, and in our own hearts we know the price.

It will not suffice for us simply to long for some earlier, halcyon day when we all really did love our neighbors as ourselves. We are not the people of any earlier age; we know what we know, we have faced our own challenges, and citing old texts will not fully answer our need. For the mystics, it is not enough to search for old truths in the sacred texts. In religious dialogue, in the invocation of the most basic truths, old ways of thinking hinder the ability to see what might be learned about the way back to connectedness, and wholeness – and to God, the ground of that truth, that connectedness, and that wholeness.

There is ancient teaching about Torah study: "Turn it over and over, for everything is in it."[392] It is not the wellspring of Torah that is exhausted of new insights, but rather our customary perspectives on it that may have reached the limits of their usefulness. There are many overlooked aspects of Torah. Let us consider just one: the underrepresentation of women in traditional sacred narratives. Aviva Zornberg writes that, for our questions about truth, Torah, specifically midrashic literature, "presents a heterogeneous, even – consciously and ambivalently – a heretical multiplicity of answers."[393] Regarding the census taken of the Israelite people just before entering the Land, Rashi noted:

> "No man survived from the original census of Moses and Aaron, when they had counted the Israelites in the wilderness of Sinai" (Num. 26.64): But the women were not subjected to the decree against the spies, because they loved the Holy Land. The men said, "Let us appoint (*nitna*) a leader to return to Egypt (14.4); while the women said, "Appoint (*t'na*) for us a holding among our father's brothers" (27.4).

Zornberg points out that all Rashi does is to take the text literally so as to tease out a teaching that is "provocative in the extreme":

With barely a hint in the text to support him, he presents a startlingly asymmetrical demographic image of the people who entered the Holy Land, women being in the large majority. His basis in the text is the expression, "No *man* survived ..." and that the story of the daughters of Zelofkhad, who were inspired by love of the Land, immediately follows.[394] Women are not, as the literary and religious convention would have it, included in the word "men": "All along, women have been *really* absent, *really* elsewhere."[395] What other indications of truths we have yet to assimilate are already present in the text, and in normative rabbinic commentary such as Rashi's?

The popularity of the story of Miriam's well among feminists is one indication of the re-energizing sustenance that awaits. The story of the miraculous well is derived from the juxtaposition of two Torah verses: the first, Numbers 20.1, ends with, "Miriam died there and was buried there," and verse 20.2, directly following, begins with the words "The community was without water." The well followed Miriam throughout her life and sustained the Israelites in their wanderings. It is clearly symbolic of the sustaining presence of Miriam – the feminine aspect of leadership. Moses' own ability to lead is compromised: it is just after the death of the strong female leader in the same chapter of Numbers that he, on his own in his maleness, loses his patience with the Israelites and strikes a rock he had been commanded only to speak to. From a mystical perspective, Miriam's absence has created an imbalance that is felt on the physical and the emotional levels of the people of Israel's existence. If we are not connected both to our feminine and to our masculine sides, if we are cut off physically or emotionally from the integrity of our own or our community's wholeness, there will be no water, no patient leadership, no healthy and functioning self, individual or communal.

Much of the feminine insight that is waiting to be learned is found most clearly in mystical theology in the doctrine of the strength of the "among and between" connectedness, which is instrumental to the existence of the system, and which is described as a naturally feminine approach to relationships in at least two ways: first, in its insistence that the world depends on the balancing of opposites, not on the suppression of one side or the other; and, second, on the realization that the power that is above, often characterized as male, cannot function without interaction with that which is in the feminine position below. One cannot give if there is no one to receive.

A tremendous strain on the contemporary Jewish community is traceable to the fact that some current halakhic and ethical positions do not correlate well with the meta-ethical awareness of the Jewish people in the 21st century Western world, which is where most Jews live. A theology of connectedness that first and foremost prohibits disconnectedness as a diminution of the presence of God - the *Shekhinah* - in the world would bring a new perspective and a new urgency to questions of belonging for groups now marginalized.

Such an emphasis on connectedness, on evoking God's holy presence, as a priority, would also offer a welcome *tikkun*. It would bring Jewish ethics into line with the ethics of many Jews who are loyal to the tradition but troubled over any number of painful issues: the Orthodox father whose daughters must stay behind the *mehitzah*, the rabbi who cannot find a way to release an *agunah*, the community with no guidance in a compassionate response to the person who "comes out" as gay.

On the other side of the equation, a theology of connectedness offers us a new approach to explaining theodicy and evil.[396] If we do not increase our sense of connectedness to one another and the tradition that guides us, we will matter less and less to one another; our tradition will cease to be relevant, and we will wander in a wilderness of confusion about who we are and where we are going. The meaning of our lives will become an even more indefinable source of anxiety.

To have a sense of self, one must be connected to others: Relationships make possible the concept of the self. Previous possessions of the individual self – autobiography, emotions, and morality – become possessions of relationships. We appear to stand alone, but we are manifestations of relatedness.[397] To be connected, one needs have a sure sense of knowing from where one came and to which community one belongs. Knowing where home is gives one the ability to explore beyond it. The Hebrew patriarch Abraham went forth to find his place in the world by leaving home and family, and the land of his birth; while much else about Abraham's election is unknown, he clearly knew from where he had come.

Bridging: Reaching Beyond Hod and Netzakh Toward Tif'eret

Like Joshua and the Israelites standing at the shore of the Jordan River, we reach a stream that must be forded here. That generation of the community of Israel faced a most difficult transition in leaving the wilderness wandering that had been the circumstances of all their lives until this moment.

All Israel, with their elders, chieftains, and judges, stood on either side of the Ark, opposite the Levites, who carried the Ark of the Covenant of YHVH; strangers and natives alike, half facing Mt. Gerizim and half facing Mt. Ebal, as Moshe had commanded, that the People of Israel might be blessed.[398] One who is "all Israel," who has fully integrated the lessons of the wandering and its physical challenges, sees both Gerizim and Ebal (representing blessing and curse in the Torah's account[399]) and maintains a balance, with the Ark in the center.

Many traditional commentaries remark that the Israelites were reluctant to leave the wilderness. In the stark desert landscape they could experience an elemental closeness to God; a pillar of fire by night and a pillar of smoke by day provided certain guidance. There was no need to settle down and make a living, for they were always on the move. But to rise toward a higher level of being, and seeing, they must move beyond preoccupation with the physical and its enduring challenges and temptations. Having confronted and learned from *Malkhut* and *Yesod*, from *Hod* and *Netzakh*, they find themselves here on this bridge that leads beyond them, to *Tiferet*. The blessing is on the other side of this crossing.

It is not easy. Having achieved a certain level of balance, and perhaps even comfort, with our physical sense of self, we might be sorely tempted to try to stay in that place, to do whatever possible to maintain the newly created stasis. Here is the challenge of the human love of routine: change is attractive to us because we imagine that we will arrive at a place where no further change is necessary – a paradox, because, of course, it can never be true that change in the world will cease. But, in human terms, once we define a place for ourselves and it becomes familiar, the system as we know it to that point becomes the comfortable, the known, the predictable.

The challenge confronting those who would rise further, beyond *Hod* and *Netzakh*, is in the seductive nature of the regular routine. Fear of the unknown is the greatest obstacle to the next step; one needs a readiness to look toward tomorrow, beyond the categories by which one defines one's life today. Doing so requires a willingness to see the incompleteness even in the definition one has already achieved for one's own life. The alternative is an idolatrous clinging to the system one has created for oneself, as if it were perfect.

To see that the physical patterns that define our lives is to deny them the power to narrow our emotional vision; to recognize that they are temporary and subject to thoughtful change is to allow empathy to upset our own physical need for security. Thus we begin to learn how to balance even the most difficult of contradictions: the realization that, even though we put all our faith in a system of belief by which we live, that does not make it right for everyone.

Every system of thought is intolerant and breeds intolerance, because it fosters self-righteousness and self-satisfaction – it is significant that the most ruthless of inquisitors have come from the ranks of the systematizers. Fixing its focus of vision at a certain definite range, a system cuts itself off from all outside that focus of vision and thus prevents the living development of truth. On the other hand, the prophetic word is a living and personal confession of faith that cannot be circumscribed by rigid boundaries; it possesses a breadth and a freedom carrying within itself the possibilities of revival and development.[400] One who mistakes the system of the *Sefirot* for a stable, fully defined framework has not achieved the integration of *Netzakh* and *Hod* that open up the gate of prophecy; such a person is trapped in her own insistence that there must be consistency and predictability. The paradox is that the insistence on certainty becomes less and less linked to reality as it truly is, and changes.

Above the level of the physical, we rise toward that of the emotional, and *Tiferet* is the gateway. Our emotional state may be less obvious than our physical situation, sometimes, but the two are intimately linked. Our physical state influences our emotional well-being, and the reverse is also true. We cannot approach our emotions, nor expect to understand and integrate their power, unless we have accepted and come to terms with our physical nature. To understand the nature of our physical creation is to find clues to the higher levels of our being.

Sin, with its attendant discomforts of regret, shame, and disconnection, creates emotional conditions that we prefer to avoid. But it is the turmoil of our emotional being that, in some ways, brings us closest to God. As the Psalmist wrote, "You have created us little lower than the angels." The mystics, however, point out that in some ways we are actually higher than they are. And it is only because we have fallen lower.

> Angels have no power of choice; they simply do what God tells them to do. But humans, created in God's image, have this very special asset [*segulah*], which is the sphere of independent human power. Like God, who does whatever He wants, humans have the ability to do whatever is desired. They have the power of choice. This is hinted at in the passage *v'hayitem k'Elohim yodey tov vera'*, "You have become like God, knowing good and evil."[401]

The medieval theologian and mystic Rabbi Judah Loew of Prague (the Maharal) here points out that it is only after the first people disobeyed God's command that they achieve their full human potential – which is to be like God. In the Torah's account of the sin the first humans committed in the Garden of Eden, the Maharal observes that

> [T]he human certainly is capable of knowing good and evil, because humans are created in God's image. But when the human lived cleaved to his Cause, a situation which is all good, the human knew good but not evil. When the human turned away from his Cause, then the human knew evil. After the sin the human became the one "who knows good and evil."[402]

Knowledge of good and evil and the act of disobedience are what make us human. Before we sin, we only know good. Knowledge of sin, on the other hand, makes us savvy. When Eve and Adam ate the forbidden fruit, "their eyes were opened."[403] What must come into our view as we rise above the balancing of mercy and judgment, of the good and the evil that are both contained there? To reach the highest levels of our human potential is, paradoxically, not to leave our awareness of sin behind. "Man is able to know good and evil, which was not possible before he sinned."[404] It is taught by the Sages that a completely righteous person cannot stand where the one who has sinned and achieved repentance, can stand.[405]

The reality of our nature requires that we find a way to achieve a sense of balance between characteristics that, though they sometimes seem opposed to each other, are all necessary, all part of us: the physical and the emotional, the capacity for good and for evil, human potentials and human limits. It is our experience of the opposing parts of ourselves, and our responsibility to choose between them, that is an essential piece of our humanity, the very definition of being created in God's image. Only by embracing and accepting them, and seeking the knowledge that comes from that openness, do we come to reflect the Image of God most fully in our human lives. Only thus do we rise.

Tiferet – The Gate of Connecting Below with Above

ATTRIBUTES: POLARITY – THE BLESSED HOLY ONE – THE CONNECTION OF SHEKHINAH AND TIFERET – SEEKING BALANCE ABOVE AND BELOW – HARMONY – PERFECT CENTER – RAKHAMIM *b'shem yikhudo shel Kudsha Berikh Hu v'Shekhintey* for the sake of the unification of *Tiferet,* the Blessed Holy One, and *Shekhinah,* the Presence of God; for the linking of the upper worlds and the lower; and for the integration of the Left and the Right.

Polarity

Below the name *Ehyeh* there is a duality of opposites: front and back, right and left. There is no attribute below *Ehyeh* that does not consist of polarities.[406]

Recall the seven-branched *menorah,* the candelabrum of ancient origin in Jewish tradition, in which the *Zohar* saw both the antecedent for the Shabbat candles and a chance to bring heaven and earth together. Modeled on the almond tree in the Book of Exodus, in which the plans for the first *menorah* are divinely revealed, this lamp is made up of seven light-bearing branches. The *menorah* stands balanced between three branches on each side, which proceed outward, reaching upward until their height equals that of the center part of the stand. The central branch is the keystone to the entire outspread illumination, and it is in this central, steadying place that we locate the principle of polarity – the eternal movement of the pendulum between truth and its opposite, which is also truth.

As we have recognized already, Jewish theology proceeds from Jewish traditional teachings – including the teaching that one must bring one's own insights to the interpretative process. Among the teachings of our tradition, one comes to know a seamlessness between God, God's creation, and one's own self-conscious sense of self. Jews come to know God by coming to know themselves and by close study of the truths expressed by the world and the way it works. Nothing is beyond or outside this mission, and we are limited only by our limitations in sight and in perception.

Consider the magnet; see the world itself, a rather large magnet. Remember that the north pole is defined by its opposite, and that for every action there is an equal and opposite reaction. We find that in

Torah and in every observation we can make, when we identify a reality we also invoke its balance, far beyond the small list included in the *havdalah* blessing: day and night, Israel and the other nations, Shabbat and the week – let us consider also the polar divine - and human - attributes of truth and compassion, of judgment and mercy, of male and female. There are polarities of meat and milk, male and female, gay and straight, young and old, heaven and earth, life and death. Each of these realities depends on its opposite for its self-definition and thus, in a way, for its very existence.

It is significant that such polarities by and large are not necessarily defined as good or bad. There is no moral quality necessarily attached to the fact that they are complementary opposites, and it begs the question as to why certain polarities, such as gay and straight, are so judged by the tradition. Perhaps there is an insight in the fact that, while each half of the polarity is generally seen as morally neutral, the mixing of the opposites is problematic; *sha'atnez,* the mixing of wool and linen, is one example (cheeseburgers are another). Most interesting of all, we observe from the phenomenon of polarity in nature that it is not static. There are flowers, fish, and trees, including the Land of Israel's carob, which alternate their sex. Similarly, Jewish mysticism envisions God as the source of, and possessed of, female and male attributes – and those attributes seem quite flexible: they are described very differently in different mystical sources. In the same apparently contradictory way, the science of biology has discovered that we ourselves possess both ends of human sexual polarity. Physically, we harbor within ourselves both male and female attributes; spiritually, we know that we are made up of both heaven and earth. We are capable visions of eternity and of petty blind spots, and we know, too, somehow, that the contradictions within us balance us.

God as *atah,* or "Thou", is the God of the intermediate *Sefirot,* the forces that coalesce around *Tiferet* or the blessed Holy One. *Atah* represents the "male" energy within God, the one to whom *Shekhinah* is partner. This is the God we meet in Other, the One before whom we stand in both love and judgment. *Atah* is the God with whom we exist in relationship as with another. We address prayer to God as *atah,* even though we know that God's "I am" is also within us and all around us.[407]

The Blessed Holy One, and the Union of Shekhinah and Tiferet

> "Come, and I will show you the place where heaven and earth kiss."[408]

The union of *Tiferet* and *Shekhinah* is a central focus of the mystical effort to rejoin the sundered connections between *Sefirot*. For the mystics, the coming of Shabbat each week was an opportunity to recreate the original wholeness of the world by bringing together the upper, *Tiferet,* with the lower, *Shekhinah,* aspects of God. The mystical ritual is part Rabbinic custom, part ancient *hieros gamos*.[409] *Yesod* is the pathway on which all depends: it channels the memories that orient us, the covenant linking individuals to the people, and the sowing of the next generation's seed. *Yesod* is also, and especially, the place of the connection between heaven and earth. Through *Yesod, Malkhut* (*Shekhinah*) links to the worlds above. *Shekhinah* is associated with earth, with the people of Israel, with observing *mitzvot,* and with the exiled presence of God among us; she connects through *Yesod* to *Tiferet,* which is associated with heaven, with the Holy Blessed One, with balance and harmony, and with *El Nikdash b'Tzedakah,* "God sanctified through justice".[410] The two are meant to be together, but without the free flow of *shefa'* through *Yesod,* this joining of the upper and the lower worlds, on which all depends, cannot occur.

When the world was beginning, heaven and earth, *Tiferet* and *Shekhinah,* were brought into being, as the *Zohar* recounts:

> When the world above was filled and impregnated, like a female impregnated by a male, it generated two children as one, male and female, who are *heaven* and *earth,* as above. *Earth* is nourished by the waters of *heaven,* released into her, though the upper are male and the lower female, the lower nourished by the male.

> The lower waters call to the upper, like a female opening to the male, pouring out water toward the water of the male to form seed.[411]

One of the implications of the covenant is that we are not alone. The Jewish people inherit a mutually pledged responsibility to one another and to God. For the Kabbalists, our interconnection with one another implies that we affect others by our actions. In an interactive system, all the parts affect the whole. Even the smallest part can affect the entirety. This understanding requires us to treat one another in ways that move us toward the positive, fostering a creative flow between and among us. Our interconnection with God in this system of mutuality similarly indicates our ability, even as the lower partner, to "call to the upper." Sometimes the action is initiated from below, as Jacob's vision of a ladder showed us: "A ladder was set upon the ground, and its top reached the sky, and angels of God were going up and down upon it."[412] The word for angel in Hebrew is *mal'akh*, "messenger." We are these messengers, originating on the earth but always reaching toward heaven. This striving to rise is our unique human longing and our responsibility. We call God forth by our actions to encourage the free flow of the *shefa'*, the emanation that is the power of the world's life.

In the creation story we see the positioning of humanity balanced between heaven and earth.

> These are the generations of the heaven and of the earth when they were created, in the day that the Eternal God made earth and heaven. No shrub of the field was yet in the earth, and no herb of the field had yet sprung up; for the Eternal God had not caused it to rain upon the earth, and there was no one to till the ground; but there went up a mist from the earth, and watered the whole face of the ground. Then the Eternal God formed the human of the dust of the ground, and breathed into his nostrils the breath of life; and the human became a living soul. The Eternal God planted a garden eastward,

> in Eden; and there He put the human whom He had formed. ... And the Eternal God took the human, and put him into the garden of Eden to till it and to tend it.[413]

From this Biblical passage we see that rain has not yet fallen to earth from the sky. There is a mist that comes up from the earth and waters the ground, but it is not enough to sustain shrubs and herbs. The upper waters, which are the masculine *Tiferet,* and the lower waters, which are the feminine *Shekhinah,* both exist, but they have not yet joined; as the *Zohar* puts it, "the lower waters" have yet to "call to the upper." Following Kabbalistic teaching, we, *Knesset Israel,* are the lower waters, who, in our need for sustenance, call to the upper waters. The garden of Eden, the meeting place of the upper and lower waters on which creation will depend, needs our hand to bring together the upper and lower and to tend the Garden. In just this way, the lower waters, the dust of the ground, and the breath of the Eternal come together, through the longing of the lower for the upper and the upper for the lower. The human being comes into existence as the child of that longing.

The four teachings that encourages us to believe that by our acts we enable the same acts to occur within God is reflected in prayer techniques meant to unify *Shekhinah* and *Tiferet.* For example, in the liturgical poem *Lekha Dodi,* the first line of the refrain contains fifteen Hebrew letters, which correspond to the letters *yud* and *hey,* the half of the Four Letter Name of God associated with *Tiferet.* The second line has eleven Hebrew letters, which correspond to *vahv* and *hey,* the other two letters of the Four Letter Name, which are linked to *Shekhinah.* To sing the refrain for *Lekha Dodi* with the appropriate, focused intention, therefore, is to spark the unification of *Shekhinah* and *Tiferet* by linking the two halves of the Divine Name.

Seeking Balance Below and Above

One of the more interesting descriptions of the male–female balance in relationship is found in the word *k'neged,* which in Hebrew usage can mean "beside," "over against," or "equal and opposite." The word's complexity suitably mirrors the reality of an intimate partnership. In its discussion of the creation of the first, androgynous human being and the subsequent intimacy, in the marital relationship, of the two gendered halves, the *Zohar* includes the following passage:

> [W]e have established: *Asher* is her husband, and she is named after him: *Asherah*. So it is written: "For *Baal* and *Asherah* (2 Kings 23.4). So, "do not plant *Asherah* ... beside the altar that you make for YHVH your God" – beside "the altar of YHVH," for the altar of YHVH is based on this, so "do not plant" another *Asherah* beside Her.[414]

In the *Zohar* "the name Asher is associated with the male sefirotic potency, *Yesod;* so *Shekhinah*, wife of *Yesod*, is named after Him: *Asherah*." The point of the *Zohar*'s interpretation is that one should not "substitute the false goddess *Asherah* ("another *Asherah*") for *Shekhinah*, the original *Asherah*, who is the genuine *altar* of *YHVH*."[415] Most fascinating about this discussion of *Asherah* is that it stands in stark conflict to the Tanakh's repeated prophetic denunciations of the goddess and those who sanctified her.[416] In the theology of the Canaanites, alongside (and in opposite to) whom the ancient Israelites developed their religious beliefs, *Asherah's* domain was the sea, and the god *El*, her husband, ruled the heavens. *Asherah* was mother of all the gods and a powerful nurturer of her human devotees. Biblical evidence indicates that *Asherah* was probably represented by the Hebrews who worshiped her as a carved wooden image, placed, according to Deuteronomy 16.21, next to the altar of YHVH. The repeated accounts of the religious reformations in which *Asherah* was once again cleared out of the Israelites' praying places is the best evidence for the tenacious hold the people kept on their goddess, despite the official YHVH-centered monotheism of the nation.

> [King Josiah] brought out the *Asherah* from the house of YHVH, outside Jerusalem, to the brook Kidron, and

burned it at the brook Kidron, and stamped it small to powder, and cast the powder upon the graves of the common people. He broke down the houses of the *k'deyshim* that were in the house of YHVH, where the women wove coverings for the *Asherah*.[417]

At times, the presence of the goddess *Asherah* seems to have been accepted "as [YHVH's] inevitable, necessary, or at any rate tolerable, female counterpart,"[418] probably because "she answered the psychological need for a mother-goddess which was keenly felt by the people and its leaders alike."[419] In the Hebrew kingdoms of Israel and Judah shrines were built to her, and her image was found alongside that of YHVH in the Holy of Holies, to which it somehow returned each time it was removed owing to occasional sovereign fits of monotheistic piety.

The Biblical texts hold many direct references to the goddess, referred to rather obliquely as a "pole" or a "tree" but with the use of her name. Other references are partial: Leah's utterance of joy at the birth of her second son, *b'oshri!* has been explained as a form of *ashrey*, "joy." Leah named that son Asher,[420] and some scholars see a note of thanks to *Asherah* in both the exclamation and the name. The worship associated with the goddess is expressed repeatedly in references to broad, leafy trees and high places:

> The sin of Judah is written with a pen of iron, and with the point of a diamond; it is graven upon the tablet of their heart, and upon the horns of your altars. Like the symbols of their sons are their altars, and their *Asherah*s are by the leafy trees, upon the high hills.[421]

The prophet Jeremiah railed against the people's idolatrous behavior; he compared them to an adulterous woman who lies beneath that same leafy tree, waiting for a chance to give herself away:

> YHVH said unto me in the days of Josiah the king: 'Have you seen what backsliding Israel did? she went up

upon every high mountain and under every leafy tree,
and there she played the harlot.[422]

There are a few places in the Tanakh where the Hebrew word *Asherah* or *Anat* (another local Canaanite goddess, *Asherah*'s daughter) catches one's eye, but the translation gives no hint of the presence of a goddess of any sort. In one instance, the scholar Raphael Patai shares a new, possibly corrected text of an obscure passage in the book attributed to the prophet Hosea. Verse 14.9 reads, in part, *ani 'aniti va'ashurenu* and has been translated in ways that are awkward. For example (the difficult passage's translation is italicized):

> Ephraim, what have I to do any more with idols?
> *I [YHVH] respond and look upon him,*
> I am a like a leafy cypress-tree
> from me is your fruit found.

Given the discovered archaeological evidence relating to "YHVH and His *Asherah*," Biblical scholars now suggest that the best way to understand the verse from Hosea is (compare second line):

> Ephraim, what have I to do any more with idols?
> *I [YHVH] am his Anat and his Asherah,*
> I am a like a leafy cypress-tree
> from me is your fruit found.[423]

The association of the goddess with a tree is clear; so is her popularity with the Israelite people, who repeatedly place a "pole" or wooden image in the shrine that is at the heart of their belief – the altar of YHVH. We find its antecedent in the Torah's description of the tree-shaped *menorah* near the altar of YHVH, separated only by a curtain from the Ark itself.[424]

The mystical connection of the *Asherah* to the *Shekhinah* reveals a deep and necessary link from the ancient Hebrews' Divine Feminine Presence to the medieval Jewish mystical Great Mother God. It flows like *shefa'*, below the surface of history, like a subterranean stream of life-giving water waiting to be rediscovered and reunited with *Yesod* for the sake of the fulfillment of the first *mitzvah* of creation, "Be fruitful and multiply." The "tree" or "pillar" of *Asherah* that stood in the Temple was never successfully eradicated; rather, it was transformed into the *menorah*, described in the Book of Exodus as a seven-branched candelabrum modeled on an almond tree. The light of that *menorah* evokes the past memory of a burning bush, and is echoed by every woman who kindles light to welcome Shabbat each week.

Now we can better understand the *Zohar*'s warning cited earlier, "Do not plant *Asherah* ... over against the altar of YHVH, for the alter of YHVH is based on this, so do not plant another *Asherah* over against Her." The warning is against depicting the feminine in the world and in God in a way that would contradict the reality of the *Shekhinah*. The *Shekhinah* – divine partner, half of God and therefore half of God's creation and each one of God's reflected images – is a necessary half of a balanced world. The danger of images is that they inevitably narrow our sense of what is being imaged. Rabbi Abraham Joshua Heschel taught that "the reason graven images are forbidden by the Torah is not that God has no image, but because God has just one image: that of every living, breathing person."[425] The feminine, the *Zohar* seems to be telling us, must not be suppressed or otherwise disenfranchised. Because the woman and the man are equally necessary, and their power must be equally balanced, the world is catastrophically unbalanced if one is dominated by the other.

There is no question that the feminine half of the divine and of the human has been suppressed and relegated to a secondary status in traditional Judaism. But we see throughout the archetypal literature of Torah and Talmud many conflicting images of women – some depicted by the men who told their stories as powerful, accepted as teachers and leaders, significant decisors in their lives and the lives of the men around them. The picture that emerges from Jewish culture is not static. Similarly, in Judaism women are identified with the moon, which constantly waxes and wanes. Its light is reflected, true, but if it were not there to do the job of reflecting, the night would have no beacon.

The *menorah* in the wilderness Tabernacle and in the Temple was to be lit so that its light would shine forward, outward. The *menorah* has no light of her own – she receives the light and turns it to shine on us.

Thus the suppressed feminine emerges, in wordplay, in sacred ritual objects, and, most powerfully, in the Kabbalah. And, as mystical teachings make clear, it is up to us to rescue her from exile, and restore her to her place – and, in so doing, we shall ourselves be restored.

Harmony – Perfect Center

If *Tiferet* is the place of perfect harmony in the *Sefirot*, what is it that is being balanced?

> [T]he second triad is the source of the moral order. *Hesed* stands for love of God; *Gevurah* for the power of justice manifested as severity or punishment. From the union of these emanates *Tiferet*, compassion or beauty of God, medating between *Hesed* and *Gevurah*, between the life-giving power and the contrary power, holding in check what would otherwise prove to be the excesses of love.[426]

True judgment comes from the balance between *hesed* and *gevurah*, as Gikatilla teaches in his study of the *Sefirot*. Where it appears in the Torah, the name *Yud-Hei-Vav-Hei* is associated in mystical tradition with *hesed*, "mercy," and the name *Elohim* with *gevurah*, "judgment."

Wherever you find in the Torah YHVH ELoHIM mentioned – which is a full Name – everything in the section which refers to YHVH ELoHIM was made with both the attribute of judgment and the attribute of mercy, as you will see in the Creation of the primordial Adam, his judgment, his exile, and other matters....in all these cases they attended with the combined attributes of judgment and mercy, and they all contained the ultimate perfection of judgment and mercy as is fitting for true judgment. ... "The Rock," the Dispenser of decrees, does not do so with force, nor with cruelty does He administer justice, but

"His deeds are whole (*tamim*)"; before the judgment is dispensed, He consults with these two attributes, *hesed* and *din*. This is what is meant by, "His deeds are perfect." For the word *tamim* is the essence of both attributes and it is as if the word "twins" (*t'umim*) were being uttered.

A true and complete manifestation of God's presence requires a full Name – both of these contradictory qualities must be evoked. The qualities are actually twins: they can exist together, Gikatilla insists, and they must if wholeness is to be achieved. One quality or the other may be hidden, at one time or another, if their co-existence seems too contradictory to bear. But it is only to the limited vision and capacity of human beings, that

> below they appear as two entities, as one thing and its opposite, as a defense and a prosecution; but above, all comes from a singular intention, the defense and prosecution have the same intent, there is no hate or love and there is no favoritism, only true judgment.[427]

Only when one achieves balance between above and below, between right and left, between inner and outer, between and among all that exists can one begin to rise beyond the lower level of the physical, and toward the challenges of the emotional level of the *Sefirot* as they are reflected in one's own life.

Achieving balance between such powerfully conflicting opposites is rather like resolving a logical paradox; it will be seen only in the End of Days. And, indeed, that is how Jewish mysticism describes the Redemption that brings about the World to Come. The present broken state of the world came about because of a catastrophic imbalance between evil and good; the world's healing requires us once again to find a balance between these two. Redemption and the end of exile will be brought about by overcoming what seems to be an irredeemable contradiction: that which is evil will merge with the good, and even this most difficult balance will be achieved and transcended. In *Sefirotic* terms, the left, associated with evil, will be found in the right, associated with good and contained by it.[428] The left, expressed as a harsh overabundance of judgment in the world, will finally be overcome by the mercy of the right side. Redemption, then, is dependent on

> the containment of the divine left within the divine right. ... Exile is a condition of pure judgment, redemption one of mercy balanced with judgment. The severing of this balance is, in the first place, one of the causes for the emergence of an independent demonic realm.[429]

Exile is an expression of the left, that is, of evil; balancing evil with good requires engagement and challenge. Dismissal of that which is evil, through attempts to isolate oneself from its effects, for example, but without any effort to redeem it, only strengthens the evil. The mystics ascribed the darkest evil, the "demonic realm," to evil unchallenged by good; in modern terms, "All that is required for evil to triumph is for good men to stand by and do nothing."[430]

Here and now, the left may usefully restrain and contain the abundance and overflow of the right in the *sefirotic* system, but at the time of redemption the right will contain the left, and both will exist in harmonious balance. Note that it is not that the right will vanquish the left and rise alone, ever upward; left and right will meet, and mercy, on the right, will be appropriately balanced by judgment, on the left. There is a power in the left side that cannot be dismissed. The *Zohar* recognizes this in its discussion of the verse, "Thy right hand, O Lord, glorious in power; thy right hand, O Lord, shatters the enemy."

> [T]he left is found in the right and is contained therein. R. Shimeon said: It is as we have explained, for a man is found divided. What is the reason? In order that he may receive his mate, and they will make one body. So "thy right hand," i.e. it is divided. What is the reason? In order to receive the left hand with it. Thus is everything: one [part] with another. Therefore, with one hand He strikes and heals.[431]

When there is harmony in the *Sefirotic* realm, then the left is united with, nay contained in, the right, as male unites with female;, and all acts, including those of the left, are carried out with the guidance of the right: "With one hand He strikes and heals."

Rakhamim

Tiferet is not half-just and half-merciful. It is the place of *rakhamim*, of compassion. The word *rakhamim* invites the comparison to *rekhem*, "womb." The perfect center of the *Sefirot* is the place where judgment is overcome by mercy and gives birth to compassion.

> The divine right hand is the hand of mercy, whereas the divine left hand is the hand of strict justice. When God's right hand of mercy overcomes the left hand of justice, then the left hand is transformed and becomes also a hand of mercy. As Rashi interprets the verse, "your right hand, God, is adorned with strength (*ko'akh*); your right hand, God, smashes the enemy" (*Shemot* 15.6). Rashi asks: why does the verse repeat the phrase, "your right hand"? When Israel fulfills God's will, God's left hand of justice is turned into God's right hand of mercy.[432]

Tiferet is the place of balance between the physical and the emotional. As the bridge to the emotional level, it is both physical and emotional. As the middle attribute, it balances all the others and contains them all. It is the place where the physical is overcome; here, physical desire does not rule over the emotions.

Tiferet, "glory," also called *rakhamim*, "compassion," is the ability, no matter what one's physical circumstance, to bear it separately from one's emotional mood. God's compassion is cited in the forbearance of Divine Anger when the Israelites committed the sin of the golden calf: "*YHVH, YHVH Elohim*, merciful and gracious, long suffering, abundant in goodness and truth, maintaining mercy for thousands, forgiving iniquity and transgression and sin."[433] *Tiferet* is a quality of compassion that is aware of suffering as well as well-being; it contains within it the truth of all experience, balanced, integrated, and complete. In this way *Tiferet* balances the effects of good and evil in human behavior:

> What [was the purpose] when Scripture wrote: "Long-suffering" [*erekh apayim*, a dual form] where the singular [form] might well have been used? Only this: long-suffering towards the righteous, and long-suffering also towards the wicked.[434]

Rising toward *Tiferet*, considering what it has to teach us, invites us to contemplate the glorious splendor of the compassion that grows from physical integrity, despite our physical limitations. We will never completely overcome the handicap of a physical body while we inhabit it; but we can refuse to let the weaknesses which circumscribe our physical activity to limit our emotional range. We can deliberately choose to inhabit *Tiferet*, to be generous in response to the gift of life rather than pensive and angry because it is fleeting, incomplete, and often unjust.

> [I]t could all go in a minute. It WILL all go in a minute. This life is a brief stop, whether I die tomorrow or in fifty years. I would love not to know this, to have the innocent certainty that, when loved ones set out on a journey, they will return unharmed, that I can go out to sea in my boat, play in the waves and not be swallowed up. But I am more grateful now than I ever was in my innocence. In the end it is all a gift, is it not? The brief entwinement of body and soul, the breath of God that gives and sustains human life, creates such a colorful, sparkling trail as it arcs through time. It is so ephemeral, and yet it affects everything. As we say when we open our eyes every morning: "*modeh ani l'fanekha* - I give thanks to you, God of life which is eternal, for

returning my soul to me this morning. Great is your faithfulness."[435]

Din – The Gate of Judgment

JUDGMENT [DIN] – SEVERITY – MEASURING OF DIVINE LOVE – THE RESTRAINING HAND – SARAH – EVIL – ISAAC – POWER (GEVURAH) – EVIL IS PART OF THE ALL – THE YETZER HARA' – COMPLEXITY

> *b'shem yikhudo shel Kudsha Berikh Hu v'Shekhintey* – for the sake of the unification of left hand and right, of restraint and of outpouring, of lack and of fulfillment.

Judgment [*Din*] - Severity

From a mystical perspective, the world is broken; that much is clear. Things do not happen as they should; life is not fair. People suffer who should not suffer, and evil triumphs over good. Cynicism is a real danger to any effort to heal the world, and as we experience increasing alienation from one another and from communities of meaning, social networks attenuate, and many choose not to "get involved," unaware or uncaring of the cost to themselves. For mystics, human society is experiencing a paradox: too much *gevurah,* and not enough. Too much severity, and not enough judgment. These are two sides of the *sefirah* called *Din* or *Gevurah,* "judgment" or "power." In the early twenty-first century, many, if not most, people recoil from judging one another. While it is true that many are happy to judge another's acts in the form of *lashon hara',* "evil speech," to a third person, almost no one wants to be in the position of actually judging the merits of another's behavior. Individuals assert that no one else has the right to judge another, perhaps since doing so seems to require that another person raise herself above the rest of the human race. "Who gave *you* the power to judge *me?*" we say. The invitation to walk a mile in another's boots before passing judgment on the boots' owner is an affirmation that no one can truly judge another, because none of us can actually stand in the place occupied by another.

On the communal level of day-to-day interactions, the place of judgment is terribly difficult, for one must balance severity and compassion, or, to put it another way, balance the letter *and* the spirit of a rule or a policy. The attempt to achieve a thoughtful balance between these polarities, or complementary opposites, is complicated: where one must be placed in judgment over another person, it is easy to do a very poor job of it, making assumptions, not checking facts, going with a "gut feeling" – anything, just to finish the uncomfortable process.

Yet, judgment is an attribute of God's, as we learn in the Torah's narratives. From the prophets of antiquity to the contemporary liturgy for Yom Kippur, the theme of judgment is central to any ethical review of human behavior. Every aspect of an act is subject to judgment. "Justice, justice shall you pursue"[436] is interpreted by Jewish tradition to indicate two aspects of just behavior: first, we must look for opportunities to do justice and not wait passively for such chances to come to us. Second, we must do justice in a just way: the means and the ends must both be just.

Jewish tradition does not consider the possibility that one might decline to judge one's neighbor when necessary. If judgment is God's, then it is also ours, and to shrink from it is to abdicate an important human responsibility. We are to live as best we can as a reflection of God in this way also. Judgment is an essential quality in human community: it balances mercy and offers a restraint on it. It is recorded in the Talmud that, in a study session with the eminent Rabbi Meir, Rabbi Judah ben Koma referred to the commandment, "Execute the judgment of truth and peace in your gates," by exclaiming, "Surely where there is strict justice there is no peace, and where there is peace, there is no strict justice!"[437] Rabbi Judah was frustrated by the very same thing that bothers us in our societies: no matter what law we pass, we always end up having to make exceptions – or to pass another law to correct the first. Human beings cannot be made to fit a consistent pattern: we are endlessly variable, and so are our problems.

The Jewish tradition of judgment maintain that a judge must apply the law through careful consideration of the specific case, and carefully note the with respect to the specific people and situation involved. Judgment which that is sensitive to the individual case, not the consistent application of policy, is considered most honorable in Jewish tradition. And so it is that in a discussion between Rabbi Meir and Rabbi Judah, the example of King David, known as a righteous judge, is cited:

> In rendering legal judgment, David used to acquit the guiltless and condemn the guilty; but when he saw that the condemned man was poor, he helped him out of his own purse [to pay the required sum], thus practicing judgment and compassion, justice to the one by awardinding him his dues, and compassion to the other by assisting him out of his own pocket. And, in this way, therefore, Scripture says, David practiced justice and compassion towards all his people.[438]

As the Yom Kippur liturgy insists, no one can live under the rule of strict justice; every human being is dependent on compassion to live. Jewish ethics teaches that the gates of justice will remain closed to us until we extend to others the compassion we need ourselves – until we treat others as we treat ourselves.

Detachment from others is only the human level at which we experience the greater, more destructive cosmic detachment from which we, too, suffer. The act of adding to that detachment is called by Jewish legal tradition "the trait of Sodom":

> the term refers to an inordinate privatism ... a degree of selfishness so intense that it denies the others at no gain to oneself. There need be no actual spite. Simple indifference may suffice....One view in the Mishna - the definitive view according to most halakhists - subsumed under it the attitude that "mine is mine and yours is yours." It thus broadly denotes obsession with one's private preserve and the consequent erection of excessive

legal and psychological barriers between person and person.[439]

A modern person might insist on the right to privacy, but Jewish tradition is not so biased. Rashi explains the Mishnah's condemnation of the building of a gatehouse between one's home and the common street:

> [F]or the gatehouse gates off the poor people who are crying out for money or assistance, and their voices are not heard. ... It is a deplorable thing since the gate of the courtyard is locked and the poor person cries out and the gatehouse which is inside buffers the voice.[440]

Voices that cry out and are not heard; pain that is suffered but no one comes to help. Life was meant to be a harmony of flow, an unimpeded giving and receiving of divine *shefa'*. But, because of the unnatural, unexpected breaks in the intended unity of the world, the system of the cosmos itself breaks down.

> Originally there was harmony between God and His final manifestations, between the upper *Sefirot* and the tenth *sefirah*. All things were attached to God and His power surged unhampered throughout all stages of being. Following the trespass of Adam, however, barriers evolved thwarting the emanation of His power. The creature became detached from the Creator, the fruit from the tree, the tree of knowledge from the tree of life, the male from the female, our universe from the world of unity, even the *Shekhinah* or the tenth *sefirah* from the upper *Sefirot*.[441]

When we judge others without having learned in our own hearts that *There but for the grace of God go I,* or, even more truly, *There go I,* we contribute to the brokenness. In such judgments, we hold ourselves separate where separation is damaging and unhealthy, and allows the evil to grow.

Measuring of Divine Love – The Restraining Hand: Sarah

Just after the second Pesakh Seder, when the *sefirat haOmer* is initiated, a Rabbi shared a text explaining *hesed,* which balances *gevurah,* with a student. "Abraham was known for his love of giving, especially to the passersby. It is said that his tent was open on all four sides so that no one could escape his welcoming hospitality."[442] At that, the student burst out laughing at the vision of what sounded like guerilla hospitality, forced on anyone unlucky enough to blunder into Abraham's range of vision. "It seems almost threatening," he said.

The *sefirah* of *Gevurah* balances the *sefirah* of *Hesed,* and with good reason. *Hesed* is the unbounded quality of love, of mercy, and of kindness. *Gevurah,* which is described as a rigorous power of judgment, provides a necessary limitation on what otherwise could be overwhelming and even negative in its impact. Kindness without judgment can be patronizing, mercy without judgment can lead to exploitation of the merciful, and love without judgment is pathological.

Sarah, Abraham's wife – and, for Kabbalah, literally his "other half" – is associated with *Gevurah.* Where Abraham gives without stint and without judgment, Sarah restrains, considers, focuses. Abraham hosts a feast for his entire extended family and followers to celebrate Isaac's birth; during that celebration, seeing the two boys interacting in ways that worry her, Sarah realizes that Ishma'el and Isaac cannot co-exist. She is the one who restrains Abraham's *Hesed* toward his family members and tempers it into meaning: Hagar and Ishma'el will be given provisions and sent away, and Isaac will survive and be the heir. Without demur, the Torah records that God tells Abraham to accept Sarah's judgment. Hers is "the lucid vision of reality that is hidden from the more entangled emotions of Abraham."[443]

"Who is wise? One who can see what is being born."[444]

Talmudic tradition, approving Sarah's ability to detect the possibility of a problem between the two boys, draws comparisons to Cain and Abel. "'She looks for wool and flax.'[445] This refers to Sarah, who said, 'Cast out that slave-woman and her son'."[446] Sarah could see, in the abundance of her husband's *Hesed,* that generosity alone was not enough.

This mystical understanding of the role Sarah plays to balance her husband's acts causes her to be associated with the *sefirah* of *Gevurah,* of restraint, channeling, and judgment. This is an important aspect of one of the highest Jewish activities – the giving of *tzedakah*. The Talmud records the teaching:

> The verse (Psalm 41.2) doesn't say "happy is the one who gives to the poor," but rather, "happy is the one who uses his insight when giving to the poor." This means that one must use all one's faculties when considering how to do the *mitzvah* of *tzedakah*.[447]

For the mystics, this Talmudic teaching means that one does not reach one's highest potential by exercising one sefirotic attribute in isolation from others; rather, one must constantly judge one's sense of the necessary balance between *Hesed* and *Gevurah*. It is not enough to hand out change randomly on the street, or to give someone a warm winter blanket when what she needs is shoes.

There must be a healthy and necessary balancing, the kind that naturally takes place in the give-and-take within working systems, as well as in our own physical bodies. As long as all the channels of social communication, and of our veins and arteries, are open, the system will find its level.

Evil

But terrible things can happen when a system's healthy flow is impeded. The medieval Kabbalist Rabbi Isaac Luria taught what has become the central mystical understanding of what happens when systems, and human nature, break down and evil is real. It begins when the powerful light, or what we might understand as presence, of God flowed forth from *tehiru,* the chaos of primordial nothing; rather like the "vacuum" of space, this is the emptiness God created in order to make room for human life. In the process of creation, God's presence, in the form of the life-giving energy of *shefa',* would fill the *Sefirot,* since they are the underlying structure of the world. The *Sefirot* were to be as vessels which would both express and transmit God's power, light, and presence. The upper vessels survived the tremendous power of the flow that surged through them, but

> the vessels that were supposed to shelter the lower *Sefirot* from *hesed* through *yesod* proved to be insufficiently strong for the task. Under the impact of the simultaneous flow of light into these six lower vessels, the latter shattered and were dispersed into the *tehiru*. This even is known as the *shevirat ha-kelim,* the "breaking of the vessels." While the vessel containing the final *sefirah,* Malkhut, also cracked, it did not completely shatter as did the others.[448]

The breaking of the vessels caused sparks of divine light and power to become scattered throughout the cosmos, hidden within the shards of the vessels that constitute the material world. Evil comes into the world at this point, in the broken shards of the vessels, which are also called *kelippot,* the dry outer "husks." Just as husks are all that is left when the life-bearing seed that was within them is removed, so the cosmic husks represent the absence, so to speak, of God's presence.[449] All that is left are the empty bits of what used to be a vessel.

In the complex development of the Kabbalistic explanation of evil, there are two significant teachings. The first is that evil is real; it cannot be explained away as a matter of mistaken perception. With this assertion, the medieval Kabbalists took a religious stance contrary to that of the Jewish philosophers of their day. The difference between the mystics and the philosophers is

> the difference between religious and intellectual motives of thought. To the intellect the problem is no real problem at all. All that is needed is to understand that evil is relative, more, that it does not really exist. ...the religious consciousness demands that evil should be really vanquished. This demand is based on the profound conviction that the power of evil is real, and the mind which is conscious of this fact refuses to content itself with intellectual *tours de force*, however brilliant, which try to explain away the existence of something which it knows to be there.[450]

The Kabbalists have this in common, despite differences in their details and expositions: "They all assume the reality of evil."[451] In this not only they not only differ with the philosophers; they are also displaying their own conservatism. The Kabbalists veil their innovative thought with a constant emphasis on the framework of the Biblical and Rabbinic sources on which they build. In the case of evil, the ancient support for their stance is clear. In the book of Isaiah, God declares, "I form light and create darkness, make peace and create evil."[452]

The second significant belief about evil that arises from Jewish mysticism is that evil is part and parcel of the world's essential structure.

> The totality of divine potencies forms a harmonious whole, and as long as each stays in relation to all others, it is sacred and good. This is true also of the quality of strict justice, rigor and judgment in and by God, which is the fundamental cause of evil. The wrath of God is symbolized by His left hand, while the quality of mercy and love, with which it is intimately bound up, is called His right hand. The one cannot manifest itself without involving the other. Thus the quality of stern judgment represents the great fire of wrath which burns in God but it always tempered by His mercy. When it ceases to be tempered, when in its measureless hypertrophical outbreak it tears itself loose from the quality of mercy, then it...is transformed into the radically evil.[453]

Some Kabbalists taught that this radical evil is part of a *sitra akhra,* an "Other Side" that is somehow separate from God; but there is a fine line, of which they were aware, between this insistence that evil must be separate from God and the heretical doctrine of the existence of any divine power other than God. The only answer to this problem, as they were aware, is that evil itself is not other than God. Certainly Abraham, Sarah and Isaac all express that reality in one of our tradition's most disturbing stories, the *Akedah* – the Binding of Isaac. Abraham hears God's voice telling him to take his son, Isaac, and offer him up as a sacrifice on a nearby mountain.

Millennia of commentary express the Jewish people's ongoing ambivalence about this narrative. Evil can be discerned in so many places in this story. What kind of God would ask such a thing? What kind of father would hear it? What was the effect on the son? And the mother of that only son? For the midrashic imagination, it is no surprise that the story of Sarah's death is related directly after the *Akedah*. According to several midrashic sources, when Sarah realized what her husband had been doing,

> she began to cry and wail. She cried three sobs, corresponding to the three *Teki'ah* notes of the Shofar, and she wailed three times, corresponding to the *Yevava*, staccato notes of the Shofar. Then she gave up the ghost and died.[454]

Sarah dies of a terrible anguish, and not only because of the anguish of her son. Aviva Zornberg points out that the midrashic connection to the Shofar leads to an entire theodicy of atonement – that a ram can substitute for a human sacrifice, that suffering itself can atone for sin. But that is not the only possible meaning. In another midrash, God replies to Jacob's complaint that his life is difficult with words that become the heart of Jewish theodicy: "Abraham did not rejoice in My world and you seek to rejoice?"[455]

> Abraham is the example of a terrible testing, which is resolved in the saving of his son and vindication of his own purity of intent. But this joy is then undercut

by Sarah's death. The implied connection between the Akedah and Sarah's death becomes a prooftext for meaninglessness, within the parameters of this life. The midrash continues to speak ultimately even of God's lack of joy in His world: joy belongs to the future, affirms the midrash, not to the troubled middle-distance of temporal reality.[456]

Sarah dies, more than anything else, bereft: of son, of husband, and of the God she had agreed to follow. God was not there for Sarah, did not speak to her, did not alleviate her doubts or soothe her terror. In the compassionate imagination of our ancestors, Sarah died, in the end, of meaninglessness; and this is one of the faces of evil.

We are left without words to respond. So it is with the world, and so it is with this *sefirah*. Here we find an imbalance that overemphasizes severity and leads to evil, of humans and of God. For if the *Akedah* was God's will, as the suffering of Job is also presented by the Tanakh, then we can learn only that sometimes, that which we experience as evil clearly comes from God.

There is, it is said, a "saving grace" in this understanding, as frightening as it is. It is hinted at in the development of Isaac as symbol. As the personification of strict justice, rather than its victim, Isaac represents that very severity that would find all of us guilty if strict justice were to have its way. Joseph Gikatilla explains Isaac's blindness in this symbolic way: "Know that God diminished the power of the attribute of justice, so that it would not scrutinize each and every sin.

> This is the essence of "and his eyes were darkened from seeing." (Genesis 27.1). ... When people sin, the attribute of justice is extended toward them and then God ... sees that if the judgment is fulfilled, then worlds will be utterly destroyed, so what can He do? He removes judgment from there and he brings it up to the attribute of mercy.[457]

It is God's eyes that are "darkened from seeing." Grace, *Hesed*, is the sefirotic balance for *Din;* it is literally that which saves us from justice. For, as the Rabbinic liturgy asks, if justice were allowed to rule, who would survive? All of us sin. In a balanced sefirotic system, justice and mercy always interact; neither is experienced as a pure state. At the moment when justice might be meted out to us, grace saves us: "'may YHVH's face shine upon you and be gracious unto you.' ... If you are not fit for mercy at the moment He shines His face from above, He will give you a gift, and that is the essence of the verse."[458]

Isaac – Evil – Might [Gevurah]

Isaac's father knew God's mercy and expressed it, this *sefirah*, which is situated opposite to Abraham's *sefirah* of *Hesed*, is known as *Pakhad Yitzhak*, "Fear of Isaac." The simple fact of this association seems obvious, given that the central story of Isaac's life is one of meaningless terror. His association with the *sefirah* of *Din*, of Judgment, allows the mystics to confront and develop their understanding of the reality of the damage that this *sefirah* can do when it is out of balance with its opposite, *Hesed*. The fire of the *Akedah* sacrifice represents the great consuming fire in which God is sometimes manifest, as also in the story of Nadav and Abihu and the "strange fire" in which they were consumed (another sacrifice of sons which is also narrated without any sense of justice). "For YHVH your God is a consuming fire, an impassioned God."[459] In the correct dosage, fear of God is the same as reverence: it is that awe which silences us when we stand in its presence. This is Rudolf Otto's description of the state of being exposed to the "numinous," a sense of mysterious and terrifying holiness. It is an amoral state, not moral nor immoral. Human categories of good and evil do not apply.[460] Feeling oneself to be in God's presence may not necessarily lead one to a state of calm goodness or blessing. The Prophet Isaiah describes terror as his initial reaction when he sees God in the Temple in Jerusalem:

> In the year that King Uzziah died, I beheld my Lord seated on a high and lofty throne, and the skirts of his robe filled the Temple. Seraphs stood in attention on him. Each of them has six wings: with two he covered his face, with two he covered his legs, and with two he would fly. And one would call to the other, "Holy, holy, holy, the Lord of Hosts! His presence fills all the earth!" The doorposts shook at the sound of the one who called, and the House filled with smoke. I cried, "Woe is me, I am lost!"[461]

Otto called this the powerful sense of a *mysterium tremendum* an overwhelming awe mixed with terror, comparable in our own modern lives, perhaps, to moments such as those of a parent in childbirth, of an astronaut floating in endless space, or any moment that stops us in our tracks with the realization that the world is so vast and we are so small. As the psalmist put it, "What are we, that You take note of us?"[462] This is what the ancients called God's *Gevurah*, "might," and they realized that we must come to a sense of awe and respect before God, before we might ascend to a real love of God. At the lower stage of moral development through which we must rise, fear of the consequences keeps us from straying too far from the path that will lead us higher.

> Even though the attribute of Isaac is fear, its intention is to bring merit to Israel. ... If it were not for the attribute of fear from hell, how many of the righteous would sin! ... This is the essence of *Pakhad Yitzhak*, about which it is said: "Happy is the man who is constantly fearful." (Proverbs 28.14). If this is so, open your eyes and see how much fear helps, for it keeps man from sin.[463]

As with any human attempt to understand the meaning of life, the mystics had to struggle with the question of theodicy: why does evil exist? Or, in their language, why were the vessels broken? The mystical answer to this question is, surprisingly enough, an empowering and visionary idea. The vessels were broken because of a divine miscalculation about just how much of the power of the *shefa'* of *Ayn Sof* they could withstand. Even as the Torah makes clear, God is not imagined in Jewish tradition as omniscient, perhaps because God is not alone. We are the other element in this world's reality.

Whatever purpose evil plays in God's creation, it must also have its source in God. But, in the early stages of God's self-unfolding, evil is only latent, as it were, in God's complete justice and mercy. It is only in the process of creation that evil comes to enjoy an independent existence.[464]

This theme was first introduced in our initial considerations: Jewish tradition teaches that there is no way around the truth that by our own acts, we either strengthen the darkness around us or dissipate it. But Jewish mysticism sees this power of ours to sin as, inevitably, balanced by an equal and opposite characteristic: to do the right thing. Because evil is not outside the All in which we live, but rather is a part of it, we have it within our power to affect evil by our acts. Accompanying this empowering teaching is an attendant ethical *mitzvah:* no other person may be demonized. Of no one may we say, that is not a human being. When we do, we deny not only our ability to reach that being and help him or her become fully human; in a mystical sense, with the denial of another's humanity we are asserting that some creative power other than God's exists in the world. This is the true meaning of idolatry: to believe that we are not all part of one All.

The mystics maintained that nothing that is of the world is beyond the human power to affect, change, and heal through the power of *mitzvot*. We can choose to do *mitzvot* that strengthen the good in the world and light up the darkness. And the power we have through the *mitzvot* not only brings a healing energy to ourselves and our world; because we are a part of God, the *mitzvot* also bring healing to God. To fulfill a *mitzvah* is a form of "participation in the vast drama of the dynamic occurrences in the divine world. The fate of the divine powers is thus relegated to the hands of human beings."[465] The power that this gives human beings is frighteningly significant. We can heal – or destroy – the world. God is not going to stop us; as the midrash puts it, "You are my witnesses, and I am God: that is to say, if you are not my witnesses, then, God forbid, I am not God."[466]

It is not sufficient to believe in an infinite God. ... Theological understanding and speculation are incomplete without deeds. Through ritual, God's inner life (the *Sefirot*) is explored and known, imitated and affected. These *Sefirot* are the manifestations of *Eyn Sof,* the divine attributes. Here God thinks, feels, and responds. The *Sefirot* link *Eyn Sof* with the world; *mitzvot* are the mystical tool that enables one to contact the otherwise unknowable God.[467]

For the Kabbalists, evil is not outside of the rest of the world, some kind of free-floating entity answerable to no one, dealing destruction and death. Rather, "the 'emanations of the left' have their origin in and are sustained by the left side of the divine realm itself.' That is to say, therefore, that the demonic has a root within the divine."[468] This means that we can own it and subsume it into the All and, in so doing, cause to come closer to reality a wholeness of the world that was last known in the Garden of Eden. Thus we make atonement for all the evil of our species, and, in the fullest meaning of that word, we return to a balanced existence, full of light and love, as life is intended to be.

Evil is a necessary part of the ethical spectrum of Creation: some people are more evil, some people are less. Some do a better job than others of suppressing the *yetzer hara',* the evil impulse with which we are born and with which we must struggle all our lives. The trespass of Adam and Eve, described mystically as the shattering of the vessels, is both a necessary part of becoming human, and a distancing from its holy and creative source.

Owing to that separation the world was thrown into disorder, the power of strict judgment increased, the power of love diminished and the forces of evil released. Man who was to exist in pure spiritual form as light in constant communication with the Divine was sunk into his present inferior state.[469]

The mythical moment at which evil entered the world is not only an inheritance. One feels the resonance in one's own acts, one's own existence. No human being is very different from the first human, and the last also will be not too unlike. If we look, we can see all around us "the power of love diminished and the forces of evil released." The question is whether or not we can also see our connection to all that is around us and our own ability to evoke change for the good. As Rabbi Abraham Joshua Heschel asserted, "In a free society, some are guilty. All are responsible."[470] The choice not to act, to decide that one's acts cannot possibly make a difference, is also an act – one that nurtures evil.

"All are responsible" is a teaching that derives directly from the mystical insight that we are all connected, to each other, to the earth, to God, and to good and evil. We have more power than we know to impact the world. We all have a good and an evil side to us; who, if not each of us, knows the evil intimately and knows how to channel it into good?

> If you ask what level this is, the level of the knowledge of evil, certainly it is the level of *hokhmah*. The wisdom of a human being includes the knowledge of good and evil, as it is written: "and the eyes of the two were opened", *v'hayitem k'Elohim yod'ey tov vera'*, "and they became like God, knowing good and evil" (Gen. 3).[471]

Evil Is Part of the All

Recall that the *Sefirot* can be imagined as three pillars of light and that the pillar on the left side is the absence of light, in which there is fear – of the darkness and of the unknown. There is also the opening onto evil, which we have seen. One of the most difficult things to imagine is that this, also, is all part of the Place which is God. But that is the implication of monotheism, finally: that if all is unified in God, then God is "the Eternal, there is none else, forming light and darkness, making wholeness and evil."[472]

Rabbi Nehuniah ben HaKana said: One verse (Job 37.21) states, "And now they do not see light, it is brilliant (*bahir*) in the skies. Another verse, however (Psalm 18.12) states, "He made darkness His hiding place". It is also written (Psalm 97.2) "Cloud and gloom surround hi..

This is an apparent contradiction. A third verse comes and reconciles the two. It is written (Psalm 139.12) "Even the darkness is not dark to You. Night shines like day – light and darkness are the same."[473]

It is very difficult to consider this inevitable conclusion, which must be drawn from the idea that God is the All, but anything less is just as difficult a theological position. If God is *not* All, then what exists outside of God? The rabbis of antiquity were adamant against any belief that there is another power outside of God; the famous story of the four who entered the mystical garden ends with the doom of one, Elisha ben Abuyah, who is described in the Talmud as having drawn precisely that fatal conclusion from what he sees there. He asks, "Are there, then, two powers in heaven?" and immediately he is rejected from the Jewish community and, in a very unusual step, not allowed the possibility of *teshuvah*, atonement and reconnection to the community.[474] As painful and difficult as it is to see all of life and its unfair tragedies all as part of one unified source, that is the clear message of the ancient Jewish sources. It is carried forth by Kabbalah in a way that is no less unflinching. There are, to be sure, evil spirits and dybbuks, as well as unexplainable horrors visited on entire Jewish communities; but, despite more than adequate provocation, Jewish religious belief has never countenanced an equal and opposite power in the world, a Lord of Darkness who could carry out any evil outside of God's will.

This is the source of the mystical hope that we can overcome evil, even malicious, destructive, insane levels of evil. For, if one God is the source of absolutely everything, then nothing is outside God's reach. The psychosocial implications are both disturbing and empowering. What is disturbing is the idea that the one who does evil is really no different at base than am I, than are you. To say that nothing is outside God's world means that we cannot demonize – dehumanize – any evil human behavior; we cannot say that the act is inhuman if a human being commits it. Rather, if we can recognize that "there but for the grace of God go I," then we can truly begin to understand the wisdom of the rabbinic teaching about the *yetzer hara'*, which all people possess. The evil within human nature cannot be eradicated, but we can develop the personal resources and discipline to control it, whether we speak of our own impulses or evil on a larger scale. All of life is linked and unified at the source, and if the evil we experience is within human reach, then it may also be compassed by human healing.

Lurianic Kabbalah, with its myth of the shattered vessels and the crippling of the intended purpose of Creation, recognizes both the disruptive power of evil and the human potential to overcome and destroy evil and repair the breach.

> Rabbi Isaac said, "The light created by God in the act of Creation flared from one end of the universe to the other and was hidden away, reserved for the righteous in the world that is coming, as it is written: "Light is sown for the righteous." Then the worlds will be fragrant, and all will be one. But until the world that is coming arrives, it is stored and hidden away."
> Rabbi Judah responded, "if the light were completely hidden, the world would not exist for even a moment! Rather, it is hidden and sown like a seed that gives birth to seeds and fruit. Thereby the world is sustained. Every single day, a ray of that light shines into the world, keeping everything alive; with that ray God feeds the world. And everywhere that Torah is studied at night one thread-thin ray appears from that hidden light and flows down upon those absorbed in her. Since the first day, the light has never been fully revealed, but it is vital to the word, renewing each day the act of Creation."[475]

The Yetzer HaRa'

> Reb Bunam said, "You must imagine the evil sprit as a thug hovering over you with a raised hatchet, ready to chop off your head."
> "What if I can't imagine it?" asked a Hasid.
> "That's a sure sign that he has already chopped it off."[476]

The realization that human beings have a good side and an evil side to them is a basic Jewish teaching, as ancient as God's realization after the flood that the human species is an inevitable blend of kindness and cruelty. The prooftext for the two *yetzers*, the two impulses, with which humans are born and that we must learn to control is interpreted from the spelling of the word *yatzer*, "formed." *Vay'yatzer Adonai Elohim et ha'Adam*, "YVHV *Elohim* formed the human."[477] The Hebrew word *vay'yatzer* is spelled with two letter *yuds* in the Hebrew; from this it is interpreted that human beings have two *yetzers*, a word that also begins with a *yud*.[478]

The good and evil that are part of each of us are also part of the world. We bring ourselves fully into our potential and into the world when we act in either sphere. Another play on the Hebrew illuminates this idea: the Hebrew word *levav'kha* is a variant that seems like a doubling of the normal singular form of the word *lev*, "heart."

One must bless God for the evil in the same way as for the good, as it says, *You shall love Adonai your God with all your heart* (Deut. 6.5) *B'khol l'vav'kha*, "with all your heart" means with your two impulses, the evil impulse as well as the good impulse.[479]

Evil is inextricably related to other aspects of existence. The creative impulse, for example, is seen as deriving its power from the *yetzer hara'*. It has its place even in Creation itself: "God saw everything that God had made, and behold, it was very good."[480] In a typical technique of Torah interpretation, midrashic commentary sees the "and" as an "extending particle," allowing the phrase to be interpreted twice:

Nahman said in R. Samuel's name: *Behold, it was very good* refers to the Good Desire; *and behold, it was very good* to the Evil Desire. Can then the Evil Desire be very good? That would be extraordinary! But for the Evil Desire, however, no man would build a house, take a wife and beget children.[481]

Evil is a necessary, therefore "good,", element in the mix of what it means to be a complete human being. One cannot avoid the evil within oneself; there is no way to erase it from one's being. One can only learn how to cope with it. The *Zohar* cites passages within Jewish tradition: "The moment a human being comes into the world, the evil impulse appears along with him, inciting him constantly, as is said: 'At the opening sin crouches'[482] – [This is the] evil impulse."[483] The opening of the womb is the initial opening of the gateway into life for a human being.

Good and evil are intertwined in the world as they are in a human being. The *Zohar's* commentary on God's appearance to Moshe in a thorn bush is symbolic:

> [T]he thorn-bush [the demonic potency] was surely within that holiness [i.e. *Shekhinah*] and cleaving to it, for everything cleaves together, the pure and the impure; there is no purity except from within impurity. This is the mystery, "Who can bring a pure thing from what is impure" (Job 14.4). The shell and the kernel are together.[484]

Coming to terms with the existence of evil is required any spiritual journey. For the mystics, one metaphor for that experience is found in Abraham's journey "down" to Egypt. There he encountered evil and learned its ways. Thus he was able to rise above it, as the *Sefirot* show, since he is associated with *Hesed*, which balances and softens judgment.

Good and evil are not only unavoidable realities; their proper relationship is to be intertwined. Attempting to separate them and to live somehow untouched by evil is not only impossible, but, for the mystics, heretical.

Rabbi Isaac said: when the Holy One, blessed be He, created the world and wanted to reveal the depth out of the hiddenness and the light from within the darkness, they were contained within one another. Therefore out of darkness emerged the light and out of the hiddenness emerged and was revealed the depth.[485]

"To separate good and evil is ultimately to deny the unity of the divine."[486] The *Zohar* attributes the sufferings of Job to the fact that he "separated good and evil instead of containing them together."[487] For the mystics, the sacrifices offered to God were to be balanced by some portion dedicated to the *sitra akhra*, the "other side." Even as the

Torah describes a goat offered to the desert "demon" as part of the Yom Kippur ritual, so this mystical understanding that evil separated from good is likely to become stronger than if it were somehow included in the world of goodness. "Paradoxically, by not participating in evil Job was overcome by evil; by separating evil from good Job strengthened the former."[488]

Job never gave any portion to [the Other Side], as it is written, "he offered up burnt-offerings according to the number of them all" (Job 1.5). The burnt-offering rises upward. He did not give any portion to the Other Side. ... .come and see: just as he separated and did not contain the good and evil [together], so in the exact manner he was judged: [God] gave him good and then evil and then returned him to the good. Thus it is fitting for a person to know good and to know evil, and then return to the good. That is the secret of faith.[489]

Although the consideration that evil must be recognized as a powerful reality may appear to be a radical departure from basic Jewish theology, the mystics are merely holding fast to the logical consequences of a belief in monotheism, in the truth that All is One. Redemption will come about only with the embrace and subsuming of evil, never by ignoring it. It is part and parcel of us, and the world.

> Given that our impulse to evil is born with us and cannot be eradicated, there is no more obvious tool with which to fight it than our impulse to do and be good. That impulse, however, does not immediately develop in us.
>
> [T]he good impulse accompanies a person from the day he begins to purify himself. When is that? when he becomes thirteen years old. Then he joins with both of them, one on the right and one on the left: good impulse on the right, evil impulse on the left. These are two real angels, empowered, accompanying a person constantly.[490]

The *yetzer hatov*, the will to goodness, appears in us only when we are mature enough to have developed an ethical conscience. For traditional Judaism, that is at the age of *bar mitzvah*, the age when one becomes obligated to the *mitzvot* and is expected to be morally sensitive to their meaning.

One of the most empowering implications of the natural link between evil and the rest of Creation follows directly from the insight that evil is an inextricable part of us, as well as of the world around us. Evil, channeled correctly, leads to the power to build a house; evil, managed by the nurturance of the impulse to good and the discipline of *mitzvot*, is not overpowering. Most of all, as we have seen, evil is not demonic; it is not outside the normal order. Every bar mitzvah boy can learn how to fight it, by balancing it with good. Every one of us is needed; every one of us is given a key to establishing the world of goodness, the world in which all the *Sefirot* are linked and balanced, and the energy, the *shefa'*, flowing through them gushes freely upon us. If we do not act for good, the connections are plugged by the detritus of evil acts, and slowly but surely we lose our ability to act for the good, buried under a million small cynical acts and despairing moments. In our very creation, we hold the links "to what is outermost and ... what is innermost":

> The keys are in the hands of humankind, both the keys to what is outermost and the keys to what is innermost. The significance of the opening is not for the individual alone; the work is holy, because its essence is answering the need on high, to unify the Great Name in all its strength unto Ayn Sof. This is [done] by way of Torah and the fulfillment of its *mitzvot*; her roots are the secret of the emanation which is emitted for humankind. It is the image and likeness of the Highest. By way of Torah and *mitzvot* the upper power is awakened and, as it were, strengthened ... if, God forbid, Israel sins, then there is a separation between those who should be

cleaving [the *Sefirot*] and the *Shekhinah*, as it were, is in exile.[491]

There can be no greater good than this: to keep the connection open and vital between us and God. All that is required is to take life, and the power of our acts, seriously.

We must be constantly aware that the world's fate is in the balance in every act. This is why it is taught in Hasidism that cynicism is a terrible sin: it robs one of the ability to take one's every act as seriously as its ramifications may indicate. Consider a small pebble thrown into a pond: its ripples will extend far beyond a small rock's scope. Chaos theory offers us the "butterfly effect": that a butterfly flapping its wings in Madagascar can theoretically, with the right climatic conditions, cause a cascading effect of air molecules that will lead to a hurricane. Jewish mystical teachings on good and evil see each of our acts in this same way. We must constantly regard each of our acts, words, and thoughts as contributing to the good of the world, or to the evil that can destroy it. The mystics see the promise of the closeness to God that they seek, *devekut*, in the Torah's words:

> This *mitzvah* which I command you this day is not hidden from you, nor is it far off. It is not in heaven, that you should say, "Who shall go up for us to heaven, and bring it to us, that we may hear it, and do it?" Nor is it beyond the sea, that you should say, "Who shall go over the sea for us, and bring it to us, that we may hear it, and do it?" The word is very near to you, in your mouth, and in your heart, that you may do it. ... I call heaven and earth to witness this day against you: I have set before you life and death, blessing and curse. Choose life, that both you and your seed may live; that you may love the Lord your God, and that you may obey his voice, and that you may cleave to him.[492]

Blessing and curse are both possible outcomes of our path through life. Our personal fate and the fate of the world depends on our acts – our choice to accept our obligation to fulfill the commandments in a way that nurtures life. The entirety of the Jewish mystical view of evil can be summed up in this way:

> The *Zohar* sees evil as originating in justice itself, when that justice is not tempered with compassionate loving-kindness. The force of *din* within God has a legitimate role, punishing the wicked and setting out to limit the indiscriminate love-flow of *hesed*, which itself can be destructive if not held in proper balance. But once *din* has escaped the demands of love, it is no longer to be trusted. It then becomes a perversion of God's justice.[493]

Evil is the imposition of judgment without love; it is the inevitable product of focusing on the letter of the law until its spirit is crushed. But the impulse to evil, tempered correctly, becomes the necessary strength behind the necessity for *Din*, judgment, as well as the self-control necessary for discipline.

Obedience – Discipline - Creativity

Gevurah has an important place in the balancing of right and left in the *Sefirot*. The Baal Shem Tov described the interactive stance of the *Sefirot* using the example of how a human thought develops.

The thinking process unfolds along this lines of the ten *Sefirot*. Your ideas are conceived in *Abba* and *Imma* [i.e. *Hokhmah* and *Binah*]. Therefore, the spark of an original Torah insight is called *Abba* and *Imma*. Your initial thought then expands in your mind and soars in all directions in an untamed flow of consciousness, in line with the *Sefirah* of *Hesed*. But now you need the power of the *Sefirah* of *Gevurah* to restrain and inhibit your free-flowing thoughts so that you can organize them, put them into words, and explain them to others. This gives you the serenity of *Tiferet*. At this point you need faith [and the inner conviction to convey your thoughts]. Faith is symbolized by the *Sefirot* of *Netzakh* and *Hod*, the "two thighs of truth" [the pillars that support the body]. The gratification you get from innovating your own Torah thoughts is akin to the *Sefirah Yesod*, which is symbolic of the male organ. Finally, you articulate your novel idea through speech, which conforms to *Malkhut*, the *Sefirah* of the mouth, the organ of speech.[494]

The scholar Louis Jacobs explained the idea of containment in thought as one's "internal editor". *Tzimtzum* is not only the process required of God to create the world, it is also the process required of human creativity. If it is to be coherent, it must be limited.

> When the idea is finally pinned down by the mind, when it is limited and thus saved from vagueness, a process operates in the mind similar to that of *Gevurah* in the Sefirotic realm. In this way the *tzimtzum* process is repeated in man's creative thinking. By controlling his thoughts and arranging them in ordered sequence so that they can be communicated to others, he repeats the *tzimtzum* process and mirrors it.[495]

It is striking to consider that, along with the logical proposition that good and evil are equal and balancing powers that occur in our world, there is another, deeper insight into *Gevurah* and creation here.

In the Torah's creation story we see clearly that darkness precedes the "let there be light" moment when the unfolding, developing new Creation is illuminated; for the *Zohar*, the initial spark of creation itself is a *botzina d'kardinuta*, "spark of impenetrable darkness."[496] The spark of creation is itself a spark of darkness, not light.

The mystics explore this paradoxical idea, that it is only from a necessary, pre-existing darkness that light emerges. "That light," the light that was commanded into existence on the second day and existed before, and independent of, the sun and the moon, "radiated from the midst of darkness hewn by truncheons of the Concealed of All". Divine blows carved the darkness "until a single secret path," a path identified as the emanation of that primordial light down toward the world, "was carved by the hidden light, leading to darkness below, where light dwells".[497] The "darkness below" is the last, lowest, closest *sefirah*, *Malkhut*, which, like the moon associated with her, receives and reflects light but does not radiate any herself. Paradoxically, it is in this place of darkness, *Malkhut*, that "light dwells."

This sense that one sees light only out of darkness, that creation itself comes forth from a contained place, offers insight not only into the artist's craft but also into the ongoing artistry that is Jewish interpretation of Torah, especially legal interpretation. *Halakhah*, Jewish law, literally means "path"; it is the continuing journey of understanding and fulfilling God's will, as presented in the system of *mitzvot* which expresses and demonstrates the covenantal relationship. Fulfilling the *mitzvot* properly is a creative process, and that creativity is vital to the mystics, because the *mitzvot* are our only way to participate in the sefirotic system and add our energy to it, so that the *shefa'* on which our own lives, and our world, depend, will flow down to us in return.

Complexity

The Israelite understanding of God and what God wants, as demonstrated in the Torah, is far from static. It grows, as does the individual's capacity to understand and respond to her world; it evolves, as does the community's ability to comprehend its limits and its potential. For the mystics, the universe itself is ever-growing, expanding from a small point of wisdom into the endless flow of *shefa'*, from that beginning point until now. The mystical description of the universe's growth is surprisingly similar to the understanding developed by modern physics: "in its own way, the big bang is a contemporary Creation story."[498]

In Judaism growth as a basic principle is manifest in a number of ways. Consider the Tree of the Knowledge of Good and Evil. The evidence of the Bible is that "knowledge of good and evil" is identified with moral awareness, and not only sexual knowledge – both essential for the process of human growth toward maturity.[499] Growth, for an individual, or for a community, or for a religious tradition, is not necessarily painless; but matters of exile and redemption are not for children. Scholars of *Halakhah* such as Menakhem Elon[500] and Moshe Halbertal[501] have shown that Jewish law is an organic entity, in which historical periods of creative expansion are followed by resting and consolidation of the new parameters and new understandings – just as an individual human being breathes in, expanding the lungs and chest and incorporating new molecules of oxygen into his or her system, and then breathes out, and the oxygen and its energy is incorporated into the body, and waste products are jettisoned.

The concept of an ongoing process is expressed in Jewish literature as part of the nature of revelation, such that the future innovation of a bright Torah student is also part of the teaching of Sinai.[502] Certainly Jewish mysticism, with its penchant for paradox and tolerance for uncertainty, is a natural Jewish expression of the sense that we do not yet know all that there is to discover. *Hiddushim*, "innovations," are still possible only when there is uncertainty about a final meaning.

One of the practical effects of tolerating uncertainty in one's theology in a Jewish context is to make problematic the finality one expects from *Halakhah*. Law seems not to admit much in the way of uncertainty, and that is among its strengths inasmuch as law offers a clear framework for organizing individual and communal human behavior. But a certain amount of uncertainty is recognized within *Halakhah*, if only because divine law can be understood only imperfectly by human beings. Added to this assertion is the ethical impact of incorrectly applying law by dismissing context, and one begins to realize that law is not a fixed point on which we can focus our sights and relax. We do better to turn it over and consider it from a different angle, and thus test our assumptions. Philosopher Menachem Fisch[503] offers the theory that the point of the peculiar arrangement of the Jewish legal texts of the Talmud is due to the fact that the rabbis were developing a process by which Jewish life might be guided, and that the results of the process were less important to them than the process itself. Their insight was that, with a good process, results would necessarily be good, whereas if the process is not sound, the effect would be, as we might put it in modern terms, "garbage in, garbage out." This is why minority arguments are included, and why an inordinate amount of Amoraic discussion centers not on the correct ruling in a given situation but on trying to ascertain the nature of the reasoning of the Tannaim who came before them.

Unfortunately, this process has been derailed in Jewish history by an inclination to rely on results: "What is the law?" we ask, not always remembering to add "in this case" to our question. Or, worse, we declare, "This is the law," even when it is clear that in this case the law does not fit. The desire for quick clarity and the concomitant emphasis on results – the "bottom line" – leads to a lack of ability to understand and appreciate the vital role of process in a living system, whether it be law or any other human organism.

The extreme of the dismissal of process in Jewish law is the formulation of a code. The factors that led to the writing of the Mishnah and have informed attempts to create a succinct code of Jewish law since have in the past included

> the desire to restore uniformity to the law, the fear that the academic level and the number of students were declining due to new tribulations, the spread of the "kingdom of wickedness" in the world, and the aim of facilitating the knowledge and study of the *Halakhah*.[504]

Codification is a gesture of containment and restraint, to use the mystics' terms; the power of *Gevurah* protects the tradition from the ravages of human forgetfulness and worse. But *Gevurah*'s virtue is rigid strength; a law that is all *Gevurah,* according to Jewish tradition, is inhuman. And so we see inhuman results. Guarding and protecting existing *halakha* also shields it from the extensive reasoning process that was a constitutive part of its formation. The containment of *Gevurah* freezes what should be a living path – *halakha* literally means "going" – into terse statements, interrupting their natural developmental relationship with the halakhic decisors of the present, making innovation and flexibility much more difficult to achieve within the system. Trapped within the parameters of a code, law becomes "reducible to formal lawmaking," no longer generated by "a universe of meanings, values, and rules"; no longer "a word to inhabit" but merely "a body of data to master and adapt".[505] It unbalances the dialogue between past and present, between ancestors and descendants.

Interestingly, although the *halakhic* literature itself records multiple opinions on the derivation of *Halakhah* throughout, controversy over the correct *Halakhah* in a given instance is not necessarily always understood as a negative. One trend in the literature is, certainly, to describe disputes over the law as a result of inadequate learning:

> At first there were no disputes in Israel. ... once the disciples of Shammai and Hillel who did not properly serve their master became many, disputes multiplied in Israel, and they became two Torahs.[506]

But this is not the only rabbinic understanding of the nature of difference in *halakhic* discussion. It is also asserted that "controversy is not a sign of the downfall of tradition or of distance from the moment of receiving it; rather, it is part of the tradition, projected backward to the moment of revelation.

> A man might think, "Since the House of Shammai declare unclean and the House of Hillel clean, this one prohibits and this one permits, why should I henceforward learn Torah? Scripture says, "Words ... he words. ... These are the words. ..." All the words have been given by a single Shepherd, one God created them, one Provider gave them, the Lord of all deeds, blessed be He, has spoken them. So you build many chambers in your heart and bring into it the words of the House of Shammai and the w who ords of the House of Hillel, the words of those who declare unclean and the words of those declare clean.[507]

This text seems to be trying to say that the understanding of the law as ideally monolithic is a vision that is not sustainable in its application to a large community of variable human beings – and that a monolithic law is not God's will.

It is inevitable that halakhic simplicity and certainty will be victims of the system's successful growth, since "once the disciples ... became many," "disputes" would follow, since each new community of Jews adopting the system would bring a new set of factors to which the *Halakhah* would be applied. This understanding of the multiplicity of halakhic meanings, the contradictory plurality of halakhic reasonings, and the variety of halakhic rulings are not as lamentably unavoidable as we might think but are as necessary and appropriate part of the system itself. "Dispute," or *makhloket*, is considered in Jewish tradition to be a vital part of good decision-making, or at least, according to the mystics, an inevitable part of *tzimtzum*. "All the words," in another famous passage, "*elu v'elu*," are of "the living God."[508] Significantly, the continuation of the *elu v'elu* passage explains that the *Halakhah* is in accordance with the House of Hillel not because they are correct halakhically, but because "they teach their rulings and also those of the House of Shammai, and what is more, they give the rulings of the House of Shammai first, before their own." At least one of the definitive reasons why the *Halakhah* of the House of Hillel is to be followed, therefore, is that the rabbis of that school offer more than one opinion.

The historical transition from rulings that relied on primary learning to those based on secondary, summary sources led to a distancing from those primary voices. If the halakhic process is to be understood as such, that is, as a growing and developing system, then the natural and understandable impulse toward codification must be guarded as would be any other *yetzer*, and kept within moderate parameters. Definitive answers must be understood as relatively applicable, and the background any code seeks to simplify must nevertheless be crucial to the final understanding of the legal issue. If we remain mired in the certainty that has characterized modern *Halakhah*, we will see only more inhuman results: *agunot*,[509] *mamzerim*,[510] and the perennial oppression of converts, Russians, and others through the "who is a Jew" issue.

The mystical treatment of paradox and uncertainty expresses the strain of that consciousness that runs through all of Jewish thought, and reminds us that what is called for in us is not some obsession with getting it exactly right but remembering in humility that such is beyond us. For us the situation is not either/or, it is both/and, and we need to hold these opposites together in our minds. Neither side of any *makhloket* covers all the ground; but in a good conflict, a conflict "for the sake of heaven", they are both necessary, because they are polar opposites which inform and balance each other, and we are called upon to consider carefully how best to apply law, or theological insight, in each situation, with respect for the uniqueness of each situation.

As each of us is a unique stamp of the Creator's image, the human condition of each of us requires investigation of its unique details. As the insights of mysticism remind us, it is the balance that is vital. The balance between principle and application, between process and result, and between text and context, must be maintained. Most of all, we must find a way to restrain in ourselves the evil impulse to control others by insisting that they fit into predetermined definitions.

There were two conflicts: one, beginning; one, ending. This is the way of the righteous: beginning harshly, ending gently. Korakh was the beginning of the conflict: seething in wrath, he was compelled to cling to Hell. Shammai was the end of the conflict, when wrath subsides and one must arouse the conflict of love and be reconciled by heaven.[511]

Korakh, a Levite who is cousin to Moses and Aaron and a member of the priesthood, is characterized in midrash as the ultimate example of a Biblical rebel[512] who used democratic language but whose ulterior motive was personal advancement. Shammai disagreed with his colleague Hillel on every conceivable matter of *Halakhah*, but their conflicts were celebrated as "for the sake of Heaven."[513] The conflict of love is found in "the tension between left and right, [which,] when resolved, yields the harmony of *Tiferet*, also known as *Rakhamim*, Compassion, who eventually unites with *Shekhinah*."[514]

Abraham Joshua Heschel wrote in defense of religious complexity: "one thing God has spoken, two things have I heard":

> Just as we are obligated to observe, so are we required to remember. The Torah cannot be fulfilled unless one safeguards the plain meaning of the text and also remembers the revelation at Sinai. Torah can only be acquired in two ways: with reason's lens and the heart's

lens. One who is blind in one eye is exempt from the pilgrimage.

Here is another rule of thumb: there is no verbalization of wisdom that does not contain within it both give and take, that does not both wax and wane. Negative statements have positive connotations, and vice versa. Thought develops only through dialectic: through the synthesis of concept that are opposed to one another and complement one another. A knife can be sharpened only by the blade of its counterpart.[515]

Heschel cites the Talmudic axiom, "A controversy that is for a heavenly purpose will in the end endure."[516] Agreement, then, seems to indicate shallow thinking, at best. The insight that one must bring a mystical tolerance for complexity to halakhic thinking if one would plumb its depths is articulated by one of the greatest mystics and halakhists:

> When the blessed God gave the Torah to Israel, every matter in the Torah was given just as it was, meaning that God said that this particular case has within it an aspect of innocence and an aspect of guilt; in matters of ritual prohibition, it was said that a particular case has an aspect of permissiveness and as aspect of prohibition, and similarly in matters relating to family relationships: there were always opposing aspects. Just as in the world generally, everything is composed of opposing elements ... and you will not find any completely simple substance, so in the Torah there is no such thing as something so completely impure that it has no pure facet to it, though it has a facet of impurity as well. when one examines something from the point of view of purity, and applies his intellect to proving its purity, he has revealed one aspect of it ... and when another gives reasons for saying "impure" of the same object, he has revealed another aspect of it. And that is what it

means to say that all were said from the mouth of the Master of all.[517]

"A foolish consistency is the hobgoblin of little minds," declared Ralph Waldo Emerson. A similarly foolish insistence on certainty will throw off our *Sefirotic* vision, obstructing the balance between our need for certainty and our ability to open the gates to the World to Come.

Balancing Gevurah and Hesed

To balance *Gevurah* and *Hesed* requires both the strength and the courage to judge *and* to show mercy. In our own human communities, we clearly demonstrate that some of us are drawn more toward *Hesed*, and some toward *Din*. Mystics see the balancing as between *hesed*, "mercy," and *pakhad*, "fear." This is not the fear, *yir'ah*, that is rooted in reverence, but the more basic, "lower" fear of punishment.

Avraham admonishes humankind with the attribute of *hesed*, while Yitzhak rebukes humankind with the attribute of *pakhad*. Each one urges the community in accordance with his attribute: one through the attribute of *hesed* and reward, the other through *pakhad* and punishment; one through the positive commandments, the other through the negative commandments.[518]

Both of these qualities, fear of punishment and awe, appear in the Biblical use of the term *yir'ah;* in rabbinic development, *yirat shamayim* refers to a religious sense of ethics and right conduct.[519] Simple *yir'ah*, fear, of God, is considered the least developed impetus for obedience to Divine Law, but it does serve a function, at the very least, to keep one from sinning.

> Let him incline his heart upwards, to the other place from which he was created, that he might come to know his Creator who created him from nothing [*ayin*], and let him understand and know that the Holy One sees his deeds, and that all is known before Him, every secret of the heart and every thought, and all his deeds are

> written in a book, and in the future judgment will be brought before him for every trivial conversation that ever came out of his mouth. Let him see his Creator before him always, and let him be in fear, and tremble in dread, as it is written, "I have set Adonai always before me" (Psalm 17.8). Thus he will restrain himself from transgressions, and conquer it [the evil impulse].[520]

Ideally, one should rise above such fear in a life of moral growth. But the power of fear to undermine love and mercy can skew the world dangerously off balance. When a person who is ruled by fear has power, the results are uniformly disastrous in human history.

In any human community, people demonstrate different strengths and different tendencies. On any committee, philosophical disagreements show us more about the fundamental leanings of each person toward *Hesed* or *Gevurah* than about the subject at hand. As in the cosmos itself, different aspects of reality each have a place where they are clearly expressed; the challenge is in the overall balance of the world, and of the committee.

> When Yaakov Avinu [Jacob our Father] came, there was no third attribute for him to cling to, so he attached himself to both the attributes of Avraham and Yitzhak, *Hesed* and *Pakhad,* and he announced to the world the significance of their truth, and never veered to the right or the left.[521]

Because Jacob could balance the attributes represented by his ancestors, he is identified in Jewish mysticism with *emet,* "truth." He is described in the Torah as a man who "dwelled in tents"[522]: he knew how to be at home in both the tent of *Hesed* and that of *Gevurah.*

The third patriarch is also called *tam,* a word meaning "simple," "innocent," "perfect." Here the mystics see the essential quality that defined Jacob. To reconcile the two *Sefirot,* one must learn "how to perceive the unity hidden in the world and how to transform the ego.

In other words, one must think of oneself as simple and minimize one's own ego.

One of the founders of Hasidism, Dov Baer, the Maggid ("preacher") of Mezeritch (in the Ukraine), encouraged his followers to look at the self differently. Playing with the Hebrew letters of *aniy,* the word for "I," the Maggid permutes them into *ayin,* challenging his listeners to reconfigure the ego. Only by attaining awareness of *ayin* can one imitate and express the boundless nature of God.[523]

Heschel describes the *Sefirot* as three columns of various shades of light. Din is on the left side, in the column that is devoid of light.

> The *Sefirot* are divided into a *right* column, signifying Mercy, or light, a *left* column, signifying Severity, the absence of light, and a *central* column, signifying the synthesis of the right and left.[524]

This description is reminiscent of the mystical teaching about the quality of the light that is reserved for the righteous. It is a light that was too intense for the world in which we live. Our lives are a play of light within shadows, and shadowed light.

Hesed – The Gate of Mercy

GRACE – FREE-FLOWING LOVE OF GOD – GREATNESS (GEDULAH) – MERCY – ABRAHAM – GENEROSITY – OPENHEARTEDNESS – RIGHT HAND

> *b'shem yikhudo shel Kudsha Berikh Hu v'Shekhintey – for the sake of the unification of mercy and judgment, of outpouring and ingathering, of abundance and containment*

Grace – Free-Flowing Love of God – Greatness (Gedulah) – Mercy

> Because What Do I Know about Love
> Except that we are at sea in it –

and parched for its lack?

Let down your buckets, my dears.
Haul up the sweet, swaying spill.

Tilt your face to the stream.
Be washed. Be drenched. Turn loose

the dripping dogs to shake
themselves among you.

Flood the decks; fill the cisterns.
Then drink, and find it fresh.

You have sailed all unknowing
into your home river.[525]

Hesed is the free-flowing, abundant, unstinting, unconditional love of God. While *Din* necessarily judges correct limits to this flooding, overwhelming cloudburst of mercy, rising toward *Hesed* requires an understanding that the world cannot exist on the basis of strict justice. According to the Sages, if the world were to be judged strictly for even one moment, it would cease to exist.

> [S]aid the Holy One, Blessed be He, "If I create the world with compassion, its sins will be great; if with judgment, how will the world exist? Rather, behold, I create it with a measure of judgment and a measure of compassion, and then, may it long endure."

Hesed exists over and against *Din,* as its *ezer k'negdo,* its equal and supportive partner. *Din,* the power of judgment, cannot be justly expressed without the influence of *hesed,* the power of love; conversely, *Hesed,* which flows forth without constraint, cannot be withstood if it is not measured and limited by the restraining hand of *Din*.

Hesed is a word found throughout Jewish liturgy; we seek God's *khen*, *hesed* and *rakhamim*. These word are alliterative but not synonymous. Their meaning, and their English translations, flow together in Jewish prayer even as the *shefa'* that transmits them flows forth: "grace, mercy and compassion." The Psalms assert: "*hesed* will build the world."[526] Acts of *gemilut hasadim*, "loving kindness", are one of the three pillars that uphold the stability of the entire world. The centrality of this attribute, and its location beyond that which is merely just, cannot be too strongly emphasized: "All pathways to *YHVH* are *hesed*."[527] The mystic Gikatilla explains that "*hesed* is that which is done by someone who acts even though it is not required from the perspective of *din*, but rather is done of one's own desire and one's own will without coercion, for the sake of goodness."[528]

Hesed is a higher level than *din;* it requires a more fully developed, deeper understanding. To be generous requires more courage than to judge; this is the step beyond judgment, where it is balanced by the vulnerability required of us in order to be open to others. *Hesed* is practiced against a background of poignancy; grace appears awkwardly among us, in precious, barely articulated moments. Given the hierarchy of the *Sefirot*, this is not a "low" level, nor is it easy to reach; it is a level we begin to achieve only after we have learned to see beauty (*Hod*), feel compassion (*Tiferet*), and accept limitation (*Din*).

The conflicting tendencies that require balancing at this level are many; navigating between them without losing one's balance is difficult. And so much depends on it.

> Freedom and law, possibility and necessity: these are the poles between which the electric current of redemption must run ... this means a dialectical tension between *peshat* (plain meaning) and midrashic narrative. In philosophical or psychological terms, this means an awareness of the tension between "finitude and infinitude," to use Kierkegaard's expression. The central issue ... is freedom: "freedom is the dialectical aspect of

the categories of possibility and necessity." Each mode has its own danger, its form of despair.
Between finitude and infinitude, possibility and necessity, we struggle for authentic freedom."[529]

And, we might add, for an authentic sense of mercy.

Life is experienced at this level through a heightened awareness of love, as expressed in the daily prayers: *ahavah rabah ahavtanu*, "You have loved us greatly," *v'ha'eyr eyneynu b'Toratekha, v'dabek libeynu b'mitzvotekha*, "open our eyes in the light of your Torah, cause our hearts to attach to your *mitzvot*."[530] We can know great love, if we are open to receiving it. This highest form of connecting to God is not beyond or despite the everyday level of fulfilling the *mitzvot* that are expected of every Jew; rather, it is precisely through fulfilling the *halakkhah*, as expressed in the *mitzvot*, that a Jew comes to know God, and to love God. It takes time to develop this love; each *mitzvah* done "with all your heart, with all your being, with all your resources"[531] is a step that brings one closer to an unending river of *shefa'*, inviting us to immerse ourselves in it.

> One may love a river as soon as one sets eyes upon it; it may have certain features that fit instantly with one's conception of beauty, or it may recall the qualities of some other river, well known and deeply loved. One may feel in the same way an instant affinity for a man or a woman and know that here is pleasure and warmth and the foundation of deep friendship. In either case the full riches of the discovery are not immediately released - they cannot be; only knowledge and close experience can release them. Rivers, I suppose, are not at all like human beings, but it is still possible to make apt comparisons, and this is one: understanding, whether instinctive or grown by conscious effort, is a necessary preliminary to love. Understanding of another human

being can never be complete, but as it grows toward completeness, it becomes love almost inevitably.[532]

It is all the same love, for the mystics: one loves the world, another person, God, out of the same overflowing heart. "If someone tells you he loves God, but hates his neighbor, don't believe him," warns one piquant Hasidic saying.

For the mystics the *mitzvot* do not obstruct one's relationship with God; rather, as the prayer indicates, it was an act of love on God's part to provide us the pathway by which we can attach ourselves to God. *Halakhah* means "path" - not simply a path through life that is mindful and ethical, but a way of making every act of one's life part of the trail one's life blazes toward the ultimate light of God. [T]he Holy One made us holy through His commandments and attributes, and when we make our acts and attributes like those of our Creator, we achieve *devekut* [attachment] to the Holy One. "Become attached to His attributes" (BT *Sotah* 14a). The *mitzvah* is so called because it indicates connection and *devekut* as in the verse: "they are a linking of grace ..." (Proverbs 1.9). God's giving us the *mitzvot* was an act of unearned love. The Holy One offers Israel merit that by way of the *mitzvot* out of a love drawn from *Hesed*. The 613 commandments purify the 248 limbs and 365 sinews in a person. In this way we achieve the love of God.[533]

Abraham – Generosity – Openheartedness

In the Torah we find that *Hesed* is the attribute demonstrated by Abraham's practice of desert hospitality. The Patriarch kept his tent flaps open for all strangers:

> God appeared to him by the terebinths[534] of Mamre, as he sat in the tent door in the heat of the day. He lifted up his eyes and looked, and saw three men in the distance; and when he saw them, he ran to meet them from the tent door. Bowing down to the earth, he said: "My lord, if now I have found favor in your sight, do

not go on, I pray you, from your servant. Let a little water be fetched, and wash your feet, and recline under the tree. I will fetch a bit of bread to sustain you, and after that go on your journey – since you have come by your servant." And they assented, saying: "Do as you have said."[535]

In this account, the grammatical ambiguity regarding Abraham's visitor is resolved by Jewish tradition with the explanation that the "men" who visited Abraham were actually angels bringing him God's message – or, possibly, literally an embodied manifestation of God.[536] The mystical interpretation is significantly different, informed as it is by the medieval teaching that we are each *helek Eloha mima'al,* "a part of God from above." The mystical interpretation, informed as it is by the medieval teaching that we are each *helekh Eloha mima'al,* "a part of God from above", maintain that what Abraham saw were three men who each reflected the divine image. They were not angels, but unique and precious human beings, possessed of a divine spark within them, as we all are. What makes Abraham a *tzaddik,* a righteous man, was not the special nature of the visitors, but the special ability of Abraham to see a stranger as a valuable human being, worthy of respect and care.

There are qualitatively different accounts of *Hesed* demonstrated throughout our sources, and the kind that Abraham demonstrates is the highest of all. As we compare instances of the term found elsewhere in the Torah and Tanakh, *hesed* is seen to be a quality of merciful treatment resulting from the mutual regard expected between covenanted partners, or, more broadly, between members of the same tribe. *Hesed* is practiced between those who have some sort of common bond. *Hesed,* then, can be Biblically defined, in a minimalist way, simply as "taking care of tribal kin."[537] This understanding of *hesed* is called by the mystics *hasdei Zion,* and we find it expressed by the *mitzvot* of the covenant experience. When God makes a covenant with the descendants of Abraham, God shows them mercy for the sake of their ancestor, who was God's friend.

Of the three levels of *Hesed* defined by Jewish mystical tradition, *hesed Avraham* occupies a high level, flowing forth into the daily life of the world and asserting that tribal bonds are no boundary to *Hesed*. *Hesed Avraham* challenges the reasonable limitations of *Din* with a never-ending expansion of generosity, reaching out to strangers and practicing "random acts of kindness and senseless beauty" as a popular bumper sticker urges. The highest kind of *hesed, hesed Elyon,* comes forth directly from above, and showers itself paradigmatically upon Abraham. The first Patriarch experiences a radically different kind of *hesed* from God, who, for no reason given in the text, chooses Abraham to be the recipient of fame, fortune, offspring and a land to raise them on. Abraham simply is the Chosen One of God, and God showers upon him an abundance of blessing. This "*hesed* from above" with which Abraham is blessed for no reason is unalloyed with judgment; it simply exists to flow forth. Abraham receives *hesed Elyon* from God, and, as an open and joyful channel of *shefa'*, he transmits *hesed Avraham* in turn, through his own behavior. *Hesed Avraham* is a quality somewhere in between God's *hesed Elyon* and the "lower" *hasdei Zion* of Jewish daily life as defined by the *mitzvot*. *Hesed Avraham,* the *hesed* of Abraham, incorporates both the upper and the lower forms of *hesed*. In the story of Abraham's life we see the human balancing of heaven and earth, in the oscillation, back and forth, of the quality of the *Sefirah Hesed* that he is able to express.

Early in the story of Abraham in Genesis, he is described as responding to the command to *lekh l'kha*, to "go forth":

> Abram took his wife Sarai, his nephew Lot, and all their belongings that they had gathered, and the souls that they had acquired [*asu*, literally, "made"] in Haran. They went forth toward the land of Canaan.[538]

Rashi explains that *hanefesh asher 'asu*, "the souls they had gotten," means

> they caused them to enter beneath the wings of the *Shekhinah* – Abraham converted the men and Sarah

converted the women, and it was accounted to them as if they had created (*'asu*) them.[539]

Because they are the first members of this new covenant relationship with God, Abraham and Sarah have no kin to whom to restrict their practice of *hesed;* they offer it to all who cross their path. Those who respond become their followers and companions in the *lekh l'kha* journey. Even later, when Abraham's camp is large, he continues to reach out beyond family, an attitude symbolized by those open tent flaps. Abraham's generous openness in his practice of *hesed* is modeled on the inexplicable *hesed* God showed him.

There is another aspect of *hesed Avraham* with which we are acquainted: there is in this level a lack of clarity of transmission of the attribute. The difficult balance of *hesed* and *din* is played out in the story of the *Akedat Yitzhak,* the binding and near-sacrifice of Isaac by his usually loving and merciful father, Abraham. Whether we understand this story as Rashi does, as due to Abraham's having misunderstood God's command, or whether we detect in it a lesson about how parents can be so blind to their children as nearly to sacrifice them to their own parental vision, in either case the price is fearful for Isaac.

Hesed Avraham is a attribute that reaches out into in the world beyond the safe place of the tribe, a *Hesed* that seeks God in every passerby; it is much more a "shot in the dark" precisely because it reaches out to the unknown. It exists without reason, and it flows forth without limit. Therefore it must be translated through *Din*. It is a kind of *Hesed* that is difficult and sloppy, because without *Din* it cannot be withstood, and it must be mediated by *Din* without creating destructive results.

The ultimate significance of this balance can be expressed through the relationship between the Hebrew words *pakhad,* fear, and *hesed,* mercy. They share two letters in common: *khet* and *dalet*. According to the mystics' Hebrew/Aramaic dialect, these two letters spell out the word *khad,* Aramaic for "one." Each of these attributes, *din* and *hesed,* are easily misconstrued as the Whole of the One, the Most Important Attribute of Existence. It is easy for us to see *Din*, judgment, problematic, because of the dangers we have traced which are born of it. But *Hesed* cannot exist in the world as a pure substance; we could not survive it. Consider the simple act of breathing: oxygen is an ultimate good – one cannot live without it. But if one only breathed in, one could not survive. *Hesed* is like breathing in; each inhalation must be balanced by an exhalation. *Din* is exhalation; it is the limitation of the good; it is that which makes the good *good*.

This is a difficult lesson for us, the concept that endless good is not good, at least in this world of our human existence. It is written that we know the good only because we also know bad; Jewish ethics teaches that we are all naturally composed of a *yetzer ra'*, an evil impulse, and a *yetzer tov*, a good impulse – and that we cannot banish the *yetzer ra'*, since it is an essential part of our human nature. Rather, we have to learn to balance them. The stakes? We return to the words *pakhad* and *hesed*. The letters that are unique to each word, the *samekh* of *hesed* and the *pei* of *pakhad*, come together to spell *saf*, "threshold." That which is unique in each of these two attributes must be recognized and respected; each is as real and necessary as they are irreconcilable. Unless we reconcile *Din*'s quality of judgment and *Hesed*'s opposing quality of mercy, we will not cross over this threshold toward *Binah*, the attribute of Understanding, and thus toward a higher and deeper awareness of the purpose of our lives.

The ultimate expression of the *Hesed* of God is, as the Psalm hinted, the existence of the world. *Hesed* is

> "the *tzedakah* of God" (Deut. 33.21), His mercies and kindness with the entire world. This is the right hand of God.[540]

The idea of the *tzedakah* of God is intriguing, since *tzedakah* is understood in Jewish tradition as both righteousness and justice, and, in a derivative sense, as "charity." And perhaps that is the only explanation for the gift of our lives, as an act of "charity," altruistic and bestowed regardless of the worth of the recipient. How else can we understand such a gift except as an act of love, given unconditionally, undeserved and nearly unbelievable?

The emergence of God from hiding is an act filled with love, a promise of the endless showering of blessing and life on all beings, each of whom will continue this process of emerging from the One. This gift of love is beyond measure and without limit, the boundless compassion of *keter* now transposed into a love for each specific form and creature that is ever to emerge. This channel of grace is the original divine *shefa'*, the bounteous love of God of which the Psalmist says: "his mercies are over all his works." We too, as we emerge from oneness, are filled with love for each and every creature.[541]

We are told in the story of creation that we are reflections of God, created in God's image; the Jewish teaching derived from this is, simply, that we reflect God. We ourselves are vessels of *Hesed,* and our function as God's image in the world is to let God's *Hesed* fill us and flow through us into the world. Of course, our human capacity for love and mercy is a pale shadow of God's. So is a small stream but a tiny hint of the mighty and far-away sea. But the one flows with the same water as the other.

How does one reflect God's *Hesed* into the world? Jewish tradition translates the idea of our being commanded to be like God because we are created in God's image into specific, concrete terms:

R. Hama, son of R. Hanina, further said, "What does the text mean: 'You shall walk after the Eternal your God?'" (Deut. 13.5) Is it, then, possible for a human being to walk after the *Shekhinah*; for has it not been said, "For the Eternal your God is a devouring fire"? (Deut. 4.24). But [the meaning is] to walk after the attributes of the Holy One, blessed be He. As He clothes the naked, for it is written: "the Eternal God made for Adam and for his wife coats of skin, and clothed them" (Gen. 3.21), so should you also clothe the naked. The Holy One, blessed be He, visited the sick, for it is written: "the Eternal appeared unto him by the oaks of Mamre" (Gen. 18.1), so should you also visit the sick. The Holy One, blessed be He, comforted mourners, for it is written: "It came to pass after the death of Abraham, that God blessed Isaac his son" (Gen. 25.11), so should you also comfort mourners. The

Holy one, blessed be He, buried the dead, for it is written: "He buried him in the valley" (Deut. 34.6), so should you also bury the dead.[542] This is a classic text, illuminating much about how mysticism inspires the practice of Jewish ethics. First, what does it mean to "walk after God"? One might guess that this is an exhortation to follow God's laws to the letter, or in some way to become God centered, and separated from everyday worldly concerns. But for R. Hama, to walk after God is to be like God, to follow after and imitate God's "attributes," or ethical qualities (*middot*). To understand the mystical implications of a human being acting as a reflection of God in the world is to read the descriptions of God's attributes and understand that they are also one's own attributes. It is to read about God's acts of kindness and see in them one's own marching orders. This passage is a definitive description of God's *Hesed*, and of the way in which human beings who are connected to it become themselves conduits of God's *shefa'*, the abundance of God's presence, allowing the messenger to convey blessing not only to the world, but also to its source.

> Love is the root of unification... Unification, which is the ultimate goal and purpose, depends upon the doing of the *mitzvot* and their activation. They come from the side of *hesed*, and this is the great secret of love. ... the *mitzvot* are done for the sake of the need on high, and the need of humanity.[543]

Right Hand

Physically, the *sefirah* of *hesed* is associated with the right arm, not only of God but of the human being. Located on the right side of the *Sefirot*, it carries all the expected connotations with which we are familiar: to be on the right is to be, literally, right, not wrong. To be right is to be favored, special. The favored one "sits at the right hand"; the one on which we can depend is "like my right hand." Of course, none of this holds true for those of us who are left-handed, but we'll entertain the metaphor for now, while remaining conscious of its limits.

The "right hand of God" is the power hand; it vanquishes foes, rescues one from destruction, and is eternally as reliable as it is awesome. This is the quality that split the Sea. How may we compare this idea to our own sense of the significance of our right hand – or, shall we say, the dominant hand, whichever it may be? Consider what our dominant hand does: it is a primary physical connector between the individual and the world in physical, concrete terms. An outstretched hand brings either help or harm, depending on its intent. The *birkat hamazon*, the blessing after meals, implores God to "open your hand and sustain every living creature."

Rising Requires Recognition of All That Is a Part of Me

One of the teachings that emerges from the sefirotic structure and its multilevel connectedness is that one cannot rise toward God except by way of the integration of each vessel, and each channel, as one seeks to advance. Only after one discovers how to achieve a sense of balance in one's life, on any level, can one reach forward. This is a lesson clearly taught on the physical level: one's two feet must be firmly planted before one can reach forward with one's hands toward the fruit one would pick from the tree, or to caress a loved one's face.

It is interesting to consider the color white, with which *Hesed* is associated, at this point. *Hesed* is the highest of the emotional attributes, and this higher attribute contains within it all the aspects of the attributes beneath it, even though it might seem to us that it has overcome them and left them behind. In truth, one cannot reach the level of *Hesed*, either to express it or to understand that one receives it, unless one holds within oneself the integrity of all the lower attributes, held in balance and in their proper development. This is just the same as the color white, which seems to be empty of all color but, in reality, contains within it all the colors of the spectrum within it.

Similarly, we seem to be individuals, yet we contain within us all the colors of our personal, familial, and communal interactions within us. Understanding this foundational concept, that we are individuals who harbor worlds of connectedness to others within us as part of our very essence, moves us above the level of emotion and toward the intellect, the highest of the *Sefirot*. The level toward which we move now is *Binah*, Understanding and Deepest Source of Return, and the Womb of the Universe. To achieve this rising we must come to know that we cannot get there alone. The example of group prayer is revealing:

The congregation acts like a circle of dancers giving constant support to one another, helping the individual to overcome weariness and continue further than one might do alone. The Ba'al Shem Tov explains this by means of a parable: In order to reach the heights, the worshippers create a kind of human ladder, each one standing on the shoulders of the next, thus enabling the individual to climb high. nyone who leaves this ladder not only removes a rung, but destroys the entire ladder. On the other hand, one who finds a congregation suited to his prayers is invigorated and elevated through it and by his participation in it.[544]

The Meeting of Hesed and Binah

The meeting of *Hesed*, the highest of the second triad of *Sefirot*, and *Binah*, the lowest of the highest level of *Sefirot*, forms a bridge from the world of emotion to that of the intellect. One can only hope to rise toward *Binah*, Understanding, if one has calmed the emotional currents of the soul. Strong emotion, especially anger, is a great danger from which one should shield oneself.

Anger, in contradistinction to sins that pollute only the body, pollutes also the soul and, in fact, the whole being.[545] Even when it is permissible to be angry, that is, when one has a justifiable reason, one should still "not hold on" to it.

This idea is comparable to our sages' explanation of the verse "When you see the donkey of your hated enemy struggling under his load ..., *azov ta'azov imo*, "you shall surely help him" (*Shemot* 23.5). They explain the cause of the hatred mentioned in the verse as being that he saw his enemy transgressing, and, being a lone witness, he cannot testify in the rabbinical court. Thus, he is permitted to hate the fellow as regards his sin. Even so, the Torah demands, *azov ta'azov imo*, "you shall surely help him", meaning, "abandon – *azov* – the anger in your heart." It is a *mitzvah* to draw the person closer with love, for perhaps this method will be effective. This is exactly the attribute of "He does not maintain His anger forever."[546]

Here is where *Hesed*, "mercy," and *Binah*, "understanding," meet. The quality of their relationship is an embrace of the image of God in all its challenging human manifestations. *Tiqqunim*, a collection of mystical writings that comments on the *Zohar*, offers a concrete way of understanding the link between these two *Sefirot* by asserting that these qualities are found in the faces of the *kheruvim* that were part of the Ark of the Covenant: "They are Mercy and Understanding, which are the faces of the *kheruvim*."[547]

What are the *kheruvim?* In the Torah, the detailed directions given by God concerning the Ark specifies a wooden box to be covered with gold, a pure gold *kaporet*, "cover," for that box, and two *kheruvim* of gold to be affixed to it. In many religions of the ancient Mediterranean, a god's or goddess' sanctuary included a representation of the divinity standing or sitting on a throne or footstool. The Ark of the Israelites served a similar function for an invisible deity. It was a focusing place for the people to seek God's presence.

> *v'natata et hakaporet ah ha-Aron*, "place the *kaporet* on the Ark; put inside the Pact that I will give you. It is there that I will meet with you, and I will impart to you – from above the cover, from between the two *kheruvim* that are on top of the Ark of the Pact – all that I will command you concerning the Israelite people."[548]

In a list of Biblical words and their *sefirotic* associations that he supplies in his *Or Neerav*, the mystic Moshe Cordovero links the *kaporet* to *Yesod*.[549] The *kaporet* is the cover of the Ark on which the *kheruvim* stand, of a piece with it: "from the *kaporet* they were made."[550] The word, however is fraught with more complex associations. *Kaporet* is translated as "mercy-seat" in some sources, from the literal translation of the word's root, *k.p.r*, "atone." Cordovero explains that the *kaporet* is the foundation, which stands upon the Ark, which is *Malkhut;* thus the interpretation in *Tiqqunim.* It is only called thus when it is specifically located above *Malkhut,* covering her, as expounded by the *Zohar* in the matter of *ben porat Yosef.*[551]

At the end of his life, Jacob blesses Joseph with the words *ben porat Yosef,* "Joseph is a fruitful bough."[552] The *Zohar* imagines *Tiferet* as a bough, heavy with fruit, hovering over *Malkhut,* the one to be protected. This is *Hesed* in a most elemental form: the protection the lover offers the beloved. *Yesod* stands over *Malkhut* and covers her with his own presence, just as the *kheruvim* cover and protect the Ark with their spread wings.

R. Kattina said: Whenever Israel came up to the Festival, the curtain would be removed for them and the *cherubim* were shown to them, whose bodies were intertwined with one another, and they would be thus addressed: Look! You are beloved before God as the love between man and woman.[553]

The balancing of mercy and understanding, these elements of *kaporet,* bring about atonement through their embrace. Similarly, not by way of avoiding or overcoming physicality, but by embracing its place in human and divine expression do we achieve its integration with the emotional level of existence. Thus we are empowered to reach upward toward the highest levels of being.

Where mercy and understanding embrace, literally, we find God's presence: what is evoked is the Presence of God which is the *Shekhinah,* associated with Rachel, Mother of Israel.

> Rachel has achieved more than all of them by standing at the crossroads whenever the world is in need. Mystery of the matter: Ark, *kaporet,* and *kheruvim* in the share of Benjamin, who was born by the road, and *Shekhinah* above all.[554]

Rachel was buried, by herself, on the road near Bethlehem. She died giving birth to Benjamin, "who was born by the road." The road is the truest symbol of the Israelites, born as they were in wilderness wandering. Mercy and understanding embrace in the one who maintains the sense of wandering, even when settled; mercy and understanding bring about the presence of God in one who knows how to welcome the wanderer, include the stranger, and comfort the exiled.

Rachel, who was buried by the side of the road, achieved even more than did the patriarchs, constantly comforting the people of Israel and evoking divine compassion for them. The mystery is that in her death Rachel gave birth to Benjamin, in whose territory the Temple was eventually built. Benjamin completed the full count of twelve tribes, upon whom the *Shekhinah* rested; later She dwelt in the Temple, which contained the Ark, its cover, and the winged cherubim. Rachel, symbolizing the *Shekhinah*, conveyed her blessings to the people and aroused compassion above.[555]

Only one who knows what it is to bury a loved one by the road, who experiences the truth of life as a wanderer, will be able to show *Hesed* to another wanderer, as Abraham learned to do, and as we must, too.

Bridging: Integrating All That Has Come Before, Rising Toward the Heights

When the lower, *Malkhut,* joins with the upper, *Tiferet,* according to mystical tradition, they merge; and, in creating the wholeness to which they each bring themselves, they complete each other, since each has something the other lacks. The lower physical and the upper mental, when linked, temper each other; when the flesh and the spirit are joined, outer appearances and inner meaning connect and create an integrity of self. Thought and deed become one, and we doo as we meant to do – and are meant, ideally, to do. Hypocrisy becomes impossible.

In classical Jewish terms, this completion is effected through the joining of act and intention. For the mystical path, mindfulness is not only a private practice.

> Know that there is no act which is complete without direct intention, for the *mitzvot* need intention in order to be an act of true completeness, which includes the speaking and the thought. The speaking, since one should say "This is me, about to do what I have been commanded by my Creator, for the sake of the unification of the *Kadosh Barukh Hu* and his *Shekhinah*. And the thought, which is the intention of the commandment and its hidden meaning."[556]

Intention, *kavanah,* is the linking of thought and word, or word and deed; it is a balancing of that which is within with that which is without, in every moment. To see oneself in God's image through the prism of the *Sefirot* is to see for the first time how, through one's thoughtful, everyday human acts, one is on the path to personal integration and wholeness. Take one example: a person aspires always to react to others with kindness, even if judgment, and even disagreement, is later required for an honest interaction. One must look deeply within oneself, and discover one's own need to defend one's own heart from possible "attack." One learns to repeat over and over, "I will not assume that I am about to be criticized. I will not counterattack before I listen closely. I will follow the Jewish ethical teaching of giving the other the benefit of the doubt at all times. And as I attempt to radiate *Hesed,* mercy, toward others, I will try as well to be open to receiving it myself." And one tries again and again to be mindful to make that careful behavior one's new default – a success that, neurologists say, takes dozens of repetitions to become one's normal behavior. One perseveres in the emotional exaltation of *gadlut*, forgets in the darkness of the soul called *katnut*, makes mistakes, regrets, tries again, and finally, perhaps, reaches up from below to grasp the rung of that behavior more firmly, and make it part of one's soul.

In so doing, one merges one's own attributes of *Hesed* and *Gevurah*, integrating one's own tendencies toward mercy and judgment. One becomes a more integrated self, more likely always to react consciously as the person one means to be. Others will notice that one is reliably kind, or at least calmer, and naturally respond in kind. The *Sefirot*, given the opening, will shower well-being upon that response; and it is sorely needed. Mystics calculate that, in the larger sefirotic rhythm of creation, we are in the cycle of *Gevurah:* the world is overmuch ruled by harshness. It requires all our dedication to balance that *sefirah* and the negative effects of too little *Hesed* in the world and in our own lives.

Judaism defines much of the world's differences as complementary opposites, as Eve was *ezer k'negdo,* equal and opposite, to Adam. The *havdalah* ("separation") prayer recited at the close of Shabbat lists several:

> [B]etween holy and everyday, between light and darkness, between Israel and the peoples, between the seventh day and the six days of work.[557]

These distinctions between opposites do not imply a moral judgment; each of these "equal and opposite" pairs, between them, encompasses all of reality. This prayer, listing pairs of opposing words, means to represent a whole spectrum between them. This is a common feature of Biblical verses, which refer to such word pairs as "moist and dry," "heaven and earth," and "male and female," which are meant to include everything that lies between the two extremes.[558] An interesting case for complementarity has even been made for the terms *tahor* and *tamey,* usually translated, inaccurately and simplistically, as "ritually pure" and "ritually impure."[559] The balance of each of these opposites, which each evoke between their poles an entire world of meaning, must be incorporated into the sefirotic vision of wholeness, and balanced precisely and correctly, so that each can release the contribution of its power into the world.

Opposites must be seen as complementary, not conflicting. Suppression of one to favor the other exacts a price from both. The cost of the separation between what is below and what is above damages the very primordial structure of the All. Gikatilla teaches that "all that was created was *tov m'od"* – "very good"[560]. *Tov,* "good", is associated with the *yetzer tov,* and *m'od* with the *yetzer ra'*. When *Malkhut,* which is associated with the level of God's presence called *Adonai,* draws from *Yesod* (the *sefirah* directly above it, which is associated with *tov*), all the works of *Adonai* are

Tov, and all that comes to the world, life and death, all is *Tov*, "good." *Tov* comes to connect all things. There cannot be *Tov,* i.e. goodness cannot be manifest, where there is division and separation.[561]

In the process of this work of balance and integration, there is the creation of something new. Out of the meeting of *Hesed* and *Gevurah* one develops in oneself the *sefirah* that is born out of that meeting: *Rakhamim,* Compassion, the glorious place of *Tiferet* which is associated with *rekhem,* the nurturing womb of all that exists. Through the work of becoming more the person one aspires to be, by way of acting out *gemilut hasadim,* "loving kindness" in relationship with others, one creates in oneself the compassionate place one longs to inhabit, symbolized by the unconditional, nurturing, dependable love of Mother. Popular psychology has it that, in the human quest for security and love, we would all "crawl back into the womb," but the compassion of this womb is a reward for the most difficult and emotionally maturing work of all. This is the work of ascending the *Sefirot.*

Binah – The Gate of Understanding

IMPENETRABLE MYSTERY – PALACE OF REFLECTION – WOMB OF EXISTENCE – TESHUVAH – RETURN TO THE DEEPEST SOURCE – LEAH – THE HIGHER FEMININE – THE TENT

> *b'shem yikhudo shel Kudsha Berikh Hu v'Shekhintey –*
> for the sake of the unification of understanding and wisdom, the lower feminine and the upper feminine, the mother and her children

Impenetrable Mystery

The great mystic Moshe Corovero warns about the place where we now find ourselves. He maintains in his writings that it is not appropriate for us to go further in exploring the *Sefirot.* As we approach *Binah,* we rise toward the last triad of *Sefirot.* These three, *Binah, Hokhmah* and *Ayn Sof,* correspond to the level of the intellect, the highest and most inner aspect of existence. The three highest and innermost *Sefirot* are also the source of the others: as we will see, it is the union of *Hokhmah* and *Binah* that leads to *Binah's* birthing of the lower *Sefirot* as offspring of the highest. It is because we are inquiring into the level of birth, of the mystery of beginning, that Cordovero's words express a sense of propriety, almost of modesty, in inquiry into this area. Even as we would toward a friend or family member, Cordovero expresses a respect and sensitivity toward the privacy of the innermost, the cosmic version of the Holy of Holies, which only the High Priest entered.

> It is improper for the seeker to probe the essence of the first three *Sefirot*, since they constitute the Divine Mind, Wisdom, and Understanding. It is also improper to probe the essence of the hidden substance that creates all that exists. Since it is one with its Will, Wisdom, and Understanding – its essential qualities – it is not proper to probe. However, it is not wrong for us to explore from *Hesed* and *Gevurah* on down, for these qualities have been emanated to conduct the beings below. Whoever explores them thoroughly is rewarded for his zeal. Concerning this it is written: "Let the mother go," referring to *Binah* (Understanding); "the children you may take," to search and explore.[562]

Yet we are drawn to that probing. Seeking wisdom is one of the highest aims of a human life; Cordovero is, in a way, telling us that there is something very intimate, very inner, about such a search. If *Hokhmah*, wisdom, is the highest, ultimate goal, it is *Binah*, understanding, that we must come to know first. In Rabbinic sources and in Jewish liturgy, they are often found paired. One may not be achieved without the other, and understanding comes first. Without it, one will never reach wisdom.

> The first three *Sefirot* are mentioned in the verse *vehahokhmah me'ayin titzmakh, ve'ey zeh makom binah*, [literally "from where, *me'ayin*, shall wisdom be found?

And where is, *ve'ey zeh*, the place of understanding?"] (Iyov 28.12). Iyov is saying that the *sefirah* of *Hokhmah* ["wisdom"] emanates from the *sefirah* of *Keter*, which is also called *ayin*, and that the *Sefirah* of *Binah* ["understanding"] flows from *Hokhmah*.[563]

Understanding, *Binah*, derives from *Hokhmah*, Wisdom. *Hokhmah*, in turn, comes *me'ayin*, literally "from *ayin*," which can mean "from where" or "from nothing"; from that which is beyond us – and which we experience as nothing, since it is no thing that we know – comes wisdom. Wisdom comes from a place we cannot know.

The *Zohar* does not attempt to give a clear description of the emergence of *Hokhmah*. As we will see in the study of that *sefirah*, what is said about it is also, in a way, unsaid. Wisdom and its source are beyond us. But *Binah*, understanding, is a bit more approachable. After all, she is *Imma*, the Mother of All. But we go on aware of Cordovero's warning. Let it remind us of our inability to reach the heights we would grasp, and the difficulties, confusions, and *katnut* caused by our limitations.

Binah is the frustrating crossroads of our sorely limited human ability to understand and to love. That is why the mystics linked the Matriach Leah with *Binah*:

> "God saw that Leah was unloved, so He opened her womb: but Rachel remained barren. [Genesis 29.31]" You cannot love something you cannot understand. You may even dislike it. For example: when you have solved an intricate problem, you feel a sense of joy and delight, but when you are stumped by a question that is beyond your grasp you feel low and depressed. That explains why Leah was unloved. For [in Kabbalistic thought] Leah represents inwardness, the mystical world, the realm that is beyond human understanding; [remember, Leah had "weak eyes" [Genesis 29.17] symbolizing the unfathomable]. And that's why Yaakov

did not love Leah [as much as Rachel]. Rachel, on the other hand, represents outwardness, the revealed, the tangible world.[564]

Let Cordovero's warning remind us of our inability to deserve or achieve that which we most long for, and let it remind us to give thanks for the gift that we are able to reach. The traditional *honen ha-da'at* prayer mentions three aspects of intelligence for which we strive, and includes our awareness that all knowledge is a gift of God, a gift that comes, literally, from God.

> "You grace humans with *da'at* [knowledge] and teach mortals *binah* [understanding]. Grace us with *dey'ah* [knowldge], *binah* [understanding] and *haskel* [insight] from you."[565]

Let the warning remind us of the dangers the mystics sensed in trying to rise further, delve deeper. In every epic myth, ancient and modern, the hero's last and greatest challenge is always to confront that which is closest to, and deepest within, herself. Grasping each higher rung of the ladder linking earth to heaven becomes more difficult and more challenging as one rises, and requires more honesty, more strength, more determination. Otherwise the light becomes too blinding, too disorienting, and one risks a fall.

Palace of Reflection

> "When you arrive at the place of marble, do not say, 'Water, water!' for falsehood cannot be established before God." Ben 'Azzai cast a look and died . . . Ben Zoma looked and became demented . . . Aher mutilated the shoots. R. Akiba departed unhurt.[566]

Binah is the Palace of Reflection. Reflections are misleading things. One looks into a body of water of any depth and sees one's own face, but because that reflection fills the eyes, one cannot see the large fish that floats just below the water's surface. The brighter the light by which we think we are seeing, the stronger the reflected image that fills our eyes and the less likely are we to see what is truly there, beneath the surface that hides it. As we know from a hundred stories about adventurers wandering in the desert, light at certain angles seems to reflect off the surface of water even when there is no water. In a famous Talmudic story, four mystical adepts make an attempt to enter the *pardes*, "garden" of God and seek out the divine Throne. One of the dangers of their journey is that things are not what they seem, and to misunderstand is a fatal mistake; thus, "One who works deceit shall not dwell in my house; one who tells lies shall not remain in my sight."[567] The first challenge of *Binah* is to look deeply at what is seen and not be misled by surface reflections in the attempt to achieve understanding – lest one live in a world of lies, unaware.

The ancient insight of the mystics – that my behavior ripples through the interconnected cosmos in a way that affects you, me, and the world – is borne out not only through modern studies in sociology, but also in physics. The "observer effect" of quantum physics has taught us that the first thing we see when we look at the world is the effect of our seeing. In one fascinating example, a scientist realized that the act of shining a light on a small enough physical particle would have an effect on the particle: the wave, or stream of particles, of which light is composed,[568] would literally bump into it and actually change its position slightly.[569] This physical observation about the world offers us an interesting insight into the effects of our own seeing. One person looks at another, and the other becomes aware of being observed; the bearing of the observed may change, and behavior become more self-conscious. The effect of a gaze is all the more powerful if the observer has power of any kind over the observed: a boss watching a subordinate, a good-looking man staring at a woman, a man sizing up another man on a city street.

The way a human being sees is literally a result of the physical development of human vision. Scientists suggest that the form of the human eye results from eons of adaptations of survival mechanisms, and sight is not a simple and straightforward ability (which is why our eyes can "play tricks" on us).[570] This awkward physical reality leads to an inevitably incomplete perception: when a person looks at something, there are other things she does not see that exist in the same general vicinity. She can look straight at something and not see it. Or she can see it without being able to understand what she sees. This last was the problem suffered by three of the four comrades during the mystical journey led by Rabbi Akiva. They could not cope with the concept that the image of what they thought they saw was not the reality.

When we look at the others with whom we share our lives, we may tend to assign a great deal of importance to the surface impressions our sight gives us. Yet even as each word and verse of Torah harbors deeper meanings of *drash, remez* and *sod,* so also is each human being made up of layers of stories and events, insights, and desires. Thus we caution each other, "Don't judge a book by its cover" and suggest that we "walk a mile" in another's shoes before we pretend to understand her. Similarly, when we look at our own lives we may be missing something. "A self-made man is about as likely as a self-laid egg," said Mark Twain; none of us can see the extent of the influence of others on us. We may deny the effect of our family of origin, by disowning it or by dismissing it as something we've long ago resolved. We may think that our ethics and values are our own creation, freely chosen and not beholden to any system of belief. Even those of us who seek to minimize our impact on the planet still flick electric switches provided by a network of workers and power sources, buy bread that began as wheat someone sowed and that made its way through many changes of hand to come to ours, and depend on the idea of a shared social contract[571] and a functioning police force to cross a city street safely.

Each of us is part of a vast network of connectedness, although the image we see reflected back at us from any mirror seems quite individual. In the language of the *Sefirot,* I am an emanation from many different vessels of *shefa',* and I myself am a vessel infusing that abundance into all others with whom I connect in a way that allows the flow to freely move, from you to me and from me to you.

To understand the place where I stand, that is, to stand in the palace and not be derailed by the falsehood of what I think I see, I must look beyond myself, and, at the same time, I must look within myself. Only in that way will I see my connectedness to everything of which I am a part, within which I function, and that will be at least partly defined by my choices. Even with regard only to the implications of my Jewish identity, this conscious stance touches on my personal, immediate connection to Jewish culture, community, history, and environment. All this I see, when I truly see. "The secret of seeing is, then, the pearl of great price."[572]

Womb of Existence – Return to the Deepest Source

Binah itself was born, or emanated, from *Hokhmah*. As the Kabbalists envisioned it, *Binah* emerged from the unity of all being, differentiating itself in the same way that, in the human process of gestation, identical molecules come into existence and then differentiate and specialize into molecules meant to build the brain, the heart, the hand. *Binah* emerged because without this *sefirah*, existence could not have come into being. It is not enough, the mystics sensed, to create with high, remote, intellectual wisdom. Understanding, tempered with emotional experience and physical knowledge, is also necessary. The primal point of wisdom might pierce the cosmos all day long with its pulsating light, but until there was a vessel to hold the light, a womb to be penetrated by that point and to contain what it brought forth, physical creation would not exist. Birth and growth require not only an idea, or a seed, but also the fertile ground to receive it.

> [B]before the emanation of the [*Sefirot*] these qualities were utterly hidden within Him in the greatest possible unity. It is not appropriate [to ascribe to them] any image or point at all. They were, rather, united in Him. Afterward He emanated one point from Himself. [This] one emanation is *Keter*, which is called *'ayin* ("Nothingness") on account of its great transparency

and closeness to its source, such that being (*yesh*) cannot be posited of it. From [*Keter*] a second point was emanated in a second revelation. It is *Hokhmah,* and it is called "being" because it is the beginning of revelation and being. It is called "being from nothingness" (*yesh me'ayin*). Because it is the beginning of being and not being itself, it required a third point for the revelation of existents. That is *Binah*, which [constitutes] the revelation of the existents. *Hokhmah* is the beginning of existence, and *Binah* is the end of existence.[573]

Binah is "the *sefirah* which is also described as the womb of the universe; 'souls emanate from this place', all life clings here."[574]

> *Binah* is ... the womb of God as Great Mother, the Source of life to which all life longs to return. *Teshuvah*, or "return to God," is another name for *Binah*. In *Binah* we go back to our deepest source, our most ancient memory.[575]

Binah is not only the womb of the world. It is the beginning of time as well. From the womb *Binah* emerges all that will be real, all that will exist; and she is the place of all that has been and all that will be remembered, as well. The pregnant pause that leads to the articulation of a thought; the impulse racing along a system of nerves that leads to the movement of a muscle; all of that which will be, before it exists, is found here.

> The seven *Sefirot* which flow from the maternal womb of *Binah* are the seven primeval days of creation. What appears in time as the epoch of actual and external creation is nothing but the projection of the archetypes of the seven lower *Sefirot* which, in timeless existence, are enshrined in God's inwardness ....In describing this division of the divine consciousness, the *Zohar* in

one of its profoundest symbolisms, speaks of it as a manifestation of God's progressive unfolding.[576]

Binah, Understanding, is the necessary quality linking the Upper to the Lower, according to Gikatilla's *Shaarey Orah.* Understanding is the place of Absolute Mercy; above the court of *Elohim,* that dispenses mercy mixed with judgment. The mercy flowing from *Binah* extends the limits of tolerance, as it is said, *El Rakhum v'Khanun, Erekh Apayim v'Rav Hesed v'Emet,* "God is compassionate and full of grace, long-suffering, and full of mercy and faithfulness".[577] For the mystic Rabbi Nakhman of Bratslav, existence can endure only when it is based on the quality of *rakhmanut. Rakhmanut,* "compassion," is related in the Hebrew to *rekhem,* "womb." "It is the capacity of the *rekhem* to open up, to make an empty space in the heart of fullness of the person and to make room for the embryo, for a being Other. *Rakhmanut* is essentially the ability to conceive something other than oneself."[578]

> For the Name, blessed be He, because of his uterine capacity (*rahmanuto*), created the world, because he wished to reveal this uterine capacity. Now if the world had not been created, to whom could he have revealed his uterine virtue? And because of this, He created the whole of creation, from the beginning of the emanation, right up to the central point of the material world, in order to show his uterine capacity.[579]

Teshuvah

> They asked the Rabbi of Lublin, Why is it that in the holy Book of Splendor [the *Zohar*], the turning to God which corresponds to the emanation "understanding" is called "Mother"? He explained, When a man confesses and repents, when his heart accepts Understanding and is converted to it, he becomes like a new-born child, and his own turning to God is his mother.[580]

Binah is also the mother of *Gevurah,* Judgment. And, like a mother, *Binah* is the *sefirah* that regulates Judgment and reins in its excesses. *Binah* offers this potential for restraint of Judgment through the power of *teshuvah,* of repentance, which is found here, in Understanding. Without Understanding, there can be no atonement.

There is a mystical wariness about *Gevurah,* the place of Judgment; it is, of course, necessary to contain the otherwise overwhelming quality of the *sefirah* of *Hesed,* but *Gevurah's* power is too often destructive. *Teshuvah* offers the power to subdue *Gevurah,* as the Rabbis declared, "Great is repentance, because it brings about redemption, as it is said, 'And a redeemer will come to Zion, and unto them that turn from transgression in Jacob,' i.e., why will a redeemer come to Zion? Because of those that turn from transgression in Jacob."[581] In other words, "turning," *teshuvah,* will save the world from Judgment. Jewish tradition has long suspected that human beings are not being judged as we deserve to be – and that we could not survive it if we were.

> As [God] was about to create Adam, Torah exclaimed: If a human being is created and then proceeds to sin, and You punish him – why should the world of Your hands be in vain, since he will be unable to endure Your judgment? He replied, I have already prepared *teshuvah,* returning, before creating the world. Once He had made the world and created Adam, the blessed Holy One exclaimed, "O world! world! You and your laws are based solely upon Torah. That is why I created the human being in you, so that he might engage in her, strive for her. If not, I will turn you back into chaos and void."[582]

The saving grace is the invitation extended to us to do *teshuvah,* the "repentance," which is a return to the path that leads toward God. But repentance is not simply about admitting sin. Achieving the difficult goal of true repentance is a sign that one's attempts to become wise through Torah study have been effective. "The goal of wisdom," according to the Talmudic sages, is atonement and *mitzvot*. It is impossible that one who has become truly wise through study of Torah and Mishnah would be the same person who shows disrespect or indifference to one's father and mother, or teacher.[583]

The world depends on the balancing between the two *Sefirot* of *Gevurah* - Judgment, and *Binah* - Understanding. Judgment itself, like any other attribute of a *sefirah*, is already present in potential in the first pulsing into reality that is the beginning of the All. Moshe Cordovero explains that the quality of judgment "is on high"; it is traced from *Keter,* another name for *Ayn Sof.* But Judgment does not emerge into expression until it descends "below" the highest three *Sefirot.* Its appropriate emergence is not only balanced with *Hesed,* mercy, it is also "suspended" in, or dependent on [*taluy*, literally "hangs upon"] Understanding.[584]

> [T]he Judgment of *Gevurah* is suspended in *Binah*. If *Binah* adds to it and influences Judgment, it is able to function, for the branch goes after the source. [However,] if *Binah* does not influences the Judgment in *Gevurah*, it has no power to execute. Now that which the rabbis have explained is clear, that in the innermost houses [of the divine] there is a grief which is related to the heart, and in the rest of the organs which are the outer houses there is not.[585]

The innermost houses, that is, the uppermost *Sefirot,* are the place of "a grief which is related to the heart." The outer, lower *Sefirot* are not sensitive to, or, at least, do not reflect, this inner grief.

Why does grief suddenly appear here? How is grief related to Judgment, or to God? The Talmud preserves a perspective according to which God, like a human king, has outer chambers for public appearances and inner ones in which God, like any public figure, can enjoy privacy.

> But is there any weeping in the presence of the Holy One, blessed be He? For behold, R. Papa said: There is no grief in the Presence of the Holy One blessed be He; for it is said: *hod v'hadar l'fanav,* "Honor and majesty are before Him"; *oz v'khedvah bim'komo,* "strength and beauty are in His sanctuary"! (Psalms 96.6) — There is no contradiction; the one case [refers to] the inner chambers, the other case [refers to] the outer chambers. But behold, it is written: And in that day did YHVH, the God of Hosts, call to weeping and to lamentation.[586]

Ancient tradition asserts that even God needs a private place in which to weep over tragedy. "Honor and majesty," which the mystics associate with the lower, physical *sefirah* of *Hod,* is only the outer appearance of God. There is an inner world that, as we know, requires investigating beneath the veils of *peshat,* the level of what is apparently true and real. This inner world, for the mystics, is higher and closer to God; we, as reflections of God, come closer to our own essential reality when we go beyond the physical and try to understand our own innermost heart. Thus we reach higher, and come closer, to God.

This innermost place, the "still, small voice" of the soul, is the "sanctuary" of God – the true place of "strength and beauty". This inner world is also the small, quiet place of grief: the grief of coming to the Understanding that one is often wrong, usually fails, and will invariably lose.

> It is important that we be strengthened by the wisdom of our grievings. ... until each individual maintains a responsible relationship to his or her own losses and changes, there will be no such thing as a hopeful future. For, as in the Taoist description of the wheel in terms of the strong, empty spaces *between* the spokes, one's future depends not only on the visible spokes of the present, but also on those invisible elements from the past, those

> things we are missing, are grieving for, have forgotten and left behind, so that they may be recovered.[587]

Binah, teaches Gikatilla, is the place of all redemption and liberation, from Egypt, from forgetting, even from the certainty that surely indicates that there is something we are missing.

"The vessels were broken, and from there the husks came into being, as is known." Rabbi Nakhman of Bratslav considers the problem of evil that reaches beyond our capacity to answer it – or its own capacity for redemption.

> *Apikorsut* comes from there, from this area of empty space, since within this empty space there is no God [*Elohut*], so to speak. And if so, the difficulties that come from there, from that empty space, can never be answered [or, "can never be atoned"], because an answer [*teshuvah*] is only possible where God is present.[588]

There can be no answer to certain questions, such as those which come from "outside." Nakhman was referring to "outside wisdom," the secularism that was challenging the Jewish community of his day. What he was confronting was the difficulty of having a dialogue with another person who does not make the same assumptions about reality. For an atheist, there is no God. There can be no common ground for a conversation about God with someone who will not posit the reality of God as possible. That person is in a place without God.

And Nakhman asserts that there is no *teshuvah*, neither an answer for the secularist's question nor a possibility for redemption for him, as long as he occupies a place without God. This reworking of Kabbalistic concepts for the early modern world includes the possibility of taking the idea of *tzimtzum* to its radical extreme: God's Presence does not exist in the world. "But he does exist beyond the world; so there will always be an infinite distance between man and God, whose surmounting (or nonsurmounting) constitutes one of the essential aspects of the life of man."[589]

> The absolute separation from God, his absolute transcendence, is the logical condition for the existence of man and the world. ... but the divine has to be reintroduced, given the possibility of immanence. This reintroduction of the divine into the "space empty of God" is the origin of the fundamental paradox. Two opposite things have to be asserted at the same time: (1) God is absent from the world (as a consequence of *Tsimtsum*); (2) God is in the world, because the world cannot exist without him.[590]

That is the enduring agony of questions of theodicy. We do not understand the existence of radical evil; and we cannot comprehend how God can exist as a presence – or imagine even an idea of any worth at all – when people act out of *apikorsut,* the denial of God. The aspect of God the mystics associate with judgment is *Elohim,* and Gikatilla, in an expression of the ultimate uncertainty, teaches that

> this is the secret of the saying "Torah has seventy faces," if you you're your eyes you will see that wherever in Torah the name *Elohim* is written it alludes to the Sefirah *Binah,* just as we have alluded to here, and sometimes it refers to the attribute *Gevurah* for whom it is suited, while at times it refers to the attribute *Malkhut,* when it dons the garments of *Gevurah.*[591]

In other words, the higher one rises toward God, and the closer one gets to seeing, the less one can be certain. Clarity may be achievable in the lower realms of being, but when one rises high enough, when one reaches the realm of Understanding, then one arrives at "sometimes."

Binah, Understanding, is a tempered quality; as one of the highest *Sefirot,* it births the attributes of the physical body and of the emotional heart. One does not achieve Understanding without much life experience and much effort to overcome the massive distractions of physical needs and emotional desires and fears. Grief comes, inevitably, from that life experience; as Rabbi Akiba taught, when grief opens the heart, then we can begin to learn what may be learned from life.

"Words that are spoken from the heart reach other hearts," assert the sages of Jewish tradition.

> Words spoken from the heart reverberate in the world and in my memory, and they come back to me, opened to unexpected resonances of meaning, for one who is able to hear, able to feel – one who learns to be humble, and listens for the inner holiness of the words.[592]

Now may we begin to reach understanding. There can be no true repentance without understanding; and there can be no true Judgment, no *Gevurah*, that does not depend upon, "hang upon" *Binah*, Understanding.

> How should a person train himself in the attribute of *binah*? Through returning in repentance, for there is nothing as important, in that it repairs every flaw. And just as the way of *binah* is to sweeten all judgments and neutralize their bitterness, so one should turn in repentance and repair all flaws. One who thinks of repentance all his days causes *binah* to illuminate all his days, so that all his days are spent in repentance. He merges himself with *binah,* which is repentance, and all the days of his life are crowned with the secret of highest returning. See, all existence is rooted in turning.[593]

Thus: all existence hangs upon the Understanding that one achieves through repentance, and repentance is gained by way of Torah study. We are not referring here to Torah-quoting; we do not mean the act of pointing to a verse and insisting on its *peshat* fulfillment. This is the Torah study of Moses, who did *teshuvah* in this sense, as noted in the introduction to this study, when he "turned aside to look." That is, because he was humble enough to realize that he did not already know what he was seeing, he was rewarded with a revelatory moment of seeing what was truly there. This kind of understanding comes from the thoughtful, quiet, humble Torah study that seeks what is beyond the *hod v'hadar*, the sound and fury of the outer chambers, looking within for the "still small voice."

> Behold, YHVH passed by, and a great and strong wind tore the mountains, and broke in pieces the rocks before YHVH; but YHVH was not in the wind; and after the wind an earthquake; but YHVH was not in the earthquake; And after the earthquake a fire; but YHVH was not in the fire; and after the fire a still small voice. And it was so, when Elijah heard it that he wrapped his face in his mantle, and went out, and stood in the entrance of the cave. And, behold, there came a voice to him, and said, What are you doing here, Elijah?[594]

The still, small voice asks us what we are doing here. We cannot do *teshuvah* without answering this question from the innermost place of truth within us. And as the mystics see it, we cannot express judgment, either, until we are ready to see the truth of the limited person from whom our judgment comes – our human self.

> Among the manifestations of God there is one – for several reasons the Kabbalists identify it with *Binah*, the divine Intelligence – in which He appears as the eternal subject, using the term in its grammatical sense, as the great Who, *Mi*, who stands at the end of every question and every answer. ... [one] reaches a point where it is still possible to question "Who, but no longer possible to get an answer; rather does the question itself constitute an answer.[595]

When we are able to see that we cannot even ask, we have arrived at the place of Understanding.

The Upper Feminine - Leah

Once upon a time, ancient Israelites knew a mother-God as well as a father-God. Traces of that feminine power still exist, for those who know how to look for them; there are examples of wise women and prophets throughout the Tanakh and Talmud. A fascinating primordial example of the Upper Feminine and its power emerges through a careful reconstruction of the character and symbolism of Eve, whose name means "mother of all the living."

Eve is defined in Biblical tradition as *ezer k'negdo,* which is often translated as "helper," *ezer. K'negdo,* however, means "over against him," which indicates an equal and opposite partner, not a handmaid or second-class citizen. Very often the source of help in the Tanakh is, after all, God. Eve and God do share a similar power, as life-givers. As Biblical scholar Ilana Pardes has demonstrated through linguistic parallels in the Tanakh as well as ancient cognate languages, Eve's words upon her first experience of giving birth, *kaniti ish et YHVH,* mean, "I have created a man with YHVH" (and not, as the traditional translations have it, "I have acquired." Pardes quotes the modern Biblical commentator Umberto Cassuto to explain that

> the first woman in her joy at giving birth to her first son, boasts of her generative power, which approximates in her estimation to the Divine creative power. The Lord formed the first man (ii 7) and I have formed the second man. ... I stand together (i.e., equally) WITH HIM in the rank of creators". Note that for Cassuto *et YHVH* means not only "equally with" but also "together with." Eve's position in the rank of creators allows her to become God's partner in the work of creation; it allows her to "feel the personal nearness of the Divine presence to herself."[596]

The divine feminine is associated with wisdom in many ancient Near Eastern myths that touch on those of Judaism, such as the personification of wisdom as a woman in the book of Proverbs. The word *hokhmah*, "wisdom", is itself a feminine word in Hebrew. The central story connecting wisdom to women in the Torah, however, is that of the serpent in Eden.

> [This] "wisdom tale" ... does concern the function of a wise agent (the "cunning" serpent) and the conferring of wisdom (3.6). ... Unlike the pragmatic, instructional wisdom of a book like Proverbs, the third chapter of Genesis – like Job, Ecclesiastes and certain Psalms – belongs to the speculative type of wisdom that deals with the meaning of the paradoxes and harsh facts of life.
> The prominent role of the female rather than the male in the wisdom aspects of the Eden tale is a little-noticed feature of the narrative. It is the woman, and not the man, who perceives the desirability of procuring wisdom.[597]

The mystics who assign wisdom to the "male" side of the *Sefirot* are perhaps engaged in a simple polemical act of deliberately arrogating this most respected of Biblical qualities to themselves. But it is also possible to see *Binah* as exactly the "speculative type of wisdom" that might be well associated with the quality of Understanding. The "piercing" kind of wisdom associated with the "male" *sefirah Hokhmah* is in itself not enough to support us in facing the "paradoxes and harsh facts of life".

There is something about the quality of the intellect associated with Eve, and with the feminine aspect of the intellect that was a necessary prerequisite for God's highest creation, the human being, to emerge into its full form, that is, with the capacity for free choice and all that it implies:

> Eve is seen in the Genesis tale as an intellectually curious person whose quest for knowledge ends in the rash act of violating God's law. As a consequence of this act, man and woman are forced to make themselves clothes, till the land, and invent tools – in short, to launch human civilization as we know it. There is no indication in the original story that Adam is perceived as superior to Eve in any way; man and woman are equally culpable in the eyes of God, and equally responsible for the consequences of their deed. However, in [midrashic tradition]. ... Adam is described as far better than Eve – he is the "dough" of the world.[598]

As the Torah narrates the story, after the humans ate of the Tree of Knowledge, "YHVH *Elohim* said, Behold, the man has become like one of us, knowing good and evil."[599] Eve's power in this story is parallel to God's: God first creates a human out of pre-existing matter and then instills a soul into it. In this second phase of the creation of the human being, Eve takes the created human and adds the power of choice, the last necessary ingredient for human beings to become God's partners in creation. Adam is the passive character, placed in a privileged position by others – God and Eve. In other words, Adam may be the "dough," but Eve here certainly is the yeast.

The Torah depicts Eve as the central "player" who, by eating of the Tree of Knowledge, moves the first humans toward full awareness of their human powers, a knowledge "not restricted to moral awareness only, but as denoting a 'full possession of mental and physical powers'."[600] The narrative ends with the naming of Eve as giver of life, "mother of all the living."[601] She is clearly a partner with God in creating the paradigm from which "all the living" will proceed. In overtly identifying a feminine side of God, the mystics resurrect and re-establish Eve's early work:

> Eve's naming speech may be perceived as a trance from an earlier mythological phase in which mother goddesses

> were very much involved in the process of creation. ... her speech is a critique not only of monotheistic principles but also of the underlying patriarchal presuppositions of monotheism. Unlike the inhabitants of Babel with their scandalous phallic creation, the first woman challenges *both* the divine restrictions on human creativity and the exclusion of the feminine from the representation of creation.[602]

Here we touch on an important power shared by the first woman with her descendant, the Matriarch Leah. Naming her children is an overt and noticeable power that Leah, Jacob's first wife, wields. For The *Zohar*, Leah is the most powerful of the matriarchs, and so she is associated with the Upper Feminine aspect of God, of the world, and of each of us.

> Come and see: Leah gave birth to six sons and one daughter, fittingly so, for six directions stand above her; these six and one daughter emerge.[603]

The *Zohar* associates Leah with *Binah* and the seven lower *Sefirot* that emerge from *Binah* – the six sons being *Hesed, Gevurah, Tiferet, Hod, Netzakh*, and *Yesod*, and her daughter Dinah, of course, is *Malkhut*, the "lower" feminine aspect of God, also called *Shekhinah*. Leah is the Upper Feminine, the Womb of the World, the Concealed, Hidden World, where all is one. "She stands in unity; from here below is the World of Division."[604]

In our *Sefirot* graph (see Figure 1), *Binah* is the "lowest" of the three uppermost *Sefirot*. Her presence between the *sefirah* of *Hokhmah,* which is represented in mysticism as masculine, and the lower *Sefirot,* which are represented by her children, evokes the traditional family image: wise father, remote and beyond the reach of the child, and mother, embracing the gap between her child and her husband as only she is capable of doing through her ability to understand both the physical and the emotional expression of the children and the lofty wisdom of the father – and how they are, and must be, linked in one family, one unity.

The Tent

The word *Leah* contains the same letters as *ohel*, "tent." The tent is not only the place where people take refuge for sleeping and other private, vulnerable acts which require safety. It is the place where Isaac is consoled after the death of his mother. In the Torah and in Jewish mysticism, the tent is also associated with the presence of God. Sarah's tent is "a prominent feature in the narratives" that describe her life with Abraham in Canaan.

> In Genesis 18 reference is made to a tent five times in ten sentences: Abram is outside the tent (v.1, 2); Sarah is inside it (v. 6, 9); and Sarah is at the entrance to the tent with the divine visitor (v. 10). This emphasis on the tent makes it the pivotal point around which the mystery of the annunciation of Sarah's conception takes place. Genesis does not specify what Sarah's tent was like, but it is certainly an abode of significance, seeing that it is mentioned so frequently, is located in a (sacred) grove, and is visited by a deity.[605]

The Torah tells us that Moses set up the *ohel mo'ed*, Tent of Appointed Times (for meeting God), but the *Zohar* tells us why he set it up outside the camp. Moses set up the Tent outside the camp, above the "world of division." "When Moses discovered that Israel had sinned ... he brought Her outside"; this act of protection shielded the *Shekhinah*, God's presence, from any further taint as a result of the behavior of the people of Israel.[606] Seen as feminine, the Tent itself is vulnerable; just as women's power to shelter and nurture is easily overcome by violence and destruction, the ability of the Tent of God's presence to shelter is not inviolable. Joshua, for example, although he spent much time in the Tent, could not be protected by the Presence of God within it, since human sinfulness weakens the strength of the Tent. "She was not empowered to sustain Joshua forever, nor anyone else. Therefore he called Her 'Tent of *Mo'ed,* Slated Time,' a tent housing allotted time for the entire world."[607] The "allotted time," the *mo'adim,* are the appointed times of Israel's holy days.

The tent is a dark shape, shrouding mystery in, for there are no windows. From the open doorway there is a light beckoning one to enter. This vision of the Tent, as the manifestation of celestial light, is an expression of *Malkhut,* which is the place of the *Shekhinah.* Here the Upper Feminine evokes the Lower Feminine; they are linked, even as Leah and Rachel were linked as sisters, then wives to the same man. The *Zohar* refers to Rachel as the *Alma d'itgalya,* the "revealed world," and Leah as the *Alma D'itkasya,* the concealed, hidden world.[608]

> Always the revealed and the hidden, Rachel and Leah, without jealousy, both build the house of Israel.[609]

The light is emitted from below and above; a light by which to enter, a light by which to find one's way within. The light of God's presence, the *Shekhinah,* after all, has withdrawn from the world of division, and appears only to the righteous, and only once in a while. This is "the radiance that shone and was treasured away, the radiance of the letter *tet* in Creations, the 'heat of the day' – mystery of Abraham sitting 'at the opening of the tent; (Genesis 18.1), the opening from below to above, while 'the heat of the day' shines on that opening, shining from there."[610]

> "[O]pening of the tent" – opening of righteousness, as it is said, "Open for me the gates of righteousness" (Psalm 118.19). This is the first opening to enter; through this opening all other supernal openings come into view. Whoever attains this attains all other openings, for all abide here. Now – when this opening is unknown, since Israel is in exile – all those openings have withdrawn from it; they cannot know or grasp. However, when

Israel will come forth from exile, all those supernal rungs are destined to alight upon it fittingly. Then the inhabitants of the world will discover precious, supernal wisdom, previously unknown to them, as is written: "the spirit of YHVH will alight upon him: a spirit of wisdom and understanding, a spirit of counsel and power, a spirit of knowledge and awe of YHVH" (Isaiah 11.2). All those are destined to alight upon this lower opening, "opening of the tent."[611]

All the matriarchs had tents. Deborah the Judge refers to "women in tents" in her Song:

> Blessed above women shall Yael the wife of Heber the Kenite be
> blessed shall she be above all women in tents.[612]

When The Torah speaks of Abraham pitching his tent, the word for *tent* is written in the feminine gender (*ohalah*) but vocalized in the masculine (*ohalo*), leading Rashi to comment that "first he pitched a tent for his wife and afterward one for himself."[613] The tent has significance as a feminine abode. That is, a tent is "hers," not "his," even when a man resides in it.[614]

> "And Isaac brought her into the Tent [of] Sarah his mother" R. Yose said, "This verse is difficult: *ha-ohelah*, 'to the tent, Sarah his mother'. It should read: *le-ohel*, 'to the tent of Sarah his mother.' Why *ha-ohelah*? Because *Shekhinah* returned there. As long as Sarah existed, *Shekhinah* never departed from her. A lamp would burn from one Sabbath eve to the next, illuminating all the days of the week. After she died, that lamp died out; as soon as Rebekah appeared, *Shekinah* reappeared and the lamp rekindled. 'Sarah his mother' – resembling Sarah in all she did....Rebekah's image was precisely

Sarah's; so, 'Sarah his mother', literally....even though Sarah died, her image never departed from the house.[615]

The ultimate *ohel*, then, is Mother's Tent; it is the womb of the world.

Hokhmah emanates from the third *Sefirah*, *Binah*, also called *Imma* (mother). *Binah* is impregnated with the archetypes found within *Hokhmah*. Within *Binah*, the embryonic archetypes becomes more distinct and differentiated into specific phenomena. *Binah* is the second aspect of God that is knowable. *Hokhmah* impregnates *Binah* with the archetypes, ideas, and principles of all things. They grow within *Binah* as within a womb. *Binah* is the receptive power in God that allows all the archetypes, ideas, and principles to develop. *Binah* is the totality of divine ideas. *Binah* is the archetype of God as mother. It is *Binah* who is called *El* in the Torah.[616]

Children come forth first from the "tent" of mother's womb. From the darkness of the moment of creation all human beings emerge into the light of the world at the door of that tent. Normal human growth proceeds from the infant's dependence on mother's arms and breasts, to the toddler underfoot in the kitchen and other intimate spaces – the "tent" of enclosed, safe surroundings. As the child matures, she emerges from the womb to the world of adult, developed selves, growing into the "archetypes, ideas, and principles" implanted within her. And, like Isaac, she brings with her something of the image of that tent, and the Mother within it, into the world – seeking, in some way, this image of her own forming. When a mystic beholds the Light by which he seeks to understand his life, there is within it some of this first light. In just this way an individual's journey through life brings the memory of the Garden with her, looking for its echo in the World To Come.

The longing to reach that understanding, to see in that Light, drives the mystic forward, onward, inward, upward, despite setbacks, frustrations, and bad days. The effort is daily pursued in prayer, religious acts, and other *mitzvot*, along with meditative techniques that are meant to enhance the individual mystic's natural link to the *Sefirot*. Some mystics even seek to draw the Light and the Presence closer to themselves, as indicated in commentaries on the longing in the *Song of Songs*. "I would lead you, and bring you into the house of my mother":

> "I would lead you, and bring you": I would lead You from the upper world to the lower. "I would bring you into my mother's house": this is Sinai. R. Berekiah said: Why is Sinai called "my mother's house"? Because there Israel became like a new-born child. "That you might instruct me": in precepts and good deeds.[617]

The desire to come closer to God, to bring God closer to the world, compares the world to "my mother's house," Sinai, the place where God and humans meet, in the *ohel mo'ed*, the tent, which here becomes a place for transformative and healing Torah study.

The longing to be close to God persists even in the face of the awe and fear we experience in numinous regions, because despite the awe, there is a sense of belonging. This the image in which we are created; we are part of this structure of life. If we are naturally linked to the *Sefirot*, then in our attempts to make the sefirotic flow of *shefa'* come down more strongly on us, we are only seeking more of the elixir of life that already sustains our existence.

The mystic is caught between trying to slake a human thirst with the small flow from a drinking fountain, or with the cascading force of water bursting from a fire hose. The eagerness to see, finally to know and understand, is dangerous. We overestimate our ability to cope with what we want; and our desires can so easily overwhelm us. Ben Azzai, one of the "four who entered the *pardes*" with whom we began our study of *Binah*, is described in an anonymous Kabbalistic commentary:

> He gazed at the radiance of the Presence, like a person who looks with his weak eyes[618] at the full light of

the sun and his eyes are weakened, and sometimes he becomes blinded because of the strength of the light that overcomes him. Thus it happened to Ben Azzai: the light that he gazed upon overwhelmed him from his great desire to cleave to it and to derive pleasure from it without interruption, and after he cleaved to it he did not want to separate from that sweet radiance, and he remained immersed and hidden within it. His soul was crowned and adorned from that radiance and splendor to which no creature can cleave and afterwards live, as it says, "for no man shall see Me and live" (Exodus 33.20). But Ben Azzai only gazed at it with a slight vision, and his soul departed and remained hidden in the place of its cleaving, which is a most precious light. The death was the death of the pious whose souls are separated from all the affairs of the lowly world and whose souls cleave to the ways of the supernal world.[619]

The best death, for the mystic, is to come so close to the light of God's presence that one exceeds the boundaries of one's own ability to see and "cleaves" to it: one's soul connects to the Soul of the World and disappears into it, as a drop of water becomes part of, and disappears into, the ocean.

> Just as the light of the *Sefirot* spreads out and emanates directly from above to below like [natural] light ... so the light, after it descends to its [proper] place, returns and spreads from below to above ... this is the mystery of the light which returns from below to above, it is the secret of the reversed light which strikes the mirror and returns to its source.[620]

The closest that we can normally come to this overwhelming, soul-swallowing moment is Shabbat, a time when that which is closed opens. Through the opening we see visions of *Binah,* in a safety and wholeness that evokes the World to Come. "The whole world is full of divine presence.

> [T]he goal of prayer is to open this point. On Shabbat this gate is open, as it is written, "the gate of the inner courtyard will be closed on the six workdays, and on Shabbat it will open. (Ezekiel 46.1) We see that the Shabbat is holy among days; even though it is in time, it is of the World to Come. The difference between Shabbat and weekday is the opening of inwardness.[621]

The prayers of Shabbat bring each praying Jew closer to God; and God is brought closer to the world, as well.

> As Israel below is sanctifying the day, the Tree of Life (*Tiferet*) rouses. Its leaves rustle as a breeze comes forth from the World-to-Come [*Binah*]. The branches of the Tree sway and waft forth the scent of the World-to-Come. The Tree of Life is further aroused and at this moment, brings forth holy souls which it gives to the world. Souls exit and they enter, and the Tree of Life is filled with joy. All Israel is wreathed with crowns, which are these holy souls. Now the cosmos is joyous, and at rest.[622]

Hokhmah – The Gate of Wisdom

ATTRIBUTES: PRIMAL POINT – SPARK OF EXISTENCE – DEEP WELL – GOD'S WATER – HIDDEN TORAH

> *b'shem yikhudo shel Kudsha Berikh Hu v'Shekhintey* – for the sake of the unification of darkness and light, for the sake of the upper compassion which is unalloyed with judgment, for the sake of the sometimes within the forever

Primal Point – Spark of Existence

The second sphere contains the essence of where questioning begins.[623]

What is there, what exists, at the moment of beginning? What happens before the initial *bereshit*, "in the beginning"?[624] Consider a small version of *creatio ex nihilo:* the thinking of a thought. What happens in the moment before that thought emerges? Where does it come from? At first in one's mind there is nothing, that is, no specific thing; yet all things, all thoughts, come from that nothingness. This nothingness is not emptiness; it is no one thing because it is all possible things. This mysterious "place" is the unlimited location of all potential thought. From nothing – No Thing, no one thing, nothing yet real – comes A Thing, all things, that which becomes real – an act, a thought, a word. Something now exists where there was nothing.

This mystical intuition of how all emerges from nothing resonates with the modern theory of the Big Bang. "Oneness is grounded in scientific reality: We are made of the same stuff as all of creation. Everything that is, was or will be started off together as one infinitesimal point: the cosmic seed."[625] All that exists came into being through an initial very small, very dense point that expanded into the entirety of the universe.

> When Concealed of all Concealed verged on being revealed, it produced at first a single point.[626]

From one small point of heat and light, all that we know exists.

These two beginnings – of everything, and of a single thought – are not so different. Both are births. Here is the *Zohar*'s mystical description of the beginning of All:

> "In the beginning" (Gen 1.1) ... A spark of impenetrable darkness (*botzina d'qardinuta*) flashed within the concealed of the concealed, from the head of Infinity – a cluster of vapor forming in formlessness, thrust in a

ring, not white, not black, not red, not green, no color at all. ... Deep within the spark gushed a flow, splaying colors below, concealed within the concealed of the mystery of *Ayn Sof*. It split and did not split its aura, was not known at all, until under the impact of splitting, a single, concealed, supernal point shone. Beyond that point, nothing is known, so it is called *reyshit*, "in the beginning", first command of all. *Zohar*, "Radiance!" ... With this "beginning", the unknown concealed one created the palace.[627]

Because the *Zohar* does not speak at all of the first *sefirah*, *Keter*, it presents a story of the initial moments of creation in which a spark somehow comes out of the "concealed of the concealed", from the "head of infinity." More than this the *Zohar* does not offer. While perhaps frustrating, this is exactly what the creation account in Genesis narrates: the Presence of God is described as "moving over the face of the waters."[628] The existence of God precedes the creation of the world: God's existence is not explained.

The Talmud interprets this idea by using the letter *bet* ב with which the Torah begins: it is a letter closed above, below. and before. The Rabbis interpret from the nature of the letter *bet* that what is before, above, or below the story of the world's creation is closed to us. It is no surprise, then, to see that, while the *Zohar* seeks to describe the mystery of how God created the world, it does not go back before this; it does not inquire into how God comes to be.[629] The story begins with the existence of *Ayn Sof*, the aspect of God that is "without end," already assumed. To say that it is referred to is not to say that it is described, however: *Ayn Sof* is "the concealed of the concealed," about which nothing is known. There is a point beyond which we literally cannot see with human eyes, even with the most powerful microscopes; similarly, there is a reality beyond our ability to comprehend, not only "out there" but also up close. Rabbinic tradition describes God's presence as utterly transcendent and beyond us but also as utterly immanent – and in that way, perhaps, also beyond us. There is that which is very close to us, or even part of us, which we cannot fully grasp. Human vision and human understanding are both limited.

The *Zohar* the inner process of creation that took place in God before it could extend beyond God and into the world, and thus finds itself having to explain how something comes from the great Nothing, how diversity proceeds from the great Unity. Somehow – and the *Zohar* does not really tell us how, as it denies the very terms it uses ("It split and did not split") – somehow a point beyond understanding extends from nothing into the "palace" it creates by reaching out beyond itself, as it were. And what does it create first of all? The second *sefirah*, which is *Hokhmah*, "wisdom." *Hokhmah* is thus called "Beginning," because it is the first of all the *sefirot*, attributes of God, that can be known.[630]

> Within a primal point, at once infinitesimally small and great beyond measure. ...The move from *keter* to *hokhmah*, the first step in the primal process, is a transition from nothingness to being, from pure potential to the first point of real existence. ... As being exists first in this ultimately concentrated form, so too does truth or wisdom. Here we begin to see the Kabbalists' insistence that Creation and Revelation are twin processes, existence and language, the real and the nominal, emerging together from the hidden mind of God. As the primal point of existence, *hokhmah* is symbolized by the letter *yod*, smallest of the letters, the first point from which all the other letters will be written. Here all of Torah, the text and the commentary added to it in every generation – indeed all of human wisdom – is contained within a single *yod*.[631]

According to the kabbalistic understanding of the inner nature of God, the first and highest characteristic of the divine being is wisdom. It is interesting that the schema indicates that wisdom is located between the *sefirot* of understanding (*Binah*, the mother) and *Ayn Sof*, the

Beyond. True wisdom is a mixture of that which we can understand and that which we recognize as being beyond us.

Now we are in a position to understand how the *Zohar* would have us interpret the first three Hebrew words of Genesis, *bereshit bara' Elohim*. The verb *bara'*, "created," requires a direct object – the question for the mystics is, what is the direct object? Since the letter *bet* can be translated not only as "in" but also as "with," and since we now understand that *reshit*, "beginning," may be translated as "wisdom," we can follow the *Zohar*'s suggested answer to that question: "with Wisdom God was created".

We are taught that we are created *b'tzelem Elohim*, in the image of God. During the Days of Awe and at other peak times of Jewish reflection and self-judgment, we are encouraged to consider what that means for our lives. As we have seen, the Kabbalists who developed the sefirotic system as a way of understanding God also assume that the same system is echoed in our own makeup – and in the cosmos around us. Thus, we cannot contemplate God without staring right back at ourselves as well as at the universe in which we find ourselves. This is not such an unusual idea for physicists and astronomers, who are discovering that the larger and smaller structures of the universe are patterned in the same way as the larger and smaller structures of the human body. What, however, is fascinating to contemplate is that our ancestors somehow had this same insight, without benefit of microscopes, telescopes, atom colliders, or knowledge of quantum mechanics physics. And it is also the hidden lesson of *lekh l'kha*, God's command to Abraham: "go to yourself." Explore your inner universe if you would come to understand the outer world in which you live, move, and craft your life.

As we consider the creation of our world, then, we are also considering the creation of ourselves – and our relationship with that world, and with the God which we envision to be behind and before it all. Jewish tradition teaches that we are to strive to gain – or regain – a sense of unity with the world and with God, with each other, and with ourselves. In English there is a nice play on words that expresses this thought: the word atonement, a synonym for repentance, may also be read as at-one-ment. To do true *teshuvah* is to become *at one* – with the world and with God, with each other, and with ourselves. Considering the creation of ourselves using the sefirotic system, in which all the diversity is nevertheless clearly part of the All that is the One, offers us a way of coming to terms not only with the conflicting diversities within ourselves, but also with those of the world around us. All of it is part of the world; all of it is part of the meaning of our lives. We will not be able to know and understand every aspect of that meaning – the sefirotic structure suggests that there is a part of us, and part of our world, that is beyond knowing. Yet that which is unknown is still a part of us. It is the unknown that is the key to our capacity both for holiness and for sin – for exalting a life and for missing the mark we sought. According to Jewish tradition, we know that we live between blessing and curse: what remains unknown is the human choice.

We can interpret another piece of rabbinic wisdom from this story: in the work of atonement, as in the ongoing work of creation in which we are called on to participate, we are not required to complete the work – only to do our part, aware that we are part of a greater whole that is either nurtured or undermined by our individual acts. What we may understand from the teachings of the *Zohar* is that the essence of our humanity, that which we share with God, is to be willing to begin the work.

> Existence will remain meaningless for you if you yourself do not penetrate into it with active love and if you do not in this way discover its meaning for yourself. Everything is waiting to be hallowed by you; it is waiting to be disclosed in its meaning and to be realized in it by you. For the sake of this your beginning, God created the world. He has drawn it out of Himself so that you may bring it closer to Him. Meet the world with the fullness of your being and you shall meet Him.[632]

The invitation to humility and, beyond that, submission, to awe and reverence in the face of that which we cannot understand, is fully expressed in rabbinic sources and our ethical literature, as well as in the Torah itself: we are not capable of seeing the world clearly. As our ethical teachings remind us, we cannot know the hidden faults of others, but, more important, we cannot even fully comprehend our own.

> Seven things are hidden from human beings:
> the day of death,
> the day of comfort,
> the extent of judgment,
> one human being does not know what is in another's heart,
> nor does he know from what he will earn a living,
> nor when the Kingdom of David will return,
> nor when the Evil Kingdom will end.[633]

There are so many things we do not know, many that are more important to us than knowing whether or not our neighbor is really repentant – such as knowing for certain how we will support ourselves and our families. Our tradition encourages us to realize all that we do not know and to refrain from the presumption that we can know exactly what that neighbor should be doing. Better to concentrate on the only thing we can possibly control – knowing what we ourselves should be doing.

> "How should a person train himself in the attribute of *hokhmah?*
> Although it is hidden and exceedingly exalted, the attribute of *hokhmah* Above is spread out over all creation. As it is written, *mah gadlu maasekha YHVH, kulam b'hokhmah asita*, "how many are Your words, YHVH; You have made them all in *hokhmah*" (Psalms 104.24). Similarly, a person's *hokhmah* should pervade all his actions, and he should be ready to benefit and influence others.[634]

> Where are we from, what has influenced our development, what past choices are we living with ... but, even before that, how did we come to be? Why are we the way we are? The *Zohar* seems to warn us that we cannot know, with a paradoxical description of "a spark of impenetrable darkness." There are things that are beyond us, a point of mystery we cannot penetrate. This is the point at which we become inarticulate, faced with the profound mystery of our own nature and that of the world. As the psalmist sings, *l'kha dumiyah tehilah* – "to You, silence is praise."[635]

There is a point beyond knowledge. This is the meaning of *Ayn Sof*, the great Nothing – the pregnant nothing out of which something is born. It is the moment before the intake of the breath that you will then turn into a word, or a song, or a sigh, when you expel it. That nothingness is not empty. Recall that, in our tradition, there is speculation about what we actually heard when we stood at Sinai and "heard" the voice of God: one teaching has it that all we heard was the silence of a word about to be spoken. Nothing more was necessary for us to learn that the world is full of the potential that gives way to the actuality of creation, over and over again; nothing more was necessary for us to grasp that there is a source of that potential, and of that creation – of the world, of us ourselves, of each moment.

Similarly, the furthest reaches of God's presence are not explored by the *Zohar;* that ground is ceded. Human beings cannot grasp some things. *Reshit hokhmah yir'at Adonai*, "the beginning of wisdom is awe of God"[636]; Gikatilla warns, "from here on, be wary of contemplating His great might, and of entering beyond that which separates you." When one stands in a place of awe, of *yira*,' "there is no strength for contemplative thought here; there is neither boundary nor measure."[637] The beginning of wisdom, paradoxically, is the place where one realizes that one *does not know*. "Beyond that point, nothing is known." Wisdom, in mystical tradition, is not the accumulation of knowledge to the point of certainty, but, paradoxically, the accumulation of understanding to the point of realizing that we are not wise, we do not know, and we never will.

This sense of paradox, of uncertainty, pervades the *Zohar*'s attempt to speak of the esoteric; the spark "split and did not split": "the flow somehow broke through, but the nature of the breakthrough is impossible to describe, so the act is stated and immediately denied."[638] The image, suggesting that the spark broke through yet did not break through, is reminiscent of the process of birth, as if the spark were struggling to break through a membrane, or a chrysalis. In the *Zohar*'s narrative of the beginning of all, the light breaks through to "the palace," which is the third *sefirah*, *Binah* ("Understanding"). This is the womb of the world, the place where the emerging light of *Hokhmah* penetrates in an act of cosmic intercourse. With the second *sefirah*, *Hokhmah*, *Binah* gives birth to the seven lower *Sefirot*, and the world comes to be.

The *Zohar*'s reference to the "single, concealed, supernal point," which is the second *sefirah*, *Hokhmah*, is called *reshit*, "beginning," "because it is the first ray of divine light to appear outside of *Keter*, the first aspect of God that can be known."[639] That blinding spark is the first impulse of emanation emerging from the unknown transcendence of God; it births the *Sefirot*.[640] The spark itself, however, deserves close attention: this "spark of impenetrable darkness" is utterly counterintuitive. A spark should be light, a brilliant flash of fire. This one is, perhaps, the sort of spark that is too bright to see; the kind of blinding light that one senses through closed eyes and that leaves a black spot on the inside of the eyelids. Like a star that is a black hole, like a presence that cannot be envisioned but only comprehended in its impact, it is a spark of darkness. "You cannot see My face and live."[641] This spark of birth, of the world's creation, keeps emerging from concealment, rather like a pulsation of light.

The knowledge that we cannot know everything, the understanding that we cannot understand all that is, the wisdom to know that wisdom will remain beyond us – these realizations, for the mystics, leave us with the ultimate expression of humanity in God's image: compassion. The highest compassion expressed by God is beyond the balancing of mercy and judgment; it is above any admixture of *Din*. It is pure compassion, radiated from *Keter* through *Hokhmah*.

> [O]ne should be compassionate to all creatures, neither despising nor destroying them, just as the *hokhmah* above extends over all of creation —objects, plants, animals, and humans. ... Just as the Supernal *hokhmah* despises nothing, since everything is created from there — as it is written, "you have made them all with *hokhmah*" (Ps. 104.24) — a person should show compassion to all the works of the Holy One, Blessed be He. That's why our holy Rabbi was punished: he had no pity on a calf that tried that hid behind him, saying to it, "Go! for this purpose, you were created." For this reason, suffering — which derives from the aspect of severity[642] - came upon him, for compassion shields against severity. Then, when he had mercy on a weasel, saying, "it is written, 'His mercies extend to all His deeds' (Ps. 145.9), he was delivered from severity, for the light of *hokhmah* spread over him, and his suffering abated.[643]

The ebb and flow, the dance of life and death, of light and darkness, of healing and suffering, continues forever; it echoes in every aspect of the created world. Even elementary particles betray their own participation in the movement of which they are a part. On every level, we are part of a shared existence that swells and recedes like the tide. Sometimes in human history and in our own lives God seems more present to us, sometimes less; sometimes compassion and peace expand to fill our world, and sometimes they fade from our acts.

The light of the primordial spark of creation pulsates; it is not constant. There is darkness, then there is light, then — darkness again. Similarly, the light of wisdom in a human life is elusive. We live with an abiding, poignant tension between potential and reality, between the spark and the world, between what we mean and what we can, almost, manage to utter in words.

> Sometimes, perhaps, instead of a great sea, It is a narrow stream running urgently
>
> Far below ground, held down by rocky layers, The deeds of mother and father, helpless sooth-sayers
>
> Of how our life is to be, weighted by clay, The dense pressure of thwarted needs, the replay
>
> Of old misreadings, by hundreds of feet of soil, The gifts and wounds of the genes, the short or tall
>
> Shape of our possibilities, seeking And seeking a way to the top[644]

Why does that light come forth in the first place? Rabbi Akiba taught: "As much as the calf desires to suck, the cow desires to suckle."[645] The light comes forth and illuminates out of the darkness; light, then, is a way of answering a hunger, an emptiness, which is symbolized by darkness: "The world was without form and void."[646] Astonishingly, God needs Creation as much as we need God as the Source of Life, our life, and the world's. God is also seeking us.

> When Adam and Eve hid from His presence, the Lord called: *Where art thou* (Genesis 3.9). It is a call that goes out again and again. It is a still small echo of a still small voice, not uttered in words, not conveyed in categories of the mind, but ineffable and mysterious, as ineffable and mysterious as the glory that fills the whole world. It is wrapped in silence; concealed and subdued, yet it is as if all things were the frozen echo of the question: *Where art thou?*[647]

The piercing of understanding by wisdom brings forth the world; the light coming forth is the presence of God, we might say, coming forth to seek us. For the legendary ancients of our tradition, God's presence was manifest in a sense of communication so clear that only the metaphor of real words sufficed to express it. For us, so far away from that sense of certainty, we seek God through the siren call of the fascinating nuance of a Torah text. *Darsheni*, "interpret me"; the obscurity of an unexplored text seems to invite us to explore. It has been said that if Torah is God speaking to us, then prayer is us speaking back to God; perhaps that is why a good Torah study, filled with learning and new insights and moments of *aha!* can fill one with a sense of prayerful awe.

Deep Well – God's Water

> And what is this "tree" of which you have spoken? He said to him: All powers of God are in layers and they are like a tree: just as the tree produces its fruit through water, so God through water increases the powers of the "tree." And what is God's water? It is *hokhmah*, and the fruit of the tree is the souls of the righteous.[648]

We are vessels, filled with the *shefa'*, the abudance and vitality, of the Source of Life through all that Creation gives us. And we, like Rebekah at the well, draw to fill ourselves, and by our acts (the *mitzvot*) transmit to others the life-giving *shefa'* that flows through all creation. The *Sefat Emet* transmits a midrash on the verse *gerim anakhnu l'fanekha*, "we are strangers before You."[649]

> [H]uman beings were not created in this world in order to be attached, God forbid, to this world. The opposite: by way of human *devekut* to the root of life, even things of this world are drawn to God. The word *ger* [stranger] means "drawing forth," a movement that speaks of the act of bringing water up from a well. "The same is true of the exile in Egypt: it is written "your seed will be strangers" (Genesis 15.13), that is, they will draw forth

holy sparks that were lost in Egypt. That is the meaning of the verse 'and afterward they will go out with much treasure'."[650]

The presence of a well of water is associated in Jewish legend with Miriam: according to the midrash, wherever she was, water was found to sustain the Israelite community during their desert wanderings. The well represents the source of true wisdom, according to Rabbi Mordecai Yosef of Isbitza. Commenting on Exodus 24.12, "God said to Moshe, come up to me, to the mountain, and be there," he taught "to the mountain" refers to the end of the renewal of all the levels. At first one must pass through all the different kinds of wisdom in the world in the necessary order, before one reaches true wisdoms. "Be there" indicates the place of purity and the root of life, as it is written in Numbers 21.17, "and from there to the well". All wisdoms come from the well. The important thing is that one find oneself, finally, in the place which is the end of all wisdoms which is called "there."[651]

The beginning and end of wisdom is to know, when one has ascended the mountain, how to be there, to be present for that moment.

The well of water itself is more than the most vital single aspect of a landscape for ancient life in the arid ancient Land of Israel. The well is also a rich and complex concept in Jewish mystical thought. We explore its depths using the mystical tool of PaRDeS – *peshat*, "surface meaning"; *derash*, "interpreted meaning"; *remez*, "hint"; and *sod*, "secret." What is the significance of a well in the Torah?. In all of the following texts, it is a symbol of survival.

> And God opened Hagar's eyes, and she saw a well of water; and she went, and filled the bottle with water, and gave the lad drink.[652]

At the level of *Peshat*, "surface meaning," the well simply and profoundly means survival for Hagar and her son. However, it is presented as a miraculous well; Hagar does not see it until God opens her eyes.

For the level of *Drash,* "interpreted meaning," the appearance of a well of water when it means the difference between life and death can serve as a metaphor for the gift of clarity when one is unsure of one's path forward or the way in which one can be rescued from all manner of situations by the "miraculous" appearance of a new reality.

On the yet deeper level of *Remez,* "hinted meaning," the miraculous appearance of a well reminds us of the well of water that was always near the Israelite camp because of Miriam's merit. This well is also associated with a woman, Hagar the Egyptian, who has just been banished from her home and position in the household of Sarah. Is it her own merit that causes this well to appear? Why is God so solicitous of this Egyptian woman? Is it something about not oppressing Egyptians even though they oppressed us, because we know what it means to be oppressed? Or is it possible that the well appeared through Hagar's female power, just like Miriam?

Note that water drawn from a well comes from below, as compared with water that falls from above as rain. Using traditional spatial understandings regarding male and female positions vis-à-vis each other, we see an important hint of a mystical insight: since the "above" position is the dominant, rain from above is male water; and since the "below" position is the dominated, water that wells up from below is female water.

We come to the deepest level, that of *Sod,* "secret." The level of *sod* is the level of secrets, of that which is hidden from us. How can we consider that which is hidden from us? A midrash compare the study of Torah to standing outside a doorway: "Happy is the one who listens to Me...who hovers outside my doorways. (Proverbs 8.34)"[653] [O]ne must always be ready to receive and hearken to the words of the Holy One, since there is in every word the sound of God's word; every word which is uttered has within it the hidden creative power of God's word. One must listen for that which is hidden. There is a profound innerness, without measure. This is the meaning of "doorway": one should not assume that one has already arrived; one must bear in mind that one is always standing at an opening. "Doorway" [*delet*] is related to poverty [*dalut*]; by remembering that one has achieved nothing, door after door is opened for one. Especially for the Jew whose living soul constantly hears the voice to Torah, but it is hidden from him. This is what is written: "listen, listen" – listen to that which you can already hear.[654]

What sort of well might we see if we allow God to open our eyes? A second text to consider:

> Isaac dug again the wells of water, which they had dug in the days of Abraham his father; for the Philistines had stopped them after the death of Abraham; and he called their names after the names by which his father had called them. Isaac's servants dug in the valley, and found there a well of living water. The herdmen of Gerar strove with Isaac's herdmen, saying: 'The water is ours.' And he called the name of the well *Esek* ("contention") because they contended with him. So they dug another well, and they fought for that also. And he called the name of it *Sitnah* ("hatred"). He left there, and dug another well; and no one fought over that well. He called the name of it *Rehovot* ("wide open spaces"), saying: 'For now the Eternal has made room for us, and we shall be fruitful in the land.' He went up from thence to Beer-sheva, and the Eternal appeared unto him the same night, and said: 'I am the God of Abraham thy father. Fear not, for I am with you, and will bless you, and multiply your seed for My servant Abraham's sake.' Isaac built an altar there, and called upon the name of the Eternal, and pitched his tent there; and there his servants dug a well.[655]

Peshat, "surface meaning": Isaac encounters difficulty establishing himself in the aftermath of his father's death. Apparently the locals do not respect him as they respected his father. Isaac is patient, and he finally determines where God means for him to dwell. He arrives in *Beer-sheva* ("well of the oath" or "well of seven") after the well *Rehovot* is dug, and there God blesses him with the same blessing that his father received. Isaac responds to the blessing by digging another well.

Drash, "interpreted meaning": One of the few stories the Torah preserves of Isaac as an adult shows him digging wells. Recalling the association made in midrash between women and wells, we might interpret a seeking here, for his mother. Or is this perhaps an expression of Isaac's own feminine side?

Remez, "hinted meaning": In Isaac's digging of the wells, he is establishing his own relationship to the Land of Israel. We also see a hint of our own future in the land: *esek* – "contention," *sitnah* – "hatred," and, finally, we hope, *rehovot* – "wide open spaces."

Sod, "secret meaning": what is the way to establish oneself, the way to dig, that will lead to God's presence and a sense of personal blessing?

> And from to *Be'er*; that is the well of which the Eternal said to Moses: "Gather the peo there ple together, and I will give them water." Then Israel sang this song:
> Spring up, O well, sing unto it, the well, which the princes dug, which the nobles of the people delved, with the sceptre, and with their staves.[656]

Peshat: This is an aside during a recitation of a journey narrative. The people traveled from here to there, and then from there to there, and then from there ... to *Be'er*, a well called, simply, Well. The people of Israel sing to the well, which princes either dug or caused to be dug. This song is neither well known nor often cited (although it was recited in the Jerusalem Temple on Shabbat alternately with the Song of the Sea[657]).

Drash: Finding water is the most important factor in survival in arid country, such as the wilderness of the Israelites' wanderings. The water is a gift from God, even if it is human princes who pick the place to dig. This is reminiscent of the phrase in the *birkat hamazon*, the blessing after meals: "may I not depend upon the largess of princes, but only upon that of God."

Remez: There is an instance in the Torah in which God tells Moses to gather the people so that God can give them water. The incident culminates with Moses making an unfortunate choice to hit a rock, rather than speak to it as God has commanded him to do. In this case, the well is mentioned as a significant aside during a longer recitation of traveling and battles. Does it hint at the importance of balancing the male with the female side of our existence, even during fighting and war?

Sod: Why was this fragment of song preserved in the Temple service? What did it mean? What is the significance of song to survival? Who are the princes, who the nobles – and what does it mean that they, not workmen or slaves, are the ones who dig the life-giving well, with scepter and stave?

Hidden Torah

> The scroll of the Torah is written without vowels, so one can read it in different ways. ... The Torah scroll must not be vocalized, for the meaning of each word accords with its vowels. Once vocalized, a word means just one thing. Without vowels, you can read it in many wonderful ways.[658]

In the image borrowed from the poet, Torah and all it symbolizes is like a "narrow stream running urgently / far below ground, held down by rocky layers." On so many levels, Torah is hidden. Let us consider several examples from the simplest, *peshat* level of Torah study.

Sometimes the sense of a verse is unclear. In the following passage, sacrificial law of the Harvest Festivals is specified. In that context, what does the second half of the last verse (*italized*) mean?

> Three times you shall keep a feast to Me in the year. You shall keep the Feast of Unleavened Bread; you shall eat unleavened bread seven days, as I commanded you, in the time appointed in the month *Aviv*; for in it you came out from Egypt; and none shall appear before me empty; the Feast of Harvest, the first fruits of your

labors, which you have sown in the field; and the Feast of Ingathering, which is at the end of the year, when you have gathered in your labors from the field. Three times in the year all your males shall appear before the Lord God. You shall not offer the blood of my sacrifice with leavened bread; nor shall the fat of my sacrifice remain until the morning. The first of the first fruits of your land you shall bring into the house of the Lord your God. *You shall not boil a* kid in its mother's milk.[659]

In the context of the verse, first fruits are clearly analogous to a kid (a baby goat). But very little else is clear. For some reason, cooking it in the milk of its mother is not an acceptable means of observing the harvest. Learning from archaeological sources that Canaanite religious practice included exactly this sort of meal as part of a fertility ritual further complicates our study, as we must now decide just which sources of information from the larger world also qualify as Torah. As Rabbi Akiba said after observing his rabbi in mundane household activities, "This too is Torah, and I need to learn it."[660] Where is the boundary to Torah study? Is all learning acceptable as we seek to illuminate the meaning of a verse?

Even if the Torah's words are coherent, the reality they describe is sometimes confusing or contradictory. One example is that of the red heifer. Why does one who handles that which ritually purifies become ritually impure?

> Eleazar the priest shall take its blood with his finger, and sprinkle its blood directly before the Tent of Meeting seven times; one shall burn the heifer in his sight, with its skin, and its flesh, and its blood, and with its dung. The priest shall take cedar wood, and hyssop, and scarlet, and cast it into the midst of the burning of the heifer. Then the priest shall wash his clothes, and he shall bathe his flesh in water, and afterward he shall come into the camp, and the priest shall be unclean

until the evening. And he who burns it shall wash his clothes in water, and bathe his flesh in water, and shall be unclean until the evening. And a man that is clean shall gather up the ashes of the heifer, and lay them up outside the camp in a clean place, and it shall be kept for the congregation of the people of Israel for a water of sprinkling; it is a purification offering. He who gathers the ashes of the heifer shall wash his clothes, and be unclean until the evening.[661]

According to Jewish tradition, even King Solomon admitted that this text was beyond his ability to understand.

Sometimes the meaning of a list of *mitzvot* may not include explanations, thus depriving us of the ability to make inferences. Some of the following instances of admixture may seem logical, but not all:

You shall not sow your vineyard with different seeds; lest the fruit of your seed which you have sown, and the fruit of your vineyard, be defiled. You shall not plow with an ox and an ass together. You shall not wear a garment of different sorts, like woolen and linen together.[662]

The same is true for all the levels of meaning hidden in the Torah – *drash*, "interpretation"; *remez*, "hint"; and *sod*, "secret." The Sages of the Talmud taught that in every generation, more insights, more learning, more understanding were yet to be revealed. Thus medieval mystic Moshe de Leon wrote that "the written Torah is an unripe fruit of supernal wisdom." The root of Torah is the wisdom on high, secret and hidden in the mystery of the wonders that emerge from wisdom. How wonderful is the root, how great are the wonders! Who can each the root of Torah, this wisdom? That is why the sweet singer of Israel sang, "Open my eyes and I will see wonders out of your Torah!"[663]

In ancient Jewish teaching, Torah study evokes God's presence; to devote oneself to Torah is to draw near to God. A famous passage in the

Zohar compares the relationship between the Torah itself and a student to that same holy love: passionate, full of fascination and the excitement of discovery, and the promise of *devekut,* the attainment of oneness with God. Like the primordial point of wisdom, Torah initially appears from its concealment only for a moment; the devotion of a lover turns that glance into a gate leading to the longed-for intimacy.

> Human beings are so confused in their minds. They do not see the way of truth in Torah. She calls out to them every day, in love, but they do not want to turn their heads. She removes a word from her sheath, is seen for a moment, then quickly hides away, but she does so only for those who know her intimately.

A parable.

> To what can this be compared?
> To a beloved, ravishing maiden, hidden deep within her palace. She has one lover, unknown to anyone, hidden too. Out of love for her, this lover passes by her gate constantly, lifting his eyes to every side. Knowing that her lover hovers about her gate constantly, what does she do? She opens a little window in her hidden palace, revealing her face to her lover, then swiftly withdraws, concealing herself. No one near him sees or reflects, only the lover, and his heart and his soul and everything within him flow out to her. He knows that out of love for him she revealed herself for that one moment to awaken love in him. So it is with a word of Torah: she reveals herself to no one but her lover. Torah knows that one who is wise of heart hovers about her gate every day. What does she do? She reveals her face to him from the palace and beckons him with a hint, then swiftly withdraws to her hiding place. No one there knows or reflects – he alone does, and his heart and his

soul and everything within him flows out to her. This is why Torah reveals and conceals herself. With love she approaches her lover to arouse love in him. Come and see the way of Torah. At first, when she begins to reveal herself to a human, she beckons him with a hint. If he perceives, good; if not, she sends him a message, calling him simple. Torah says to her messenger: "Tell that simple one to come closer, so I can talk with him." He approaches. She begins to speak with him from behind a curtain she has drawn, words he can follow, until he reflects a little at a time. This is derasha. Then she converses with him through a veil, words riddled with allegory. This is haggadah. Once he has grown accustomed to her, she reveals herself face to face and tells him all her hidden secrets, all the hidden ways, since primordial days secreted in her heart. Now he is a complete human being, husband of Torah, master of the house. All her secrets she has revealed to him, withholding nothing, concealing nothing. She says to him, "do you see that word, that hint with which I beckoned you at first? So many secrets there! This one and that one!"[664]

We seek "hidden Torah" when we allow the *peshat* level of the text to open its doors to deeper levels; higher levels, at which, we recall from our encounter with *Binah*, the quest for certainty becomes the acceptance of "sometimes." In *Hokhmah* sometimes it will be this way, sometimes that way. And it will not be the "all good," but "all," that we encounter.

The primary Jewish spiritual act is the encounter with the holy text: it is a visual experience of reading, whether through study or in prayer. Thus, Torah is at the center of the Jewish mystical search for knowledge of God, even as Torah is the heart of any Jewish learning. Ideally, Torah study is an act not of the static absorption of information, but an expression of an active longing to seek truth and wholeness – another way of expressing the desire to draw close to God. Every act of interpreting Torah is a potential moment of once again "seeing the voices", experiencing revelation in a profound, life-changing, but also quiet, everyday, "normal"[665] way.

The Psalmist proclaimed that *yir'u tzadikim v'yira'u*,[666] "the righteous shall see and fear"; the words "see" and "fear" share two root letters, *resh* and *alef*, and sound similar enough in Hebrew that, to the ancient Israelite ear, the experience of seeing and a subsequent state of awe might have seemed like two sides of the same revelatory experience; for the descendants of those who saw what transpired at Sinai, reliving that text through reading it offers its own kind of potential for seeing. That which is seen in Jewish mysticism is, and must be, ultimately rooted in that which is read and interpreted in Torah. "The convergence of interpretation and revelation" finds its fullest form in the *Zohar*, the quintessential, and most sacred expression of Jewish mysticism:

> The imaging of the formless God in iconic forms is related in the *Zohar* to the hermeneutical act of reading. To see God is to read the sacred text of Torah, which is the embodiment of God. There is no corporeality without textuality and no textuality without corporeality. The gap between revelation and interpretation is fully closed, inasmuch as interpreting Scripture is itself a revelatory experience.[667]

Torah bridges the distance between the reflection of the divine and the divine source of that reflection. A midrashic commentary on the gift of the Torah at Sinai asks if Moses was really able to ascend to God to receive the Torah. Was Moses really able to cross the boundary between the human and the divine? The answer is "not exactly" but rather that the Torah itself acted as a sort of mediator between heaven and earth, between God and the human:

> R. Berekiah said, the length of the Tablets was six handbreadths. It is as if two handbreadths were in the

hands of the One Who Spoke And the World Came
To Be, two handbreadths were in Moshe's hands, and
two handbreadths *mafrishim beyn yad l'yad*, "separated
hand and hand."[668]

The Torah, as a product of the dialogue between God and humanity, exists in the space between; it is "the intermediary which arouses the upper Image toward the lower".[669] Torah is the necessary bridge between human and divine. Without the divine touch, we would simply be holding stones in our hands; without the human, the Torah would float away, the inheritance of angels, not of Jews.

> This ember is found in every place, its sparks are from the Torah, which is called "fire". It has been noted that *gakhelet*, "ember", has the same value in gematria as *emet*, "truth" – and there is no truth outside of Torah. Everything created is echoed in Torah and its spark is found everywhere, in everything.
>
> But it is up to the Jew to free that spark to fulfill its potential. ... This refers to the effort one makes in immersing oneself in Torah study. One can, with this effort, free words of Torah in every place.[670]

Keter – The Gate of Transcendence

FIRST RIPPLE IN STILLNESS OF AYN SOF – KETER – ALEF – ALL

> *B'shem yikhudo shel Kudsha Berikh Hu v'Shekhintey* – for the sake of the unification of the Holy Blessed One and the Shekhinah, the Transcendent and the Immanent. Humans attempting the mystical journey toward God want to go all the way "up" or "in" to *ayin*, nothingness, the dissolution of the ego into the all. One takes one's אני and transforms it into אין.[671]

First Ripple in Stillness of Ayn Sof

> You may be asked: "How did God bring forth being from nothingness? Is there not an immense difference between being and nothingness?" Answer as follows: "Being is in nothingness in the mode of nothingness, and nothingness is in being in the mode of being." Nothingness is being, and being is nothingness. The node of being as it begins to emerge from nothingness into existence is called faith. For the term "faith" applies neither to visible, comprehensible being, nor to nothingness, invisible and incomprehensible, but rather to the nexus of nothingness and being. Being does not stem from nothingness alone but rather, from being and nothingness together. All is one in the simplicity of absolute undifferentiation. Our limited mind cannot grasp or fathom this, for it joins infinity.[672]

In a body of water, the ripple caused by an action of a body sets up a counter-motion when it reaches the shore, or another physical body which stands as an obstacle to its movement. The ripples of small waves continue back and forth, back and forth, moving over and through each other from one side to the other.

In the mystical vision of God and us in the wholeness they express through the *sefirot*, the first ripple out of the stillness of the transcendence of God comes from God. It is a small point, which pierces the cosmos and emerges toward the world it creates. And this ripple continues to move; our existence may be said to be that which counter-ripples, when the movement touches us. Whether or not we are aware of it, we are part of a back and forth, a not-quite-comfortable quest for a sense of linkage that will not short out the senses, or the existence, of either of us.

> "He was like an eagle arousing its nest, hovering over its young, spreading its wings and taking them". (*Devarim* 32.11) The Sages comment on this passage: God fluttered over them, touching them, yet not touching them.[673] God is Infinite, and no one can exist in His

Infinite Light. That's why He hovers, fluttering lightly with rapid vibrations. When He touches no one can survive; that's why He instantly pulls back, as it says, "The *Hayot* ran to and fro like the appearance of a flash" (Ezekiel 1.14).[674]

For the mystics, the *Hayot*, the supernatural creatures accompanying God in Ezekiel's vision, can be seen on some level as a metaphor for the back and forth, a sort of waxing and waning of all that lives and breathes, and of the desire that brings us toward each other and then makes us recoil, as well. The beings come forth from God toward the world, in a moment of almost, not-quite-contact, like the gesture one makes to test if a stove's burner is hot – not an inappropriate approach for a people who remembers the story of the two priests, Nadav and Avihu, who carelessly approached the divine presence and were burned to death by its proximity.[675] Contact between the divine and the human is something for which, perhaps, neither side is, even now, quite ready.

The sense of the attraction of longing, and the simultaneous repulsion caused by fear, is expressed in the motion of the *Hayot* who run between God and God's creation; they move in a rhythm of *"ratzo vashov,* 'run and return', as it were, the ebb and flow of the universe.

> This rule of fluctuation dominates man's existence and is evident in the pulse of the heartbeat and the rhythm of the breathing lungs. It comes to the fore in man's desire to free himself from the bonds of physicality and unite with the Creator and the opposing urge to remain in this world and partake of life.[676]

This is a movement of longing; as Heschel put it, this is God's *ayeka?,* "Where are you?" addressed to us. To respond to it, paradoxically, we must both answer the question of self-hood and simultaneously reach beyond it. One must be an *ani,* an "I", before one can re-arrange those letters and become an *ayin,* "no thing", the no one thing which is all, in one's own way the most complete reflection of God's "no thing ness", and the *Ayin* which is the Source of All. It is a paradox: to find oneself, one must lose oneself.

The spiritual distance one travels in experiencing the struggle to reach the *ayin* of the self is the distance between believing that one has an independent existence, and understanding that one's existence is completely dependent upon God.[677] The practice of attempting to travel that distance is called *bittul hayesh*, "the negation of that which is". As Rabbi Issakhar of Zlotchov put it, the goal is "to understand that all your strength and mind and independence is nothing but a piece of God in you"[678]. Moses reaches the place where it is written *vayasteyr Moshe panav*, "Moses hid his face", (Ex.3.6) because he realized that all is God, and it was as if he, a human being with a face, did not exist.

> R. Dosa observed: It says, *For man shall not see Me and live* (Ex. 33.20). This implies that men cannot see God when they are alive but that they can see Him at their death; likewise it says, *All they that go down to the dust shall kneel before Him, even he that cannot keep his soul alive* (Ps. 22.30). R. Akiba explained: 'For man shall not see Me and live (*hay*)' implies that even the *Hayot* [literally, "living creatures"] that bear the Heavenly Throne do not see the All Glorious.[679]

The Talmud records a discussion between Rabbi Yohanan and Rabbi Eleazar, considering how to reconcile two contradictory verses describing the *heruvim* which spread their golden wings above the Ark of the Covenant in the Temple of Solomon. The question before them was whether the *heruvim* were fashioned in such a way that they stood face to face with each other, or looking away.

> One said, "They faced each other," and one said, Their faces were turned toward the House" [toward the interior of the Jerusalem Temple, i.e., away from each other]. If one holds the position that they faced each other, how are we to explain the verse "their faces were

turned toward the House" (Second Chronicles 3.13)? There is no difficulty: the first refers to when Israel does the will of the Place, and the second, when they do not.[680]

In that passage, God is referred to as *haMakom*, the Place – a Name which is particularly suited to our communal interactions, which occur in a place that we share, physically and spiritually. The place that we share, including the Place itself, and even the *heruvim* on the Ark, are affected by the way we treat each other: when we are doing the will of God, the *heruvim* respond by standing face to face. Since we are created "little lower than the angels", then, we learn that to do the will of God is to lift up our faces to each other, just like the *heruvim*. In so doing, we evoke the fullness of the Place we share. Then we will sense God's Presence between us, even God was heard, as the Torah records, in the space above the Ark, between the faces that gazed steadfastly at each other. This is the end of exile: when we can stand in a place face to face with each other, and sense God's presence, and live in harmony with the will of that Place.

Keter (Crown)

Even here, at a height so dizzy that we may not take as certain anything that we learn or intimate – for that which is transcendent will remain a mystery to human beings – even here the mystical ethicists see a path toward the emulation of the Creator:

> To be a person in the mold of the Creator, according to the mystery of the attribute of *keter*, he must possess several qualities which characterize his behavior: First and foremost is the quality of humility; one must not be arrogant and raise oneself up. The attribute of humility descends and looks downward always. ...
> There is none so patient and humble as our God in the attribute of *Keter,* for it is the height of compassion,

and before Him no blemish or transgression, no severe judgment or other quality can prevent Him from protecting and causing *shefa'* to flow and benefit constantly. So, also, a man should let no reason in the world should prevent him from doing good to others always and at every moment, and no transgression or acts of unworthy people should block him from doing good for those in need at any time.[681]

In this teaching we can detect the association of this highest attribute of God – and the human being – with Pure Compassion. All sins are forgiven here, in the overwhelming force of the Creator's love for the Creation, in the blinding "white light" of the spark of darkness which emerges from the source.

> This Sphere is called the *Rosh haLavan* [White Head]. The reason is that this Sphere is the essence of the realm of great mercy, of *ratzon* [will] and desire, and she bleaches the sins of Israel by revealing the face of *ratzon* and mercy. Let me intimate: The beginning of all visions is *loven* [whiteness] and the purpose of all visions is blackness. ... This is encoded (in the service where one separates from the Sabbath): "He who distinguishes between the sacred and secular, and light and darkness"[682]

One way of accessing one's own attribute of compassion is, possibly, by way of empathy: if one can imagine and therefore understand the situation of another person, one will be compassionate. There are, after all, fifty gates of Understanding, according to Talmudic teaching[683] - many ways of working toward the enlightened attitude we would adopt. But the medieval mystic Gikatilla reminds us that this is the "one gate that is more formidable than all of them put together": "*Keter* is not represented by a particular letter in the ineffable Name, but with the crown [*keter*] on the letter *yud*, as if it were alluding to the fact that this concept is inaccessible."[684]

Alef

> The letter *alef* stood alone and did not enter. The blessed Holy One said to her, "*Alef, alef,* why do you not enter My presence like all the other letters?" She replied, "Master of the World! Because I saw all the other letters leaving Your presence fruitlessly. What could I do there? Furthermore, look, you have given this enormous gift to the letter *Bet*, and it is not fitting for the exalted King to take back a gift He has given to His servant and give it to another!" The blessed Holy One said "*Alef, alef!* Although I will create the world with the letter *Bet*, you will be the first of all the letters. Only through you do I become one. With you all counting begins and every deed in the world. No union is actualized except by *Alef.*"[685]

To encounter *Ehyeh* is to contemplate the *alef,* that silent letter which is pregnant with the word, and the world. It is the first of letters, and the most silent of letters. The dilemma of seeing is not resolved here; in a way, it has only been brought more clearly into focus. One yearns to, but cannot, peer into the ultimate unknown: the future symbolized by the letter *alef.*

In the language of the *sefirot,* somewhere in the balance between piercing and receptive understanding, the seeker reaches the generative place of *Ehyeh*, "I will be". This is the place of the depths of transcendence. The place of *Ehyeh* is also the Source of Desire,[686] as the Psalmist cries: *mima'amakim karatikha Yah*, "from the depths I call out to you, God."[687]

In Hebrew, the letter *alef* stands for the number one and also for this first *sefirah* called *Keter*. The word *ekhad*, "one", begins with the letter *alef*.

> The thought of the blessed Holy One is the concealed, enveloped, supernal א (*alef*); no human thought in the entire world can either grasp or know it. If what is suspended in supernal thought cannot be grasped by anyone, all the more so thought itself! Within thought – who can conceive an idea? Understanding fails to even pose a question, much less to know. *Ayn Sof* contains no trace at all; no question applies to it, no conceiving contemplating any thought. From within concealing of the concealed, from the initial descent of *Ayn Sof*, radiates a tenuous radiance, unknown, concealed in tracing like the point of a needle, mystery of concealment of thought. Unknown, until a radiance extends from it to a realm containing tracings of all letters, issuing from there.
>
> First of all, א (*alef*), first and last of all the rungs, a tracing traced by all the rungs, yet called "One," to demonstrate that although containing many images, it is only one.[688]

The *Zohar* calls the *alef* the letter which "issues in the form of mystery of the beginning of thought", mysteries which include hidden light, the radiance that withstands evil, and the "radiance radiant with healing".[689]

The Maggid of Mezeritch taught that the *adam*, the human (spelled in Hebrew *alef-daled-mem*), is only *dam*, corporeality, literally "blood", (*daled-mem*) until one achieves unity with God's attributes. The *alef*, representing God, added to the *dam* completes the *adam*, each one of us. The unification of the individual with God, which entails the integration of all one's attributes, even as God's attributes are integrated, is that which leads to one's own personal fulfillment.

This silent letter *alef* nevertheless contains within it all. Gershom Scholem points out that "to hear the *aleph* is to hear next to nothing; it is the preparation for all audible language, but in itself conveys no determinate, specific meaning." Yet everything is in it.

> [The *alef*] points toward the [cosmic] unity more than all the other letters do. And even though there is no proof for this point [in Scripture], there is a hint to this effect [in Psalm 100.3]: "Know that the Lord is God. He has made us, *ve-lo' anakhnu*. His people. ..." *Ve-lo'* is written [in the Biblical text] with an *alef* [i.e. *lamed-alef*], and *ve-lo'* is vocalized [in the Masoretic tradition] with a *vav* [i.e. *lamed-vav*]. ... The meaning of *ve-lo'* when written with an *alef* is *ve-la-alef anakhnu*," (we belong to the *alef*). That is to say: we belong to [or derive from] the perfect unity, from whom everything derives blessing, constantly, and without any cessation.[690]

The sages of Jewish tradition focused upon the *alef* which begins the *Aseret haDibrot*, the Ten Utterances of Sinai. The Talmudic discussion about what was actually communicated at Sinai begins with an awareness of the great number of *mitzvot* which are implicit in the giving of the Law at Sinai:

> R. Simlai when preaching said: 613 precepts were communicated to Moses: 365 negative precepts, corresponding to the number of solar days [in the year], and 248 positive precepts, corresponding to the number of the members of a man's body. ...[This] we heard *mi-Pi haGevurah*, directly from God.[691]

Yosef Gikatilla teaches that *Keter* can only be apprehended by listening, an insight perhaps built upon the Talmud's insistence here that we actually heard the word of God *mi-Pi haGevurah*, "from the mouth of the Mighty One". The rabbis did not, however, agree on what exactly was heard, and by whom.

> Moses alone was addressed by God, and for this reason the second person singular is used in the Ten Commandments. ... The words "in order that the

> people hear when I speak with you" (Ex. 19.9) show that God spoke to Moses, and the people only heard the mighty sound, not distinct words.[692]

The idea that *Moshe Rabbeynu*, Moses our teacher, would hear more, and more clearly, than the rest of the Israelite people is very much in line with the Torah narrative, in which a frightened people beholds the thunder and lightning and, directly after the Ten Utterances have been relayed, tells Moses "let not God speak to us, lest we die."[693]

Other examples of reasoning to explain why Moses might hear more than the rest of the people are based upon his superior relationship to God, or his higher level of piety. The mystical insight which grows out of this story takes this idea further: in the struggle each of us undertakes to rise higher toward God, and go deeper into our own awareness of self, we not only integrate the diverse aspects of ourselves. We also learn how to see the myriad implications and connectedness in a word. If an *alef* can contain all the letters, then a word can contain all that we need to hear, if we learn how to hear.

> In Rabbi Mendel's view not even the first two Commandments were revealed directly to the whole people of Israel. All that Israel heard was the *aleph* with which in the Hebrew text the first Commandment begins, the *aleph* of the word *anokhi*, "I".[694]

The first word of all the Ten Utterances is the Hebrew word *anokhi*, which is the first word *mi-Pi haGevurah*, "from the mouth of God", which would have been heard on Mt. Sinai, if anyone there was capable of hearing it. But would the entire word have to be heard? The first letter of that first word is *alef*, the word in which all letters are contained. Within that *alef* is all we need to know.

But the *alef* makes no sound! All that one "hears" when an *alef* is pronounced is silence – or, perhaps, the very slight sound of the intake of a breath that one might witness before an interlocutor begins to speak. To hear when another speaks is to pay attention, to notice that something is about to be said and to listen for it. The sound of the *alef*, then, is the sound of no thing about to become some thing, some word ("thing" and "word" is the same in Hebrew: *davar*). The only *davar* that the Israelite people needed to hear at Mt. Sinai was the silence which was about to become speech, the silence full of the potential presence of God. *Anokhi*, "I am". Once we knew that there is God, all the rest follows.

All

> A person should be so absorbed in prayer that he is no longer aware of his own self. There is nothing for him but the flow of Life; all his thoughts are with God. He who knows how intensely he is praying has not yet overcome the bonds of self.[695]

The all, and how human beings live in it, is a concept which differs markedly between modern and pre-modern thinking about the world. "For traditional or premodern peoples, experience is shot through with a sense that all things are connected by an underlying life force or principle of being, a force that has been called in different cultures by names such as *mana* or *wakan* or *dharma*." These words can only be translated into modern English as "being", since inanimate objects also possess it.

> "*Mana*" or "*wakan*"...is anterior to the individuality of persons and objects; these...are rather apprehended by [the early premodern] as "stopping places of *mana*".... the human soul [is] one of the "stopping places" for *mana*, but what differentiates [the premodern] mind from ours is, that it conceives itself to be only *one* of those stopping-places and not necessarily the most significant."[696]

In Hasidic mystical thought, one attempts to become aware of the greater life force of which one is an inextricable part through prayer and meditation. The aspects of existence that seem to indicate our separateness from each other and the world are illusory at higher, deeper levels of awareness – but one must be willing to let go of the illusion before it will lose its power.

> You must forget yourself in prayer. Think of yourself as nothing and pray only for the sake of God. In such prayer you may come to transcend time, entering the highest realms of the World of Thought. There all things are as one; distinctions between "life" and "death", "land" and "sea" have lost their meaning. But none of this can happen as long as you remain attached to the reality of the material world. Here you are bound to the distinctions between good and evil that emerge only in the lower realms of God. How can one who remains attached to his own self go beyond time to the world where all is one?[697]

Holiness, connectedness to God, is an experience with meaning to the individual and to the community. Achieving it must be a personal, embodied process as well as a communal effort at ethical unity.

> "Speak to the whole community of Israel and say to them, You shall be holy, for I YHVH your God am holy" (Leviticus 19.2). This section was spoken in public assembly (so says *Sifra*), for no one can merit holiness except by negating the self within the whole of Israel. It is written: "The whole community, all of them, are holy" (Numbers 16.3). This refers to when they all are one....

The idea of the "assembly" applies to each part as well: to gather all of our 248 limbs and all our desires into one. It is by means of the *mitzvot* that one attains holiness: "He has made us holy through His *mitzvot*." And we ask, "Sanctify us by Your *mitzvot*" because it is by way of the *mitzvot* that the limbs are joined together and merit to a state of oneness. And then there is holiness.

> But the holiness of all Israel is higher than this. Therefore a gathering for the sake of heaven, its end is to survive, since the name of heaven is upon it and holiness is in it. Thus it actually was when there was unity in Israel, they had the tabernacle and the Temple, and God's presence dwelled among them. Now, because of baseless hatred there is only destruction, for there is no holiness except in oneness.[698]

The familiar verse "let them build me a sanctuary that I may dwell among them"[699] is directly related to the command to be holy: both require one's awareness that one is part of a greater whole and interdependent with it. The point is that "the holiness demanded by Torah does not come through isolation and asceticism, but on the contrary, it is demanded in the plural: be holy in your communal existence, in the midst of your interaction with other creatures."[700] We must see ourselves, each one of us, as an embodiment of one of the *sefirot,* and together in community with all other people embodying all the other *sefirot,* all are capable of embody the holiness inherent in the complete sefirotic system. We are part of an unending dance, balancing others who affect us, as we influence them; and as part of the greater web of connectedness, we comprise the embodiment of God. It is a constant dance: we embody different *sefirot* at different times. Part of the wisdom of *Hokhmah* is to discern this.

For some of us, this requires an attempt at lowering the boundaries that we have raised in the development of our individual selves; there is an alienation, a distancing that some of us are taught, or learn in order to survive harshness in significant personal relationships. For others, there may be an underdevelopment of self-hood, a lack of the appropriate boundaries which help each one of us know who we are and what we have to give – in essence, which *sefirah* we embody.

The problem may be an incorrect perception of the nature of the holy. There are four levels of holiness, according to one branch of Hasidic thought:

1. *domem*, a clump of earth
2. *tzomeyakh*, plant
3. *beheymah*, animal
4. *m'daber*, human (literally, "the one who speaks")

The holiness of *domem* is highest, because it is the highest form of *bittul hayesh*, the negation of the self. It only seems to be the least holy; this misperception is actually a deliberate concealment. The level of the *m'daber*, the human being, is the least holy, because it is the most apparent in the world, and because the human being has the highest capacity for *kiyum hayesh*, self-establishment, the opposite of the self-negation which is *bittul hayesh*.[701] Even as one's eye can get in the way of seeing, one's "I" obstructs one's ability to connect to God. Our sense of individuality, that sense of bounded self, is the opposite of the *bittul hayesh*, the "annulment of that which is" that mysticism teaches as the key to *devekut*, linkage with God, and the All.

We are left with a paradox: our sense of what we should be, and how, is actually utterly contradictory to the inner, real truth of our lives. To be something is nothing; to be nothing, for the mystics, is all.

> [I]f they think that they are something (*yesh*), then, alas, they are nothing (*ayin*). On the other hand, if, because of their fusion with the Creator, cleaving with all their physical and mental powers, they think of themselves as nothing, then they are very great indeed. They are like the branch of a tree that realizes it is part of one organic unity with its root. And the root, of course, is the One without end – the *Ayn Sof*, the One of Nothing. ... .It's like a single drop of water fallen into the sea. It has

returned to its source. It is one with the ocean. Now it's no longer possible to identify it as an independent thing in any way whatsoever.[702]

This is, however, not a final statement that a human being is nothing. Rather, typically a human being underestimates existence. We believe that we are alone, and we feel lonely, when in truth our essence is fundamentally linked to that of the universe, and what we are feeling is an inner alienation, a sense of spiritual exile, which undermines any ability we might cultivate to glory in our individualism. At the end of the day, we are part of the world and we suffer when we are distanced from it.

The anonymous author of a medieval mystical-ethical treatise muses upon the way in which the very physical structure of the human body echoes that of the world. He compares the structure of the human mouth to that of the entire world: an upper firmament corresponding to the wet human palate, and the lower waters like our wet tongue – with a separation in the middle for an air passage in both structures. In our spiritual makeup and even in our physical creation, each of us is a reflection and a microcosm of the world:

> The end of the matter is that the world of creation and the mystic world are all hinted at somewhat in man. And one who understands the secret of this thing will understand the wonders of the Lord, may He be Exalted. Therefore, man is called a world in miniature. And because the body of man is formed in the pattern of the upper world and the lower world. Therefore there has been given within him the soul which is somewhat similar to its Creator.[703]

To see that the whole world is patterned similarly to the structure of the human being is not to conclude that therefore the human being is at the center of the universe in importance. Rather, the author concludes that the glory of human life is that each of us is just another wave in the ocean, just another wondrously made part of the garden, no more and no less beautiful than spring's almond blossoms and no more and no less disgusting than the mire of a swamp. "Upon such matters should you ponder. And then you will be modest, lowly of spirit, and reverent of God."[704]

Some things will remain a mystery. How is it that apparently contradictory opposites are actually part of the necessary wholeness of the world. Why is it that faith cannot be proved, that fact and belief will always occupy separate realms of reality? Why is the Integrity, the Wholeness, the Oneness at the heart of life so difficult to realize?

> As I have written elsewhere, truth and faith are two different rungs. This is the matter of Joseph and Judah, as it is written in the Midrash "one toward the other draws near" (Job 4.18, Genesis Rabbah 93.2). "On that day shall YHVH be one and His Name one" (Zekhariah 14.9). In the future this oneness within all of Creation will become clear; it is called "the secret of oneness" (Zohar II.135b) because it is now a hidden mystery. God's oneness is beyond the power of created beings to conceive, as it is written, "all that is called by My name I have created, shaped, and made for My glory" (Isaiah 43.7), for this world was created with God's blessed name.[705]

The linking of Joseph and Judah is the balancing of truth and faith, or, to consider our opening image ("seeing is believing"), the ultimate integration of that which is seen, and that which is believed. The wholeness of the world will not come about until these two are linked, and the channels between them open to the of *shefa'*, and ready to transmit it to the world.

Mystical tradition offers a gateway into understanding this link between the two *sefirot* as symbolized by the brothers:

"I will create a new saying, says God": *shalom, shalom larakhok ulakarov,* "peace, peace for the one who is far off and for the one who is near," *urfativ,* "and I will heal him".[706]

The *Zohar* identifies two kinds of peace with the brothers: that which comes from afar, and that which is close by. The peace from afar is that of Jacob: one struggles for a lifetime and yet, at the end of life, one feels as did Jacob, that life was short and difficult, and the task still incomplete. The peace of Joseph, close at hand, is no less difficult to achieve. It requires all the discipline one can muster, and the self-control that keeps the vision of wholeness in sight despite the provocations of others with whom we are close, and share our lives.

Shalom, "peace" in Hebrew, is also "wholeness"; and in wholeness is the presence of God. One finds it first within oneself, even as Judah found it within himself when he came near to his brother Joseph.[707] For a mystic, Judah found it within himself precisely because he drew closer to his brother Joseph. According to the Torah's account, his first words were *bi Adoni,* "please, my lord". In the Torah text, *bi* is translated at the *peshat* level as "please", but may be read as "within me". Understanding *adoni,* "lord", as hinting at *Adonai,* "Lord", *bi Adoni,* then, may be translated as "God is within me". By means of faith that God is within each of us, "a person can set himself right even in times of [God's] hiding. Then you should have faith that you have within yourself the soul of the living God.

> To the one who negates the self before this life-point of the Holy One, wanting to know the truth, it will be revealed. Thus we find with Judah [after he said *bi Adoni,* "YHVH is within me"] "Joseph was no longer able to hold back" (Genesis 45.1).[708]

Judah's approach causes Joseph to respond. Here is the place where heaven and earth touch so closely that they appear to be kissing: where truth and faith embrace, and the *kheruvim* spread their protective wings over the quality of mercy that saves the world.

Jewish mystical thought, developed over centuries from esoteric, closely-guarded secrets, through ethical treatises and Hasidic storytelling, faces the insoluble mystery of being and insists that, even in times of darkness, we are on our way toward the Light. It is all within us as we are within the world, and it is only waiting for a new kind of seeing in order to emerge.

PART IV

Conclusion
Ehyeh: What Will Yet Be Seen

In Sefer Yetzirah it is said: "The heights are deep, and the depths are deep, the beginning is deep and the end is deep, the East is deep and the West is deep."[709]

Ehyeh: "I will be what I will be". We conclude with an exploration of what the view is like from the top of the ladder - although we have not actually been there. What we might be able to see from that imagined perspective that has never been visible before? and what might be, now, that could not ever have been before we learned how to see it?

CHAPTER 12

Teshuvah: Beginning to See

We end with beginning. This study concludes with one more paradox: to attempt to contemplate the highest level of the *Sefirot* is to find oneself at a place that cannot be conceived, because it is not yet.. In the grip of an extreme state of being or feeling, one might feel the need to speak, yet be unable to utter a word; there is a deep inner place that is beyond words, beyond description. Yet it is not empty. This is the pregnant silence of what will yet be, the Sinai place of the *alef*: that which is longed for but not yet heard, not yet seen. It is the place of the *Hayot,* the living creatures who forever run to and from, suspended between clinging in desire, and recoiling in awe and fear.

> Why is the language of lovemaking so hard to learn? Why is the body so often dumb flesh? Why does the mind so often choose to fly away at the moment the world waited for all one's life is about to be spoken?[710]

Because it is the place not yet articulated, this is not a place of arrival. It is a place of transcendence, which no human being can reach during a human lifetime. It is beyond human limits, yet, paradoxically, it is the place a human being on a spiritual quest seeks constantly. This is the place of the undefined space that exists in front of the lifted foot, as it moves toward the completion of its stride. It is the "not yet" of life:

the goal not reached, the desire emerging. It is the place of the hoped-for eternal peace of the End of Days, and the lost, longed-for wholeness of Eden. It is the place of *Ehyeh*, "that which I will be," of the individual, of the world, of God: of that which is yet to be seen, and known, and done.

How can the one know the One? What allows a mere human being to see what has not yet been seen? The view from the *Sefirot* has shown us: to ascend them is to accept them, and to incorporate into one's own knowledge of one's self what they represent and what they teach. It is to learn to be whole in one's learning and one's life. Only in this way is one's vision is opened up to the fullness of what it is possible to see, what may yet be seen. It is a life long journey down a path of Torah; learning and doing by which one achieves balance, and integration – the healing of the self.

The invitation is Eternal, the doorway waiting to be opened so that the Need on High, on Deep, and on Forever, can be answered. To ascend the *Sefirot* is to see and welcome their image and echo in oneself, in others, and in the world. To accept them is to unlock their power within oneself to become an intentional part of an essential linkage in a chain of Oneness, a part of the All which is more whole for the freeing of that part's spark. Like the view at the top of a tall mountain on a sunny day, to climb the limbs of the Tree of the *Sefirot* is to see that which has never been seen before, that which cannot be seen but for the ascent. When one reaches the level of understanding that transcends physical desire and emotional anguish, the path is cleared of distraction, and one reaches the serenity of understanding that there is that which cannot ever be clear. The crucial clarity that one achieves through the ascent is that now, one can accept that a lack of certainty in human terms need not destroy human serenity: one learns to live with mystery.

The difference between an honest, learning, and sincere Kabbalistic journey to the heart of life, and the quick and quacky promises of pop mysticism, is this: as one reaches higher and deeper, one is less concerned with control over one's life, and with the reassurances that are sought in power and public esteem. The true ascent is not toward control, not of the upcoming lottery or even of a loved one's health; it is a clarity of spiritual calm brought about by realizing that one does not and cannot control. It is in seeing that each one is part of All. And that All is One. Moses stands at the burning bush, standing before *Ehyeh*, that which will yet be. To see what has never been seen before required his ability to embrace the uncertainty of the *alef*, to turn toward it and away from certainty; he had to be willing to let go of that which he already knew, and to gaze long enough to overcome the eye's certain yet unseeing gaze, so that he lose that certainty and thus truly see. This turning, this *teshuvah*, is a willingness to bend the stiff neck, to leave the path and investigate what might be seen in a new direction. *Teshuvah* requires humility; one must be willing to recognize not one's knowledge, but one's ignorance. This turning offers great promise of that which might yet be seen, but only if one is willing to lose sight of the expectations and assumptions to which one clings.

This is not easy; *teshuvah* does not come to a whole heart. Very often it is a clarity of vision achieved through suffering. There is that which can be seen only through tears, and the light we create through suffering can illuminate the path to wholeness. As High Priest, Aaron continued his work for the community even when he was in mourning for his sons, even when he could not see a meaning in their deaths. Rabbi Kalonymus Kalmish Shapira, who continued leading and caring for his congregation in the Warsaw Ghetto during its darkest and most terrible days, insisted that

> even when Aaron's life was as bitter as *gidin* – wormwood – he continued to do his holy work without deviating in the slightest from God's command. This is what made it possible for Aaron to "light its lamps facing the menorah."

He did not shake his fist at the sky. He stood in the face of the darkness and continued to fulfill his obligation to light the sacred menorah daily, as a *ner tamid*, a "regularly kindled light." The light on the altar of God is not eternal; it must be tended reliably. The effect of Aaron's sacred service was not only to illuminate the interior of the *mishkan* with that light; the light of its lamps, the Torah recounts, reflected back on the menorah itself. Shapira taught that, as Aaron fed the menorah with precious olive oil, by that very light he nurtured the people of his community. "The Jewish people are 'the face of the menorah'... the purpose of the menorah was, in fact, the Jewish people. In kabbalistic terminology 'purpose' is synonymous with 'face'."[711]

In the midst of his personal catastrophe, Aaron found a way to continue to stand in the light of the faces which faced him. Out of the exile of his personal grief, the link between him and his people was re-opened and renewed, and the *shefa'*, the energy and the blessing, of that connection nurtured and illuminated in both directions. All is reflected: by bringing the light he needed, Aaron also received it. By gathering his courage and will to once again stand in it, he dispelled his own darkness as he alleviated that of others.

This turning to see, this *teshuvah,* is not for one who lives in the past, or cannot bear the idea of change. It cannot be achieved in the safety of what is already known and named and seen; whether by one who is already certain that all is well, nor by one who cannot come to terms with life-changing trauma. *Teshuvah* is a movement of the soul in which on turns around and for the first time, beholds a new and infinite horizon, a "wild surmise":

> then felt I like some watcher of the skies when a new planet swims into his ken; or like stout Cortez when with eagle eyes He star'd at the Pacific – and all his men look'd at each other with a wild surmise – silent, upon a peak in Darien.[712]

The drop of water beholds the ocean to which it belongs. This is the end of exile, from others, from the world, from God.

> Our souls are really very close, it is only sin that causes distance and separation ... there are sins which cause separation between a human being and the Place, and those which cause separation between one person and another. There is also a separation between you and

yourself. ... When all the sins are atoned for, all Israel becomes One ... the Torah is dependent upon this unity, for it is a "tradition for the community of Jacob" (Deut 33.4).[713]

Sin is that which separates from the sources of one's life and wholeness; in this context, *teshuvah* is that which overcomes the disconnect, and links individuals in nurturing and healing forms of community. Torah itself is dependent on this *teshuvah,* this willingness to turn away from distancing and see the path toward reconciliation; authentic Torah study can only exist in a healthy, holy community.

CHAPTER 13

The River Kevar

The Book of Ezekiel opens with the words *nift'khu hashamayim va'er'eh mar'ot Elohim,* "the heavens opened and I saw a vision of God". The first letters of the Hebrew words spell *emunah,* "belief". One can see only what one believes.[714] This account of a vision of God opens the Book of Ezekiel. This prophetic book recounts the exile of the People of Israel, in the aftermath of the destruction visited by the Babylonian Empire upon Jerusalem over twenty five hundred years ago. The survivors of the catastrophe were exiled to Babylon, and so it was that Ezekiel sat by the river Kevar, in despair: surely this was the end of the Jewish people.[715]

Yet it is precisely at this moment, when all seems lost and nothing is clear, that Ezekiel raises his eyes and sees something never seen before: a vision of God. Once upon a time, Abraham had lifted his eyes and beheld God in three strangers who passed his way, and his ability to see God's presence among them brought about a new hope for his own personal life and that of his people, waiting to be born. Ezekiel's vision, many generations later, becomes a powerful message of hope and rebirth for all of Abraham's descendents. In both cases, one must lift one's eyes past what is true now, in order to see what might yet be.

Ezekiel lifted his eyes above the River Kevar. In Hebrew, the word *kevar* means "already"; it refers to something that has happened in the past. It is *hayah* - that which was.

> *"Adonai l'mata, yud-hey-vav-hey ba'emtza, Ehyeh l'malah"* [*Adonai* is below, YHVH is in the middle, *Ehyeh* is above]: *Ehyeh* is the name of God which invokes the future. The Zohar's comment on Ezekiel's vision – *hayo hayah al nehar Kevar"* - is that *hayo hayah* means "what was", i.e. God was. God was the *Ehyeh* God, but the *alef* fell off. That is what happens in Exile: Ezekiel found himself by the River Kevar ("already"), where there is no future, only what was, what already has happened. Our challenge is to restore the *alef*.[716]

Thus it is with us: when we are in exile by the River *Kevar,* the River of What Was, we are only able to touch *haya,* the part of God which is in the past. At the River of What Was, the God of the future, symbolized by the missing *alef,* cannot be seen. It is only in the turning to lift one's eyes from the River of What Was that one sees *Ehyeh,* the future vision of "I Will Be," which God promises to Moses at the burning bush.

We live suspended between these two names of God, *hayah* and *Ehyeh,* between past and future, as surely as we balance each day between day and night, birth and death. The path toward meaning offered by Jewish mysticism invites us to rest in the awareness that life exists with all the subjectivities of shifting balances, conflicting truths and partially-perceived realities. Up and down, back and forth, *gadlut* and *katnut,* moving away and moving toward.[717] To be a Jew with a mystic sensibility is to know that it is precisely in the balance of these polarities that we find the fullness of our lives, and God's presence; most of all, in the balance between that which was, and that which may yet be. Like Moses, we are able to see that which is within the bush only when we are ready to "turn aside and look." It is this capacity for turning, to see that which may be seen, which opens for the seeker the way home from exile.

We have earlier in this work explored the significance of remembering, but there is yet another link of memory to consider. This connection reaches, through Torah, from today to the ancient past; it recovers layers of buried memory of that which the Jewish people used to know. This is most necessary aspect of self-integration carries out the "re-membering" of the individual, and of the people: recovering memories which should have been transmitted, but were forgotten on the way, lost along with that part of the wholeness that might have been. Nothing is yet whole. When God speaks to Moses out of a burning bush, I want to suggest that it is possible to interpret that God is proclaiming the Name as a reality yet to be completely created, and dependent on the human telling and guarding, of the word. "*Ehyeh Asher Ehyeh,*" God declares, and goes on to explain: *zeh shemi,* "this is My Name": *l'olam* "forever", *v'zeh* "and this" *zikhri* "remember," *l'dor dor* "for all generations."[718] *Zikhri* is the femine form of the command to remember; God is speaking to all of us, as the feminine sefirah Malkhut, through these words addressed to Moses.

In a perfect inverse to the traditional teaching that God said *shamor v'zakhor b'dibbur ekhad,* "'keep' and 'remember' in one utterance," in the phrase *Ehyeh Asher Ehyeh* God may be said here to say the same thing twice but to mean something different by it in each utterance. The first *Ehyeh* is "my name forever," or "my name is Forever"; the second, then, equates *Ehyeh* with *zikhri,* or, "my name is Remember." We might extend this understanding to interpret the commandment, then, that when we would rise toward Jerusalem we are to bring up not *zakhur'kha* "all your males," but *zakhor'kha,* "all that you are commanded to remember." God's name *Ehyeh Asher Ehyeh,* "I will be that which I will be", is literally a call to human beings to create That Which Will Be through our own response of remembering, and of re-membering, and recreating, a future wholeness that we already know by heart. If we would stand in the Presence of God, we must rise through, integrate, and bring along all our personal and communal memory, all of our experience, all of our self, and selves. One does not rise toward the promise of the future without intently, and intentionally, living each day that passes.

CHAPTER 14

Get Going: The End of Exile

According to a story shared among Hasidim, the Kotzker Rebbe one morning began his prayers in the usual way, saying *modeh ani l'fanekha* – "I give thanks before You". Suddenly he asked himself, "Who is the 'I'? and what is the 'before You'? and he stopped, and said no more."[719] This is the moment of "get going," of *lekh l'kha,* the command through which a spiritual journey begins. Here everything stops, and one must open one's eyes and turn aside to see that which has not yet been seen. When that moment came to Abraham, what he saw was sufficient to allow him to go forth and leave everything he knew, for the sake of learning what he did not yet know.

When confronted with his own moment of *lekh l'kha,* Moses turned his face away, from which we learn that he knew that he had to move beyond his face, his "I", in order to come face to face with the "You" before which he stood. Moshe is described in Jewish tradition as having the ability to see God *panim el panim,* "face to face." Yet at the same time Moshe is told by God that he cannot see God's face and live. Clearly it is possible that the kind of *devekut,* closeness to God, indicated here is the vision of God that ends one's life; but ancient Jewish tradition also insists that God may be seen, not only by Moshe, but by other human beings who achieve the vision and do survive it.

Recall the ancient Jewish image of the scales, balancing a pan on each side. In the context of human relationships, justice is defined in the Torah as the fulfillment of the fundamental concept of maintaining balanced scales in business dealings. The prophet Isaiah proclaimed that God is present only in conditions of human justice, i.e., God is seen only where balance is achieved between the one who gives and the one who receives. In sefirotic terms, justice is found in the balance between the overflowing right side of abundance and the restraining left side of containment – in the world, in human relationships, and in the individual human's struggle to achieve an integrated, balanced, meaningful life.

> Moses said: 'Master of all the worlds! [It is written] "For You, YHVH, are seen face to face" (Num.14.14). What is the meaning of "face to face"? Resh Lakish said: 'Behold' [said Moses], 'the scales are evenly balanced!'[720]

The ancient Israelites expected to see God *between* the *kheruvim*; for the Jewish mystic, God is seen between the balanced scales, not in any one place or face, but in a vision composed of all the different, conflicting, contrasting, complementary faces reflecting back at each human being on her journey through the world. In other words, we see God in the balancing of every act, in each day.

Jewish tradition counsels that, if we would lift ourselves up, we must focus upon the small acts which make up our lives. Rabbi Pinkhas of Koretz said:

> It could be that a man comes into being, is created and lives seventy years, only for the sake of one single word or one single gesture that he will do in truth before the Holy Blessed One. There will be many other things that he will do wrong, and he will live with the question of never knowing when he will return to the Holy One; in any case he was perforce created for that single gesture, which the world needs.[721]

In Jewish terms, to believe in the power of a simple gesture, its effect yet unknown, is poignantly expressed in the words God spoke to Abraham at the beginning of their relationship: *lekh l'kha*. To "get going" on the journey to becoming a reflection of God, one must bring oneself into the world, with each gesture.

For a Jew, to get going is to immerse oneself in Torah and *mitzvot*. Even if one is not able to do such in the correct way yet, get started; get going.

> Rav Yehuda said in the name of Rav, a person should always [*l'olam*] be busy with Torah and *mitzvot*, even if he is not able to do so for its own sake, since *mitokh shelo l'shma ba l'shma*, within the doing something not for its own sake, one comes to doing it for its own sake. ... as long as a person continues to go from level to level, his mind will expand, and he will know how to cleave to a higher understanding, and this is why the definition of a human being is *holekh*, "one who moves"; as long as he continues to move from level to level, he will achieve more of the true inner light of Torah, which is called *l'shmah*, "for its own sake"... this process will never end, which is why the Sages said "never"... the Sages meant to hint at this idea, that one never reaches the final level [and never feels that one is doing *l'shma*] but spends one's whole life moving from level to level. As he rises, from the perspective of the new position, each previous step will seem as if it was not for its own sake.[722]

L'olam, "always" or "forever", also literally means "to, or toward, the world." It may also be taken to mean "toward Eternity", that is, God. It is as if we were to answer the perennial human question "how long will it take?", or "are we there yet?" by saying, as God said to Abraham, "look at the stars, can you measure them?"

The idea that the essence of a human being as *holekh*, "one who moves", can be applied to many kinds of movement. The Hasidic teaching of *lekh l'kha* is understood not as "go forth" to some other, outer place, but as "go to yourself," explore your own inner depths, and how they connect to the outer, to the All. This process never ends; to be human is holekh – to go, to move, to walk.

> The being of a person is never completed, final. The status of a person is a *status nascendi*. The choice is made moment by moment. There is no standing still.[723]

One might also say, *status ascendi*. Meaning is not located in a promised land, a place to be discovered, but rather, as a movement toward a wholeness, a Oneness; this going on and on which requires one's entire life. As Rabbi Nakhman of Bratslav put it in a well-known saying, "Wherever I am going, I am going to Jerusalem."

The journey to the end of exile can be envisioned in at least three different forms of movement. This study has offered an exploration of the *Sefirot* using a metaphor of Jacob's ladder to describe steps we take in ascending a ladder toward wholeness; but the wholeness which the end of exile promises is found just as much as a downward deepening of groundedness and stability in the roots of one's own being, and, no less, in a third sense, as a movement inward toward one's own true center. Regardless of one's sense of direction, each step depends upon keeping one's balance – between the forces of gravity and exhilaration, between the left and right of one's waverings, and between what pulls one away and what beckons one onward to fulfill one's human potential.

> It is written (Ecclesiastes 3.11) "He has also placed the world (*ha'olam*) in their hearts [that they should not find out the work that God has done from the beginning to the end]. Do not read *ha-olam* (the world) but *he-elam* (concealment)."[724]

Once again the medieval mystics touch upon an essential human truth: it is not only what is beyond us that is hidden to us, but also what is closest to us. Every gesture counts, but we cannot know how. It is in the realm of That Which Will Be, and the mystics are daring enough to suggest that That Which Will Be depends upon the focus, and the everyday acts, of normal, ordinary human beings.

> The Holy Blessed One said to Moshe, "Go, say to them, to Israel, that My name is *Ehyeh Asher Ehyeh*." What is "I will be that which I will be"? As you will be with me, I will be with you. David said, "God is your shadow at your right hand"; what is the meaning of "God is your shadow?" As you are as a shadow, so shall your shadow be. If you play with him, he will play with you; if you weep over him, he will weep over you. ... .So the Holy Blessed One is your shadow: just as you are with him, so he will be with you. Thus ... the upper regions are aroused in accordance with the arousal of the lower regions, and in this way the upper regions appear to the lower as a shadow of a shape. Thus, according to the act which arouses the lower regions, so the upper regions are influenced, for good or for evil.[725]

The Jewish people invokes its memories of what came before. What was it like to feel a harmony and a wholeness of one's being, moving in awareness and in concert with Being? Each year on the holy day of Simkhat Torah, the cycle of Torah readings begins once again, moving Jewish memory through the Exodus from Egypt and toward Sinai. The movement of Jewish historical memory is from *katnut* to *gadlut:* from narrow places to exultant, expansive freedom, from slavery to liberation, and finally, from brokenness to wholeness. Home from exile.

CHAPTER 15

Standing in the Light

> You are like one who has been given a ladder; the light that shines in you is a gift from above.[726]

In light we see; in light we are seen. "A *mitzvah* is a lamp, and the Torah is light,"[727] declares the author of Proverbs; by way of *mitzvot*, the Jewish framework for communal interaction, individuals and communities create the light which illuminates the path forward. For a mystical perspective, this is not a movement whose face is turned inward, or backward, but rather an effort to face up to, and learn from, bitter experience. In human experience, light is derived not from the avoidance of darkness but out of one's encounter with the darkness itself, even as the light of the first day was created out of darkness. Unlike other creation myths, the surviving version of the Jewish myth does not require conquering and destroying darkness in order to create light; rather, light is drawn from the darkness, even as forms are drawn from formlessness. "Out of chaos He formed substance, making what is not into what is. He hewed enormous pillars out of ether that cannot be grasped."[728]

Seeking out the light of that first day, the mystical path is understood by those who follow it as the real force maintaining the divine Garden, as Adam was commanded to do by God. This cultivation of the Garden is an ongoing activity rather than a return to, or attainment of, a primordial state. The theosophical Paradise is ... a dynamic attempt to maintain this world in the best status quo ... by the effort to construct it continuously and actively.[729]

By the light of God's presence in the Garden of Eden, the *or ganuz,* "hidden light", we see and are seen in our fullness, our wholeness. What would it mean to be, and to be seen, in such a way for the first time? We experience God as hidden from us; the mystical insight which teaches that all is reflected from above to below to above suggest that we in some way are also hidden from God. God calls to the first humans, in the moments after the unity of the Garden was first broken, *ayeka?* "Where are you?"[730]

To reveal oneself is to step into the light, and thus to become complete in one's creation; it is to stand in the light of the menorah as Aaron did, and thus to stand in the light of the presence of the Jewish people. From a mystical perspective, these seven lights, representing the seven lower *Sefirot* from *Hesed* through *Malkhut,* are all part of the same sefirotic structural wholeness; each light gives light to all the others. To stand in that light is to see oneself as only a small part of the All, and yet,

> not to be embarrassed, and to do what one has to do. "Thus Aaron did in front of the menorah" (Numbers 8.3) and did not change. This means that he did not change what he was doing, nor hide.

To reveal oneself to God is to reveal oneself also to oneself: to accept all of oneself, and in that way to come to know an acceptance of all of creation in its fullness.

> [T]hen human beings will be able to stand and serve before the Blessed Holy One even though the Blessed

Holy One is high and exalted above all the ministering angels, even as God is above the lower regions. Before the exaltedness of the Creator there is no recognizable difference between ministering angels and the lower regions, except that angels have a wholeness which allows them to do what they are commanded to do even though they see and understand the exaltedness of the Creator.[731]

To function, to fulfill what is expected of one even when one is overwhelmed by the sheer scale of the All in which one participates, is to stand before God at the level of angels – in wholeness, at peace. And then, anyone lighting Shabbat candles will fulfill the role of the High Priest, and by the kindling below evoke Aaron's lighting of the Menorah. And then all will be raised up by that light, up unto the Upper World.[732]

When we stand in wholeness, integrated and balanced, before the menorah, we reveal ourselves to God, and to the other human beings with whom we share the life of the world. We can see that we touch all, because we are part of the All. By our own raised light, then, we shall yet see the Oneness that has yet to be seen, and bring it into being.

ENDNOTES

1. Hayim Vital, *Shaarei Kedushah*, 3.2.
2. *Zohar* 2.23b, trans. Daniel Matt. Pritzker Edition, Volume 1 (Stanford: Stanford University Press, 2004). Unless otherwise indicted, all *Zohar* translations are Matt's either entirely or foundationally.
3. Genesis 2.7.
4. BT *Bava Batra* 74a.
5. Ecclesiastes 1.8.
6. See Byron Sherwin's treatment of this theme in *Crafting the Soul: Creating Your Life as a Work of Art*.
7. Psalm 145.18.
8. Moses de Leon, *Sefer haRimmon*, in Elliot R. Wolfson, *The Book of the Pomegranate*, p. 388.
9. BT *Berakhot* 29b.
10. Related by Martin Buber without attribution in *Ten Rungs*, p. 31
11. Abraham Joshua Heschel, *God In Search of Man*, p. 238. Italics in the original.
12. BT *Yoma* 85b.
13. A quote attributed to H.L. Mencken, who used it to describe a philosopher. "A theologian," he went on to say, "is the one that finds it."
14. The idea that God is seen, but only through a dark looking-glass, is an ancient attempt to reconcile divergent Biblical accounts; what Ezekiel, Isaiah, and even Moses saw was only a distant glow of the presence of God (although the power of Moses' leadership was that he could see more clearly). In the future healed world, the mystical tradition promises, humankind will see more clearly.
15. Micah 7.20.
16. Moses Cordovero, *Or Ne'erav*, p. 38.
17. Zekharyah 14.9.
18. Exodus 4.1.
19. Exodus 3.2-4.
20. Elliot Wolfson discusses the "iconic/visual and aniconic/aural representations

of God" and makes his case for the priority of the visual, against Scholem, in his *Through a Speculum That Shines.*
21 Exodus 20.15.
22 Rashi to Exodus 20.15.
23 Exodus 20.15
24 Rabbi Yehudah Leib Alter of Ger, *Sefat Emet, Yitro* 1, p. 31 (Hebrew), in Arthur Green, *The Language of Truth.*.
25 There is an alternate belief, demonstrable throughout the Bible but beyond this study's scope, that images of God were acceptable, such as the golden bull worship in the northern kingdom of Israel.
26 Howard Eilberg-Schwartz', *God's Phallus and Other Problems for Men and Monotheism,* and Benjamin Sommer, *The Bodies of God and the World of Ancient Israel* both examine the evidence for seeing God, and theological difficulties with that idea within the Bible.
27 Exodus 33.20.
28 Elliot R. Wolfson, *Through A Speculum That Shines,* p. 4.
29 Max Kadushin, *The Rabbinic Mind,* p. 209.
30 Jacob Z. Lauterbach (ed.) *Mekhilta deRabbi Ishma'el,* p. 24.
31 Benjamin Sommer, *The Bodies of God and the World of Ancient Israel,* pp. 41-42.
32 Rabbi Joshua b. Karkhah, *Exodus Rabbah* II.5.
33 Annie Dillard, *Pilgrim at Tinker Creek,* p. 35.
34 Exodus Rabbah II.6.
35 Aviva Gottlieb Zornberg, *The Particulars of Rapture,* p. 80.
36 Annie Dillard, op. cit., p. 81.
37 The sacred space built by the Israelites during their wilderness wanderings, in which the Divine Presence, the *Shekhinah,* would dwell among them.
38 Exodus 36.18-20.
39 I owe this idea to Lily Robbins, who, called to the Torah at Congregation Shir Tikvah in Portland, Oregon, as a bat mitzvah on Shabbat *VaYakhel* 5768, offered this insight in her *d'var Torah.*
40 T.S. Eliot, "Little Gidding," *Four Quartets,* p. 4.5.
41 Leviticus *Rabbah* 4.6.
42 M *Avot* 1.2.
43 Kenneth Gergen, *The Saturated Self,* pp. 97–98.
44 *Sefat Emet* cited in Aharon Yaakov Greenberg (ed.), *Itturei Torah,* p. 104.
45 A phrase used by Arthur Green.
46 This important aspect of mystical theology is discussed at length in Part I.
47 Psalms 65.2.
48 Psalms 118.28.
49 Yitzhak F. Baur, *Galut,* pp. 109–-110.
50 Psalm 137.5-6.

51 Blessing after the Haftarah, third paragraph.
52 *Sheva Berakhot* (wedding blessings), seventh blessing.
53 From the Torah service.
54 Gershom Scholem, *The Kabbalah and its Symbolism..*
55 BT *Rosh HaShanah* 31a.
56 BT *Rosh HaShanah* 31a.
57 The reference is to the mystical Shabbat hymn *Lekha Dodi:* the complete line is, "At hand is Bethlehem's David, Jesse's son, bringing redemption to my soul."
58 Abraham Joshua Heschel, *The Jews: Their History, Culture and Religion*, p. 616.
59 Abraham Joshua Heschel, *The Jews,* p. 616.
60 This *kavvanah*, "intention," is a statement of purpose used by Kabbalists to focus the mind on the inner mystical significance of the fulfillment of a *mitzvah*, in this case, that of prayer. To unify the Name is to bring together the two letters associated with Judgment, *yud hey,* with the two letters associated with mercy, *vav hey.* "The blend of both leads to the desired goal for creation" (Nosson Scherman, *Mahzor,* p. 37).
61 Abraham Joshua Heschel, "No Religion Is an Island," in Abraham Joshua Heschel and Susannah, *Moral Grandeur and Spiritual Audacity,* p. 242.
62 Joseph Gikatilla, op. cit., pp. 86–87.
63 Moses Cordovero, *Or Ne'erav,* I.2
64 Proverbs 25.11.
65 Maimonides, *Guide for the Perplexed,* p. 6.
66 For a discussion of the traditional boundaries set about Kabbalah study and a modern interpretation, see my discussion "Is Kabbalah Jewish?" below.
67 Joseph Gikatilla, *Shaarei Orah,* pp. 56–60.
68 Abraham Joshua Heschel, *Who Is Man?* p. 31.
69 See Figure 1.
70 Deuteronomy 13.4.
71 Ibn Gabbai, *Avodat haKodesh* II, 6 fol.29a, cited by Gershom Scholem, *Major Trends,* p. 54.
72 A Talmudic coinage originally meant to refer to the needs of the Jerusalem Temple, first used Kabbalistically by Nahmanides. See *Problems and Parables of Law: Maimonides and Nahmanides on Reasons for the Commandments,* p. 173, n.31.
73 BT *Pesakhim* 112a.
74 Attributed to Rabbi Isaac the Blind.
75 Benjamin Sommer, *The Bodies of God and the World of Ancient Israel,* p. 74. Sommer suggests that Divine longing for immanence is the central theme of the Biblical priestly tradition.
76 BT *Sanhedrin* 64a.
77 The phrase is found in Job 31.2, where it refers to one's destiny; in the 16th

century the usage emerged that referred to the human soul as an actual part, *helek*, of God. See, among others, Elijah de Vidas, *Reishit Hokhmah haShalem*, p. 362.
78 BT *Sotah* 14a.
79 Cited in Byron Sherwin, *Mystical Theology and Social Dissent*, p. 125.
80 Deuteronomy 4.4.
81 Included in the *siddur's* daily morning prayers from BT *Shabbat* 127a; also see JT *Peah* 2a.
82 Moses Cordovero, *Tomer Devorah*, pp. 42–43.
83 Rabbi Azriel, *Perush haTefillot*, cited in Isaiah Tishby, "Prayer and Devotion in the *Zohar*," in Lawrence Fine, *Essential Papers on Kabbalah*, p. 351.
84 Isaiah Tishby, "Prayer and Devotion in the *Zohar*," in Lawrence Fine, op. cit., p. 52.
85 *Zohar*, 110b, cited in ibn Gabbai, *Avodat HaKodesh, VaYikra, Behar*.
86 Genesis 2.5-6.
87 Genesis 1.27.
88 Benjamin Sommer, *The Bodies of God*, p. 70.
89 Judah Loew of Prague, *Derekh Hayim*, p. 143.
90 a phrase from Maimonides' Articles of Faith.
91 Elimelekh of Lizhensk, *Noam Elimelekh*, p. 102b.
92 *Shiur Komah* is the name of what is considered to be the most ancient work extant of Jewish mysticism: it contemplates the dimensions of the Divine.
93 Elimelekh of Lizhensk, ibid.
94 David Shapiro, "The Doctrine of the Image of God and *Imitatio Dei*", p. 135.
95 M. *Avot* 1.14
96 Abraham Joshua Heschel, *Who Is Man?* p. 31.
97 Ibid.
98 D. H. Lawrence, *A Propos of Lady Chatterly's Lover*, p. 323.
99 Charles Guignon, *On Being Authentic*, pp. 9–10.
100 Robert Bellah et al., *Habits of the Heart: Individualism and Commitment in American Life*, pp. 147–148.
101 Eleazar Azikri, *Sefer Haredim*, p. 219.
102 Nel Noddings, *Caring: A Feminine Approach to Ethics and Moral Education*.
103 BT *Sukkah*, 53a.
104 Robert Putnam, *Bowling Alone: The Collapse and Revival of American Community*.
105 Mordecai Yosef Leiner, *Mei haShiloah*, p. 87.
106 Bellah, Robert et al., *Habits of the Heart: Individualism and Commitment in American Life*, p. 282.
107 For example, an early Aramaic translation of the story of Cain and Abel in *Bereshit* supplies the cause, missing in the Hebrew version, of the murderous argument between the brothers as a theological dispute; Cain held that *leyt din*

v'leyt dayyan, "There is no justice and there is no judge", which is an important religious issue for the *Targum* author's time.
108 See David Stern, "The First Jewish Books and the Early History of Jewish Reading," pp. 163–202.
109 Rachel Adler, *Engendering Judaism: An Inclusive Theology and Ethics*, p. 3.
110 BT *Pesakhim* 116b.
111 Cited by Rabbi Louis Jacobs, transmitted by Rabbi Byron Sherwin.
112 Abraham Joshua Heschel, *God in Search of Man: A Philosophy of Judaism*, p. 107.
113 Elizabeth Barrett Browning, *Aurora Leigh: A Poem*.
114 Exodus Rabbah 2.5.
115 Ibid.
116 Lurianic Kabbalah explains that if God fills all existence, then there can be no creation of anything outside God. Therefore God had first to contract God's essence in order to make room for human beings to exist, and to enable them to act freely of their own choice.
117 Deuteronomy 11.26.
118 Kotzker Rebbe, *Ohel Torah*, 84, cited in Victor Cohen, *The Soul of the Torah*, p. 344.
119 Abraham Joshua Heschel, *God in Search of Man*, p. 101.
120 Emmanuel Levinas, *Totality and Infinity*, p. 215.
121 Annette Baier, *Moral Prejudices: Essays on Ethics*, p. 24.
122 Ibid., p. 25; reflecting on Carol Gilligan's *In A Different Voice*, in *Moral Prejudices*.
123 Byron Sherwin, "An Incessantly Gushing Fountain: The Nature of Jewish Theology," p. 9.
124 Louis Jacobs, *A Jewish Theology*, p. 13.
125 Exodus 34.7.
126 M. *Avot* 5.22.
127 The word "orthodox" refers to the concept of only one correct and true doctrine, especially in religious usage.
128 Rachel Adler, *Engendering Judaism: An Inclusive Theology and Ethics*, p. xvi.
129 ibid., p. 29.
130 At least not halakhically. There are aggadic examples of women teaching Talmud and demonstrating halakhic wisdom superior to men's. This seems to be typical of the interestingly subversive quality sometimes demonstrated by *aggadah*, but by definition does not bear on the halakhic issue.
131 Abraham Joshua Heschel, *God in Search of Man*, 5.
132 Leviticus 19.36.
133 Deuteronomy 16.20.
134 Leviticus Rabbah 34.1.
135 Robert Alter, *The Art of Biblical Narrativ*, p. 22, slightly misquoted in Gilligan, *In A Different Voice*, p. xviii.

136 Abraham Joshua Heschel, *Man Is Not Alone*, p. 147.
137 Genesis 22.13-14.
138 *Bereshit* 32.25-32.
139 Rabbi Byron Sherwin: "It used to be that 'Jewish' was the Jews' first language, and the language of the dominant culture in which they lived was their second language. Now that has been reversed, and 'Jewish' is the Diaspora Jew's second language" (personal communication, February 2006).
140 Rachel Adler, *Engendering Judaism*, p. 26.
141 BT *Berakhot* 6a.
142 Ibn Gabbai, *Avodat haKodesh* II, 6 fol. 29a, cited by Gershom Scholem, *Major Trends*, p. 54.
143 *Hesed*, "kindness" or "mercy," is a Biblical term defined by Nelson Glueck (*Hesed in the Bible*). as the "loyalty, mutual aid, or reciprocal love" one may ask from – and owes to – another within a mutually covenanted community. In the Jewish community, then, *hesed* is the kindness we may ask from God, and that we owe God, as well as each other, because of the covenant relationship we share. *Hesed* as a *sefirah* is explored in depth in the Ten Lessons section.
144 The *Zohar*'s authorship is currently attributed either partially or fully to Moses de Leon of Castile, but the scholar Yehudah Liebes has recently put forward the theory that the work is more accurately defined as a true group project. The tradition that holds it to be a sacred text on the level itself of the Talmud, if not the Torah itself, attributes it to the first-century Talmudic Rabbi Shimon bar Yohai.
145 On the authorship and nature of the *Zohar*, see Gershom Scholem, *Kabbalah*, pp. 213–235; Moses Idel, *Kabbalah*, pp. 1–7; Arthur Green, "The *Zohar*, pp. 27--66; Yehudah Leibes, "How the *Zohar* Was Written," pp. 85–138.
146 Moses Idel, *Kabbalah*, describes this as a prohibition originally applied specifically by one Kabbalist to his teachings, which was then transmitted as a general warning that became applicable to all Kabbalah.
147 See, for example, William James, *The Varieties of Religious Experience*, and Evelyn Underhill, *Mysticism*.
148 Louis Jacobs, *Jewish Values*, p. 116.
149 Shalom Rosenberg, "Ethics," p. 202.
150 *Devarim* 30.19.
151 Yehiel ben Yekutiel, *Ma'alot haMiddot*, 206.
152 Menakhem Mendel of Kotzk, *Emet v'Emunah*, p. 12 n. 56.
153 BT *Berakhot* 10b
154 Daniel Matt, *Zohar*, p. xvi.
155 Menakhem Mendel of Kotzk, p. 12 n. 56.
156 Baal Shem Tov, *Tzavaa'at haRivash*, 6b
157 Rabbi Isaiah Horowitz, *Beit HaBekhirah* 47b. The vital status of human activity

in the creation of the world will be discussed in more depth below in the introduction to the Ten Lessons.

158 Moses Idel, *Kabbalah:*, p. 185.
159 Micah 6.8; Knohl's translation in *The Divine Symphony*, p. 58.
160 *Zohar*, 1.15a, ed. Matt, 107-108.
161 *Tanhuma, Tetzaveh*, 6.
162 Genesis 1.3.
163 *Zohar* 1.32a.
164 *Zohar*. 1.31b
165 Psalm 36.10
166 Genesis 12.1
167 He was known by the acronym of his title and name: **Ra**bbi **Sh**lomo **Y**itzhaki.
168 Rashi, comment on *parashat Lekh L'kha*, Genesis 12.1.
169 Variations on this interpretation of *lekh l'kha* are attributed to the second Karliner Rebbe: *atzmo*, "one's self"; Shlomo Ephraim of Luncicz: *atzm'kha*, "yourself," d several other sources; elsewhere, *l'kha* becomes one's "root," as Levi Yitzhak of Berditchev, *Kedushat Levi*, p. 20.
170 Moses Cordovero, *Tomer Devorah*, 5.27–-28
171 Hayim Vital, *Derush she-Masar*, p. 20, cited by Lawrence Fine, *Physician of the Soul, Healer of the Cosmos*, p. 135.
172 Luria transforms *tikkun ha'olam*, a Talmudic concept cited to support a specific and circumscribed legal category, and applies it in a way that far transcends its origins. The modern interpretation of *tkkun ha'olam* derives much more from the mystical redefinition than from its Talmudic origins. For historical surveys of the meaning of *tikkun ha'olam* in Jewish usage, see Lawrence Fine, "Tikkun: A Lurianic Motif in Contemporary Jewish Thought"; Eugene Lipman, "*Mipne Tikkun Ha'Olam* in the Talmud: A Preliminary Exploration"; and Gilbert Rosenthal, "Tikkun ha-Olam: The Metamorphosis of a Concept."
173 Lawrence Fine, "Tikkun: A Lurianic Motif in Contemporary Jewish Thought," p. 39.
174 BT *Sanhedrin* 37a
175 The *'omer* period, especially the first 32 days, is associated in some traditions with bloody and tragic losses sustained by the Jewish army leading the rebellion against Rome in springtime battles; others maintain that the period of "semi-mourning," during which no weddings are held and observant Jews observe mourning customs, commemorates the deaths of many of Rabbi Akiba's students due to a plague.
176 M. *Rosh HaShanah* 1.2
177 Proverbs 3.18.
178 M. *Avot* 1.2.
179 Moses Cordovero, *Or Neerav* and *Tomer Devora*. p. 10

180 *Zohar,* 1.135a, cited in Isaiah Tishby, *Mishnat haZohar* II, p. 399
181 John W. Gardner, founder of Common Cause and the Urban Coalition, among other community-building organizations, and a 1964 recipient of the Presidential Medal of Freedom.
182 BT *Yevamot* 49b: "[A]ll the prophets beheld God by way of a mirror that did not shine; Moses looked by way of a mirror that did shine."
183 *Mekhilta deRav Ishmael,* cited in Reinhard Neudecker, *The Voice of God on Mount Sinai,* p. 55.
184 BT *Shabbat* 88b.
185 *Shemot* 20.15-16.
186 *Shemot* 20.2.
187 Gershom Scholem, *On the Kabbalah and Its Symbolism,* p. 30.
188 Abraham Joshua Heschel, *Who Is Man?* p. 78
189 Genesis Rabbah 39
190 These three specific translations are suggested by Arthur Green, *Ehyeh,* p. 48.
191 *Zohar, Haqdamat haZohar,* 1.4a.
192 However, German Protestant theologians did attempt to articulate the Name and as a result gave us the unfortunate "Jehovah."
193 See Rachel Adler, *Engendering Judaism: An Inclusive Theology and Ethics,* especially pp. 93 and 103, for a striking discussion of the problem of "liturgical idolatry."
194 Avraham Yaakov Finkel, *Kabbalah,* p. 158.
195 Moses Cordovero, *Pardes Rimonim,* p. 1.1
196 Susan Last Stone, *"The Emergence of Jewish Law in Postmodernist Legal Theory."*
197 Abraham Joshua Heschel, *God In Search of Man,* p. 316.
198 Isaac of Radvil, *Or Yitzhak,* p. 190.
199 Swarm behavior, shared by ants, bees, birds and humans, is the fascinating subject of Peter Miller's "The Genius of Swarms."
200 Abraham Joshua Heschel, cited in Byron Sherwin, *Studies in Jewish Theology,* p. 141.
201 Exodus 3.15.
202 Byron Sherwin, *Studies in Jewish Theology, p.* 279.
203 Marcia Falk, *The Book of Blessings,* 170.
204 M *Avot* 2.1.
205 Baal Shem Tov, *Tzava'at haRivash,* 17a.
206 *Tzava'at haRivash,* 14a
207 Martin Buber's philosophy of the two levels of relationship is developed in his *I and Thou.*
208 *Avodat Yisrael, parashat Shemini.*
209 Genesis 27-28.
210 This form of the word "head" occurs only eight times in the Tanakh, twice

in Genesis, once in I Kings 19.6, and five times in two separate instances in I Samuel 19.13–16 and 26.7–16; interestingly, the *k'ri* (the Masoretic guide to pronunciation) corrects the *k'tiv* (the written form, which reads as an attempt to render the expected singular) three times in the latter instance.

211 Genesis 28.12–17.
212 Gershom Scholem, *Major Trends in Jewish Mysticism*, p. 207.
213 M. Avot 1.2.
214 Numbers 6.24-26.
215 Rashi to *BaMidbar*, 1.1.
216 Menakhem Mendel Schneerson, *Torah Studies, BaMidbar*, cited in Victor Cohen, *The Soul of the Torah*, p. 257.
217 Abraham Joshua Heschel, "The Mystical Element in Judaism", *The Jews*, p. 608.
218 This diagram of the Divine is from Arthur Green, Shalom Hartman Center Rabbinic seminar, 2002.
219 Yehudah Leib Alter of Ger, *Sefat Emet, Shavuot* 1, p. 117 (Hebrew) in Arthur Green, *The Language of Truth*.
220 Joseph Gikatilla, *Shaarei Orah* (Mossad Bialik) p. 252.
221 Exodus 34.5-6.
222 Rabbi Isaac the Blind, cited in Moses Idel, *Kabbalah: New Perspectives* p. 138
223 See figure 1.
224 *Sefer haBahir*, 1.3, p. 206 (Hebrew), in Aryeh Kaplan *The Bahir: Illlumination..*
225 Moses Idel, *Kabbalah: New Perspectives*, p. 177, citing ibn Gabbai, Meir. *Sefer Avodat HaKodesh*.
226 Moses Cordovero, *Tomer Devorah*. 1.1.
227 BT *Sotah* 14a.
228 *Zohar* 3.113a
229 Moses Idel, *Kabbalah*, pp. 186–187.
230 Ibid., p. 180.
231 Genesis 1.27.
232 See the entire scope at http://micro.magnet.fsu.edu/primer/java/scienceopticsu/powersof10/.
233 *Midrash Bereshit Rabbah*, 1.1.
234 The listing of qualities associated with the attributes derives from several sources but is not limited to them: (1) Joseph Gikatilla, *Shaarei Orah*, (2) Daniel Matt, *Zohar*, and (3) Arthur Green, "Images of God in Kabbalah," a lecture given at the Shalom Hartman Institute, Jerusalem, summer 2002. The list is by no means exhaustive.
235 BT *Yoma* 85b..
236 BT *Hagigah* 14b.
237 The listing of qualities associated with the attributes derives from several sources: (1) Joseph Gikatilla's *Gates of Light*, (2) Daniel Matt's critical edition of the

Zohar, and (3) Arthur Green, "Images of God in Kabbalah," a lecture given at the Shalom Hartman Institute, Jerusalem, summer 2002. It is not exhaustive.
238 "To begin with oneself," Martin Buber, *Hasidism and Modern Man.*
239 A good close mystical reading would not miss the *gematria* of this chapter and verse as, appropriately enough, indicating two living beings, since "life" in Hebrew, *hai,* has the numerical equivalent of 18.
240 On Soviet identity papers, the first four "points" were one's surname, patronymic, personal name, and birthplace. Fifth was ethnicity. When a Jew did not get a job, was not admitted to the University of Kiev, or was passed over for some form of recognition, everyone knew what was meant when one shrugged and said, "Because of the *pyaty punkt,* the fifth point" (on one's identity papers).
241 Observations based on the author's own experiences living in Kiev, Ukraine in 1993--1994.
242 Isaiah 6.
243 Exodus 25.8.
244 Exodus 19.6.
245 *Kedoshim* 2.
246 Leviticus 11.44-45, 19.2, 20.26, and 21.8.
247 Isaiah 5.16.
248 Abraham Joshua Heschel, *Who Is Man?* pp. 94–95.
249 Gershom Scholem, "The *Zohar* II," p. 215.
250 M. Avot 3.17.
251 Numbers 6.1-21 provides guidelines for an Israelite who vows to become a *nazir,* temporarily taking on ascetic religious practices, and describes the sin-offering a *nazir* must bring when his or her vow is completed.
252 Gershom Heschel, *The Jews,* p. 608.
253 Psalm 90.
254 Heschel, op. cit., p. 105.
255 Ibid, p. 30.
256 Ibid., p. 39.
257 Abraham Joshua Heschel, *The Jews,* p. 609.
258 Jewish ethicist Byron Sherwin's categorization, following the medieval Rabbinic scholars *Maharsha* and the *Maharal,* in the introduction to *Crafting an Ethical Jewish Life* among other places. They are commenting on BT *Baba Kama* 30a, in which three definitions of pious behavior are given. One deals with damages, one with personal morality, and one with blessings.
259 *Ma'alot haMiddot,* 295.
260 Hillel Goldberg, "Israel Salanter and *'Orkhot Zaddikim:* Restructuring Musar Literature.". *Tradition*
261 R. Nakhman of Bratslav, *"Ma'aseh 6: MiMelekh Anav,"* in *Sipurei Ma'asiyot,* p. 60.

262 *Orkhot Tzaddikim*, p. 41.
263 Hillel Goldberg, "Israel Salanter and *Orkhot Zaddikim*."
264 Yosef Dan, *Jewish Mysticism and Jewish Ethics*, p.18.
265 Israel Salanter, op. cit.
266 Emmanuel Levinas, *Nine Talmudic Readings*, pp. 14–15.
267 Ibid., p. 48.
268 Abraham Joshua Heschel, *Who Is Man?* p. 66.
269 Ibid., pp. 100–101
270 Ibid, p. 95.
271 Daniel C. Matt, *The Essential Kabbalah*, p. 9.
272 Elimelekh of Lizhensk, *No'am Elimelekh*, Vol. 1, p. 19b.
273 Jeremiah 31.14.
274 Cited in Chava Weissler, "Woman as High Priest,": A Kabbalistic Prayer in Yiddish for Lighting Shabbat Candles", p. 533.
275 *Zohar*, I.48b, cited in Chava Weissler, op. cit., p. 535.
276 Howard Eilberg-Schwartz, *God's Phallus and Other Problems for Men and Monotheism*, p. 3.
277 Genesis 1.27.
278 *Zohar*, Genesis 1.22b, *Zohar* scholar Daniel Matt identifies this text as belonging to *Tikkunei Zohar*, a later level of writing in the *Zohar*.
279 *Zohar*, Genesis 1.47a, Soncino.
280 Daniel Matt, *Zohar*, p.1.47a.
281 Judy Chicago, excerpt from "The Dinner Party," in *Cries of the Spirit*, p. 235.
282 Exodus 24.10.
283 BT *Bava Batra* 74a.
284 Exodus 24.7.
285 BT *Masekhet Berakhot* 3a.
286 I am indebted to Dr. Jonathan Cohen, Professor of Philosophy at Hebrew University and the Mandel School for Educational Leadership, for this insight.
287 *Fun di Chasidishe Otzsros*, 302, cited in Victor Cohen, *The Soul of the Torah*, p. 217.
288 Audre Lorde, "Use of the Erotic: The Erotic as Power," pp. 210–211.
289 Marge Piercy, "Interpretive *Nishmat Kol Khai*," p. 232.
290 From the evening *Shema uVirkhoteha* prayers..
291 This point is better understood when contrasted with Christianity's definition of the significance of the person, a definition focused more on the soul, allowing for a certain de-emphasis of the body and sexuality. See Daniel Boyarin, *Carnal Israel*, for a discussion of this difference and its importance for Jewish theology.
292 Wine, for example, is that over which we bless God on Shabbat and holy days, and it is also an effective key to the destruction of one's own world as well as that of one's family.

293 Daniel Matt, *Zohar*, p. 71.
294 Arthur Green, "Images of God: Images of God in Kabbalah I."
295 Raphael Patai, *The Hebrew Goddess*, pp. 141–142
296 Ibid., p. 142.
297 *Tikkun Leyl Shavuot, Zohar* I.8a., p. 1318.
298 See Figure 2.
299 The second blessing of the *Birkat haMazon,* the "Blessing After a Meal."
300 Genesis 9.16.
301 Weinstein, Avi, *Gates of Light*, p. 78.
302 Exodus 34.27, cited in Weinstein, op. cit., p. 77.
303 Exodus 6.12 and 6.30.
304 Exodus 20.6 and 20.12.
305 My gratitude to my teacher Byron Sherwin for pointing this out to me.
306 Genesis 24.1-3.
307 *Sifre* to Deuteronomy, 346.
308 The Hebrew letter *bet* can be vocalized as both "v" and "b."
309 Daniel Matt, op. cit., 1, p. 3b.
310 *The Bahir,* 1.102.
311 This is Arthur Green's suggested translation of the word *tzaddik* as applied to the *sefirah Yesod.*
312 Psalms 10.25.
313 Daniel Matt, op. cit., 1.59b, pp. 339–340. The passage referred to is: Now Joseph was well-built and handsome. After a time, his master's wife cast her eyes upon Joseph and said, "Lie with me." But he refused. He said to his master's wife, "Look, with me here, my master gives no thought to anything in the house, and all that he owns he has placed in my hands. He wields no more authority in this house than I, and he has withheld nothing from me except yourself, since you are his wife. How then could I do this most wicked thing, and sin before God?" And much as she coaxed Joseph day by day, he did not yield to her request to lie beside her, to be with her. One such day, he came into the house to do his work. None of the household being there inside, she caught hold of him by his coat and said, "Lie with me!" But he left his coat in her hand and got away and fled outside (Genesis 39.6-12).
314 Ibid., p. 422, n 610.
315 Ibid., p. ii.
316 Yosef Hayim Yerushalmi, *Zakhor: Jewish History and Jewish Memory,* p. 5.
317 *Shemot* 20.8.
318 Exodus 20 and Deuteronomy 5.
319 Daniel Matt, op. cit., pp. 159b–160a.
320 *Shemot* 3.15.
321 Shabsai Sheftl Horowitz, *Kabbalah*, pp. 159–160.

322 Yosef Hayim Yerushalmi, *Zakhor: Jewish History and Jewish Memory*, p. 94.
323 BT *Berakhot* 58a.
324 BT *Menakhot* 43b.
325 *Tosafot* to BT *Menakhot* 43b.
326 Deuteronomy 8.10
327 1.207b. Daniel Matt explains in Zohar that "the 'blessing of nourishment', recited after each meal, focuses on *Shekhinah*, rung of faith. When one blesses Her while satisfied after eating, he ensures that She will be nourished from above and sustain the world below." p. 273 n82.
328 Chronicles 1.15, cited in BT *Hagigah* 5.
329 BT *Berakhot* 10a.
330 Robert Alter, *The Book of Psalms*, p. 362; I have replaced "Lord" with *Adonai* to emphasize this Name's association with the level of the physical that *Hod* expresses.
331 Robert Alter, *The Book of Psalms*, p. 362 n1.
332 Robert Alter, op. cit., p. 368; "Lord" is again changed to *Adonai*.
333 Arthur Green, *Seek My Face*, p. 149.
334 Matt, op. cit., p. 162 n. 434.
335 Proverbs 20.27.
336 Joseph Gikatilla, *Shaarei Orah*, p. 150.
337 Isaiah 6.1-4.
338 Rudolf Otto, *The Idea of the Holy*, p. 40.
339 The *Akedah*, "the Binding," refers to the disturbing account of Abraham nearly completing the sacrifice of his son Isaac in Genesis 22. The insight is Hebrew University Professor Israel Knohl's, shared in a Jerusalem seminar in 2003.
340 See Leviticus 10. No moral reason is given for their summary death.
341 BT *Zevakhim* 115b.
342 Numbers 27.20.
343 Daniel Matt, op. cit., p. 164, and n45.
344 Edwards, B. P. *Living Waters*, p. 273.
345 Art Green, *Ehyeh*, p. 53.
346 BT *Hagigah* 15a.
347 Joseph Gikatilla, op. cit., p. 124.
348 Daniel Matt, *The Essential Kabbalah*, p. 72.
349 Elliot Dorff and Louis E. Newman, *Contemporary Jewish Theology*, p. 1.
350 Bava Metzia 31b and others.
351 Reuven Margolis, *Yalkut Peninim* (Lemberg, 1929), cited in Kushner and Olitsky, *Sparks Beneath the Surface*, commentary on *parashat Metzora*. p. 144.
352 Israel Knohl, *The Divine Symphony*, p. 5.
353 Rachel Adler, *Engendering Judaism*, p. xvi.
354 JT *Peah* 2, *gemara* to *halakhah* 6.

355 James Kugel, *God of Old*, 107, cited in Benjamin Sommer, *The Bodies of God*, 178, n 41.
356 Genesis 17.1. *Tamim* can mean "innocent," "pure," or "whole."
357 *Bereshit Rabbah* 30.10
358 BT *Eruvin* 54a.
359 Ecclesiastes 1.2.
360 *Raziel HaMal'akh* p. 27, cited in Abraham Yaakov Finkel, *Kabbalah*, p. 29.
361 *Zohar, Pinkhas*, cited in Finkel, op. cit.
362 *Zohar*, 1.146a.
363 *Zohar*, 1.146a
364 Genesis 32.32.
365 Cited by *Shem miShmu'el* in *Itturei Torah*, Vol. 6, p. 50.
366 Isaiah 45.8.
367 Joseph Gikatilla, *Sha'are Orah*, p. 127.
368 Joseph Gikatile, op. cit., p. 134.
369 ibid., p. 130.
370 ibid., 130-131.
371 Joseph Gikatilla, *Sha'are Orah*, p. 131.
372 Exodus 33.7.
373 Moses Maimonides, *Guide for the Perplexed*, p. 384
374 *Maggid Devarav l'Yaakov* 69a, cited in Arthur Green and Barry Holtz, *Your Word Is Fire*, p. 56.
375 M. Avot 1.2.
376 Moshe Idel, *Ascensions on High in Jewish Mysticism*, pp. 75–76.
377 M. *Avot* 1.2.
378 I Kings 7.21.
379 Byron Sherwin, "Fear of God," *Contemporary Jewish Religious Thought*, p. 245. Fear and love as attitudes toward God will be explored more thoroughly in the discussion of *Din*, anon.
380 The four Hebrew letters spell out the word *ahavah*, "love.".
381 *Zohar*, 2.145b-146a.
382 Song of Songs, 3.6-10
383 Op. cit., 5.15.
384 Moshe de Leon, *Sefer haMishkal*, cited in Daniel Matt, *The Essential Kabbalah*, p. 148.
385 Isaac Luria, cited in Daniel Matt, op. cit., p. 149.
386 A popular aphorism based upon M. *Avot* 3.1: "Akavya ben Mehalalel said, think about three things and you will not be tempted to sin: know where you came from, where you are going, and before Whom you will render an accounting for you life."
387 *Zohar*, 2.161b–162a..

388 Alice Walker, *The Color Purple,* p. 203..
389 *BT Kiddushin* 66b, cited in Danny Siegel, *Where Heaven and Earth Touch,* p. 25.
390 *Shemot* 25.8.
391 Abraham Joshua Heschel, *Who Is Man?,* p. 99
392 M. *Avot* 5.22.
393 Aviva Gottlieb Zornberg, *The Particulars of Rapture,* p. 5.
394 ibid., pp. 7–8.
395 ibid., p. 9.
396 See discussion of *Din* later.
397 Gergen, p. 170.
398 Joshua 8.32..
399 Deuteronomy 27.12.
400 Leo Baeck, *Essence of Judaism,* p. 43.
401 Rabbi Judah Lowe of Prague, *Derekh Hayyim,* 148.
402 Iibid..
403 Genesis 3.7.
404 Rabbi Judah Lowe of Prague, *Derekh Hayyim,* p. 148.
405 BT *Berakhot* 34b.
406 Joseph Gikatilla, *Shaarey Orah,* p. 207.
407 Arthur Green, *Ehyeh: A Kabbalah For Tomorrow,* pp. 79–80.
408 BT *Bava Batra* 74a.
409 Described in *Yesod.*
410 Psalms 5.6.
411 Daniel Matt, *Zohar,* 1.30a.
412 Genesis 28.12.
413 Genesis 2.4-15.
414 Daniel Matt, *Zohar,* 1.49a
415 Ibid., .49a. note 1260-1261, Matt notes the existence of several pieces of archaeological evidence, inscriptions that refer to *YHVH* and His *Asherah.*
416 The following depiction of *Asherah* is based on Raphael Patai's description in *The Hebrew Goddess,* pp. 34–53..
417 II Kings 23.6-.7
418 Patai, op. cit., p. 43.
419 Ibid., p. 46
420 Genesis 30.13.
421 Jeremiah 17.1-2.
422 Jeremiah 3.6..
423 Patai, op. cit., p., 53.
424 Exodus 25.31-37.
425 Cited by Art Green, *Seek My Face,* p. 27.
426 Abraham Joshua Heschel, "The Mystical Element in Judaism," p. 607

427 Joseph Gikatilla, *Shaarey Orah*, p. 179.
428 The expression of evil as "left" and good as "right" is a cultural commonplace: in Latin, left is *sinister,* in French, *gauche,* and in America, until recently left-handed children were forced to use their right hands. God's favorite as well as that of a human king is "at the right hand," and in Arab culture one never offers the left hand in greeting. More problematic is the association of the evil side with the feminine.
429 Elliot Wolfson, "Left Contained in the Right," p. 45
430 Attributed to the English philosopher Edmund Burke (1729-1797).
431 *Zohar*, cited by Elliot Wolfson, "Left Contained in the Right," p. 44.
432 Shabsai Sheftl Horowitz, "The Mystery of Twenty-Eight," cited in Avraham Yaakov Finkel, *Kabbalah,* p. 159.
433 Exodus 34.6-7.
434 BT *Eruvin* 22a.
435 Margaret Holub, "A Cosmology of Mourning", p. 351.
436 Deuteronomy 16.20.7.
437 BT *Sanhedrin* 6b.
438 BT *Sanhedrin* 6b.
439 Lichtenstein, Aharon, "Does Jewish Tradition Recognize an Ethic Independent of *Halakha*?" in Menachem Marc Kellner, *Contemporary Jewish Ethics,*
440 Aryeh Cohen, *The Journal of Textual Reasoning.*
441 Abraham Joshua Heschel, "The Mystical Element in Judaism," P. 609.
442 Michael L. Kagan, *The Holistic Haggadah,* p. 236.
443 Aviva Gottlieb Zornberg, *The Beginning of Desire, p.* 135.
444 BT *Tamid* 32a.
445 Proverbs 31.13.
446 *Midrash Tanhuma* on *Mishle,* cited by Aviva Zornberg in *The Beginning of Desire,* p. 135. Torah forbids the mixing of wool and flax in clothing, which it calls *shaatnez.*
447 Talmud *Yerushalmi, Pe'ah,* 8.8.
448 Lawrence Fine, The Contemplative Practice of *Yihudim,* p. 67.
449 Martin Buber, informed by mystical and Hasidic teaching, formulated the idea that evil is the result of the absence of the presence of God's face. Evil, for him, is that which was devoid of God. The Holocaust could occur, he said, because God's face was turned away from humanity.
450 Gershom Scholem, *Major Trends in Jewish Mysticism,* p. 236.
451 Scholem, p. 236.
452 Isaiah 45.7
453 Gershom Scholem, *Major Trends,* 237.
454 *Pirke d'Rabbi Eliezer,* cited in Aviva Zornberg, *The Beginning of Desire,* p. 124.
455 *VaYikra Rabbah* 20.2

456 Aviva Zornberg, *The Beginning of Desire*, p. 126
457 Yosef Gikatilla, *Shaarei Orah*, p. 204.
458 Ibid., p. 205.
459 Deut. 4.24.
460 This insight was shared by Dr. Israel Knohl in a course he taught at the Shalom Hartman Institute in Jerusalem in the fall of 2002. In Knohl's opinion this approach might be applied to understanding the *Akedah,* an archetypal amoral experience.
461 Isaiah 6.1-.
462 Psalm 8.5.
463 Yosef Gikatilla, *Shaarey Orah,* p. 202.
464 Louis Jacobs, *Seeker of Unity,* p. 54.
465 Joseph Dan, *Kabbalah,* p. 57.
466 *Sifre* to Deuteronomy, 346.
467 Daniel Matt, "The Mystic and the Mitzvot," p. 396.
468 Elliot Wolfson, Left Contained in the Right, p. 29.
469 Abraham Joshua Heschel, The Mystical Element in Judaism, *The Jews,* p. 609
470 Abraham Joshua Heschel, *Moral Grandeur and Spiritual Audacity,* p. 231.
471 Rabbi Judah Loew of Prague, *Derekh Hayyim,* p. 148.
472 Isaiah 45.7.
473 Aryeh Kaplan, *The Bahir,* p. 1
474 BT *Hagigah* 15a.
475 *Zohar,* 1.31b-1.32a.
476 Cited in Abraham Joshua Heschel, *A Passion For Truth,* p. 37.
477 *Bereshit* 2.7.
478 BT *Berakhot* 61a.
479 BT *Berakhot* 54a.
480 Genesis 1.31.
481 *Midrash Rabbah, Bereshit,* 9.7.
482 Genesis 4.7.
483 *Zohar,* 1.165b
484 *Zohar* 2.69b, cited in Elliot Wolfson, Light Through Darkness: the Ideal of Human Perfection in the Zohar, p. 86.
485 *Zohar,* 3.80b, Ibid, p. 89.
486 Elliot Wolfson, op. cit., p. 89.
487 Elliot Wolfson, "op. cit., p. 87.
488 Elliot Wolfson, op. cit., p. 88.
489 *Zohar* 2.34a, op. cit., p. 87.
490 *Zohar,* 1.165b.
491 Isaiah Horowitz, *Beit HaBekhirah, Shaar haGadol,* 15b.
492 Deut. 30.11-20.

493 Arthur Green, The *Zohar*: Jewish Mysticism in Medieval Spain, p. 55.
494 *Sefer Baal Shem Tov, Bereshit* 64, cited in Avraham Yaakov Finkel, *Kabbalah*, p. 288
495 Louis Jacobs, *Seeker of Unity*, p. 57.
496 *Zohar*, 1.15a.
497 *Zohar.*, p. 1.32a, with my interpolations.
498 Daniel Matt, *God and the Big Bang: Discovering Harmony Between Science & Spirituality*, p. 35.
499 Israel Knohl, *he Divine Symphony: The Bible's Many Voices*.
500 Elon, Menachem. *Jewish Law*.
501 Moshe Halbertal, *People of the Book: Canon, Meaning and Authority.*.
502 PT *Pea*.
503 Menachem Fisch,. *Rational Rabbis: Science and Talmudic Culture*.
504 Menachem Elon, op. cit., p. 1148.
505 Following Robert Cover, as cited by Rachel Adler, *Engendering Judaism*, p. 34.
506 BT *Sotah* 47b, cited in Moshe Halbertal, op,. cit., p. 53.
507 *Tosefta, Sotah* 7:12, op. cit., p. 53.
508 BT *Eruvin* 13b
509 Literally, "chained women," wives whose husbands abandon them yet refuse to grant them a divorce.
510 "Bastards", any offspring of a halakhically invalid marriage.
511 *Zohar*, p.1.17b.
512 Numbers 16.
513 M. *Avot* 5.17.
514 Daniel Matt, *Zohar*, p. 130. n 177.
515 Abraham Joshua Heschel, *Heavenly Torah*, p. 708.
516 Ibid., p. 709.
517 Maharal, *Be'erHaGolah*, Be'er 1, cited in Ibid., pp. 703–704.
518 Gikatilla, "the fourth *sefirah*", cited in *Kabbalah*, 97.
519 For a comprehensive survey of *yir'ah* in Jewish thought, see Byron Sherwin, "Fear of God" in *Contemporary Jewish Religious Thought*. Sherwin points out that, in contrast to much of rabbinic, legal and ethical development of the term, the *Zohar* "identifies religious consciousness with *yirah* of God. While identifying both *yirah* and love and with the various pairs of the divine emanations (*sefirot*), the *Zohar* consistently equates *yirah* with the higher emanation." p. 251.
520 Yehiel ben Yekutiel, *Ma'alot haMiddot*, p. 202.
521 Gikatilla, cited in *Kabbalah: Selections From Classic Kabbalistic Works*, p. 97.
522 Genesis 25.27.
523 Daniel Matt, *God and the Big Bang*, p. 75.
524 Abraham Joshua Heschel, The Mystical Element in Judaism, p. 609.
525 Author unknown.

526 Psalm 89.3.
527 Psalm 25.10.
528 Joseph Gikatilla, *Shaarei Orah*, 2.37.
529 Aviva Gottlieb Zornberg, *The Particulars of Rapture*, pp. 14–15
530 The daily *Shakharit* prayers.
531 A variant translation of Deut. 6.5.
532 Roderick Langmere Haig-Brown, *A River Never Sleeps*, p. 344.
533 Rabbi Yehudah Leib Alter, *Sefat Emet* (Hebrew), p. 87.
534 The terebinth (*Pistacia terebinthus*), also called the turpentine tree, is a small deciduous tree native to the Mediterranean
535 Genesis 18.1–5.
536 Benjamin Sommer, *The Bodies of God and the World of Ancient Israel*, examines this idea in the light of evidence of a "lost theology" he traces in the pages of the Bible. See especially p. 40–41.
537 Nelson Glueck's study *Hesed in the Bible* explores the nuances of this important Biblical concept in depth.
538 Genesis 12.5.
539 Rashi to Genesis 12.5.
540 From *Bahir*, 1.144. Translation influenced more by Art Green's *A Guide to the Zohar* than by Aryeh Kaplan's *The Bahir*.
541 Arthur Green, "Images of God in Kabbalah I: Additional Sources.
542 Talmud Bavli, *Sotah* 14a.
543 Isaiah Horowitz, Shnei *Lukhot haBrit, Masekhet Shavuot*, p. 95b.
544 Adin Steinsaltz, *A Guide To Jewish Prayer*, p. 44.
545 *Zohar*, 2.182b.
546 Moshe Cordovero, *Tomer Devorah*, 1.5.
547 *Zohar Hadash, Tiqqunim*, 95a.
548 Exodus 25.21-22, translation adapted from *Etz Hayim*.
549 Moshe Cordovero, *Or Neerav*, p. 63.
550 Exodus 37.8.
551 Cordovero, *Pardes Rimonim* p. 339.
552 Genesis 49.22.
553 BT *Yoma* 54a.
554 *Zohar*, 1.225b.
555 Matt, *Zohar*, p. 357 n299.
556 Isaiah Horowitz, *Shnei Lukhot haBrit, Masekhet Shavuot*, p. 95b
557 Birnbaum, Philip, ed. *HaSiddur haShalem* – Daily Prayer Book. (New York: Hebrew Publishing Company, 1977), p. 551
558 This understanding of the terms "male" and "female", of course, offers an interesting theological opportunity to address questions of gender identification in a completely different way.

559 see, for example, Lakme Batya Elior, "*Tumah* and *Taharah* Reexamined" in Gershon Winkler's *The Way of the Boundary Crosser*. Edited by Gershon Winkler, Appendix 1. Northvale: Jason Aronson, 1998.
560 Genesis 1.31
561 Joseph Gikatilla, *Shaarei Orah,* Weinstein p. 64
562 Moshe Cordovero, *Or Neerav*, 6.3, cited in Daniel Matt, *The Essential Kabbalah*, p. 44.
563 Moshe Cordovero, *Pardes Rimonim* 8, p. 194
564 Rabbi Shneur Zalman of Lyadi, *Torah Hayim, VaYetzei*, cited in Avraham Yaakov Finkel, *Kabbalah*, p. 328.
565 Traditional weekday *Amidah*.
566 Rabbi Akiba's warning to his companions, and the aftermath, in the famous and ill-fated descent to the *pardes*, which is a mystical *locus classicus*, BT *Hagigah* 14b.
567 Psalms 101.7.
568 There is ongoing scientific disagreement over whether light is a wave or a stream of particles.
569 James Gleick brought popular attention to the fascinatingly indefinable properties of physical life explored through quantum physics in his *Chaos: Making a New Science.*
570 This has to do with the way the eye and the brain interact, which is piecemeal and has gaps.
571 Jean-Jacques Rousseau wrote *The Social Contract* in 1763; it extended to all members of society John Locke's idea of a social contract between the governed and the governors.
572 Annie Dillard, *Pilgrim at Tinker Creek*, p. 35.
573 Moshe Cordovero, *Or Neerav*, 6.1, p. 116.
574 Joseph Gikatilla, *Gates of Light*, p. 300.
575 Arthur Green, *Ehyeh*.
576 Gershom Scholem, *Major Trends*, p. 220.
577 Exodus 34.6
578 S. Trigano, *Le Recit de la disparue*, p. 25, cited in Marc-Alain Ouaknin, *The Burnt Book*, p. 273.
579 Nakhman of Bratslav, *Likkutei Mohoran* 1:64, cited in Marc-AlainOuaknin, ibid., p. 268.
580 Martin Buber, *Tales of the Hasidim*, p. 314.
581 BT *Yoma* 86b.
582 *Zohar*, 1.134b.
583 BT *Berakhot* 17a.
584 Moshe Cordover, *Or Neerav*, p. 46.
585 Ibid., p. 123.
586 BT *Hagigah* 5b

587 Tess Gallagher, "The Poem as a Reservoir for Grief (excerpt)," quoted in Marilyn Sewell, *Cries of the Spirit,* pp. 127–128.
588 Rabbi Nakhman of Bratslav, *Likkutei Mohoran, parashat bo el Par'o,* p. 64.
589 Marc-Alain Ouaknin, *The Burnt Book: Reading the Talmud,* p. 273.
590 Ibid., p. 274.
591 Joseph Gikatilla, *Shaarei Orah,* pp. 44-45.
592 From *Noam Elimelekh, Bereshit, VaYetze,* expounded by Aviva Gottlieb Zornberg, notes from public lecture.
593 Moshe Cordovero, *Tomer Devorah,* 4.25.
594 I Kings 19.11-13.
595 Gershom Scholem, *Major Trends,* pp. 220–221
596 Ilana Pardes, *Countertraditions in the Bible,* p. 202.
597 Carol Meyers, *Discovering Eve,* p. 90.
598 Nehama Ashkenazy, *Eve's Journey,* p. 11.
599 Genesis 3.22.
600 E. S. Speiser, cited by Nehama Ashkenazy, *Eve's Journey,* p. 42.
601 *Bereshit* 3.220.
602 Ilana Pardes, op. cit., pp. 4–47.
603 Danial Matt, *Zohar,.,* p.
604 Ibid., p.
605 Savina J. Teubal, *Sarah the Priestess,* p. 100. For more about the sacred grove, see her discussion of oracular shrines; Raphael Patai's *The Hebrew Goddess,* for his description of Asherah; and Merlin Stone's *When God Was a Woman* for links between the divine feminine and trees in the ancient Near East.
606 It is important to remember that the Israelites' sinful acts had the capacity to drive the *Shekhinah,* the presence of God, out of the Temple and out of Jerusalem itself, according to the midrash.
607 *Zohar,* 1.53a.
608 Gideon Weitzman, *Sparks of Light:* p. 46-47, citing the *Zohar* 1.154.
609 Abraham Isaac Kook, *Igrot HaRiyah,* in Gideon Weitzman, *Sparks of Light,* p. 43.
610 *Zohar,* 1.21a
611 *Zohar,* 1.103b
612 Judges 5.24.
613 Gen. 12.8.
614 So suggests Judith Antonelli, *In The Image of God.*
615 *Zohar,* 1.133a
616 David S. Ariel, *Kabbalah: The Mystic Quest in Judaism,* p. 76.
617 *Midrash Rabbah,* Song of Songs 8.2.
618 Note the reference to Leah, associated with this uppermost *sefirah* and described in the book of Genesis as having "weak eyes."
619 MS Vatican 283, fol. 71b, cited by Elliot Wolfson, *Through a Speculum That*

Shines, p. 362.
620 Moshe Cordovero, op. cit., 6.5.
621 Yehudah Leib Alter, *VaYigash* 1, *Sefat Emet*.
622 *Zohar*, 3.173a
623 Joseph Gikatilla, *Shaarei Orah*, p. 326.
624 Or, more correct grammatically, "with beginning." But that's a different *remez*.
625 Daniel Matt, *God and the Big Bang*, pp. 35–36.
626 *Hakadamat haZohar* 1.2a.
627 *Zohar*, 115a.
628 Genesis 1.2.
629 This is also expressed by Psalm 131: *lo halakhti b'g'dolot uv'nifla'ot mimeni* – "with things that are beyond me I will not be concerned."
630 Here the Kabbalists are basing their understanding on pre-existing ancient traditions that identify Wisdom with the Beginning of the world.
631 Arthur Green, notes for *Ehyeh: A Kabbalah for Tomorrow*, presented as *Images of God*, Hartman Institute, Jerusalem 2002, p. 3.
632 Martin Buber (1966) *The Way of Response: Martin Buber; Selections from His Writings*.
633 BT *Pesakhim* 54b in Danny Siegel, *Where Heaven and Earth Touch*, p. 14.
634 Moshe Cordovero, *Tomer Devorah*, p. 23.
635 Psalms 65.2.
636 Psalm 111.10
637 Joseph Gikatilla, *Shaarey Orah*, p. 99.
638 Daniel Matt, *Zohar*, Vol. I, p. 108 n11.
639 Ibid., p. 109 n12.
640 Ibid., p. 108, n 4: "The goal of mediation is to attain this spark and participate in the primal flow of being."
641 *Shemot* 33.20.
642 This is a reference to the *sefirah* of *Gevurah*, Judgment.
643 Moshe Cordovero, *Tomer Devorah*, p. 24-25.
644 Mona Van Duyn, excerpt from "The Stream."
645 BT *Pesakhim* 112a.
646 *Bereshit* 1.2.
647 Rabbi Abraham Joshua Heschel, *God In Search of Man*, p. 137.
648 *Sefer haBahir*, 85, cited by Gershom Scholem, *On the Kabbalah and Its Symbolism*, p. 92.
649 I Chronicles 29.15.
650 Rabbi Yehudah Leib Alter of Ger, *Sefat Emet*, 1.264.
651 Mordecai Yosef Leiner, *Sefer Mei HaShilo'akh*, Part I, p. 86.
652 Gen. 21.19
653 *Midrash Rabbah*, Deuteronomy, 7.2.

654 Yehudah Leib Alter of Ger, *Sefat Emet*, p. 95.
655 Genesis 26.18–25.
656 Numbers 21.16-18.
657 BT *Rosh HaShanah* 31a.
658 Bahya ben Asher, *Rabbenu Bahya al haTorah*, 62.
659 Ex. 23.14–19.
660 BT Berakhot 62b
661 Numbers 19.2–10.
662 Deuteronomy 22.9–11.
663 Moshe de Leon, *Sefer haRimmon*, pp.107–108.
664 Daniel Matt, *The Essential Kabbalah*, pp. 141–143.
665 "Normal mysticism" is the name Rabbi Max Kadushin used to refer to the Talmudic rabbis' teaching that an immanent sense of God's presence (*gilui Shekhinah*) is achievable in "normal" life – through the practice of such everyday *mitzvot* as Torah study (see Max Kadushin, *The Rabbinic Mind*).
666 Psalms 52.8.
667 Elliot R. Wolfson, *Through a Speculum That Shines*, pp. 10–11.
668 *Midrash Rabbah*, Exodus, 28.1.
669 ibn Gabbai, *Avodat haKodesh*, Fol. 36d, cited in Idel, *Kabbalah: New Perspectives*
670 Yehuda Leib Alter of Ger, *Sefat Emet, parashat Behar* 4, p. 61.
671 Daniel Matt, lecture (Spertus Institute of Jewish Studies, Chicago, July 2004).
672 Azriel of Gerona, cited in Daniel Matt, *The Essential Kabbalah: The Heart of Jewish Mysticism*, p. 68.
673 BT *Yerushalmi, Hagigah* 2.1
674 *Maggid Devarav leYaakov* 237, cited in Finkel, Avraham Yaakov, ed. *Kabbalah: Selections from Classic Kabbalistic Works from Raziel HaMalakh to the Present Day*, p. 297.
675 Leviticus 10.1-2.
676 Finkel, Avraham Yaakov, *Kabbalah: Selections from Classic Kabbalistic Works from Raziel HaMalakh to the Present Day*, p. 296.
677 *Yosher Divre Emet*, cited by Yehudah Gellman, Shalom Hartman Institute, Spring 2002.
678 Ibid.
679 *Midrash Rabbah*, Numbers, 14.22.
680 BT *Bava Batra* 99a.
681 Moses Cordovero, *Tomer Devorah*, pp. 14-15.
682 Joseph Gikatilla, *Shaarey Orah*, Vol. 2, p. 125.
683 BT *Rosh HaShanah* 21b.
684 Joseph Gikatilla, *Shaarey Orah*, p. 369.
685 *Zohar* 1.3b.
686 Gikatilla, *Shaarei Orah*, 23.

687 Psalm 130.1.
688 *Zohar,* 1.21a.
689 *Zohar,* 1.21b.
690 *Sefer haBahir, in* Daniel Abrams, *The Book Bahir,* p. 145, cited by Eitan P. Fishbane, "The Speech of Being, the Voice of God: Phonetic Mysticism in the Kabbalah of Asher ben David and His Contemporaries," p. 497.
691 BT *Makkot* 23b-24a.
692 Moses Maimonides, *Guide for the Perplexed* II.33, p. 221.
693 Exodus 20.16.
694 Gershom Scholem, *On the Kabbalah and Its Symbolism,* p. 31.
695 *Or HaEmet* 2b,. Arthur Green and Barry W. Holtz, *Your Word is Fire,* p. 55.
696 Owen Barfield, *Saving the Appearances,* cited in Charles Guignon, *On Being Authentic,* p. 17-18.
697 Dov Baer of Mezeritch, cited in Arthur Green and Barry Holt, *Your Word is Fire:,* p. 56.
698 Rabbi Yehudah Leib Alter, *Sefat Emet* 3.158-9.
699 Exodus 25.8.
700 Hatam Sofer, cited in *Itturei Torah,* Vol.4, *Kedoshim,* ed. Aharon Yaakov Grinberg, p. 104.
701 The *Admor haZakeyn* of Habad, *Likkutei Torah, Shir HaShirim,* cited by Yehuda Gellman, Hartman Institute, Jerusalem, spring 2002.
702 Yehiel Michal of Zlotchov, "A Drop in the Ocean," citing his master, Dov Baer of Mezeritch, in a teaching from Shavuot 1777.
703 *Orkhot Tzaddikim,* p. 625.
704 *Orkhot Tzaddikim,* p. 629.
705 Rabbi Yehudah Leib Alter, *Sefat Emet,* p. 19.
706 Isaiah 57.19.
707 Genesis 44.18.
708 Rabbi Yehudah Leib Alter, *Sefat Emet,* p. 19.
709 Joseph Gikatilla, *Shaarey Orah,* p. 166.
710 Alice Walker, *The Temple of My Familiar,* p. 396.
711 Kalonymus Kalmish Shapira, *Sacred Fire,* p. 189
712 Keats, John. "On First Looking into Chapman's Homer," *The Poems of John Keats.* J. M. Dent and company, 1906.
713 *Sefat Emet,* Yehudah Leib Alter of Ger, *Yom Kippur,* 1 (ed. Green, p. 103)
714 Nakhman of Bratslav (cited in *Sparks,* 184)
715 It is important to remember that the Israelites did not yet know that this was only the First Exile.
716 Arthur Green's teaching of the *Shem Havaya* in Yosef Gikatilla's *Shaarei Orah* points out that the difference between "was" (*hey vav hey*) and "will be" (*alef hey vav hey*) in Hebrew is the presence of the single letter *alef.* Lecture, "Images

of God in Kabbalah", Shalom Hartman Institute, July 2002
717 Consider the visual symbol used for eternity, the figure eight on its side. It traces in its form an eternal oscillation of movement, between two poles and the wavering between them.
718 Exodus 3.13-14.
719 *Emet v'Emunah,* Menakhem Mendel of Kotzk, 101 n. 647
720 *BaMidbar Rabbah* 16.25.
721 From Pinkhas of Koretz, *Torat haHasidut:*, p. 6.
722 *Yismakh Lev,* Menakhem Nakhum of Chernobyl, *Pesakhim.*
723 Abraham Joshua Heschel, *Who Is Man?* p. 41.
724 *Sefer haBahir,* 1.10, p. 5
725 Isaiah Horowitz, *Shaar haGadol, Beit HaBekhirah,* p. 46a.
726 *Likkutim Yekarim* 3d, cited in Arthur Green and Barry Holtz, *Your Word is Fire,* p. 65.
727 Proverbs 6.23.
728 *Sefer Yetzirah* 2.6.
729 Moshe Idel, *Kabbalah,* p..183.
730 Genesis 3.9.
731 *Sefat Emet, Beha'alotkha* 1, 68 (Hebrew).
732 From *Tekhine Imre Shifre;* see *Malkhut,* comparison of women lighting Shabbat candles to the High Priest lighting the Menorah, footnotes 42–43.